I0083872

The Letters of

ROBERT MORRIS

"It is the duty of every individual to act his part in whatever station his country may call him to in hours of difficulty, danger, and distress."

– Robert Morris

The Letters of

Robert Morris (signature)

ROBERT MORRIS

Founding Father and
Revolutionary Financier

By Michael Aubrecht

Heritage Books
2025

HERITAGE BOOKS

AN IMPRINT OF HERITAGE BOOKS, INC.

Books, CDs, and more—Worldwide

For our listing of thousands of titles see our website
at
www.HeritageBooks.com

Published 2025 by
HERITAGE BOOKS, INC.
Publishing Division
5810 Ruatan Street
Berwyn Heights, MD 20740

Copyright © 2025 Michael Aubrecht

Heritage Books by the author:
The Letters of Robert Morris: Founding Father and Revolutionary Financier
The Long Roll: Wartime Experiences of the Civil War Drummer Boy

Cover art: Portrait of Robert Morris by Charles Willson Peale.

All rights reserved. No part of this book may be reproduced or
transmitted in any form or by any means, electronic or mechanical,
including photocopying, recording or by any information storage and
retrieval system without written permission from the author, except
for the inclusion of brief quotations in a review.

International Standard Book Number
Paperbound: 978-0-7884-4315-2

Contents

Foreword

As winter settled in across the newly declared United States in December of 1776, the fortunes of the nascent country were likewise cold and bleak. The year, which began with the promising British evacuation of Boston, saw the ultimate failure of the American invasion of Canada and the British capture of New York and subsequent pursuit of General George Washington's Continental Army across New Jersey. Washington's rapidly shrinking force, and the country as a whole, required a drastic change in fortune. To this end, Washington envisioned a surprise assault on an isolated Hessian outpost at Trenton, New Jersey. As it stood, however, Washington's army was insufficiently equipped to carry out such an operation in the dead of winter, having bled not only men but also equipment and supplies over the preceding campaign.

It is well known that America received its Christmas miracle, with Washington's rag-tag army winning a stunning victory at Trenton on December 26th, followed by another triumph over British forces at Princeton on January 3, 1777. These twin victories changed the momentum of the war, increasing patriot morale throughout the country. Less known is the decisive role that one man, Robert Morris of Pennsylvania, played in making it possible. Morris, one of the wealthiest men in America, personally secured vital supplies, particularly blankets and clothing, that enabled Washington's surprise attack on Trenton. In the aftermath of that successful operation, right at the time that most of the soldiers' enlistments were set to expire, Morris secured a large loan that allowed Washington to pay his troops and defeat the British at Princeton. Yet, most Americans have no idea who this remarkable American even was.

Born in England and immigrating to America at the age of 11, Robert Morris was destined to be involved in world-altering events. He was apprenticed to a Philadelphia merchant and rose to become a partner in Morris, Willing and Company. In time, he became one of the wealthiest men in America, with some income realized from the firm's occasional involvement in the slave trade. Like many of his American contemporaries, Morris opposed direct taxation of the colonies, and progressively became more involved in politics, winning election to the Pennsylvania General Assembly. When war broke out in 1775, he took a moderate position, initially favoring reconciliation with Great Britain over independence. Nevertheless, Morris ultimately signed the Declaration of Independence.

As demonstrated at Trenton and Princeton, Morris worked throughout the war to obtain supplies and equipment for the Continental Army, often using his own personal credit to obtain loans. Morris was unanimously selected by Congress to become the first Superintendent of Finance under the Articles of Confederation. In this role, he instituted a number of actions to boost the nation's economy, including convincing Congress to establish the Bank of North America and issuing a more stable currency backed by his own credit.

His nationalism extended into the postwar years, where he participated in the Constitutional Convention of 1787 and signed the Constitution. Ultimately, Morris' own financial fortunes declined in the 1790's with several business and speculative efforts failing. In a sad twist of fate, the country's onetime financial wizard and savior found himself in debtors' prison and died in poverty on May 8th, 1806.

In this collection of letters, Michael Aubrecht allows this overlooked, but influential and important Founding

Father to tell his own story. Robert Morris carried out correspondence with nearly every major figure of the Revolutionary and Founding periods of American History. In the following periods, the reader will experience the momentous events of this period through Morris' writings to the likes of George Washington, Benjamin Franklin, and Thomas Jefferson. Whether a novice or expert on this fascinating period in U.S. History, researchers will find this to be an invaluable collection that illuminates how a new nation was established.

Tim Willging

Acknowledgements

There has never been a book written that hasn't been made possible without the generous efforts of individuals other than the author. I have been very blessed to have had the privilege of working with folks who are equally dedicated to producing a book that is both educational and entertaining. The first hurdle when attempting to publish a book is finding a publisher that is dedicated to fulfilling the author's vision. Leslie Wolfinger at Heritage Books Inc. has been a tremendous ally and her validation of this work is most appreciated. Debbie Riley, also at Heritage, does a wonderful job of ensuring that their books look both attractive and marketable. Timothy Willging is a historian that I have great respect for. His breadth of historical knowledge spans multiple centuries and I was ecstatic when he agreed to write the Foreword of the book. As with all of my projects, I wouldn't be able to achieve any form of success without the love and support of my family. My wife Tracy, children Dylan, Madison, Kierstyn and Jackson, and grandson Eli inspire me to do this kind of work. They are the ones that sacrifice time while I am off researching or speaking to an audience. I also want to recognize my father, Thomas Aubrecht, whose keen eye has made all of my books better. His editing and proofreading skills have been a crucial part of my writing process. Finally, I want to thank you, the reader. Thanks to you I have been able to produce four, now five books that I am most proud of. That would not be possible without your interests and support.

Introduction

One of the most satisfying things about writing a book are the opportunities you get to talk about it. As with my previous books one of the first questions people ask is "Why did you write this book?" That's always a great conversation starter. Ironically this book did not start out in any way to be what it is. Following the positive feedback I received on my last book (*Thomas Jefferson and the Virginia Statute for Religious Freedom*), I felt inspired to keep that momentum moving forward. I asked myself the obvious question. "What should I write about next?"

First, I was going to write a biography on Revolutionary War hero Hugh Mercer. Then I learned that my own publisher had already published a book on Mercer. Next, I planned on compiling a collection of letters from the noted colonial religious leader George Whitehead. Strike Two. That had also been done. Next I was going to write about twelve 18th century historic individuals with ties to the City of Fredericksburg. That book was immediately turned down by multiple publishers for being too broad. Finally, I pitched the idea for a book about a collection of letters from Founding Father Robert Morris. What prompted this approach was the fact that I was able to obtain hundreds of letters from Morris that are available in the National Archives online repository.

I must confess that, up until I started exploring the idea of writing about Robert Morris, the only knowledge I had of the man was the fact that my wife attended Robert Morris University in Pittsburgh, PA. For 49 seasons the school's teams, appropriately named the "Colonials" have proudly represented the university. After doing some preliminary research I came to the conclusion that this book had legs, as Robert Morris is not forgotten. There have been a few biographies written on the man, but this collection of letters has not been attempted. While I was preparing to start this endeavor I read, enjoyed and highly recommend the biography titled *Robert Morris: Financier of the American Revolution* by Charles Rappleye.

The more I read about the man, the more I became convinced that writing a book that essentially enabled Morris to be represented through his own words was more than just a novel idea. In this capacity I would be primarily acting as an editor. I've said in past interviews that the real enjoyable part of writing history books is the research portion of it. The writing part is the result. Conducting an investigation is where the fun is. I cannot express how much I enjoyed sifting through the National Archives collection and compiling 270 private letters written by Robert Morris to noteworthy individuals like George Washington, John Adams, Thomas Jefferson, Ben Franklin and John Jay.

Morris' critical contributions to the founding of our country are absolutely worth further examination. He served as a member of the Pennsylvania legislature, the Second Continental Congress, and the United States Senate, and was one of only two people to sign the Declaration of Independence, the Articles of Confederation, and the U.S. Constitution. From 1781 to 1784, he served as the Superintendent of Finance of the United States, becoming known as the "Financier of the Revolution." Along with Alexander Hamilton, he is widely regarded as one of the founders of the financial system of the United States of America.

This book contains over 250 personal letters and through them I am allowing Morris to reveal his own story with his own words. Throughout this book you will read letters that portray his efforts to finance and back the Continental Army, establish a new form of currency and lay out an entirely new financial system that is still used today. This collection includes letters that are both personal and professional. My goal is to present the entirety of Morris' far too overlooked contributions that are just as important and noteworthy as those he writes to. I also present the failures that Morris experienced such as going from one of the wealthiest men in the country to acquiring so much debt that he suffered bankruptcy.

My overall goal with this book is to introduce readers to one of the most complex members of our Founding Fathers and present how precarious the establishment of our country was in its infancy. Thanks to the intellect, inspiration and perseverance of men like Robert Morris we can reflect on their contributions and enjoy the fruits of their labor.

Portrait by Charles Willson Peale

Robert Morris

To call Robert Morris "a political renaissance man" would be an understatement. He was vice president of the Pennsylvania Committee of Safety (1775–76) and was a member of the Continental Congress (1775–78) as well as a member of the Pennsylvania legislature (1778–79, 1780–81, 1785–86). Morris practically controlled the financial operations of the Revolutionary War from 1776 to 1783. He was a delegate to the Constitutional Convention (1787) and served in the U.S. Senate (1789–95). Perhaps most impressive is the fact that he signed the Declaration of Independence and the Articles of Confederation, and later signed the U.S. Constitution.

At the start of the war Robert Morris was one of the wealthiest men in the colonies, but he would go on to claim bankruptcy after some catastrophic decisions. In order to fully appreciate the contributions of Robert Morris we must go back and examine him from the beginning.

Robert Morris was born on January 31, 1734 in Liverpool, England, the son of Robert Morris, Sr., and Elizabeth Murphet Morris. His mother died when he was only two and he was raised by his grandmother. Morris' father immigrated to the colonies in 1700, settled in Maryland and in 1738 he began a successful career working for Foster, Cunliffe and Sons of Liverpool. His job was to purchase and ship tobacco back to England. Morris Sr. was known for his ingenuity and he was the creator of the tobacco inspection law. He was also regarded as an inventive merchant and was the first to keep his accounts in money rather than in gallons, pounds, or yards.

In 1750 tragedy would once again strike the Morris family. In July Morris Sr. hosted a dinner party aboard one of the company's ships. As he prepared to depart a farewell salute was fired from the ship's cannon and wadding from the shot burst through the side of the boat and severely injured him. He died a few days later of blood poisoning on July 12, 1750. The tragedy had a terrible effect on Morris who became an orphan at the age of 16. Looking for a change he left Maryland for Philadelphia in 1748. He was taken under the wing of his father's friend, Mr. Greenway, who filled the gap left by the death of Morris' father. Raised with a tremendous work ethic Morris flourished as a clerk at the merchant firm of Charles Willing & Co.

Following in his father's footsteps Morris was also gifted with successful ingenuity. In his twenties he took his earnings and joined a few friends in establishing the London Coffee House. (Today the Philadelphia Stock Exchange claims the coffee house as its origin.) Morris was sent as a ship's captain on a trading mission to Jamaica during the Seven Years War (1756-1763). He was captured by a group of French Privateers, but managed to escape to Cuba where he remained until an American ship arrived in Havana. Only then was he able to secure safe passage back to Philadelphia.

Shortly after Morris' return to the colonies Willing retired and handed the firm over to his son Thomas who offered him a partnership. This resulted in the formation of Willing, Morris & Co. The firm boasted three ships that were dispatched to the West Indies and England importing British cargo and exporting American goods. This relationship lasted for over 40 years and was immensely successful. At one point, Morris was ranked by the Encyclopedia of American Wealth, along with Charles Carroll of Carrollton, as the two wealthiest signers of the Declaration of Independence.

As influential merchants, Morris and Willing were in disagreement with the changes in tax policy. In 1765, the Stamp Act was passed and was met with massive resistance. Morris was

2

at the forefront and led protests in the streets. His fervor was so striking that he convinced the stamp collector to suspend his post and return the stamps back to their origin. The tax collector stated that if he had not complied, he feared his house would have been torn down "brick by brick." In 1769, the partners organized the first non-importation agreement, which forever ended the slave trade in the Philadelphia region.

Morris married Mary White on March 2, 1769 and they had seven children. In 1770, he bought an eighty-acre farm on the eastern bank of the Schuylkill River where he built a home he named "The Hills." Due to his growing reputation Morris was asked to be a warden of the port of Philadelphia. Showing his tenacity he convinced the captain of a tea ship to return to England in 1775.

Later on Morris was appointed to the Model Treaty Committee following Richard Henry Lee's resolution for independence on June 7, 1776. The resulting treaty projected international relations based on free trade and not political alliance. The treaty was eventually taken to Paris by Benjamin Franklin who transformed it into the Treaty of Alliance which was made possible by the Continental Army's victory at Yorktown in 1781.

Scholars disagree as to whether Morris was present on July 4 when the Declaration of Independence was approved. But when it came time to sign the Declaration on August 2 he did so. Morris boldly stated that it was "the duty of every individual to act his part in whatever station his country may call him to in hours of difficulty, danger and distress." Until peace was achieved in 1783, Morris performed services in support of the war. His efforts earned him the moniker of "Financier of the Revolution."

Morris' extensive service was impressive. While in Congress he was on the Secret Committee, who helped to establish a network of secret agents. Morris was also a member of the Committee of Correspondence, which would later become the U.S. Department of State. In addition he served on the Marine Committee that ratified the American Flag.

Morris sold his best ship to the Continental Navy (renamed the Alfred), and sold a second ship (the Columbus). He later sold a third vessel (renamed the Reprisal) which was the ship that took Benjamin Franklin to France. After the British succeeded in taking Philadelphia in 1777, Morris returned to Congress and signed the Articles of Confederation. He was one of only 16 signers of the Declaration of Independence who signed both documents. Before the victory at the Battle of Trenton, Morris supplied George Washington's army with timely aid in the form of weapons, supplies and financial aid.

Morris left his post in Congress in 1778 and later returned to the Pennsylvania Assembly. Among his missions were establishing checks and balances and protecting minority rights. This was a very unpopular stance and much criticism was thrust upon the representative.

In 1779, Thomas Paine and Henry Laurens delivered charges of fraudulent transactions against Morris and his partner. In support of his defense he demanded that a congressional committee examine his books. Following the investigation Morris was exonerated. As part of their concluding report they stated that he had quote: "acted with fidelity and integrity and an honorable zeal for the happiness of his country."

In 1781, the Continental Congress called Morris to service again. This time he was appointed the Superintendent of Finance. The position was especially noteworthy as it was the first executive office in American history. Faced with a serious governmental financial crisis, Morris submitted the first national funding proposal. He then established the Bank of North America, seized control of detrimental government expenditures, purchased much needed military supplies, tightened accounting procedures, and pleaded with the states to contribute their fair share when called upon. Before he vacated his position Morris used over a million dollars of his own money to feed and pay the troops, with most of those notes to be repaid with loans from France.

Morris also became the Agent of Marine and took control of the Continental Navy. Once again he personally provided support for the army and Generals Washington and Lincoln as they marched to Yorktown. He put up 1.4 million dollars for the effort and coordinated with the French to get French ships into the Chesapeake Bay. This act resulted in a crucial victory by the Continental Army.

Following his contributions to an American victory Morris became an outspoken advocate of a more powerful government and attended the Annapolis Convention in 1786 to debate amending the Articles of Confederation. In 1787, he hosted George Washington as they both attended the Constitutional Convention in Philadelphia, and it was Morris who nominated Washington to be Chairman of the Convention. He then signed the new U. S. Constitution.

After ratification of the Constitution, Morris was elected Senator from Pennsylvania. He was the one that wrote to George Washington at Mount Vernon informing him that he had been elected President of the United States. When Washington became President, he invited Morris to become his Secretary of the Treasury. Morris graciously declined but recommended his friend Alexander Hamilton. Morris served on 41 senatorial committees and used his position in the Senate to support and advance Hamilton's financial policies. Together they established the new country's financial foundation.

Not entirely popular, Morris' critics were not disappointed to see him go. In 1795, investigations were reopened into his work on the Secret Committee dating back to the late 1770s. They refused to accept the documentation of expenses that Morris provided and charged Willing, Morris & Co., over $94,000. In order to address the fine Morris had to sign over his best remaining asset, his interest in his shipping companies.

After losing a portion of his wealth Morris moved into real estate speculation. Most impressive, he at one point owned the western half of New York State. After making peace with the Six Indian Nations, Morris sold the land to the Holland Land Company. This reestablished his wealth which he used to purchase industries. At one point Morris owned a steam engine company, a glass factory, the first iron rolling mill in America, a coal company, and several canal companies.

Things began to take a turn for the worse as Morris' debts became overextended when Napoleon's French minister, Talleyrand, did not pay for the 100,000 acres he had purchased. To make matters worse, Aaron Burr, acting as the Attorney General of New York, started a partisan lawsuit against Morris that deprived him of hundreds of square miles of New York property in the process.

At his direction Morris' partners began purchasing thousands of acres in Washington, DC. They arranged an agreement with a group of investors to take over the properties, but after the deal was signed the investors defaulted. Following this debacle Morris' group was convinced that they had a new loan from Holland that would enable them to purchase over 6 million acres, but the loan failed to materialize due to the French Revolution and the rise of Napoleon.

Morris had no choice but to declare bankruptcy in February of 1798. He was taken to Prune Street debtors' prison where he remained in custody for three and a half years. With Morris in debtor's prison, and the Federalists weakened, Thomas Jefferson won the presidency. Morris' friend and ally Senator John

Marshall, helped pass a bankruptcy law in 1801 and he was released.

Morris attempted to restart his career, but his reputation was severely damaged and he was discredited. Gouverneur Morris provided Morris with an annuity for the rest of his life. He lived quietly with his wife for another five years. Morris died of asthma on May 8, 1806 and was buried in the family vault of William White and his father Robert Morris Sr. behind Christ Church in Philadelphia.

John Adams remembered Robert Morris with great respect. He wrote, "I think he has a masterly understanding, an open temper, and an honest heart…He has vast designs in the mercantile way. And no doubt pursues mercantile ends, which are always gain, but he is an excellent member of the body."

Historian William Hogeland writes "given his seminal performance to victory in the Revolution, as well as to forming the nation, Robert Morris isn't as well known by Americans as he ought to be."

Perhaps Morris himself summed up his own legacy when he said, "I am not one of those politicians that run testy when my own plans are not adopted. I think it is the duty of a good citizen to follow when he cannot lead."

Source: Descendents of the Signers of the Declaration of Independence, Robert Morris, descendant, 2008.

Delaware Works 25 Oct.ʳ 1793

Sir

    I received some time since your
letter of the 7ᵗʰ ins.ᵗ containing a kind of offer
of some Lands in South Carolina for Sale
but in such Vague terms that I can say nothing
in answer, If your Friend wants to sell his
Lands he should give such a description of the soil
situation, Produce & Value of them & of his
terms; as to (at least) enable proper enquirys to
be made by those who might incline to purchase
which will not be my case unless the Lands
are good & cheap. I am Sir

        Your obed.ᵗ hble serv.ᵗ

        Rob.ᵗ Morris

Mr Timothy Green
    New York

Letters 1776-1802

The following letters were accessed via the
National Archives Founders Online

To John Jay, 23 September 1776

Phila. Sept. 23d 1776

Dear Sir

Altho your express delivered me your favour last Wednesday or Thursday yet I did not receive the letter from Mr. Deane untill this day and shall now send after the Express that he may Convey this safe to your hands. Shou'd he be gone I must find some other safe conveyance. You will find enclosed both Mr. D—ne's letters as you desired and I shall thank you for the Copy of the Invisible part, he had Communicated so much of this Secret to me, before his departure, as to let me know he had fixed with you a mode of writing that would be invisible to the rest of the World, he also promised to ask you to make a full Communication to me, but in this use your pleasure. The Secret so farr as I do or shall know it, will remain so to all other persons. It appears clear to me that we may very soon Involve all Europe in a Warr by managing properly the apparent forwardness of the Court of France, its a horrid consideration that our own Safety shou'd call on us to involve other Nations in the Calamities of Warr, can this be morally right or have morality & Policy nothing to do with each other (perhaps it may not be good Policy to investigate the Question at this time). I will therefore only ask you whether General Howe will give us time to cause a diversion favourable to us in Europe, I confess as things now appear to me the prospect is gloomy Indeed therefore if you can administer Comfort do it; Why are we so long deprived of your abilitys in

Congress, perhaps they are more usefully exerted where you are, that may be the case, but such Men as You, in times like these, should be every where. I am with true sentiments of respect & esteem, Dr Sir Your obedt. hble Servt.

Robt Morris

To George Washington, 21 December 1776

Philada Decemr 21st 1776

Sir

Notwithstanding there are several British Men of War cruising in our Bay, the Continental Sloop Independance Commanded by Lieutt Robinson has pushed through & got up here yesterday afternoon. There is onboard 856 Blankets which were intended with many others now expected in, for the use of the new enlistments, but the inclement weather and the severe duty the Troops now under your Command have to perform Induces me to think, these Blankets shou'd be applyed to their use in this matter however you will please to Judge & act as you see fit, for I shall send them to the Camp for your orders so soon as the Weather will permit them to be landed. there is also arrived in this Sloop a quantity of Cloths which I shall put into the hands of Mr. Mease Commissary to have made up immediately. there is also 919 Muskets onboard these I suppose you do not want, and I will send them out of Town to the other Stores unless you signify a desire for any other application of them. I have the pleasure to inform you that Mr Deane in his letters of the 30th Septr recd by this Sloop, says he *looks* upon a French War as inevitable. He expects to furnish us with ample supplys for 30 thousand Men & a Noble train of Artillery Mortars &c. so that, if you can but drive our Enemies back to New York for this Winter, we may hope for much better things.

I find my presence so necessary here in several departments that I shall stay as long as I can with safety, but as I am possessed of Publick papers that must never fall into the hands of the Enemy I shou'd be glad of a line from you whenever you think it wou'd be best for me to retire, and if you have any Commands here in which I can be serviceable, be assured of my ready attention, your several dispatches to Congress have passed through my hands & I have informed them fully of such things as have come to my knowledge respecting Publick matters.

Poor Lee, I pity him exceedingly & feel much for the Publick loss in him, Shou'd you hear any thing of the Treatment he meets with I shou'd thank you or Mr Tilghman for a line on that Subject, I fear he will meet with insupportable Insults & if so his situation must be worse than that of the Damn'd. I have been told to day that you are preparing to Cross into the Jerseys I hope it may be true & promise myself Joyfull tidings from Your expedition, You have my sincere prayers for Success as nothing wou'd give me greater pleasure than to hear of such ocurrences as your exalted merit deserves. I have the honor to remain Your Excellencys Most obedt hble servt

Robt Morris

To George Washington, 23–24 December 1776

Philada Decr 23d[–24] 1776

Sir

I had the honor to receive your obliging favour of Yesterday by Colo. Moylan, the Contents give a most mellancholly aspect to our affairs and I wish to Heaven it may be in our power to retrieve them, it is useless at this period to examine into the causes of our present unhappy situation, unless that examination wou'd be productive of a cure for the evils that surround us, in fact those causes have long been known to such as wou'd open their Eyes, the very consequences of them was often foretold, & the measures execrated by some of the best Friends of America; but in vain, an obstinate partiality to the habits & Customs of one part of this Continent has predominated in the Publick Councils, and too little attention been paid to others. To Criminate the Authors of our errors wou'd not avail, but we cannot see ruin Staring us in the Face without thinking of them—It has been my fate to make an *ineffectual* opposition to all short enlistments[,] to Colonial appointment of Officers and to many other measures that I thought pregnant with mischiefs, but these things, either suited the genius & habbits or Squared with the interests of some States that had sufficient influence to prevail, and nothing is now left, but to extricate ourselves from the difficulties in which we are involved if we can, let us try our utmost, man can do no more. I shall Urge Mr Mease to go on as briskly as possible with the Cloathing, but its impossible for him to make much progress as most of the Taylors are at the Camp. the Muskets & other Stores shall be sent out of the City, and such papers as I can spare shall be sent away. The Fleet has always been my particular care & at this time I am exceedingly anxious for its safety, but the difficulty of getting anything done is inconceivable most of the Tradesmen, necessary to finish the Delaware are at Camp I have applyed to the Council of Safety to order some few of them down & altho they wish yet they fear to do it, least the rest shou'd follow—I have now under my care, the Randolph & Delaware Frigates, the Brigt. Andrew Doria, Sloops Hornet, Independance & Fly & Schooner Mosquito all Continental Armed Vessels beside several Valueable Merchantment all which I wish to get out to Sea & think it might be effected if every man Concerned wou'd exert himself in his department, I try to give them Spirits & invigorate their exertions all in my power—The Enemy have Six Sail Cruizing about our Capes and keep a special look out, notwithstanding this, The Brigt.

Andrew Doria Capt. Isaiah Robison passed through them & got safe up this day, she left St Eustatia the beginning of this Month & on the passage took a Sloop of Twelve Guns fitted out by Admiral Gayton at Jamaica agreable to orders of the Lords of the Admiralty, she also took a Snow from Jam[aic]a & ordered both Prizes in here, but its most likely they will be retaken, before I quit this Subject, permit me to observe that there is a Lieutt Josiah of our Navy Prisoner & now at New York, and we have Prisoner at York Town in this State a Lieutt Boger of their Navy, I cou'd wish an exchange between them cou'd be effected. There is also a Doctr Hodge Surgeon to Colo. Cadwalladers Battalion of Pensylvanians now Prisoner in New York a Young Man of much Merit & his abilities in his Profession wou'd render him very usefull cou'd he be exchanged.

The Sloop taken by the Andw Doria was commanded by a Mr Jones who has the Kings Commission as master & Commander he behaved bravely & I am told he says Ld Howe will be desirous to redeem him, I suppose his Rank to be equal to a Major or Lt Colo. which I mention that your Excellency may advert to it, if you wish for an Exchange of any particular Officer of Merit of that Rank. This Brigt. was sent by the Secret Committee for Cloathing & Stores & has brought in the following cargo—208 Dozen pair of Woolen Stockings[,] 106 Dozen pair of Worsted do[,] 215 Sailors Jackets[,] 23 Great Coats[,] 50 ps. Dutch plains[,] 30 ps. 900 Yds Flannell[,] 45 ps. blue, brown & white Cloth[,] 463 Blankets[,] 218 ps. ⅞ Linen[,] 496 Muskets[,] 326 pair Pistols[,] 200 half barrells Powder[,] 14101 lb. Lead. I have enumerated these Articles that you may judge what part is wanted for your Army and your orders shall be complied with I shall only observe these Imports were intended for the new Levies but circumstanced as you are I think you shou'd judge solely of the propriety of applying them to our present exigencys, The Brigt. Lexington and Sloop Sachem may be hourly looked for with further supplys also sundry Merchantmen—but I dread their approach to our Capes, they took a French snow in sight of the Andrew Doria who protected her as long as it was possible.

I am fearfull Genl Lee may suffer for want of Money if the resentment of British officers runs as high as they have threatned—therefore to prevent present distress I enclose herein a set of Exchange drawn by the late Governor Edens Secretary Mr Smith on Messrs Thos Eden & Co. for One hundred Pounds Sterling which I beg you will Convey by a Flag to Genl Lee with an assurance of a further supply whenever he wants it, I have endorsed the bills & flatter myself that many Gentlemen now in New York to whom I am known will advance the General the Money upon them. I have no doubt but this matter may be so managed as that Genl Lee will certainly get these bills & the Money for them without putting you to much inconvenience & with the utmost esteem I remain Dear sir Your most Obedient servt

Robt Morris

P.S. having sent my Stores out of Town, this is the best paper I can Command at present.

Decr 24th. not meeting any Conveyance for this letter yesterday, I have since obtained the enclosed bill drawn by Capt. Duncan McNicol & Hugh Fraser Lieutt of the Royal Highland Emigrants for £116.9.3 Sterling in favr of Alexr Inglis Esqr. for amot of supplys to them in Charles Town it is drawn on Major Small & I dare say will be paid, therefore I think it a preferable remittance to Genl Lee than bills on London and hope you will Convey it to him immediately.

To George Washington, 26 December 1776

Philada Decr 26th 1776

Dear Sir

I have just received yours of yesterday and will duely attend to those things you recommend to my consideration, at present I have to enclose you a letter from Congress which I suppose Contains their resolves of the 20th Inst. but as the President does not say in his letter to me that they are enclosed to you & as it is necessary you shou'd have them, I take the liberty to send herewith a Copy of them.

I am well pleased to see the attention they pay Genl Lee and I shall make a point to Collect & send your Excellency soon as possible the one hundred half Johannes's they order Youl observe Mr Clymer, Mr Walton & myself, are appointed a Committee to transact the Continental business here that may be necessary & proper, and I apprehend it will frequently be necessary that we shou'd know the Substance of your Correspondance with Congress Your letters to the President if sent open under our Cover shall always meet dispatch & their Contents kept Secret, & when you think it improper we shou'd see them before the Congress Seal them & they shall go forward untouched & if you dont approve of submitting them to our inspection at all write us freely & your wishes in that respect shall be complyed with.

We have just heard of your Success at Trenton the Acct is but imperfect but we learn You are master of that place & of all the bagage & Stores our Enemies had there & of 300 Prisoners and that your Troops were still in pursuit of the flying Enemy, I have just wrote to Congress & told them this much as the Substance of an Acct just come down & I told them further I had been informed that you had executed in this matter your part of a Well Concerted plan, that Genl Heath at Hackensack had orders from you, & that

Genl Ewing & Colo. Cadwallader also had orders to Cross Delaware at the same time you did, but had been prevented by Driving Ice. Good News sets all the Animal Spirits to Work, the immagination is heated & I cou'd not help adding, that I expected Genl Heath was to Continue his March towards Brunswick which woud draw the attention of any Troops posted there & at Prince Town, while you wou'd pursue the flying Hero's to Bordenton & Burlington where Ewing & Cadwallader wou'd stop them & cut of their Communication with the 2000 Hessians & Highlanders that Came after Griffin, nay I almost promised them that you Shou'd by following up this first blow, finish the Campaigne of 1776 with that eclat that your Numerous Friends & admireers have long wished for. I Congratulate you most heartily on what is done & am with perfect esteem Dr sir Your Excellency's most obedt servt

Robt Morris

To George Washington, 30 December 1776

Philada Decr 30th 1776

sir

I have just recd your favour of this day & sent to Genl Putnam to detain the Express untill I collect the hard Money You want which you may depend shall be sent in one specie or other with this letter & a list thereof shall be enclosed herein.

I had long since parted with very Considerable Sums of hard money to Congress, therefore must Collect from others & as matters now Stand it is no easy matter, I mean to borrow Silver & promise payment in Gold & will then Collect the Gold in the best manner I can. whilst on this Subject let me inform You that there is upwards of 20,000 Dollars in Silver at Tyconderoga they have

16

no particular use for it & I think You might as well send a party to bring it away & lodge it in a Safe place Convenient for any purposes for which it may hereafter be wanted.

I gave Mr Commissary Wharton an Order for 40 thousand Dollars this morning & pressed him to attend most dilligently to your supplys I will Send for him again [to] know what is done & add Springs to his Movements if I can, I wish he was more silent, prudent &c. but I fancy he is active. Whatever I can do shall be done for the good of the Service. I ever am Dr sir Your Excellencys Obedt hble servant

Robt Morris

P.S. Hearing that you are in Want of a Qr Cask of Wine I have procured a good one which Mr Commissary Wharton will send up.

To George Washington, 1 January 1777

Philada Jany 1st 1777

sir

I was honoured with your favour of yesterday by Mr Howell late last night, & ever solicitous to comply with your requisitions I am up very early this morning to dispatch a supply of fifty thousand Dollars to your Excellency You will receive that Sum with this letter but it will not be got away so early as I cou'd wish for none concerned in this movement except myself are up, I shall rouse them immediately. It gives me great pleasure that you have engaged the Troops to continue, and if further occasional supplys of Money are necessary you may depend on my exertions either in a publick or private capacity.

The year 1776 is over I am heartily glad of it & hope you nor America will ever be plagued with such another, let us accept the success at Trentown as a presage of future fortunate Events and under that impression I do most sincerely wish you a Successfull Campaigne in 1777 to crown you with immortal honours in reward of the dangers & Fatigues of War, and that You may for many, many years after; enjoy the Sweets of Peace & Domestick happiness in reward of your Social Virtues. With Sincere Esteem & regard I ever am sir Your Obedt Servant

Robt Morris

To John Jay, 12 January 1777

Philada. Jany 12th 1777

Dear Sir

I have been possessed of your obliging favr. of the 2d Ulto a considerable time, but being too much pressed with public & private business to permit my being a regular correspondent it is needless to apologize. You undoubtedly must have been well acquainted with the rapid progress made by our Enemies through the Jerseys and the danger to which this City has been exposed for some Weeks past, and you will have heard of the removal of Congress to Baltimore in the midst of the pannic. This step has been highly censured by many of their Friends and undoubtedly lost them the confidence of some Men.

I confess for my own part I am not amongst the Number of those that Censure them for this hasty measure, for when it is considered that the Enemy s Troops were within a very few miles of us & no apparent Force sufficient to oppose their progress, it surely was time for a public body on which the support of the American cause so much depended, to provide for their safety— Meer personal safety I suppose wou'd not have induced many of them to fly, but their Security as a body was the object, had any Number of them fallen into the Enemies hands so as to break up the Congress America might have been ruined before another Choice of Delegates cou'd be had & in such an event they wou'd have been deemed criminal & rash to the last degree. Most of them dislike their present Station & complain horridly, particularly those you esteem, but it seems some others who generally carry their points, like their quarters & are for staying. I suppose it answers some of their purposes and I have but one objection in the world. They have appointed Mr Walton of Georgia, Mr Clymer & myself a Committee to transact all Continental business that may be necessary & proper in this place, the business of this Committee engrosses my whole time & encreases daily, so that I am now the veriest Slave you ever saw and wish them back to be relieved. I wish to Heaven they had removed from hence last winter, If they had, Pensylvania wou'd long since have had a wholesome constitution, its Strength might have been drawn into proper exertion & her Capital wou'd never have been made to tremble. What has happened is the fruits of that winters Cabals, Our Constitution is disliked, the People divided, unhappy, and consequently weak, the power if any there be, is placed in improper hands and in short the people seem to loose one day, the Confidence they placed in leaders of the day before.

Where it will end God only knows, Dickinson & A. Allen have given mortal stabs to their own Characters & pity it is the wounds shou'd penetrate any further, but they were men of property Men of fair private Characters & what they have done, seems to pierce through their sides into the Vitals of , Start deletion,, End, ^those who have similar pretentions^ to Fortune & good Character, the defection of these men is supposed to originate in a desire to preserve their Estates & consequently glances a Suspicion on all that have Estates to loose. I pity them exceedingly,

Dickensons Nerves gave way & his fears dictated a letter to his Brother advising him not to receive Continental money. His Judgment & his Virtue shou'd have prevented this Act of Folly, I call it such because I believe his Heart to be good & regret much that his exalted Character , Start deletion,, End, ^shou'd^ be degraded, by what , Start deletion,, End, cou'd hardly be called a Crime at the time he did it, but he thought the Game was up. A Allen deserves a better fate, than he will meet with, Aimiable in private character and deserving of the Felicity he has heretofore enjoyed he has rashly sacrificed it, by a , Start deletion,, End, hasty resolution, he has long thought it impossible for us to withstand the power of Great Britain & he complained of that Conduct amongst ourselves which has been loudly censured by America's warmest advocates & frequently exposed by the keen sentences of Mr Jay, however nothing can justify the Step he has taken & it seems wrong to paliate it, I will therefore only say, I am most sincerely sorry for him. I removed my Family & some of my effects in the heat of our Fright but determined to stay by the City to the last moment very happy have I been since, in this determination, as it is fallen in way to be very usefull on many occasions, both to this State & to the Continent, and in every instance I have exerted myself to the utmost, Congress are Sensible of it and have approved all my doings, altho I acted for a considerable time without their Authority. I join in all your Sentiments respecting our good Friend Duane and if I had not been well convinced how Ill used he was by that Cursed piece of Slander I shou'd not have troubled him with it, nor shou'd I have sent it when I did, but having heard he was coming to Congress, I thought it my duty to prepare him. I have a letter from him on the Subject and think he treats it very properly by despising the report & its Author or Authors. I wish to heaven the affairs of your State wou'd permit both your attendance at Congress, believe me you & others are wanted there, There is a leader there that you do not like and as I understand they have the rule of the roost totally since their removal to the Southward. Pray shew this to Mr Duane & tell him the next bit of leisure I get shall be devoted to answer his two letters.

I do not pretend to give you any acct of Military operations as I suppose you get them from day to day. What a glorious change in our prospects Pray Heaven Continue our Success and grant me an opportunity of Congratulating you on regaining the City of New York. I have not heard from Mr Deane for sometime past & fear he will complain for want of remittances & Intelligence those Damnd Men of War plague us exceedingly & have taken many of our Vessells, but we must persevere untill we gain success. I am Dear Sir Your affectionate Friend & Servt

Robt Morris.

To John Jay, 4 February 1777

Philada. Feby. 4th 1777

Dear Sir:

Your favour of the 7th Ulto came safe to hand, Timothy Jones is certainly a very entertaining, agreable Man, one woud not judge so from any thing contained in his cold insipid letter of the 17th Septr. unless you take pains to find the Concealed beauties therein, The Cursory observations of a Sea Captain wou'd never *discover* them, but transferred from his hand to the penetrating Eye of a *Jay* the Diamonds Stand Confessed at once, it puts me in mind of a Search after the Philosophers Stone, but I believe not ^one^ of the followers of that Phantom have come so near the Mark as you my Good Friend. I handed a Copy of your discoverys to the Committee, which now Consists of Harrison, R. H. Lee, Hooper, Doct^r. Witherspoon Johnson, you, & Myself & honestly told them who it was from because, *measures* are necessary in Consequence of it; but I have not recd. any directions yet— I shou'd never doubt , Start deletion,, End, the Success of measures Conducted by such able heads as those that take the leads in your Convention, I hate to pay Compliments, and would avoid the appearance of doing it, but I cannot refrain from saying I love Duane, admire Mr. Livingston, & have an Epithet for you if I had been writing to another.

I am stationed here with Mr. Walton of Georgia and my Colleague Mr Clymer as a Committee of Congress for transacting all Continental business that may be proper &. necessary at this place abundance of it we have &, I believe we dispatch about ⅞ths of that damn'd trash that used to take up ¾ths of the debates in Congress; and give them no trouble about the matter, but we have this day wrote them pressingly to come back whether they will or not is uncertain as I am told some of them are attached to the place, other execrate it. I do not , Start deletion,, End, Condemn their flight from hence as I should have done had I been at the distance you are, but I cannot spare time to explain myself for I write in haste & proceed to unfold a little business I want to trouble you with—

Major West the Nephew of my Friend Will West was taken Prisoner at Fort Washington he had made a kind of bargain with Mr. Elliott late Collr. of New York to get exchanged for Mr. Jauncey junr. and I represented the matter to Congress, who very *wisely* passed the inclosed Resolve, the agreeement was that if Major West cou'd make interest with Congress, Mr Elliott wou'd do the needfull with Genl. Howe to effect this exchange at least so I understand it. West is an active good Officer, & has great interest in our back Country that wou'd enable him to recruit fast— Mr Jauncey I fancy may as well be in N York as Connecticut and I wish you wou'd forward this business of Exchange. My Compts To Mr Duane & Mr Livingston and I hope they will join you in it—

I wish you had done with your Convention You are really wanted exceedingly in Congress, they are very thin, Hooper gone of[f] with a Fever— Tom Nelson with an appoplectic complaint, when I say gone off; I dont mean to the other World, only to another part of this, one to Virginia & Tother for No Carolina. Harrison has barely weathered it, but he is mending. T. Johnson passed through here a few days ago a General for the Camp. Maryland is not represented Jersey &. Delaware seldom are, your state & this not so fully as they ought. I wish it may do honor to us, but much I fear the reverse from the Names now talked off Adieu my Dr Sir God Bless you, & grant Success to America in the present Contest, with Wisdom and Virtue to Secure Peace & happiness to her Sons in all future Ages. I am with true regard Your most Obedt Servant,

Robt Morris

To George Washington, 12 February 1777

Philada Feby 12th 1777

Sir

I have this Morning received the letter & two parcells of Money sent herewith, from Mr Hancock who requests you will send them in by a Flagg, the letter is for Lieutt Colo. Rawlings one parcell said to Contain six half Joes is for him & the other said to Contain ten half Joes for Lieutt Cresap but both are to be delivered to Colo. Rawlings according to the terms of the letter herewith.

A ship from France brings no later Accounts than the 16 Novr when it was not possible for Doctr Franklin to be arrived, this Ship is also loaden with Salt. I am honoured with Your letter of the 5th Instt and am now taking the necessary measures for Sending the Prisoners into New York by the way of South

Amboy, I have Supplyed Mr Palmer with fifty Pounds Sterling & Send Genl Lee his draft for it. I am Your Excellencys Obedt Servant

Robt Morris

To the American Commissioners, 18 February 1777

Philada. Febry. 18th, 1777

Honorable Gentlemen,

By this Opportunity I forward you sundry dispatches from Congress and the Committee of Secret Correspondance still at Baltimore, and from them I have just received the inclosed resolve of Congress dated the 5th Inst. Copies of which I shall transmit you by various Conveyances, in order that you may give orders for procuring the Articles required and to have them Collected ready for Embarkation. The places of their destination are not yet fixed but you will hear from the Committee or from me very soon on that subject, in the mean time the Articles may be provided and you may rest assured of our utmost exertions to make you effective remittances to answer all your Engagements.

We have at length got one of our Frigates the Randolph Capt. Biddle Cruizing on this Coast to meet any single Frigates of the Enemy and hope for good accounts from her, she sails fast is well Manned and appointed. Others will soon join her and our utmost exertions will be used to put the Navy on a respectable and formidable footing fast as possible.

No event of War of any Material Consequence has happened since the last letter from the Committee. General Washington continues to Pin up the Enemy in Brunswick from whence distress obliges them to send Foraging once or twice a week.

Rhode Island probably may render the Jersey War a little more serious again but our new Enlistments go on so fast we shall soon be too formidable for them in the Field unless they receive very great reinforcements from Europe, and I fancy they may not find that so practicable now as the year past. With the greatest respect and Esteem I have the honor to remain Honorable Gentlemen Your very Obedient humble Servant.

Robt Morris

To George Washington, 27 February 1777

Philada Feby 27th 1777

Dear Sir

I have your favour of the 22d Inst. which wears a very serious countenance and the opinion I entertain of the Strength of your judgement and propriety of your observations, creates doubts in my Mind which I confess I had discarded, as to the safety of this City. from various Accounts I have been taught to believe that the Enemy have since Christmass lost so many Horses, are in such want of Forage, and their remaining Cavalry so worn down, that the defects in this department alone wou'd render any Movement of their Main body impossible without strong reinforcements. If such be their situation, a reinforcement of Men without fresh & large supplys of Horses, Waggons & Forage, wou'd only embarras them, and oblige 'em the sooner to quit their present station. and probably this may still happen, but when I find you so very Urgent to have the public stores removed from hence, knowing as you must, that the expence & loss or Waste arising by such removal, amounts almost to the same thing as a total destruction of them It seems to convince me I have been misinformed as to the real state of the Enemy with respect to Horses Waggons & Forage, especially as you don't say one Word of their deficiencys in these articles that I remember. I have therefore complyed litterally with your wishes & the Committee have given orders to every department to remove all stores not immediately wanted, as fast as they can.

It seems to me however that the Enemy will be pressed with very great difficultys in their designs on this place. allowing some degree of truth to their want of Horses Waggons and Forage, those wants will be infinitely more felt since the late fall of Snow than before for the Snow before it Melts will exceedingly impede the Motions of the Stoutest Horses. they will require more dry food as nothing can be got from the sod and the difficulty of obtaining such food, as I apprehend, will be greatly encreased by Your parties particularly the Rifle Men. When the Snow Melts it will render the Road totally impassable for the Carriages must then be dragged through Mud instead of Snow in short my Dear Sir I cannot help concieving that General Howe's situation somewhat resembles that of a Strong Bull in Trammells, sensible of his own Strength, he grows mad with rage & resentment when he finds himself deprived of the use of it The Bull may not so well understand the causes of his disapointment & therefore may be more patient & I fancy if my picture has any resemblance to the truth patience wou'd be of great use to the British Commander. If you find him embarrassed in these trammells provided by kind Providence I hope you will be able to teaze & harrass him untill our New Inlistments shall put him in Your power, or oblige him to take Shelter onbd the Shipping provided for that & other purposes.

I do not like to be too sanguine & yet it is very necessary in a Contest like this we are engaged in to view the best side of the picture frequently. remember good Sir, that few men ever Keep their feelings to themselves, & that it is necessary for example sake, that all leaders shoud feel & think bold in order to inspirit those that look up to them, Heaven (no doubt for the Noblest purposes) has blessed you with a Firmness of Mind Steadiness of

Countenance and patience in Sufferings that give You infinite advantages over other Men this being the case You are not to depend on other Peoples exertions being equal to your own, One Mind feeds & thrives on misfortunes by finding resources to get the better of them, another sinks under their weight, thinking it impossible to resist and as the latter description probably includes the Majority of Mankind we must be cautious of alarming them, under this Idea I have been backward about removing the public Stores, well knowing that a panic is sooner Caused than retrieved, and I confess myself much hurt At finding you Concerned your admonitions on that score were not attended to; during our greatest alarm here and when our prospects were at the Worst, when my inward feelings were most wrung, I put a good face on things and was then Convinced it was of infinite use. I hate deception and cannot wish any thing like it shou'd ever escape You, but I really think if the bright side of our affairs were sometimes to be painted by your pen or Sanctifyed by your Name it wou'd draw forth the exertions of Some good Men sooner than distress does from others. I hope you will excuse me for this stile of writing which almost amounts to the Confidential and was I sure of such being received in the same light in which I write it, I shou'd lament to You the absence of many great good & Valuable Men from Congress, for if great care is not taken that Body, so respectable from the Nature of the appointment, the Importance of its objects and the respectable Characters of its heretofore individual Members, will loose great part of its Weight & Consequence in the Eyes of our own people, We have now to lament the absence from the public Councils of America, of a Johnson, a Jay R. R. Livingston, Duane, Deane, W. Livingston Franklin, Dickenson, Harrison, Nelson, Hooper Rutledge & others not less Conspicuous, without any proper appointments to fill their places and this at the very time they are most wanted, or wou'd be so, if they had not very wisely supplied the deficiency by Delagating to your Excellency Certain powers that they durst not have entrusted to any other Man, but what is to become of America & its cause if a constant fluctuation is to take place amongst its Counsellors & at every change we find reason to view it with regret, however this is deviating from my own plans, I am holding up the wrong side of the picture, altho I am one of those People who think the best part of the Community will ultimately swim at top, notwithstanding others get uppermost during the general jumble, and I can see the way to liberty & happiness through the Cloud or mist before us. I beg your Pardon for takeing up so much of your time & remain Your Excellencys most Obedt & very hble Servant

Robt Morris

P.S. I venture to tell Mr Tilghman here that I recd his letter & sent the enclosure to his Father. I hope my letter herewith to Genl Lee may go in safe & the Money be pd to him.

To George Washington, 6–15 March 1777

Philada March 6[-15]th 1777

Dear Sir,

I am honoured with yours of the 2d Inst. the good opinion you are pleased to entertain of me makes me very happy because there is no mans opinion I reverence more and that very circumstance is at the same time the source of trouble in my mind as you force me to abandon that Idea of Security which I was desirous of maintaining; it is truely lamentable that we have never been able to this day to Conquer that Fundamental error made in the outset, by short enlistments; it was not untill Conviction of the absolute necessity of it, stared every Man in the Face that the wholesome measure of enlisting for three years or during the War, cou'd be carried in Congress & since it was carried there, it meets with insuperable obstacles raised by the former practice, for the Bounties, high Wages & Short Service has Vitiated the Minds of all that Class of people & they are grown the most mercenary beings that exist I dont confine this observation meerly to the Soldiery but extend it to those who get their livings by Feeding & entertaining of them, these are the Harpies that injure us much at this time, they keep the Fellows Drunk whilst the Money holds out When it is gone they encourage them to enlist for the sake of Bounty, then to drinking again that Bounty gone & more Money still wanted they must enlist again with some other Officer receive a fresh Bounty & get more Drink &c. this Scene is actually carrying on here daily & does immense injury to the recruiting Service, but still I hope our New Army will be got together before long, at least so many as will enable you to put a good Face towards your Enemies and if that is accomplished I think they will not Venture this way, at present it seems to be their Object and in Your situation I really do not see what is to prevent their taking possession of it, unless the want of Horses Forage &c. retards their movements or renders it impracticable for them to come on, In the mean time the public Stores are removing, and Congress have adjourned back to this place many of the Members are come up & the rest on the road, I dont expect they will make a House sooner than Monday, but your late dispatches Shall be delivered to the President soon as he arrives. I wish with you Sir, that they had Complyed with General Lee's request, and when I sent forward those dispatches to Baltimore I wrote my Sentiments to some of the Members & altho it wou'd have been inconvenient for me and I urged not to be appointed on that errand Yet I wou'd have gone rather than he Shou'd have been disapointed, Whether they will take up the matter again or not I don't know, but I much doubt it as from the Little conversation I have had with some of the Members now here they seem very averse to it, however I expect this matter as well as the Confinement of the Hessian Field Officers will at least be referred to the Consideration of a

Committee in Consequence of your letters on the Subject, and if I can influence a Complyance with Your Wishes it will give me pleasure for my own Sentiments coincide with yours exactly in these two points and at the same time I must hint to you what I take to be one of the most forcive Arguments that probably has been used in Congress against this Measure, I have not heard that it was used, but as it occured to myself on reading Genl Lee's letters, I mean the effect it may have at the Court of France shou'd they hear as they undoubtedly wou'd that Members of Congress Visited Genl Lee by permission of the British Commissioners. The Meeting with Ld Howe on Staten Island last Summer injured Mr Deane's Negotiations much & retarded supply's intended for us. I am now at the 15th March & must appologize to you Sir for not answering fully your Letter & for not having sent this away long since, but I have been attacked by a Weakness in my Eyes, and Writing is the most dangerous thing I can do whilst it Continues on this Account I am obliged to absent myself from Congress & refrain from (business) but in all situations of life I shall ever remain with the sincerest esteem Your Excellcys most obedient hble Servant

Robt Morris

To the American Commissioners, 7 March 1777

Philada. March 7th. 1777

Gentlemen

I have wrote you several letters and sent you dispatches from Congress and Committee of Correspondance by Mr. Reed who will probably be longer in reaching you than this but he goes by a much safer Conveyance as I apprehend. The Congress have adjourned from Baltimore to this place again but I think rather at an improper time as it appears to me that Genl. Howe is now forming another expedition against this place and I shall not think the City safe whilst the principal part of its defence depends on Militia, and altho our New Army has been recruiting a Considerable time yet we do not find them so forward as cou'd be wished, the want of cloathing &c. keeps them back a good deal, but we are spurring them on as much as possible. I do most sincerely hope you will negotiate the Loan and send out the Articles Wanted as we might then have leisure to make remittances with greater security than we can if done precipitately. We have bought considerable quantities of produce in various parts and shall export it as fast as the times, Seasons and Enemies Ships will permit, this you may depend on, and the Produce of this Country if it coud once be exported freely will soon discharge the Debt it may be necessary to Contract.

The Committee will all be here next Week and write you fully themselves. In the mean time I remain with perfect Esteem and respect Gentlemen Your obedient humble servant

Robt Morris

To the American Commissioners, 28 March 1777

Philada. March 28. 1777

Honorable Gentlemen

I wrote you a few lines the 7th Inst. by Monsr. Coleaux and sent you the News papers to that time; by this Conveyance I send another packet of them under Cover to Mr. Delap at Bordeaux. There are only two Members of the Committee of Correspondance here at present, the rest being absent on leave.

Genl. Howe's army in the Jerseys still remains inactive, and greatly distressed for want of Forage and Fresh provisions which they cannot obtain in any tollerable plenty as our Army are posted all round them, have removed most of the Hay, Corn and Provisions that was near Brunswick and never suffer a Foraging party of the Enemy to stir out but they attack them and altho' they come out strong enough to drive our People from their Posts very frequently, yet it has always happened the reverse, for they are constantly driven back into Brunswick with considerable loss of Men Horses, Waggons &c. Their Situation is disagreable and for that and other reasons I cannot think they will be Content with it much longer, especially as desertion is become frequent amongst their best British Troops, the Grenadiers, more or less of them, come over to us every Week. You being at so great a distance may probably think we ought to have destroyed Mr. Howe's Army by this time, and we undoubtedly shou'd had we an Army to do it. But when it is considered that Genl. Washington has drove them from their Cantonements on Delaware to Brunswick and confined them there the whole winter, during which he has killed and taken between 3 and 4000 of their Men, 4 to 500 Horses, a Number of Waggons and considerable quantities of Stores, Cloathing &c., kept them pent up in a place where they are Ill supplyed with provisions and other Necessarys which has produced desertion, discontent and sickness, it will astonish all mankind to learn that he had not during that whole time one half their Numbers in the Field, and the greatest part of the Troops he had, consisted of raw Militia that never saw a Gun fired in anger untill opposed to this very formidable army. It is now evident to all America that if in the beginning of this Contest we had enlisted our army for a Number of Years or during the War, Genl. Howe cou'd not have wintered here unless as a Prisoner, but alas our Army were disbanded by the nature of their enlistments when they cou'd have been most usefull and the militia are too much their own masters to expect from them a steady adherence to the extream Fatigues of a long and hard Winters Campaign. They turn out for a month or six weeks shew great Bravery whilst they stay, but curiosity once being gratifyed and some feat performed to make a good story at home, they become impatient to return to their Familys and neither perswasion nor principle can detain them. For this reason Gen. Washingtons army since Novr. last has consisted every month of fresh raw hands, a constant shifting Scene of comers and goers, you might suppose him 10 to 15 or 20 thousand strong by the Commisarys and Quarter Masters returns but never 5000 by the Adjutant Generals for he never had so many at any one time with him. These constant movements of Militia and the large Bountys and high wages given them has hurt the recruiting service exceedingly for those that would have enlisted, by turning out as militia for a short time have got more money than their pay and Bounty as soldiers wou'd amount to and they are more their own Masters. In short the Systems adopted by Congress respecting the Army were formed without experience and have not been equal to what was expected from them. They are now and for sometime have been Correcting their errors, so that I hope to see a formidable army under wise and wholesome regulations in a very short time as the General is now drawing all the new recruits together and as his hands are strengthened with sufficient powers I have no doubt he will do business with them this summer if the Numbers raised are sufficient to Face the Enemy and this I am inclined to believe will be the case. The Garrison at Ticonderago will be strong enough to dispute the passage there with Mr. Carleton and if you do but effect an European War to employ the British Navy, this Country will become Free and independant in a shorter time than cou'd have been expected. I fancy Genl. and Ld. Howe have it in View to attack this City. They may possibly get possession and if they do it will probably bring on their ruin, for they will there raise a Nest of Hornets that they dont expect and are taught to believe very differently. I am most truely Gentlemen Your Obedient humble servant.

Robt Morris

To John Jay, 1 April 1777

Philada. April 1st. 1777

Dear Sir

The enclosed letters came by a French Ship to New Hampshire & were sent under Cover to me by Mr Langdon with many others, I believe they are from England, and wish they may convey agreable Tidings. Last Week a Brigt arrived here with 6800 Muskets & 2100 Gun Locks, another in Maryld With 633 bbls Powder & this ship into Portsmouth brought with her about 12,000 Muskets, 1000 bbls Powder a Number of Blankets & Cloathing all these are for Continental Account and many others may daily be looked for— An offer was made to our Comrs. at Paris of two Millions of Livers without Interest to be repaid when these United States have established their Independancy in Peace & quietness, no Security or Conditions required, You may be sure they accepted this Noble Bounty & 500,000 Livers was paid down the 20th. Jany.—500,000 more was to be paid every three months untill compleated or Sooner if our affairs require it. The Comrs. were well received & promised protection of the Court and that their propositions shou'd all by duely attended to, Great Armaments & preparations for war &c. I fancy however, we must try our Strength alone for a while longer altho I firmly believe a general War will & must Eventually take place in Europe this Summer I wish our army was in the Field we want nothing else to make the day our own. Wth great regard & esteem I am Dr sir your affectionate hbl Servt

Robt Morris.

PS My best Compts to Mr Duane & Mr Livingston.

To George Washington, 10 May 1777

Philada May 10th 1777

Dear Sir

I have not taken the liberty of giving You any trouble for sometime past and indeed I never do it but with great reluctance because I know how much Your attention & time must be engaged in the most important pursuits.

The bearear of this the Marquis Armand de la Rouerie is entitled to my Warmest recommendations because he brought from his own Country letters to me that I am obliged to attend to & put great faith in as they come from persons Worthy of the utmost Credit, one of them is from Mr Deane who not only mentions him as a Gentn of Rank, good Family & Fortune but also as a Man of great Merit desiring my particular attention to him & that I should supply him with Money which will be repaid in France by a Gentn to whom America is under the most important obligations. You will therefore excuse & oblige me at the same time by your favourable attention to Monsr Armand for he chooses to pass by that Name & shoud he want Money I will pay his drafts for what he Stands in need of—I find he is a little disgusted at an appointment made for him by Congress this day and I believe it was through the inattention of a Committee which I shall get set right again in a Short time. I am Dr sir with the greatest esteem & affection Your obedt hble sert

Robt Morris

To George Washington, 16 August 1777

Philadelphia August 16. 1777

Dear sir

Agreeable to your Excellencys desire in your favour of the 14th Current, I have taken from the Minutes of the Committee of Congress who resided here last Winter, an account of the Silver sent you to Trenton, as underneath. I must assure you that it affords me true pleasure to be favoured with your Commands and that my best wishes are constantly for your health and prosperity being most respectfully Dr sir Your Affte and Obedient humble servant

Robt Morris

To George Washington, 27 August 1777

Philadelphia August 27th 1777

Dear Sir

I cannot withstand the solicitations of Monsr Epiniers the Nephew of Monsr Beau Marchais (whose Services to America I fancy you are not unacquainted with), but take the liberty to introduce this Young Gentn to your Excellencys patronage & protection He has just obtained from Congress a Captains Commission, and seems to possess an Active Mind with a large fund of Good Nature that will not fail to recommend him to those who have an opportunity of observing his Conduct, I shou'd be very unwilling to trouble you on any occasion but the present is indispensible. I have the honor to remain Your Excellencys Most Obedt & very hble servt

Robt Morris

To Benjamin Franklin, 27 December 1777

Manheim in Pensylvania Decemr. 27th. 1777

Dear Sir

As Mr. Deane has been recalled by Congress, it is uncertain wether he may be in Paris when this arrives, therefore I inclose it to you, in order that you may read the Contents of a letter I wrote to Congress Yesterday and of another to him of this Date, after which you will please to forward or deliver them to him. By these you will discover that I am intirely undeceived with respect to my Brother, and that so far from persisting in a defence of him I have determined to give him up intirely to his own Fate. Those letters will inform you so fully of my sentiments, my conduct and motives that led to it, that I think it unnecessary to trouble you with any thing further on the ungratefull Subject, except to assure you, which I most solemnly do, that I blame myself much for having written that unfortunate letter of the 29th June to Mr. Deane, and more so for having given way to Suspicions that I am now perfectly convinced were injurious to you and him. Mine has been an error founded on the misinformation of other People and backed by what I then thought a laudable partiality to a Man that I had taken much pains and gone to much expence to make a good Citizen and usefull Member of society. It is said that repenting Sinners are entitled to forgiveness and in that case I am sure Mr. Deane and you must receive me back to that share of your Friendship and esteem that I once thought myself honoured with. Happy will you make me by a line to this effect as I entertain the greatest veneration and respect for your Person and Character and am Dear Sir Your most Obedient humble Servant

Robt Morris

To George Washington, 9 May 1778

Manheim in Pensylva May 9th 1778

Dear Sir

I was honoured with yours of the 27th Ulto which needs no reply, I also rec'd your answer to what I had wrote respecting Colo. Armand & did not think it necessary to trouble you further on that Subject.

In a letter from my Friend Isaac Governeur Esqr. dated Curracoa 11th Feby 1778, which reached me a few days since, is the following paragraph "there is also a small Box Containing one dozn Bottles of Constantia Wine, its made at the Cape of Good Hope is an excellent Stomatick & very refreshing when fatigued its directed to his Excelly Genl Washington & begs his acceptance hopeing he will pardon the Freedom."

I believe this Box has been landed in North Carolina under the care of Jos. Hewes Esqr. and I will desire him to send it forward by the first safe Conveyance—when I congratulated your Excelly on the great good News lately received from France, you will not expect me to express my Feelings, was I in your Company my Countenance might shew, but my pen cannot express them. Most sincerely do I give you joy, Our Independance is undoubtedly Secured, our Country must be Free & to compleat this Work I most ardently pray, that Victory may be your Handmaid the ensuing Campaign. With the most perfect esteem I remain Your Excellys Obedient hble servt

Robt Morris

To Benjamin Franklin, 18 September 1779

Philada. Septr. 18th. 1779

Dear Sir

I have never rec'd a line from you in reply to the letters I wrote you & Mr. Deane in Decemr. 1777 and confess it surprized me a little, but the matter is entirely cleared up by the receipt of your favour of the 19th Feby last as in a P.S: thereto you mention having answered my said letters which had been entirely satisfactory, desirous of retaining your good opinion you may be sure I was well pleased at the expressions in this postscript; the business recommended in the body of that letter falls under the management of my Friend Mons Holker but you may depend on my attention to all Your recommendations. The Chevr Luzerne has not yet reached this City, but he sent me your Letter of the 2d June last, the Character you give him is very agreable & I hope he may compensate for the loss of Mr Gerard who carries with him the perfect esteem of all Men not biassed by Selfish or Party Views. I shall pay the attentions in my power to the Chevr Luzerne both on account of your recommendation his own Merits & Public Station—

Mr Gerard will no doubt give you every information respecting our situation here he knows it well & I dare say will do it impartially. My opposition to the Constitution of this State & opposition to Parties in Congress has procured me abundance of unmerited abuse, but supported by conscious innocence & unshaken Integrity I have never failed to get the better of my Enemies on the day of tryal—

With the best wishes for your health & happiness I remain Dear Sir Your most Obedt & very hble servt.

Robt Morris

To George Washington, 1 February 1780

Philada Feby 1st 1780

Dear Sir

As I make it a rule never to claim any share of your attention without some sufficient cause, it gives me pleasure when an occasion does offer to pay my Compliments with propriety. Don Digges (a Gentn whom I do not know), residing in Theneriffe has given me the present opportunity, by shipping a Pipe of fine old wine onboard a Schooner Called the Hancock Capt. Scott intended for this place, which my Friend Mr Pasley requests I shou'd take charge of and forward it to You, it is marked G.W. & branded *Pasley*. You know with how much alacrity I shou'd have executed this Commission but the Schooner was forced from our Coast by the Severe Weather and got into Edenton in No. Carolina where I have requested Messrs Hewes smith & Allen to receive this pipe of Wine and keep it in their Custody untill orders from you or some person by Your authority appear for its removal, as I did not know but the Commissaries or Quarter Masters might find a better mode of transporting it to Camp than they or I could but if this conjecture is not well founded I shall most readily take measures for bringing it forward on the opening of the Navigation.

Mrs Morris joins me in the Sincerest & best wishes for health & happiness to Mrs Washington & your Excellency assuring You that you wou'd make us happy by a Visit to Philada during this long Severe Winter. We will endeavour to amuse you & afford some relaxation from the severity of discipline & duty which your exalted Station keeps You in the constant exercise of. With the most sincere regard & Veneration I am Your Excellencys, most obed. hble ser.

Robt Morris

To Benjamin Franklin (Two Letters), 31 March 1780

I.

Philada. March 31st 1780

Dear Sir

I have just recvd by the hands of our mutual Friend Mr Holker your favour of the 22d Octr last recommending the affairs of Monsr De la Freté with Mr. Roulhac of Edenton to my assistance. I had already engaged in that service and you may depend that every recommendation of yours has the Force & effect on my mind that you wou'd wish for. I shall ever feel myself pleased in the execution of Your Commands. I beg to trouble You with a letter for your Friend Monsr Dumas in Answer to one from him & with sincere attachment & Esteem I remain Dr Sir Your most obedt hbl sert

Robt Morris

II.

Philada. March 31st 1780

Dear Sir

I do not know that what I am now going to write is in the least degree necessary or that Mr. Deane will thank me for it but the thought has just struck me, that as he has constantly & invariably manifested a Warm attachment to your Person and Character, in his examination before Congress in his Publications, & in all his private Conversations at which I have been present, it might be some satisfaction to you & him, to have a testimony of this kind from a Friend to you both, who having nothing to seek or ask for himself can mean nothing but to promote that Harmony & Friendship which he wishes to continue in existence between two Worthy Men; I consider Mr. Deane as a Martyr in the Cause of

America after rendering the most signal & important Services he has been reviled & Traduced in the most shamefull manner. But I have not a doubt the day will come when his Merit shall be universally acknowledged and the Authors of those Calumnies held in the detestation they deserve.

My own Fate has been in some degree Similar, after four years Indefatigueable Service, I have been reviled & traduced, for a long time by whispers & insinuations which at length were fortunately wrought up to Public Charges; which gave me an Opportunity, to Shew how groundless, how Malicious these things were, how Innocent & Honest my Transactions, My Enemies ashamed of their persecution have quitted the pursuit and I am in the peaceable possession of the most Honourable Station my Ambition aspires to, that of a private Citizen of a Free State. Yourself my Good Sir have had a share in these Calumnies but the Malice which gave them Vent was so evident as to destroy its own Poison, they coud not cast even a Cloud over your justly & much revered Character. These things have taught me a lesson of Philosophy that may be of Service. I find the most usefull members of Society have most Enemies because there are a number of Envious beings in the Human Shape and if my opinion of Mankind in general is grown worse from my experience of them, that very circumstance raises my veneration for those Characters that justly merit the applause of Virtuous Men, in this light I view Doctor Franklin & Mr. Deane and under this View of them, I assert with an honest Confidence, that I have a just & equitable title to a return of that Friendship which I think it is honourable to profess for them with that degree of truth & affection which impresses me to it. I am Dr Sir Your most Obedient & very humble Servt.

Robt Morris

To John Jay, 6 July 1780

Philada. July 6th. 1780

Dear Sir

I am absolutely ashamed to think how long you have been gone & that in all that time I have not found , Start deletion,, End, ^leisure^ to write you a line, & even now sit down in the midst of hurry & Confusion occasioned by the dispatch of several Vessels under my care all going away together; just to enclose a letter from Mrs. Meredith at Trenton to Mrs. Jay. I regret that I did not fix a Cypher with you, as the want of it will prevent me from writing (when I do begin) many things I might wish to Communicate. I hope Mrs Jay is recovered from the Indisposition that attacked her at Cadiz. Kitty stayed the Winter with us, & went to the Jersey's in May or beginning of June. Mrs Livingston about that time moved with the Family to Elizabeth Town and was there when Mr. Knyphausen came out the other day, at first the Family were treated politely but after a while they found it necessary to leave that place, being threatned hard by the *Brutish* as our Soldiers now call the British— Mrs. Jays Brother John is now here a Midshipman onboard the Saratoga Capt Young nearly ready to go out on a Cruize. We are anxiously looking out for Monsr De Ternay and hope the Campaigne will still end favourably for the Allies—

Mr Duer & Lady Kitty are at their Farm on the North River— poor Gouverneur Morris you will have heard has lost his Legg but is getting well again—

Mrs. Morris is out at Springsetsbury *next the Hills* & dont know of my writing or she woud have much to say to Mrs. Jay & yourself for I can truely say she holds warm affection for you both.

Having already wrote more than I intended or expected I can only beg you to believe that I am Dear Sir Your sincere & affectionate Friend & Obedt Servt.

Robt Morris

PS I beg to be remembered to Mr Carmicheal & hope he is in the enjoyment of health & happiness—

To George Washington, 28 September 1780

Philada Septr 28th 1780

Sir

I am indebted to Andw Elliot Esqr. of New-York for many Acts of Friendship, Civilty & Humanity shewn by him at my request to various American Prisoners in that place, He has obtained them liberty to return on Parole, to be exchanged, or advanced them Money just as their Circumstances required, and I have had no call to make return's untill now, that a Captn Mure of the 82d Regt lately taken onboard a Packet bound from England to New York, is a Prisoner at Lancaster, and Mr Elliot desires me to obtain leave for him to go into New York on Parole and an exchange if possible as he will interest himself to have any American Officer that shall be Named of equal Rank sent out immediately in return for Capt. Mure who is a near relation of His. As I am sure your inclination will not only lead you to oblige me but also to enable any Friend of this Country to return obligations of the Nature of those, I owe to Mr Elliot, it is not necessary that I urge a compliance with this request which will not be refused unless the interest of our Country or the Rule of your duty, forbid what I ask, and in either case, I wou'd neither make nor persist in such an application. I applied to the Board of War, they informed me that Doctr Withersp⟨oon⟩ had interested himself on behalf of Capt. Mure, but from the Tenor of some late Resolutions of Congress on the Subject of Prisoners, they thought it more proper You shou'd alone decide on these points, otherwise they were disposed to permit Capt. Mure to go in on Parole—With the most perfect esteem & respect I have the Honour to be Your Excellencys most Obedt hble Servt

Robt Morris

To Benjamin Franklin, 25 October 1780

Philada. Octr. 25th. 1780

Dear Sir

I take the liberty to introduce an Old acquaintance of mine to your Patronage & Protection whilst he may Stay in Paris which I apprehend will be but a Short time, it is Mr. Isaac Hazelhurst of this place who Visits Europe on Commercial Views and who I fancy will transact his business chiefly in France & Holland. Your Countenance cannot fail to be usefull to a Stranger and I wou'd not ask it, but in favour of a deserving Man.

Your Enemies are busy here but I hope their operations will not be able to touch you, If I can help to bear the shield that protects Your honour & your reputation I shall deem it no small happiness for I am Dr Sir Your sincere admirer & Obedt hble servt

Robt Morris

To Alexander Hamilton, 26 May 1781

Philada. May 26 1781

Sir,

It is Some time Since I Received your performance dated the 30th. April last. I have read it with that attention which it justly deserves and finding many points of it to Coincide with my own Opinions on the Subject, it naturally Strengthened that Confidence which every man ought to possess to a certain degree in his own judgement. You will very Soon See the Plan of a Bank published and Subscriptions opened for its establishment, having already met with the approbation of Congress. It only Remains for Individuals to do their part and a foundation will be laid for the Anticipation of Taxes and Funds by a Paper Credit that can not Depreciate.

The Capital proposed falls far Short of your Idea and indeed far Short of what it ought to be, but I am Confident if this is once Accomplished the Capital may afterward be encreased to almost any Amount, to propose a large Sum in the Outsett, and fail in the Attempt to Raise it might prove Fatal, to begin with what is Clearly in our power to accomplish, and on that beginning to establish the Credit that will Meritably Command the future encrease of Capital Seems the most Certain Road to Success. I have thought much about Interweaving a Land Security with the Capital of this Bank, but am apprehensive it would Convey to the Publick Mind an Idea of Paper being Circulated on that Credit and that the Bank of Consequence must fail in its Payments in Case of any Considerable Run on it; and we must expect, that its Ruin will be attempted by External and Internal Foes. I have therefore left that point to the future Deliberations of the Directors of this Bank to whom in due time I shall Communicate your address. I esteem myself much your Debtor for this piece not merely on account of the personal Respect you have been pleased to express but also on account your good Intentions and for these and the pains you have taken I not only think, but on all proper Occasions Shall Say, the Publick are also Indebted to you.

My office is new and I am Young in the execution of it. Communications from Men of Genius & abilities will always be acceptable and yours will ever Command the attention of,   Sir Your obed hble Servt.

Robt. Morris

To George Washington, 29 May 1781

Philada May 29th 1781

Dear Sir

I find by several letters that have come before my view, you have been informed of what has passed between Congress and my self relative to the office of Superintendant of Finance. The unmeritted abuse I had formerly received as the reward of Exertions as disinterested and pure as ever were made by Mortal Man had determined me against a very public Station, and God knows my Sentiments are not changed; Contrary to my inclination to my Judgement and to my Experience have I consented to make an other Attempt in favour of this poor distressed Country at a time when only one consideration could have influenced me thereto, that only consideration is, the absolute Necessity of a Reformation being attempted and the difficulty of getting any other person on whom Congress could agree. If my abilities were equal to the undertaking I might have less dread & less reluctance but conscious of my own deficiency I cannot help trembling at the prospect before me, at the same time could I depend on that steady Support which I ought to receive from Congress from the Governments of the Several States, and from the Worthy part of the Citizens of every State, I shou'd be encouraged to expect that the Sacrifices I am asking wou'd not be in vain, and believe me Good Sir, that Inspired with a virtuous Emulation from your bright Example I will not begrudge all I shall feel and suffer; if my Country derives real benefit from my Exertions, Since I have agreed to engage in this move these Herculean Labours I promise assiduity in the pursuit of what I shall think Honest Measures, calculated to promote a vigourous Collection of Revenue and an Œcomonical Expenditure of it. If I can by plain Systems and punctual performance of engagements restore Confidence If I can by degrees bring about a Revenue nearly proportioned to our Expences, and by punctual pay, constant supplies of Provisions and Regular Cloathing encourage Your Army and thereby give some ease to your Fatiques and Anxiety I shall be more than paid for every exertion, but when I look at the detail by which all these things are to be accomplished When I consider the difficulty of getting disinterested able Men for assistants, when I reflect on the opposition to be expected from those who are my personal Enemies and from those whom Ambition, Envy, disapointment and disgrace will make Enemies not only to my person but to my measures. Where am I to look for support. I shall answer the question by telling you Candidly I depend in the first instance on the integrity and disinterestedness of my own Conduct, and next on those Virtuous Men whom such Conduct will engage in my Favour, and to You Sir, as the first of that Class: but at the same time that I thus bespeak your favour, I scorn to ask it on any other terms than those of desert.

I may err in Judging of Men measures & things but I think it will never be a supported charge against me that I have done Wilfull wrong. In short I have promised nothing but honesty and assiduity and these I trust will not be wanting As to the rest, I must rely on the best information intelligence assistance and advice that I can procure from you. I have much to express in this way and I woud

48

fain hope that a force, Candid sincere Communication may take place between us, much confidential intercourse must ensue and I promise myself that you will never regret the having placed it with me if so it should happen. I am not fairly intended on the Execution of my Office yet, that being delayed a while that I may meet our assembly once more and that I may clear myself of private business. Congress however are pressing Committees & Conferences on me contrary to stipulations, one of which was that they shou'd give time to form <u>my</u> arrangements and carry on the present Campaigne under the <u>old</u> ones, without expecting aid from me therein, but you will see by another letter I shall address to You this date, that I am obliged to engage and as it is for your Relief I shall rejoice if my letters produce the Effect expected from them, I expect to have the pleasure of a personal interview with you either at Camp or here before long, I say here because some Members of Congress have thought Your presence here might be very usefull which is all that I know in that Respect, I am glad you approve of my sending Genl Robertsons Command. Mrs Morris joins in the Sincerest Compts to Mrs Washington and Yourself, be assured You have no greater admirers nor any more tru9ly attached to you; I am Dr Sir Your most Obedt hble Servt

Robt Morris

To George Washington, 29 May 1781

Philada May 29th 1781

Dear Sir

A Committee of Congress having communicated to me the distress of Your Army for want of Bread and shewn me a Motion that had been made in Congress in Consequence thereof, but which was Committed in order to a Conference with me on the Subject. I found myself immediately impressed with the Strongest desire to afford you Relief and also to avoid such measures as are proposd in the said motion, such being calculated like too many others that have been adopted to procure immediate relief, at the same time Sowing the seeds that never fail to produce plentifull Crops of future distresses and disapointments, Not being prepared in my official Character with Funds or means of accomplishing the supplies you need, I have wrote to Major Genl Schuyler and to Thomas Lowrey Esqr. in New Jersey requesting their immediate Exertions to procure upon their own Credit 1000 bbls of flour each and to send the same forward in parcells as fast as procured to Camps delivered to your Excellincys order and I have pledged my self to pay them in hard Money for the Cost & charges within a Month Six Weeks or two Months, I shall make it a point to provide the Money being determined never to make an engagement that cannot be fullfilled for if by any reasons I shou'd fail in this respect I will quit my Office as useless from that Moment. I hope therefore the letters written will produce the flour very soon at Camp and I rather chose to direct the delivery of it to Your Excellancys order than to send it into the hands of the Commissaries because there are many assertions made (whether with Truth or not I do not pretend to decide at this time) that Provisions are not delivered out with that Oeconomy which circumstances like ours require, and if you have any reason to suppose there is foundation for such reports, perhaps it wou'd be time well spent to appoint an Officer to attend the receipt and delivery of this flour. I desired the Gentn to have the weights marked on the head of every barrell in order that proper Account might easily be taken thereof at Camp, and if the Superintendg Officer attends to this, to the quantity of Rations that of right shou'd be delivered daily, sees that no more are given out, he will finally be able to ascertain the whole Account and shew what the consumption is or ought to be, shou'd you think this matter worthy of your attention it is probable that such a mode of Issuing under proper checks may now be devised and experimented as will lay

50

the ground Work for future regulation all which I only offer as hints which you will make use of or not, as your own situation and circumstances will permit, but this is certain, we must introduce the Stricktest Oeconomy into the Issuing departments or the Army will for ever be exposed to wants which are not less disgracefull than painfull. I sent the letters by Mr Govr Morris who promised to call at Mr Lowrys House to enforce the execution of business there, & to send the Letter for Genl Schuyler to your Excy that it might be forwarded by Express. I have the honour to be Dr Sir Your Excellys most Obedt

Robt Morris

To John Jay, 5 June 1781

Philada June 5th. 1781

Dear Sir

I must freely acknowledge the justice of Your charge against me as a bad Correspondant, for the force of Truth wou'd Convict were I to deny, and perhaps Friendship will hardly bear with paliatives but knowing well your attachment to and practice of Sincerity, I shall honestly tell you I did not like to write on political matters, and in what may be called Domestick you had constantly better information than twas possible for me to give, having also very ample employment for my time you will reflect that all these Circumstances combined to make me silent altho not inattentive or forgetfull of my Friends abroad.

I am sorry to learn that Messrs. Joyes the Bankers did not answer my expectations, their interested connection with Britain must account for it, and the Slender intercourse our infant Country had commenced with the Rich Citizens of Europe must give way, untill *rendered* more important by the Natural progress of things those interested beings shall *feel* their interest most advanced by that intercourse being renewed & strengthened then and not 'till then will they give us a preferance.

I have three letters from you dated the 28 May 16 Septr and 19th Novr. last and feel myself exceedingly indebted to that partiality which prompted you to say many Civil things, these are stamped with an unusual Value not because I suffer myself to think they are merited, but because, you thought so. We have heard more of you & Mrs. Jay than these letters tell me, and upon the whole have not found much cause to be pleased with your situation. Hers must too often have been very disagreable, the loss of the little *one* was truely distressing and your almost constant absence extreamly hard. But you must comfort yourselves with the Reflection that still more Cruel things might have happened had you remained in your own Country, suppose you had been with your Father when some of the Enemies Ruffians broke into the House and after satiating themselves with Plunder they had carried you my Dear Friend a Prisoner to New York, think of the Triumph of your Enemies, the distress of your Friends and what you must under such Circumstances have suffered, happy that you have escaped such an event I will not prolong the Idea of it. Upon enquiring after Francis Child I was told he had gone to settle at Richmond in Virginia and of course he must be in distress at present as the Enemy are in possession of that place Shou'd he retreat this way I will pay him the Money you desire and under such circumstances there is little doubt of its being acceptable, I told Kitty on the Reciept of your letter that I shou'd pay her twenty pounds Sterlg for the use of little Peter whenever she pleased but she has not yet taken it, She is now here and no doubt will write you every thing you can wish to know, as she commands a ready and Communicative Pen, through which flow the Sentiments of Genius, Prudence & Judgment conducted by Penetration and a well informed mind.

You are very attentive to our little junto at Springetsbury, a Cursed Fever obliged me to desist last Winter; and now, with regret I say it, Public employment will not permit the Renewal of those Social parties, but still the time may come when our enjoyments shall Return with redoubled Gust. having the blessings of an honourable Peace added thereto—. Mrs. Morris is very well and ever will feel herself strongly attached to Mrs Jay and you I suppose she will write for herself either by this or some other opportunity, altho not fond of her Pen. As this letter is entirely of a private nature I do not have recourse to a Cypher, but as I shall by this or the next Conveyance write you on Public business that which you sent me the 19th Novr. must be made use of. Our Friend Governeur has acquainted you with my appointment to be Superintendent of Finance, the motives of my acceptance are purely Patriotic and I wou'd this moment give much of my property to be excused but pressed by my Friends, acquaintances, Fellow Citizens and almost by all America I could not resist, I will therefore most assiduously try to be usefull and if in this I do but Succeed my Recompense will be ample. Governeur and others have promised me the assistance of their abilities, Congress promise Support if the Legislatures and Individuals will do the same we will soon change the face of our affairs and show our Enemies that their hopes of our ruin through the Channel of Finance is as vain as their hope of Conquest.

Your Brother Sir James is here and calls sometimes to see us, he has been long in this City but I understand has not been to you a much better Correspondant than myself he desired me the other day to think of Foedy if any employment offered that wou'd suit him, this I shall gladly comply with. I wish He & H. Brockholst Livingston were with me just now if not better provided for than the views that now offer, I want Honest, Active, able Men about me.

This Campaigne as usual opens to our disadvantage, but I expect it will also as usual close favourably for us, The Vices and Follies of our Enemies may justly be counted among the Number of our Fast Friends, they never fail to work for our Relief in the hours of distress, for at those times the Pride, Insolence and Tyranny of the British Heroes are too insufferable to be borne even by the Peasantry of America. It affords me much pleasure to find the assistance I have given towards delivering supplies at Havannah is known and approved by the Ministry at the Court of Madrid as a favourable impression there may be serviceable to my administration of the Finances and I hope still to return more important Services , Start deletion,, End, for those I expect from them to this distressed Country Adieu my Dear Sir with Sincere affection I am your Obedient hble Servt.

Robt Morris

PS Governeur Morris is in Jersey at present

PS

I find that in enumerating the letters I have recd. from you that of the 18 Decr. is omitted, it was Mislaid, Arnolds Plot is no longer of any Consequence to us, he very deservedly will & inevitably must be despised to all Eternity for his base Treason Our News papers swarm with too much personal abuse, very few Characters escape being attacked at one time or other and I fear it does much more hurt than good—

To Benjamin Franklin, 6 June 1781

Philada. June 6th. 1781

Dear Sir

Your very obliging letter of the 3d of June last year has been with me some time altho it was long in reaching my hands. My intention in troubling you at this time is only to Announce the Appointment I have received from Congress of Superintendant of the Finances of the United States, which my Friends, Acquaintance & Fellow Citizens have pressed me to Accept in such terms as have to me proved irresistable altho my Interest Tranquility & Domestic happiness must suffer beyond Compensation. Indeed the only Compensation I can have, will be the reflections that will arise from rendering essential Services to this (at present) embarrassed Country Shou'd I succeed in the attempt and if I do I will be well content with that payment for my sacrifices. If I do not succeed it Shall not be for want of Assiduity or exertion nor through any default that my small Abilities can prevent.

As I engage in this Arduous undertaking upon the most disinterested Principles and with the Sole View of Serving my Country I have a right to look up to, and call upon, all those Virtuous Sons of America who really wish to promote the interest of their Country, to assist and support My Measures so long as they have that object in View and further I do not presume to ask their Countenance. To you then Good Sir, as a Staunch Friend, an Able & Faithfull Servant to your Country, I turn my Eyes, honoured with your Friendship, esteeming your Virtues & Admiring your Abilities. You must think that a promise of Patronage & Support to me as a Public Officer so long as my Conduct Shall justly Merit it, will be most gratefully received, especially as that Spirit of envy, Jealousy & Faction which appears too strongly planted in this Country generally directs its poisoned darts at the most usefull characters, which from that cause only, are frequently in need of Support from Honest disinterested Men. I shall have occasion to write You in my official Character probably by this same Conveyance and therefore I will not longer trespass on your patience than to assure you of that respect & esteem with which I ever am Dear Sir Your most Obedt Servt.

Robt Morris

To Benjamin Franklin, 8 June 1781

Philada. June 8th. 1781

Dear Sir

In a private letter which I did myself the honour to write you the 6th Inst. I announced the Appointment I have received from the Honourable Congress to the Office of Superintendant of the Finances of the United States of No America And now beg leave to address you in my official Character. Congress have thought proper to Commit to me the disposition & management of the Money Granted to the United States by His Most Christn Majesty in aid of our operations for the present Campaigne, in order that the same may be solely applied to that use; and for this reason I have found it necessary to keep the whole business of this Grant seperate and distinct from any other, so that its application may at any time be clearly seen, instead therefore of drawing upon your Excellency, who have many other bills running upon you, I have judged it expedient to Name Messrs. Le Couteulx & Compy Bankers in Rue Montorgueil, Paris, to receive the Money in Gales, from His Majestys Ministers so that they may be enabled to honour my Bills with acceptance whenever they appear, and punctually to acquit them as they fall due. I have written to Messrs. LeCouteulx & Co. that you wou'd join & support them in any application that may become needfull to His Majesty or His

Ministers which I hope you will readily do, And on the other hand, your attention to the interest of this Country will lead you to inform yourself whether the House of LeCouteulx & Compy are as perfectly safe & Rich as they ought to be, to entitle them to this trust. They are represented to me as one of the safest & most prudent Banking Houses in Europe, and His Excelly The Minister of France at this place now writes to have five hundred thousand Livres Tournois deposited with them on Acct of the United States Subject to my drafts or Orders. Shou'd their Credit not entitle them to this Trust, you will please to interfere and consult with Mr Necker what Banker to employ in such case directing those you do employ to Accept & pay my drafts, however I immagine these Gentn. will be found sufficiently safe. Shou'd it be more agreable to Mr. Necker that any other Banker be made use of, give me the name and write me the propriety of such alteration and I shall acquiesce in such change immediately on the receipt of your letter, for I have no partiality in Public business, all I wish is to Act with Security and to the best advantage. If you think it proper to inquire into the terms on which the Bankers will receive & pay this Money and settle their Coms.[Commissions] on the most moderate footing I shall be happy in your doing so. I do not however wish to give you any trouble that is not proper & necessary, being with the highest esteem & regard, Your Excellencys Most Obedient and most humble servant

Robt
Morris
S. I. of Finances

To Thomas Jefferson, 11 June 1781

Philadepa. June 11th 1781

Sir

No doubt you have seen in the Publick Papers, the plan of Establishing a National Bank, the necessity of which every body sees that allow themselves the least time for reflection on the present State of Public Credit. All the Publick Bodies in America, have more or less lost the Confidence of the World as to Money Matters, by trying Projects and applying Expedients to stop a Course of depreciation which Original errors had fixed too deep to Admit of any radical Cure. It is in vain to think of carrying on War any longer, by means of such Depreciating Medium and at same time an Efficient circulation of Paper that Cannot depreciate is Absolutely Necessary to Anticipate the Revenues of America. A National Bank is not only the most Certain but will prove the Most Usefull and Oeconomical Mode of doing so. It is therefore of the Utmost Importance that this first Essay, confined as it is in point of Capital, should be brought into Action with the greatest Expedition. I am sensible that Plans of Publick Utility however Promising and pleasing they may be on their first Appearance soon grow languid unless it be the Particular Business of some Man or set of Men to Urge them forward. This may be said to be my Duty in the present instance but I cannot be every where. I must apply for Support to Gentlemen of your Character and Zeal for the service of their Country requesting in the most Earnest Manner you will urge your Friends and Fellow Citizens to become Proprietors of this Bank Stock. Every Subscriber will find his Own Interest benefitted, in proportion to the Capital he deposits. And I dare say few will find the Other parts of their Fortunes to yield them so large or so certain an income as the Stock they have in the Bank. And at the same time they will have the Satisfaction to be Consider'd for Ever as promoters of an Institution, which has been found beneficial to other Countries, and inevitably must be so in the highest degree to this. An institution that most probably will Continue as long as the United States, and that will probably become as usefull to Commerce and Agriculture in the days of Peace as it must to Government during the War.

The Capital proposed is but small when the Extent and Riches of the United States are Considered, but when put in Motion, the Benefits flowing from it will be so perceptible that all difficulty about Encreasing the Capital will vanish, And we shall only have to Appeal to the interest of Mankind, which in most Cases will do more than Patriotism, but there have been and will Continue to be instances where Interest have been Sacrificed to Patriotism And in that belief, I ask you to devote some of your time to Promote this infant Plan which as it gathers Strength may in the end prove the means of saving the Liberties, Lives and property of the Virtuous part of America. My good Opinion of you is an excuse for Giving you this interuption. I am Sir Your Most Obedt. Servt.,

Robt Morris

To George Washington, 15 June 1781

Philada June 15th 1781

Dear Sir

I have been honoured with your very kind & obliging letter of the 4th Inst. and shou'd sooner have replied, but I am kept here in a kind of Suspense by the very slow manner of proceeding in the Assembly of this State. I am Financier Elect, but that is all, for had I taken the Oath & my Commission my Seat in the assembly must have been Vacated, and I think it of the utmost consequence to preserve my right of appearing there, untill the Tender & Penal Laws are totally repealed, for I consider those Laws, as destructive of all Credit, even amongst private People in dealings with one another, but to the Public officers, after the experience we have had, it is evident that the existence of such Laws any longer must totally preclude them from every possibility of Credit and in our circumstances the War cannot be carried on without it. I have already made such an impression on this Subject, that I feel pretty sure those Laws will be repealed in this State within these Few days, and I expect that the other Legislatures will readily follow the example. I am also pressing our assembly to Levy effective Taxes in hard Money, there are stronger objections made to this than the other measure, and they are more pertinaciously insisted on, but still they will either wholly or partially come into this also, and if once the Ice is broken they will see such advantages flowing from these foundations as will readily induce them to follow up the plans that evidently prove in the operation how beneficial they are to the Country. Insuperable obstacles have hitherto prevented me from bending my course towards your Camp, and it seems yet uncertain when it may be in my power, for altho' I stipulated with Congress that they should not rest any part of the present Campaigne on me, Yet they cannot refrain and already much of my time and attentions are engaged in that way, not having taken any Commission prevents me from Calling on the several departments for such returns as I should choose to have with me when I wait on your Excellency, for my objects are to reduce our public Expenditures as nearly as possible to what they ought to be and to obtain revenues in our own Country to meet those Expenses as nearly as can be and then to Shew Foreign Nations engaged in the War, that we must look to them for the balance, and I am very confident that when they shall see exertion on one hand & Oeconomy on the other they will be willing to assist us all they consistantly can. The promise you so chearfully make of granting all the support in your power increases my own Confidence and I will before long engage in the Duties of my Department with all the Energy I can master of, that is provided these Tender & penal

Laws are done away. I have the pleasure to hear that Mr Lowry has sent 1000 bbls of Flour to Camp, from Genl Schuyler I have not yet heard. I have the honor to be Your Excellency's Most devoted hble Servt

Robt Morris

P.S. I hope Mrs Washington is perfectly recovered & beg my best wishes & compts. Mrs Morris is at Trenton.

To George Washington, 21 June 1781

Philadelphia June 21st 1781

Dear Sir

Mr Lowrey having inform'd me of his sending forward the Thousand bbls Flour. and I find the Expence saved by it half Crown in the Ct. Weight, have thought proper to Agree with him for 1000 barrells, more fresh & Sweet, to be delivered to Your Excellencys Order. should you desire any particular rout to be taken with this Supply, and dispatch, or time, used in furnishing it, Your Excellency will be kind enough to give him the necessary information. With the most Respectfull Attachment I have the Honour to be Your Excellys Most Obdt Servt

Robt Morris

To Benjamin Franklin, 22 June 1781

Philada. June 22d. 1781

Dear sir

This Letter will I hope be in due time happily delivered to you by Mr. Geo. Harrison of this City— a Young Gent. of Good Family and Fortune whom I beg leave to Introduce to your Notice and Friendship— I doubt not his own Personal Merit will entitle him to these and I shall be thankfull to you for any Services it may be Convenient for you to Render him—Remaining very Respectfully Dr sir Your Obedt. hble servt.

Robt Morris

To John Jay, 29 June 1781

Philada. June 29. 1781

My dear Sir

I did expect to have written you official letters before this time, having now received my Commission and fairly entered upon the duties of my Station, but Congress press business on me so exceedingly, that I cannot yet command the time necessary for writing all I have to say to you. This I write at the request of a most worthy man, my friend Mr. John Ross, to whom Congress have made a partial payment out of a considerable debt which they owe him. I shall give him this letter open, that he may inclose in it a list of the bills he has received, part of which being drawn upon you, I am to request particularly that you will not only cause those to be paid, but also urge the payment of those on Holland, if you have any opportunity of doing so; for it is absolutely necessary for the preservation of Mr. Ross's credit in Europe that these remittances which he makes to the friends who enabled him to send such ample & seasonable supplies to these States should prove effective, & I hope your situation will enable you to afford him most chearfully this relief, which he is so well entitled to. I saw Govr. Livingston last week at Trenton very well & grown fatter than usual. Kitty is next door to me. She goes out to Springetsbury in a few days with our children.

time. We all join in best wishes for you & Mrs. Jay & I am, Dear Sir, Your affectionate friend & obedt hble Servt.

Robt Morris—

To George Washington, 2 July 1781

Office of Finance July 2d 1781

Dear Sir

I am honoured with yours of the 28th ulto and am happy to have contributed to your relief in any shape, be assured that it shall be my study to guard you as much as possible against, the distress and perplexity that arise from want of Provisions &c. and if the several Legislatures will only do their part with vigour I shall have the strongest hopes of putting a much better face on our monied affairs in a short time, but without their aid, the wheels will go heavily round, I shall therefore ply them closely. In order to bring about changes gradually I have advertized for Contracts to supply Rations to the Troops artificers & Prisoners that are now in this City or which may happen to be here from time to time between this and the 1st Jany next. another contract is also advertized for Lancaster; as the proposals are required to be delivered in to my office this week, and [the] next I expect to gain some insight from them and the treatys that will ensue, and will then go on advertizing for every Post that the Board of War & your Excellency may think necessary to continue. I believe it may, not answer so well, to Contract for Rations to be delivered at the Main Army, as to make one Contract for bread, another for fresh Beef, another for Salted Meat, another for Rum, Vinegar & Salt &c. because by dividing these Contracts I can oblige each Contractor to allow convenience in time of payment for certain part of the supplies, and it is most consistent with demonstrated Ideas to divide things of this kind amongst a number of Freemen rather than permit any one to grasp all the advantages that may arise from the Contract and there is no danger of prices rising so as to create Artificial Scarcity under the management of several Contractors, because they will all be actuated by <u>one principle</u> that operates effectually against that kind of Competition which raises prices whereas a number of purchasers who have no other [rule] for their Government, than a desire to obtain what they want, never fail to raise prices by the measure they pursue, even tho they mean to serve the Public ever so well.

The letter you mention to have been written by Genl Schuyler respecting a greater plenty of flour than he expected, has not come to my hands, but I am not under any apprehensions on the score of Provisions well knowing that we are blessed with abundance, for this I pledged myself when I got the Embargo taken off last Spring, and was then told I must Answer for it, if the flour was all sent away and your Army Suffered by it, the Consequence has been just what I then foretold, All over Ships have been and Continue to be constantly employed in carrying flour to the French & Spanish Islands, our Post is filled in return with West India produce, some European Goods and many Spanish Dollars, and flour remains so plenty that there has not been a day in which I could not buy 5000 to 10,000 bbls in this City and the price has fallen from 28/ & 30/. which was asked and given at first, to 17/ which is now asked, but I think 15. or two hard Dollrs will buy 102 lb. very soon. I wou'd not take up your time with this detail, only for the sake of this one observation which I think shou'd be impressed on the minds of all persons in power and which I believe exactly Coincides with your Sentiments, It is that Commerce shou'd be perfectly free, and property Soundly secure to the Owner, the only exception that shou'd be admitted, are Legal restraints on the first, founded on such evident public Utility as convinces the Community at large of their propriety, and such restraints should Continue no longer than that propriety is evident and on the last, the only exception should be as to that part of property which is taken from all with an equal hand by Taxation. for whenever the hand of power is [Stretched out] for the partial Seizure of property upon the Plea of Necessity, a good Government ought upon principles of Justice & Policy to make ample satisfaction to the Individual. whenever these measures have their proper force in our Governments, these United States will abound with the greatest plenty of their own produce of perhaps any Nations in the world, the People are by Nature & habit industrious; feeling themselves secure in the possession of their property they will labour incessantly, that labour lays the foundation for Commerce unrestrained liberty in this, will find Vent for our own Superfluities and bring us in return whatever we stand in need of from other Countries, universal plenty will succeed, that plenty ,will produce and Maintain Numbers of Men and from those Numbers we shall always be able to collect an army equal to the defence of the Country, but I beg your pardon my Dear Sir I have been inadvertantly led into this discussion, when my intention was only to mention that you cannot want provisions so long as I can find Money to pay for them and this shall be my care & study as well as to husband it well in the Expenditure which is most essentially necessary I am much more anxious about cloathing than provisions and wish you Could tell me that the Ship Marquis de la Fayette was arrived. I shall endeavour to wait on you when certain points are attained here and in the interim I remain Your Excellencys most Obedt hble Servant

Robt Morris

To John Jay, 4 July 1781

Phila: 4th. July 1781

Dr Sir

The Derangement of our Money Affairs. The Enormity of our public Expenditures. The Confusion in all our Departments. The Langour of our general System. The Complexity and consequent Inefficacy of our Operations. These are some, among the many, Reasons which have induced Congress to the Appointment of a Superintendent of Finance. I enclose you Copies of their Resolutions on that Subject, with such other Papers as will fully explain to you my Appointment and Powers.

The Use of this Office must be found, in a Progress towards the Accomplishment of these two capital Objects; the Raising a Revenue with the greatest Convenience to the People, and the Expenditure of it with the greatest Oeconomy to the Public.

The various Requisitions of Congress to the several States, none of them entirely complied with, create a considerable Ballance in Favor of the united States; and the Claim of this Ballance is delivered over to me as Revenue; while on the other Hand the dangerous Practice of taking Articles for the public Service and giving Certificates to the People, has created a very general and very heavy Debt. The Am^t. of this Debt is swelled beyond all reasonable Bounds, nor can the Extent of it be at present estimated. These Things need no Explanation, but it may be proper to observe, that, if the Certificates were not in my Way, there is still an infinite Difference between the Demands of a Ballance from the States, and an effectual Revenue. The latter can be obtained only in Consequence of wise Laws generally adopted, and as generally executed with Vigor and Decission. Were all that is necessary on these Heads accomplished, Something further would still remain to be done in Order that the Produce of Taxes should be subject to the sole and absolute Disposition of the united States or of their Officers. To you, who are acquainted with republican Governments, it is unnecessary to observe on the Delays which will arise, the Obstacles which will be raised, and the Time which will be consumed in placing the Revenue of America on a proper Footing. Yet this is absolutely necessary before Credit can be established, and the indispensable Supplies obtained on Terms of Oeconomy.

To reform our Expenditure is an Object of equal Importance with the other; and it is in some Degree within my Power, as you will perceive it to have been subjected to my Authority. But even here I find myself entramelled by the Want of necessary Funds. To contract (for Instance) with any one in Order to obtain Bread for our Troops, requires the previous Certainty of being able to make the stipulated Payments; and so, in every other Case, I shall be unable to act with Decission unless I have the Command of Money. On the other Hand, the People will bear, with great Reluctance, the necessary Emposition of heavy Burthens, while they can perceive any Want of Arrangement Method or Oeconomy in the administration of their Affairs.

If for a Moment we suppose, that this Country, amid the Confusions of a Revolution and the Rage of War, could be governed with all the Regularity, Wisdom and Prudence of antient and peaceable Nations; Yet we must be convinced, that no annual Revenue she is able to raise, could equal the annual Expence, in an offensive War against so powerful a Nation as that which we now contend with. A great Ballance therefore must remain, and it *must* be provided for by Loans or Subsidies.

To expect Loans within the united States, presupposes an Ability to lend, which does not exist in any considerable Numbers of the Inhabitants. The personal Property not immediately engaged either in Commerce or the Improvement of Lands was never very considerable. Little as it was, it has been greatly diminished by the pernicious Effects of a depreciating Medium. This Expedient which was adopted in the beginning from Necessity, and too pertinaciously adhered to in the Sequel; has not only exhausted the Funds of those who might have been willing to trust the united States, but it has so wounded our public Credit, that even the Will would be wanting if the Ability existed, which as I said before, it really does not.

While we neither have Credit or Means at Home, it is idle to expect much from *Individuals* abroad. Our foreign Credit must be nurtured with Tenderness and Attention, before it can possess any great Degree of Force; and it must be fed by substantial Revenue before we can call it into active Exertion, or derive beneficial Effects from it's Application.

All reasonable Expectation therefore is narrowed down to the friendly Interposition of those *Sovereigns* who are Associates in the War. From Holland we can properly ask Nothing; nor is she I beleive in Capacity to grant, , Start deletion,, End, if we did ask. The active Efforts of France require all the Resource of that great Nation, & of Consequence, the pecuniary Aid which she affords us can but little advance the general Cause, however it may releive our immediate Distress. We must then turn our Eyes to Spain, and we must ask either Loans or Subsidies to a very considerable Amount. Small Sums are not worth the Acceptance. They have the Air of Obligation, without affording Releif. A small Sum therefore is not an Object of the united States, for they do not mean to beg Gratuities, but to make rational Requests.

As Congress have impowered you to remove the Obstacles which have hitherto impeded your Negotiations; you will doubtless proceed with prudent Dispatch, in forming the important Treaties which are to be the Basis of our national Connections. Your own Integrity, and the Dispositions which you certainly feel, as the true

Representative of your Sovereign, to gratify the Wishes of his catholic Majesty, will give you just Claim to the Confidences and friendly Support of his Ministers. And on the other Hand, his Majesty's known Piety and Justice will certainly induce him to facilitate a permanent Union between the two Countries, & to overturn that Power whose impious Ambition is known, felt & detested throughout the habitable Globe.

Having a perfect Confidence in the Wisdom of his Majesty's Ministers, I must request that you will submit to their Consideration the Reasons which operate in Favor of the Advances we expect. In doing this, it will immediately strike you and them, that the Enemy carries on the Operations against us at an Expence infinitely greater than that by which they are opposed. By enabling us therefore to increase our Resistance, and redouble our offensive Efforts, the British will be reduced to the Necessity of increasing their Force in america, or of submitting beneath a decided Superiority. Either must be fatal to them. In the first Instance, they will be crushed by the Weight of Expence; and in the second, they must (while they loose an actual Force, and part forever with the Object in Contest) feel the increased Weight of the american Arms, and make Head against those Resources applied to a Marine, which are now consumed in Land Operations.

Money ought therefore to be supplied to us from the Havanna; which will at the same Time save the Risque of transporting it to Europe, while, as I have already observed, it must when employed among us absolutely ruin the common Enemy. For when once they are driven from the united States, they must at a considerable Expence defend, or at a great Loss relinquish the Rest of their american Possessions; & in either Case, the Resources of this Country will enable France and Spain to carry on Operations for the Subjection of the British Islands.

With Respect to our Finance, I am further to observe, that the Resolutions of Congress of the 18th. of March 1780, have neither been so regularly adopted by the States as was hoped and expected, nor been productive of those Consequences which were intended. It is unnecessary to travel into the Causes or to explain the Reasons of this Event. The Fact is clear. The new Money is depreciated; and there is the strong Evidence of Experience to convince us, that the issuing of Paper at present must be ineffectual. Taxation has not yet been pursued to that Extent which was necessary; neither is it reasonable to expect that it should. Time has been required under all Governments, to accustom the People by Degrees to bear heavy Burthens. The People of America have so patiently endured the various Calamities of the War, that there is good Reason to expect they will not shrink at this late Hour from the Imposition of just and equal Taxes. But many Arrangements are necessary to this Purpose, and therefore an immediate pecuniary Assistance is the more necessary to us. Our Debts, under which I comprise as well those of the individual States as those of the Union, are but trifling when we consider the Exertions which have been made. The Debt I have already mentioned in Certificates is heavy, not from the real Amount, but because it is beyond what the Supplies obtained were reasonably worth, and because it impedes Taxation & impairs its Effects. But the Amount of our other Debts is so small, that a few Years of Peace would bring it within the Bounds of a Revenue, very moderate when compared with the Wealth of our Country. You well know the rapid Increase of that Wealth, & how soon it would releive us from the Weight of Debts which might be in the first Instance very burthensome, there can therefore be no Doubt that we shall be able to pay all those which it may be necessary to contract. But, as I have already observed, our great Difficulty is the Want of Means in our People and of Credit in our Government.

It gives me however very great Pleasure to inform you, that the determined Spirit of the Country is by no Means abated either by the Continuance of the War, the Ravages of our Enemy, the Expence of Blood and Treasure we have sustained, or the Artifices Falsehoods and Delusions of an insidious Foe. These last become daily more and more contemptible in America; and it appears equally astonishing that they should longer attempt them here, or boast the Success of such Attempts in Europe. Uniform Experience has shewn the Futility of their Efforts & the Falsity of their Assertions. I know They take Advantage of every little Success, to vaunt the Prowess of their Troops and proclaim Hopes of Conquest which they do not feel. But those who know any Thing of our History or Situation, must have the utmost Contempt for all these Gasconades. It is impossible they should make Impression upon any but weak Minds, and I would hardly have thought of mentioning them, but I learn, by Letters from Spain, that Men who are uninformed, have been led into Apprehensions from Circumstances which were here considered as trivial and even favorable.

I could hardly have supposed that our Enemies had still the Folly to repeat, as I am told they do, that there is an english Party in America. Bribes and Deceit have induced some wicked and weak Men to join them, but when we consider the Sums they have expended, & the Falsehoods they have used, our Wonder is, not that they have got so many, but that they have gained so few. The Independence of America is considered here as established so much, that even those of equivocal Character accustom themselves to the Idea, for, the Doubt is not now whether an Acknowledgement of it will take Place, but when that Acknowledgement will be made. Our Exertions also in the present Moment, are not so much directed to establish our Liberties as to prevent the Ravages of the Enemy, abridge the Duration & Calamities of the War, and faithfully contribute to the Reduction of a Power whose Ambition was equally dangerous and offensive to every other.

All Reasoning on this Subject must be deeply enforced by paying Attention to what has happened in the southern States. The Progress of the Enemy, while in Appearance it menaced the Conquest of that extensive Region, tended only in Effect to exhaust him by fruitless Efforts so that at length a handful of Men have rescued the whole from his Possession. The Attack on Virginia (if the piratical Incursions there can deserve that Name) has been equally futile. The Commanders may indeed have enriched themselves by Plunder, and many worthy Families have been distressed. But what is the Consequence? Indignation and Resentment have stimulated even the weak and indolent to Action. The wavering are confirmed & the firm are exasperated; so that every Hour, and by every Operation, they create Enemies instead of gaining Subjects.

Our Armies, tho not very numerous, are powerful. The regular Troops are so much improved in Discipline and the Habits of a military Life that they are at least equal to any Troops in the World. Our Militia are becoming more and more warlike, so as to supply the Want of regular Troops when the Enemy (taking Advantage of that Convenience which their Ships afford them) transfer the Scene of Action from one Place to another. The Number of the British diminishes daily, and of Consequence our Superiority becomes daily more decisive. The greatest Plenty of Subsistence is to be had for our Armies, & the Prospects from the present Harvest are beyond all former Experience. I wish I could add that Cloathing and military Stores were as abundant as those other Requisites for War. This is not the Case. Our Soldiers indeed are well armed, and in some Degree they are cloathed, we have also Amunition abundantly sufficient for the common Operations of the Field; but many of our Militia are unarmed, the Sieges which will be necessary to expel the Enemy, must make a heavy Deduction from our military Stores.

The proposed Siege of New York will soon be commenced, and it would , Start deletion,, End, undoubtedly be successful, if we could maintain a decided Superiority at Sea. This must depend on Contingencies which are not in our Power, nor perhaps in the Power of any human Being. I am not without Hopes even if we should not possess that Superiority; but the Expence will, from the want of it, be very considerably inhanced, and this is a Circumstance which I cannot but deplore; for I repeat it again, the want of Money can alone prevent us from making the greatest Exertions. What our Exertions have already been our Enemies themselves must acknowledge, and while from insidious Views, *they* assert that they could not make an Impression on us with ninety thousand Soldiers and Seamen, *we* are certainly authorized to conclude from this Confession that these States form a considerable Ballance in the Scale against them.

I am now therefore again led to reiterate my Request of a considerable Sum of Money from Spain, for I also again repeat that small Sums are not worth our Acceptance; and I may add, they are unworthy the Dignity of his catholic Majesty. There can be no Doubt, nor will the spanish Ministry deny, that there is a very considerable Risque in transporting their Money from the new World to the old; besides that, when expended there, it necessarily runs thro the different Channels of Commerce to feed the Wants and invigorate the Forces of the Enemy. There is therefore a double Policy in expending a Part of it here, where it can not only be brought with Safety and Dispatch, but employed to an immense Advantage when compared to it's Effects in Europe. If it be asked what advantages Spain will derive in particular during the War, and what Recompence can be made her after the Peace, I answer. That the Weakening more the common Enemy by a given Sum is in itself a great Advantage; and that to do this by sparing the Blood of spanish Subjects is an Advantage still greater. I add, that, when relieved from the Enemy, we may assist her in the Reduction of the Floridas and Bahamas and perhaps of Jamaica. We shall then also be in a Situation to secure Nova Scotia, thereby depriving Great Britain of her principal Resource for Ships Timber, & enabling us to furnish that essential Article to the Navy of Spain on cheaper and better Terms than it can be had elsewhere. On this last Subject I am further to observe, that there is hardly any Thing in which the maritime Power of Spain is so much interested. For if we do not possess that Country, it will be impracticable to furnish those Supplies of Masts and Spars which both France and Spain may stand in Need of; so that, of Consequence, their positive and absolute Strength at Sea will be the less while that of the Enemy is positively and absolutely greater, the comparative Inferiority therefore will be still more considerable. Nor is this all. A Marine requires Men as well as Ships. The Fisheries & Collieries are two Pillars which support the Marine of Britain, so far forth as Seamen are required. But it is evident that the Fisheries could not long continue in her Hands, if she were deprived of Nova Scotia. Here again we are also to consider, that there is an immense Difference between that patient Resistance whose Opposition must at length weary the Enemy into granting our Independence, and those vigorous active Operations which may wrest from them their present Possessions. Money is necessary for the Latter, and I can say with Confidence that money alone is necessary.

But to return, the Advantages which will flow to Spain, at a Peace, from giving effectual Aid to our Finances now, will be in the first Place the common Compensation of Repayment, should his catholic Majesty prefer Loans to Subsidies. The having expelled the English from the Bay of Mexico & having by that Means prevented the contraband Commerce so destructive to his Revenue will be another striking Advantage which cannot have escaped the Penetration of his Ministers. But this is not all. The opening a Port in East Florida, on the Shores of the Atlantic, under proper Regulations and Restrictions, would enable us to carry on a Commerce very advantageous to Spain; because we could furnish all such Supplies of Provisions &ca as their Possessions might stand in Need of, and in Return take at that Port Cocoa Log Wood Nicaragua Wood and indeed any other Commodities, which his catholic Majesty should find it for the advantage of his Dominions to permit the Exportation of. Our Commerce with Spain is also in itself a very considerable Object. At this Moment we take from thence Wine, Oil, fruit, Silk, Cloth &ca. and, after the Conclusion of the War, our Remittances of Wheat, Corn, Fish & naval Stores will be of very great Consequence to the Commerce of that Country. Another Article of Commerce will be the Building of Ships; which can be had on cheaper & better Terms here than elsewhere: and there can be no Doubt, but that the Construction of Ships in this Country is equal, if not superior, to that in any other. Even now Ships might be built on his Majesty's Account, tho by no Means so cheaply as in Times of Peace; besides that, as there is *now* no *seasoned* Timber in the Country, such Ships would not be durable, and therefore it might perhaps be imprudent to get any more than are immediately necessary.

To all the other Advantages which would arise to his Catholic Majesty, I may add (altho that is *not* so properly within my Department) the Security which his Dominions woud derive from our Guarantee. This is an Advantage which must be the more evident from a Consideration of what might have happened, had this Country continued in Union with Great Britain, & had Great Britain pursued those Schemes of universal Empire wich the Virtue and Fortitude of America first checked, and which it is the Object of the present War to frustrate. The serious Refutation of such absurd Contradictions, would involve an Absurdity. It may not, however, be improper to observe that the Attention of this Country for a Century past has been, and for a Century to come most probably will be, entirely turned to Agriculture and Commerce. We must always therefore be useful Neighbours and never dangerous, except to those who may have Views of Dominion. Spain can never be in this Predicament, tho the British may and will: Their Solicitude therefore to inspire Apprehension of us, is, and ought to be, the strongest argument against entertaining them. But if this evident Reasoning did not exist, still the Conduct of Congress, with Regard to his catholic Majesty, has been so just and even generous, not only in being willing to secure *his* Rights, but to gratify him by foregoing their own, that there is not Room for the Shadow of Suspicion. This Conduct, I should suppose, would alone have Weight sufficient to procure what is my Object to request; if the other very cogent and conclusive Reasons for it did not apply. And, after all, if it be considered how much greater is the Interest of Spain in the vigorous Continuance of the present War, than that of any other of the Associates, I cannot permit myself one Moment to doubt of your Success. I am the more sanguine, from the Character of the Catholic King and of his Ministers for Wisdom Candor and Integrity. These Qualities will, I am sure, meet such corresponding Dispositions in the United States, that the most thorough Harmony and Coalition must inevitably take Place. This is an object of the greatest importance to both Countries. Mutual Benefits and the Reciprocation of good Offices will endear a Connection between them; and their Interests require that their Connection should be of the closest Kind.

In every Point of View, therefore, that we can consider the Subject, the Advance I have mentioned must appear alike beneficial. If the Governor of Cuba, or any other Person, were duly authorized, Stipulations might even now be entered into, for furnishing all necessary Supplies of Provisions to the Fleets and Armies of his Catholic Majesty which would certainly facilitate their Operations. The Advance of Money also by Spain, would enable the Fleets and Troops of France to subsist cheaper than at present, because it would tend to raise the Exchange here which is now too low.

Your own Good Sense will suggest to you many other forcible arguments, as well as the proper Time and Manner of applying them. It is necessary to mention, that the Sum of five Million Dollars may perhaps be sufficient for our present Emergencies; but if a greater Sum can be obtained we shall thereby become more extensively useful. Whatever the Grant may be, it will be proper that it be sent hither in some Spanish Ships of War from the Havannah, or advanced to us there; in which latter Case we will devise the Means of bringing it away. Whether to ask for Subsidies or Loans, as well as the Terms on which either are to be obtained; these, Sir, are Objects which you are fully competent to determine upon. I have only to wish, that your Applications may meet with that Success which I am confident you will not fail to merit. As the Means of facilitating your Views, I shall apply to the Minister of his most Christian Majesty here, to write on the same Subject to the french Ambassador at Madrid. The generous Conduct of France gives just Ground of Reliance on his friendly Assistance, and you are too well convinced of this not to act in the most perfect Harmony with the Servants of that Court, especially on an Occasion so important as the present. I need not stimulate your activity, by observing how precious is every Moment of Time, in those Affairs on which the Fate of Empires depend. Nor need I suggest the Importance of a Treaty, and particularly a subsidiary Treaty, with Spain, in that Moment when the Judgment of Europe is to be passed on the Fate of America. For, however impracticable it may be to subdue us, it is undoubtedly of Moment to hasten the Approach of that Period when the Acknowledgement of our Independence shall give the Blessings of Peace to so many contending Nations. To spare the present lavish Effusion of Blood and Treasure, is a serious Object with those who feel, as you do, the Emotions of Benevolence. And I am confident that the Patriotism which has inspired your Conduct, will prompt you to obtain a Peace, *honorable* for your Country and *advantageous* to her Friends. The only probable Method to effect these Things, is a thorough Union of Forces and Resources, to reduce the Pride and the Power of that aspiring Nation whose Ambition embroils the Universe— With all possible Respect I have the Honor to be Your Excellency's most obedient and humble Servant.

Robt Morris
S.I. of Finances

P.S.

The Papers I mention as enclosed are, Resolutions of Congress of 7 Feby. 1781. 20th. Feby., 20, 21st March, 21, & 27 April 22d may, 4 June & 28th June—a Copy of my Commission, & Letters from me of 13 March 1781 to the President of Congress of 1781 to Messrs. Burke Houston and Woolcot & 14 May 1781 to the President of Congress.

To George Washington, 5 July 1781

Philadelphia July 5th 1781

Dear Sir

You Will find enclosed herein the Copy of an Act of Congress of the 4th June whereby I am vested with Powers to dispose of the Specific supplies required from the several States in such manner as with your Excellencys Advice, I may judge will best promote the Publick interest and Answer the purposes of the present

Campaigne—some former acts of Congress respecting these same Specific Supplies directed the Board of War to Collect them & form Magazines thereof in Consequence of Which that Board Wrote to the several States to know what Supplies were Collected or what they might depend on, And I have long Waited for the Answers, but as yet they have only one Answer which is from the Executive Authority of Pensylvania, who said they could not assure them of a barrell of Provisions, but since the date of that Ansr the Assembly have empowered me to procure their share of specific Supplies and to pay to Congress the balance due on the [4/10] of the 18th of March 1780 Emission of Paper dollars and have Assigned me as a Fund for effecting these things. their Whole Emission of State Paper struck in Virtue of an Act of the 4th April last Amounting to £500.000 this Curry at present the paper is in the same depreciated State that disabled the Council from procuring the Supplies and consequently is of no use to me but as I think the Measures adopted by the Assembly will probably Appreciate this Money Considerably I shall charge this State with the 3000 bbls of flour supplied the Army by Genl Schuyler & Mr Lowrey, and with 4,000 bbls of flour I have Obtained here on behalf of the State, but it is not eligible to transport flour from this State, Delaware or Maryland (the upper parts), either to yours or the Southern Army because there is plenty much nearer to both, that may be purchased as Cheap as in either of the States mentioned and the expence of transportation, equal or nearly equal to the first Cost of the flour, thereby be saved, I am therefore of the Opinion it is best to Convert these Specific Supplies into Money, and Employ that money for the service of the Campaign And I entertain the same Opinion With Respect to all the Specific supplies now due, for they are so circumstanced that little if any of them will be brought into use in any other manner than by selling them where they lay for the most they will fetch What use can Beef &c. in New Hampshire, Massachusets &c. &c. or flour in Fredk County Maryland or in any of the back Counties be to

Our Armies, it would Cost more Money to transport it to the Army than would purchase an equal quantity delivered at your Camp, upon the Whole, I believe we must get your Army Supplied by Contract as soon as we can and Convert these Supplies (if they can be got) into Money to pay the Contractors &ca. probably the number of Objects that will now claim your attention may induce you to [   ] to be excused from any farther trouble on this score, if so a Letter with your Opinion and Advice in general terms will suffice for me and thereupon I will take the best measures with these supplies that I can devise for the publick interest, on the contrary should you desire to be particularly inform'd of every disposition I make it shall be complied with most Chearfully.

I believe the Board of War have Written to your Excellency relative to the Appointment of places of Deposite for Provisions that are to be supplied by Contract this is Essentially necessary before prices can be fixed, but before I enter on this Subject with you I Will have a consultation with that Board in Order to be of one Understanding respecting the terms and Modes of Contracting after Which I shall do myself the honour of addressing you again. With the utmost Respect and Esteem, I am Dear Sir Your Obediant Humble Servt

Robt
Morris
S.I. of Finance

To John Jay, 7 July 1781

Phila: 7 July 1781

Dr Sir
This will accompany my Letter of the 4th Instant, which you will perceive to be so written, as that it may be shewn if necessary to the spanish Minister. You will make such Use of

it as Prudence may dictate. I would gladly now give you Details of our Situation and Plans for reforming it But I have not yet sufficiently obtained the one, nor mastered the other. Whenever I am in Capacity to apprize you fully of these Things, you shall hear from me at large on the Subject. At present I can only inform you that a Sum of hard Money will (from particular Circumstances afford us Relief, and turn to our Advantage far beyond what might be supposed from the Amount. Altho I have stated the Demand at five Millions, yet you will take as much as you can obtain, though it be far short of that Sum. But at the same time I repeat, that a very small one is not worth the Acceptance. Knowing our Wants to be great, you will judge properly as to what we can accept consistently with our own Dignity. I enclose you a Cypher, and with the Duplicates of my Letters I will send you another. Should both arrive safe you will be so kind as to hand one to Mr Carmichael letting me know which you keep and write by, viz whether it be No. 1 or 2. I am very sincerely yours &c

Robt Morris
S. I. of Finance

To explain the Use of the Cypher and Key herewith sent to you and which is marked No 1, you will observe that by Means of the Cypher the Beginning of my Letter of the 4th. Instant to the word Operations inclusive is rendered thus 169, 76, 98, 308, 250, 120, 366, 330, 393, 95, 130, 177, 169, 18, 116, 618, 272, 120, 366, 639, 76, 179, 99, 170, 379, 177, 169, 643, 178, 437, 54, 13, 366, 168, 83, 177, 169, 17, 655, 80, 116, 170, 366, 29, 596, 421, 488, 177, 169, 43, 421, 409, 170, 481, 185, 643, 369, 320, 90, 169, [*illegible*], 32, 36, 227, 24, 120, 366, 493, 98, 123 and by a Reference to the Key it will be found to contain the Words or Parts of Words, Stops &ca.

To John Jay, 9 July 1781

Philadelphia July 9th. 1781

Dear Sir

Observing by your Correspondence with Congress that you are put to a great deal of Expence by American Seamen arriving from Captivity at Cadiz where they also grow very troublesome— I offer the following Proposal to your consideration— Authorise Mr Harrison or whoever may be your Agent at Cadiz, to enter into Contracts with Such Americans as present themselves for the Bounty of their Country to proceed from Cadiz in such Ship or Vessell as he may provide for the purpose for such Port within the United States as he may appoint at the Monthly Wages of Six or Eight Spanish Dollars, to be paid so Soon after their Arrival in America as the Cargoe of the Vessell shall be Landed. after they sign such Contract, he to supply their Wants Sparingly untill he Collects a sufficient Number to Mann a suitable vessel which he may procure either by Charter or purchase whichever may be in his power and shall appear most Eligible at the time, If he Charters, it should be on such terms that the Owners risque their Vessell putting in their Own Master and if they choose it part of the Seamen—the Vessell to be Loaden with Salt for Account and Risque of the United States freight so much p^r bushel or so much p^r Ton to America & back, but in that Case let it be always a Condition that the Vessell may be Ordered from the first place she Arrives at, to any one other Port in America, because it may happen that she will Arrive where there can not be got a Cargoe to load her back, or where the Salt would be of no use—

If your Funds will admit of it, and Vessells can be purchased cheap, this would be the more Eligible Mode of doing the business, because I could then either send the Vessells back, or sell as might suit best, in case of purchase they should be fast Sailers with good Sails Rigging well found and fitted and if Armed so

82

much the better. Honest, Active, Industrious & faithfull Masters must be provided for these Vessells and they must all come addressed to my Order directed for this Port with Liberty however to get into any safe Port they can, the Master to give me immediate Notice of his Arrival when I shall give proper Orders or probably have them previously ready, An Account of the Monies Advanced to each person on board these Vessells as well as the Cost and Outfit of such Vessell With Amo^t of Cargo must be sent me by each Vessell in order that proper deductions may be made from the people and proper Credit be given for the Costs. You will observe I am duly empowered by Congress to Export and import for Account and at the Risque of the United States and I think this Plan so likely to benefit the Publick that I very freely give my Sanction to it. Provided you can find the Money your Agent must give me regular Advice of every Expedition and inform you also Whenever he Commences thereon; When a Ship is provided and a Master Appointed all the Men shoud Sign Articles for a Voyage in the Common form— I am Dear Sir Your Obedt. Humb Servt

Robt Morris
S. I. of Finance

To Benjamin Franklin, 13 July 1781

Philada. July 13th. 1781

Sir

The unanimous appointment to the Superintendancy of our Finances with which the Congress have honoured me, and my Conviction of the necessity that some *one* Person should endeavour to introduce Method & Oeconomy into the administration of affairs have induced me tho with reluctance to accept that office. Mr. Jay will receive by this Conveyance and forward you Copies of those Resolutions and letters which may be necessary to explain my appointment & Powers—

I wish I could as readily effect as I most ardently desire the accomplishment of all proper arrangements; thoroughly convinced that no Country is truely independent untill with her own Credit and resources she is able to defend herself and correct her Enemies. It shall be my endeavour to establish *our* Credit and draw *our* Resources in such manner that we may be little burthensome and essentially usefull to our Friends.

I am sure I need not mention to you the importance of collecting a Revennue with ease & expending it with oeconomy as little need I detail, the time, the Authority the ability the favourable circumstances which must combine for these purposes, but I think I may assert that the situation of a Country just emerging from dependance and struggling for existence is peculiarly unfavourable and I may add that this Country by relying too much on Paper, is in a Condition of peculiar disorder and Debility. To rescue and restore her is an object equal to my warmest wishes, tho probably beyond the stretch of my abilities.

Success will greatly depend on the pecuniary aid we may obtain from abroad, because Money is necessary to introduce oeconomy while at the same time Oeconomy is necessary to obtain Money besides that a greater plenty of solid circulating medium is required to support those operations which must give Stability to our Credit, Fruitfulness to our Revennue & activity to our operations.

Among those things which after the experience and example of other Ages and nations, I have been induced to adopt, is that of a national Bank, the plan of which I enclose. I mean to render this a principal Pillar of American Credit so as to obtain the Money of Individuals for the benefit of the Union and thereby bind those individuals more strongly to the general cause, by the ties of private interest. To the efficacy of this plan as well as to the establishment of a Mint which would also be of use, a considerable Sum of Money is necessary, indeed it is indispensibly so, for many other purposes. Be not alarmed Sir from what I have said, with the apprehension that I am about to direct solicitations to the Court of Versailles, which after the repeated favours they have conferred must be peculiarly disagreable; On the contrary as I am convinced that the Monies of France will all be usefully employed in the vigorous prosecution of the war by her own Fleets & Armies I lament every Sum which is diverted from them— Our Necessities have indeed called for *her* aid and perhaps they may continue to do so. Those calls have hitherto been favourably attended to, and the pressure of our necessities has been generously alleviated nor do I at all doubt that future exigencies will excite the same dispositions in our favour and that those dispositions will be followed with Correspondant effects, but I again repeat my wish at once to render America independent of, and usefull to her Friends. With these views I have directed Mr Jay to ask a considerable Sum from the Court of Madrid to be advanced to us at Havannah and brought thence by us if it cannot conveniently be landed here from Spanish Men of War, I say a *Considerable* Sum because, as I have declared to him, I do not wish to labor under the weight of obligation without deriving from it any real benefit, and because I consider the advance of small Sums rather as a temporary palliative than a radical remedy, our disorder's are such that the former can be of no use and it would be better to persist in a desultory defence than to put on the delusive appearances of a Vigor we do not feel, for this lulls the People into a dangerous security and fosters those hopes of the Enemy which give duration and extent to the War.

It is the disorder of our Finances which has prevented us from a powerfull Cooperation with our Allies and which has enabled the Enemy to linger on our Coasts with the Dregs of a Force once formidable, It is from this cause that they have been permitted to extend the Theatre of their Malice and multiply the victims of their Ambition. America alone will not derive benefit from the advances which Spain may make to her. All the associates in the War will feel the *consequential* advantages. The expence of the American War now hangs a heavy weight about the Neck of Britain and enfeebles her on that Element which she called her own, an encrease of that expence or the loss of her Posts here, must necessarily follow from additional Efforts on our part, and either of these must be a *consequential* benefit to those who are opposed to her. France will derive a small immediate benefit from it as she will thereby get more Money here for her bills of Exchange than she can at present procure, but it is not so much from any *advantage* which may be expected to that Kingdom or from any motives of *Interest* as from the Generosity and Magnanimity of the Prince, that we hope for Support, I will not doubt a moment that at Your instance his Majesty will make pressing representations in support of Mr. Jays application, and I will hope that the Authority of so great a Sovereign and the Arguments of his able Ministers will shed auspicious influence on our Negotiations at Madrid.

From the best returns I have been able to collect and which are in some measure imperfect from the confusions and disasters of the Southern States, I find there is about 7,200,000. Dollars due on Certificates which bear an interest of six per Cent payable in France at the rate of five Livres for every Dollar. Many causes have conspired to depreciate these Certificates notwithstanding the interest is so well secured and has been punctually paid. This depreciation is so great that they are daily offered for Sale at a very considerable discount which is attended with two pernicious consequences, one that a considerable expence is unnecessarily incurred & the other that the Public Credit is unnecessarily impaired. If I had the means therefore I could remove this Evil by purchasing in the Certificates, and to procure the means I am to pray that you will state this matter fully to the Ministers of his Most Christian Majesty. The Interest being guaranteed by the Court of France they now pay for this purpose 2,160,000 Livres annually, a Sum which in less than ten years would pay a debt of Lrs 15,000,000. at five per Ct interest. With 15,000,000 Livrs. prudently managed the whole of these Certificates might be paid. I am sure it is unnecessary to dwell on the advantages which would result from making such Loan for this purpose and I trust that if this matter is stated to Mr. Necker that enlightened Minister will Cooperate in the plan to the utmost of his ability. I again repeat that I do not wish to lay any burthens on France but this proposal is calculated to relieve us both and in any case the expence to France will be the same— Should it be adopted I must request the earliest Notice that my operations may Commence and in any case I hope that Secrecy will be observed for the most evident reasons—

I am very sorry to inform you that we have as yet no satisfactory News of the Ship Fayette, but on the Contrary her long delay occasions the most alarming apprehensions. If as is but too probable that Ship is lost you will more easily conceive than I can describe what will be the situation of our Troops next Winter.

I could wish as soon as possible to have a State of all the Public Accounts transmitted to the end that Monies due to the United States may be paid and measures taken to provide for such Sums as they stand indebted in to others. Your Excelly will I dare say send them as soon as may be convenient and I hope the Public affairs will hereafter be conducted in such manner as to give you much less of that unnecessary trouble which you have hitherto experienced and which could not but have harrassed you exceedingly and perhaps taken up time which would otherwise have been devoted to more important objects.

I shall probably have frequent occasion to address You and shall always be happy to hear from you but the Mischiefs which arise from having letters intercepted are great and alarming. I have therefore enclosed you a Cypher and in the duplicate of my letters I shall enclose another, if both arrive you will use one and in case of your absence leave the other with such person as may supply your place, let me know however which Cypher you use, whether it be No 3. or No 4— The bearer of this letter Major Franks formerly an Aid de Camp to Genl. Arnold and honourably acquitted of all improper Connection with him after a full & impartial enquiry will be able to give you our Public News more particularly than I could relate them. He sails hence for Cadiz and on his arrival will proceed to Madrid where having delivered my letters to Mr Jay he will take his orders for you. He will then wait your orders and I hope will soon after meet a safe opportunity of Coming to America—

With the most perfect esteem & regard I have the honour to be Your Excellencys most Obedient & very humble Servant

Robt Morris.

To John Jay, 13 July 1781

Phila: 13 July 1781

Dr Sir

I enclose you in this Packet the Plan of a national Bank, which I have been induced to adopt for the following Reasons. The issuing of a large Paper Medium converted the Coin of the Country into a Commodity; so that much of it was exported, and the Remainder concealed. The Depreciation of our Paper has so lessened our Currency that there is not a Sufficiency for Commerce and Taxation without creating by the latter such Distress in the former as must injure every Order of Men in the Community. It is necessary therefore to fill up the Deficiency in such Proportion as it may be called for and with such Medium as may preserve it's Value.

I have already, in my Letter of the fourth Instant, stated the Want of ability in the People to lend and of Credit in the Government to borrow. An additional Reason, therefore, for establishing the Bank, is that the small Sums advanced by the Holders of Bank Stock may be multiplied, in the usual Manner by Means of their Credit, so as to increase the Resources which Government can draw from it; & at the same Time, by placing the collected Mass of private Credit between the Lenders & Borrowers, supply at once the Want of Ability in the one and of Credit in the other.

An additional Reason for this Institution is to supply the Place of all our other Paper, which it is my Design to absorp as soon as possible, and thereby to relieve the People from those Doubts and Anxieties which have weakened our Efforts relaxed our Industry and impaired our Wealth. But this must not be done without the Substitution of other Paper, for Reasons which I have already assigned, and because that our Commerce would suffer for the Want of that facility in Money Transactions which Paper alone can give.

Finally one very strong Motive which has impelled my Conduct on this Occasion, is to unite the several States more closely together in one general Money Connection, and indissolubly to attach many powerful Individuals, to the Cause of our Country, by the strong Principle of Self Love, and the immediate Sense of private Interest. It may not perhaps be improper to shew and explain this Plan to the Spanish Ministry. They will then perceive how, by an advance of Money, they may, in this Instance increase our Resourses and our Efforts in a Degree much superior to the immediate Sum; and they may be assured, that on a Variety of other Occasions, similar Benefits will result from it. I take this Opportunity however to observe to you, that I do not mean this or any other Communication should be absolutely made. It is, on the contrary, my unalterable Opinion that a prudent Minister on the Spot should be left to act with large Discretionary Power, being always furnished with such Details as will enable him to judge with Propriety and act with Decision.

It will undoubtedly strike your Observation, that the Sum of 400,000 Dollars is very small considering the Object which it is my Design to Effect. I acknowlege that it is so; and when I tell you, that I was very apprehensive we should be unable to fill a larger Subscription; and when I add, that it is very far from certain we shall get all of this moderate Sum; you will see still more clearly the force of those Observations which I have already made. But it is weakness, to be deterred by Difficulties from a proper Pursuit. I am therefore determined that the Bank shall be *well* supported, untill it can support itself and then it will support us. I mean that the Stock, instead of 400,000 Dollars shall be 4,000,000£ and perhaps more. How soon it will rise to that Amount it is impossible to foresee; but this we may venture to assert, that if a considerable Sum of Specie can speedily be thrown into it, the Period when its Force and Utility will be felt and known is not far off.

After I had determined to make that Application to the Court of Madrid, which is contained in my Letters, it was my next Object to obtain for you such Support as might materially favor your Operations. For this Purpose I have written to Doct^r. Franklin and have told him that "you would receive by this Conveyance and forward to him Copies of those Resolutions and Letters which may be necessary to explain my Appointment and Powers." I lay this Task on your Secretaries, because the want of Clerks in my Office, and the many Things to be done, together with the short time allowed me by the Departure of the Vessel prevent me from having Duplicates made out. I have written to the Doctor to apply to the Court of Versailles to further your Negotiations with their influence. I am confident his Application will not be unsuccessful; but how you may derive most benefit from the Cooperation of the french Court, you best can tell. Major Franks, therefore, is instructed to take your Orders for Passy, and return thence to Philadelphia, so that you will have an Opportunity of communicating fully with the Doctor on any Subject you think proper. You may write to me by any Opportunity, if this should arrive safe because our Cypher will prevent you from being exposed to interested or impertinent Curiosity.

To obtain for you still further Assistance I have applied (in the Absence of Monsr. de la luzerne who is gone to Camp) to Mr. de Marbois for Letters to their Ambassador at the Court of Madrid. I have stated my Views, my Hopes and Wishes with that Candor which is proper on such Occasions and which I wish to preserve on all Occasions. Mr. de Marbois has, in Consequence written a Letter on the Subject in which he informs the Ambassador of our Conversation, states the Disorders of our finances & make polite mention of my Operations, my Designs and Abilities, as well as of the Confidence reposed in me by Congress and by the People at large. He details the proposed Plans, and particularly that of the Bank, and shews forcibly the Advantages which would result from a considerable Advance of Money by Spain. He assigns also very proper Reasons to shew why it ought to be considerable if it be made at all. The great Interest of France in this Business, as well as the open and candid Manner which has marked all Transactions I have hitherto had with the Minister of that Nation induce me to believe that this Letter is more than Compliment and that, as it is intended so it will operate to produce the desired effect.

That Nothing in my Power might be wanting to the Success of a Business which you must be convinced I have much at Heart, I have also applied to don francisco Rendon, who at present acts here for Spain, and I have every Reason to believe that he will write to the Spanish Court such a Letter as I wish. But, after all much my dear Sir must depend on your Prudence, your Activity and your Attention to incline to Stimulate to lead the Ministry into our Views, to remove the Obstacles, surmount the Difficulties and crush the Procrastinations, which retard the Completion of an Object so essential to your Country. I am happy to add, that I have the utmost Confidence in your Abilities your Industry and Integrity.

There is a Possibility, that Money may be obtained from Portugal, and tho I confess there is not a very solid Ground to build on, and tho it must be owned that Appearances are against us; Yet I think it best not to trust too much to Appearances either favorable or unfavorable, and to leave nothing unattempted which may be useful. It was for Reasons of this Sort that my Letter of the ninth Instant which I enclose you a Copy of was written to Congress. In Consequence of it, on the eleventh they passed a Resolution of which I also enclose you a Copy, and have only to add that you will act entirely according to your own Discretion on this Occasion. I cannot pretend to know the Situation of the Court of Lisbon, and therefore I will not attempt to measure out a Line of Conduct to be pursued there. You are, for every Reason more competent to this Business than I am, and therefore I submit it to your Management entirely.

You will observe that a material Part of my Letter of the ninth remains unnoticed by Congress. The Committee had not yesterday reported upon it. Should any Thing be done previous to the Departure of this Vessel you shall know it. But you are so well acquainted with the Delays incident to public Assemblies, that you will not be surprized if you hear Nothing farther on the Subject.

It is unnecessary for me to make any other mention of Major Franks, except to inform you that after a critical Examination into his Conduct by a Court of Enquiry he was honorably acquitted of all improper Connection with his late General. For the rest, you are perfectly acquainted with him, and will therefore take that Notice of him which he deserves. With Sentiments of Esteem & regard I am Dr Sir Your obedt hble Servt

Robt Morris

To Benjamin Franklin, 14 July 1781

Philada. July 14th. 1781

Dear Sir

If Major Franks had departed yesterday as was expected, he would have left the enclosed Cypher behind, it was supposed to have been enclosed with the plans of the intended Bank, but was left out by accident—

I wish you would when leisure & opportunity will permit, converse with some of the Eminent Bankers in Paris on this plan and ask whether a Correspondance & Connection with the Directors would be agreable and whether they wou'd establish a Credit for this Bank and to what Amount, permitting the Managers to draw as occasion may require not exceeding that Amount, to be replaced again by remittances in other bills within such time as they may limit, or if they decline giving such Credit, then the terms on which they will receive Remittances and pay the drafts of the Bank— An American Bank must deal largely in Bills of Excha.—it will thereby rule the price of bills so as to keep it pretty steady, by passing most of the bills drawn on the Continent through their Channell, so as to leave a certain moderate Profit, and the use of a Credit in Europe will be to have paid for their honour such bills as may be protested on Account of the drawers by which means the Bank will secure the damages of 20 per Ct and pay only interest for advance & Commission for negotiating. Occasions may also offer when the Bank by drawing on Europe shall get a high price for bills and in a few Months replace them much cheaper. I do not wish to give you trouble on this occasion but if opportunities offer you can mention the subject, and if any of the Bankers will write me proposals I will lay them before the Directors.

You will tell them that altho the very moderate Sum of 400,000 Dollrs. is proposed as the first capital I intend to encrease it gradually to ten times that Sum, the only difficulty is to get it into Action now that People have but little Money & less Confidence.

I should be glad to see your name in the list of Subscribers to an institution I believe will be permanent. I ever am Dear Sir Your devoted humble servt.

Robt Morris

To Benjamin Franklin, 19 July 1781

Philadelphia 19 July 1781

Sir

The foregoing are Duplicates of my Letters of the several Dates there mentioned, by Major Franks who has sailed for Cadiz. I now enclose to you Duplicate Copies of the Letters and Resolutions referred to in mine of the thirteenth.—

I do not write to Colo. Laurens, because I know not whether he is still in France, and because I am confident you will make to him all necessary Communications. I pray you, if he is still with you, to present my Compliments to him, and inform him of the Reasons of my Silence.

Colo. Laurens's Letter of the ninth of April last from Versailles has been received, and I am induced to hope that the 10,000,000 Livres mentioned in it to be borrowed in Holland, will be, as he says he shall request, advanced from the Treasury of France.

He mentions also, a Promise of the Marquis de Castres to make immediate Arrangements for the safe Transportation of the pecuniary and other Succors destined hither. It would be well that the Money or as much of it as possible were in heavy half Johanneses. Whether this Letter may arrive in Time I know not, but if it should, you will, I hope, be able to effect my Views. If the 15,000,000 Livres mentioned in my Letter of the thirteenth can be obtained, it will be best that it be retained in France provided the 10,000,000 be sent to America; for, in that Case, the Exchange may, I beleive, be put upon such a footing as to answer very valuable Purposes. Of Consequence the Risque will be saved to America, and France will not suffer, as she otherwise might, by the Exportation of so much Coin. To this it may be added, that a Loan will probably be easier obtained if the Days of Payment of the Money by the Subscribers to it be somewhat distant, which will answer very well for Bills of Exchange, tho not quite so well for the Exportation of Money.

To Benjamin Franklin, 21 July 1781

Phila: 21st. July 1781

Sir

I have now to inform you that the State of Pensilvania had emitted £500,000 in Bills of Credit, funded in such Manner that there could be no reasonable Doubt of their Redemption. But the public Confidence had been so impaired, that these Bills soon after they came out, rapidly depreciated, notwithstanding the Solidity of the Funds by which they had been secured. The executive Authority of Government, therefore, declined issuing more of them than were then in Circulation (being £130,000) and called the Legislature. The Assembly, at their late Meeting, took Measures for the Collection of a very considerable Tax, sufficient to absorp all the Paper then in Circulation, and which was receivable in Taxes, as also a considerable Ballance in Specie. It is therefore evident that, if the Tax has Time to operate before any more of the Paper be issued, it must necessarily rise in Value—

The Assembly did me the Honor to commit this Sum of £500,000 to my Care, for the Purpose of paying to Congress a Ballance due on the Resolutions of that honorable Body of the eighteenth of March 1780. and of procuring the specific Supplies which had been called for, the greater Part of which remained unpaid. In this Situation, it has been my Study to effect both these Objects without making any new Issues of the Paper Money. I cannot easily describe to you the good Consequences which would follow from the Appreciation of it. You will partly conceive them, when I inform you that it is now at five for one, and that my Expectation of procuring the specific Supplies, or rather of furnishing Rations to the Amount of them, is very much founded upon the Rise of its Value.

Finding, however, that the Ballance of Money due to the united States has been already drawn for by them, and that the Holders of those Drafts are very clamorous for Payment, I must put Money into the Hands of the proper Officer immediately. To accomplish this, I have fallen upon an Expedient, which, while it answers that Purpose, will be productive of another very considerable Advantage. To explain which, I must previously inform you, that I have lately refused to draw Bills on Messrs. Le Couteulx & Co: for any other than Specie, so that the Paper will no longer answer the Purpose of procuring a Remittance to Europe. I shall, at the same time, borrow such of it as I can discover to have been hoarded, and, by paying it to the Holders of the Drafts drawn by

Congress, throw it again into Circulation. I shall then draw Bills on you for 400,000 Livres, payable at six Month's Sight, or more, for which I expect to get 400,000 Paper Dollars; a Sum sufficient to answer the Demand. I shall draw on Messrs. Le Couteulx & Co: in your Favor to this Amount, payable at sixty Days Sight; which will probably leave four Months for my Operations, But at any Rate it will leave three Months which will be amply sufficient and therefore in three Months after I shall have drawn on you, I will remit you my Drafts on Messrs Le Couteulx & Co. If, in that Period, this Money can be appreciated, it will be a Gain to the united States of the Difference; which you will clearly see to be very considerable. By this Means also, I shall so oeconomize the Funds placed in my Hands, as that I can make them productive of the Supplies from this State.

In mentioning these Supplies, it occurs to me also to make mention of what has passed relative to the Contract you entered into for a Part of them, to the Amount of 400,000 Dollars.— Colo. Menonville spoke to me on this Subject from the Count de Rochambeau, shortly after my Appointment. Upon considering the very slender Situation of our Revenue, or rather the total Want of it, and that the several States had omitted furnishing the specific Supplies demanded of them; I told Colo. Menonville, and I told him truly, that I had but little Prospect of complying with your Promise. It is not easy to convey to your Mind an Idea of the Pain I suffered from being obliged to make this Declaration. I felt for you, for Congress, for America. There is no Man in the World more deeply impressed, than myself, with the Importance of fulfilling every Compact, made by proper Authority. All my Reasonings, my Feelings & my Experience have concurred in producing a thorough Conviction that it is essential; according to the Principles of Justice, from a Regard to our National Honor, and for the Sake of our general Interests. I shall, therefore, notwithstanding what has passed between Colo.

Menonville and myself, assiduously endeavour to perform your Promise, and I am happy to add that I am not without Hopes of Success.

With Respect to the Bills I intend to draw on you, I must apologize for the Trouble they will give you which I hope will be but little. It will be only necessary to accept them, and direct the Holders what Banker to apply to for Payment. That Banker will be enabled to make Payment, by the Bill I shall draw on Messrs. Le Couteulx & Co: in your Favor. Perhaps it may be most convenient to send the Bill Holders to them, but this you will be the best Judge of—. It is unnecessary to state any Reasons to you for accepting these Bills, as I cannot suppose you will have the least Hesitation on that Subject. I take this Opportunity, however, of pledging myself to you, that you shall suffer no Inconvenience from honoring them with your Acceptance; as I shall most certainly remit in Time the Bills sufficient to discharge all I draw on you. My Reason for drawing them on you at all, arises from this Circumstance, that I am desirous of keeping the Transaction entirely distinct, and that many Inconveniences would follow from drawing Bills on Messrs. Le Couteulx & Co:, at six Month's Sight, for Paper, while I draw others, at sixty Days Sight, for Specie; especially after my Refusal to draw on them, except for Specie, which Refusal was, as you will perceive, a necessary Part of my Plan. Add to this also, that the Arrangements I had made with the Minister of his most Christian Majesty would not permit of it. When this Transaction shall be finished, that is, when my Remittances to you and my Drafts on you are all paid; be pleased to send me Copies of the Banker's Accounts.

With every Sentiment of Respect I have the Honor to be your Excellency's most obedient & humble Servant.

Robt
Morris
S.I. of Finances

To George Washington, 23 July 1781

Officer of Finance July 23d 1781

Dear Sir

I am indebted for your favours of the 10th & 13th Inst. the first regarding Mr Lowreys supplies of Flour which he is to extend in the whole to three thousand barrells, this with one thousand from Genl Schuyler and what the Commissaries may have otherwise provided will I suppose keep You in bread for some time to come, and I hope at our Meeting we may be able to Concert such measures as will in future prevent those troubles anxieties and distresses you have so often experienced on the Score of Subsistence. I find by Your's of the 13th that my intentions as to disposing of the Specific Supplies have not been understood. I know very well that the Magazines you had directed to be formed never were filled and that the States have not fully complied with the requisitions of Congress in this respect, consequently it remains for them to pay up their Respective balances due on those Requisitions and it is the Supplies that are to arive from these expected payments that I am Authorized with your Concurrence to dispose of. Pensylvania has committed her paper money to me for the purpose of procuring those supplies and I wou'd rather Receive money from every State, because I am satisfyed it may be so expended as to procure more of the Articles wanted, than the States would deliver and probably of better quality. Pensylvania has Flour & wheat lying in Cumberland County & Cut wry in Lancaster by way of Specific Supplies to your Army Maryland has the same in Frederick County but surely these cannot be brought into use, for the transportation wou'd Cost more money than would purchase the same Articles near to the Army & pay for the delivery of them where wanted, then I say it is better to Sell in Cumberland, Frederick & all such distant places the Articles lying there, because whatever they Sell for is so much Saved, but that is

99

not all, the Teams that would be employed in such transportation may be otherwise usefully employed to the purposes of Agriculture. I have ordered a small Export of Flour from this Post to bring back Silver, that Silver will probably if so employed produce in Your Camp four times the same quantity of flour & save all the expence of [Carriage] I wou'd make Sale of Provisions in Maryland & Pensylvania and with the money purchase them in New York & Connecticut for your Army & in Virginia & No. Carolina for the Southern Army, and so of New Hampshire, Massachusetts &c. except only of those kinds that cannot be had in proper abundance nearer to the places of Consumption. I have said enough to shew you that my views are to have supplies delivered to the Armies on more Oeconomical plans than have been adopted heretofore As to Salt Provisions they are scarce here and I do not believe the quantity of 2000 barrells cou'd be got in this place on any terms, therefore I am of opinion it will be best to let the magazine at Rhode Island Remain there.

We have been making some humble attempts to lead the way for Contracts of more importance This Post is agreed to be Supplied with Rations Consisting of 1 lb. bread 1 lb. Beef or 3/4 lb. of Pork, 1 Gill of Country Rum & 8 lb. Soap, 3 lb. Candles 2 Quarts of Vinegar & 1 Quart of Salt to every 100 Rations at 9 d. ℔ Ration to which is added 1/2 d. for Issueing—Lancaster is agreed for at 8 1/4 d. & 1/2 for Issueing, advertizements are out for Reading, York & Fort Pitt all the other Posts in this State to be broke up and these except Fort Pitt, are retained principally on Account of the Prisoners, I expect to pay these Contracts out of the Money confided to my management by the Assembly of this State, and I am well assured that all the rations Issued for years past at these same places have Cost the public from 3/ to 4/ [per] Ration Specie Value. The Issueing Commissaries at these Posts will in course be dismissed by the Board of War—and I shall proceed to further

Contracts after seeing Your Excellency as fast as I can be assured of Funds to pay the Contractors.

I have supplied the Commissary Genl with money & Credit to procure supplies for Your Table and he also desires One thousand hard Dollars to be sent you for that purpose wherefore I inclose herein a draft made by the South Carolina Delegates the 20th Inst. at ten days sight in my favour on Guy Richards & Comssy of New London Connecticut for two thousand five hundred Specie Dollars this bill they assure me will be paid and I have endorsed it to your Excellencys order in expectation that Messrs Wadsworth & Carter or some of the Commissaries that Supply the French Troops will give you the hard Dollars for it, or that the Gentlemen of your Family will find means of obtaining the Money from New London.

This Sum your Excelly will appropriate as you shall think proper, only directing proper information to be given me that I may know how to have it charged in the Treasury Books—Your letter resp[ecting] the Batteaux providing by Genl Schuyler has been Committed to me & the enclosed letter assures him of timely reimbursement.

Daily calls for my attention to a variety of matters puts off my journey from time to time, Congress seem disposed to give me full employment and I have little chance of gratifying my own inclinations or I should have paid my Respects to you before Now however I hope that visit is not far distant and with Sincere esteem I always am Your Excellencys most Obedt hble servt

Robt Morris

To John Jay, 15 August 1781

Office of Finance
15th. August 1781

Sir

Enclosed you have a List of sundry Bills of Exchange drawn on you. I wrote you relatively to these Bills on the twenty ninth day of July last with sundry Enclosures Explanatory of my Letter I am now to inform you that the Advices contained in that Letter must from particular circumstances be totally disregarded. Should any of the Bills mentioned in the enclosed List come to your Hands you will be pleased to Protest them and assign if you please as a Reason therefore that you have express Instructions to that Purport. The Uncertainty whether you have receivd my cypher prevents my using it on this occasion. The Importance of the Subject obliges me to Write and as I send many Copies the risqué of Capture and inspection is too great to be particular— The Gazettes will furnish you with our latest Intelligence That of New York announces the Arrival of near 3000 Hessian Troops and the Capture of the Trumbull Frigate. Neither of these are very agreeable Circumstances However we must wait the Course of Events and Struggle as well as we can against adverse Fortune. Our affairs to the Southward wear no unpleasing Aspect and altho it is impossible at this Distance to determine what Effect European Movements may have on American Politicks Our Government acquires daily a Firmness and Stability which will not be easily shaken. I have the Honor to be with great Respect your Most Obedient

Robt Morris

To George Washington, 22 August 1781

Office of Finance 22d Augst 1781

D. Sir

I arrived in Town the Day before Yesterday—having taken the earliest Opportunity to acquire Information, I am sorry to inform you that I find Money Matters in as bad a Situation as possible— The Exchange, by the Concourse of Venders, has run down to five Shillings, & Bills are offered at that Rate in such great Numbers as to command all the Money which is to be disposed of; so that reducing the Price of Bills still lower would not comand Money, or answer any other good Purpose. The Paper of that State is indeed appreciating, but to issue it, in the present Moment would destroy all my Hopes from that Quarter, cut off the good Resource which I have the Chance of Comandg—& shake a Confidance which has been reposed in me, & which the public Interest calls upon me to cherish. I am sorry to observe Consequence that you must expect to meet with Disappointments; but I assure you, that I will make every Exertion probable to place you in the Eligible Situation which my Means will admit of. I am &a—

Robt Morris

To The States, 22 August 1781

Office of Finance August 22d 1781

Sir

I have already, in a former Letter, forwarded to your Excellency an account of the Specific Supplies which Congress had demanded from your State. It now becomes my Duty again to press for a Compliance with those Demands. The Exigencies of the Service require immediate Attention, We are on the Eve of the most Active Operations, and should they be in anywise retarded by the want of necessary Supplies, the most unhappy Consequences may follow. Those who may be justly chargeable with Neglect, will have to Answer for it to their Country, to their Allies, to the present generation, and to all Posterity. I hope, intreat, expect, the utmost possible Efforts on the Part of your State; and I confide in your Excellency's Prudence and Vigor, to render those Efforts effectual. I beg to know most speedily, Sir, what Supplies are collected, and at what Places; as also the Times and Places at which the Remainder are to be expected. I cannot express to you my Solicitude on this Occasion. My Declaration to Congress, when I entered upon Administration, will prevent the Blame of ill Accidents from lighting upon me, even if I were less Attentive than I am; but it is impossible not to feel, most deeply, on occasions where the greatest Objects may be impaired or destroyed by Indolence or Neglect. I must, therefore, again reiterate my Requests; and, while I assure you that nothing but the Urgency of our Affairs would render me thus importunate, I must also assure you, that while those Affairs continue so urgent, I must continue to importune. With all possible Respect. I have the Honor to be. Sir your most obedient & humble Servant

Robert Morris

This is a Copy of a letter I have written to the Governors of New Jersey, Delaware &c. and I send it to Your Excelly that You may enforce the Contents shou'd You have an opportunity.

To Benjamin Franklin, August 28[–September 7] 1781

Philada. 28th. August[–September 7] 1781

Sir

Herewith I send you No. 1 & 2. Triplicates of my Letters of the thirteenth and fourteenth July last No. 3 & 4, Duplicates of my Letters of the nineteenth and twenty first of July last. I have not yet executed the Plan mentioned in mine of the twenty first of July of drawing Bills on you for Reasons which it is not necessary to enumerate at present.

Since my Letter to you of the eighth of June last I have found it necessary to apply to the Minister of his most Christian Majesty in this Place to direct another of five hundred thousand Livres with Messrs. Le Couteulx & Co. and I am now drawing Bills for that Sum wherefore I must pray your Excellency to take Measures that they be put in Cash to Answer my Drafts— Altho I have no Doubt that this will be done on the Chevalier de la Luzernes Application yet as his Letters may miscarry or other unavoidable Misfortune happen I take this additional Precaution because it is of the utmost Importance to the United States that these Bills be duly honored.

The last Advices from Europe inform us of Mr Neckars Resignation or Removal which Occasions much Speculation as to the Causes which produced this Event. I should be glad to hear from you on that Subject.

We learn from Boston the Arrival of the frigate Magicienne with a large Store Ship laden with Cloathing &ca. for the United States another Store Ship put back to Corunna as is said having been dismasted in a Gale of Wind. If this be so it is a loss which will be more easily supplied than that of the Fayette which Ship we are now informed was taken and carried into England.

Colo. Laurens's Embarkation on Board a frigate for this Place with Money is also announced, and I hope she will spedily arrive. The Boston Account of the sixteenth of August mentions the arrival of the Magicienne in fifty Days. If Colo. Laurens had then sailed he must now have been out sixty two Days which is a very long Period for a single Frigate to be engaged in that voyage— If that Frigate arrives safe with five hundred thousand Dollars which is as I am informed on Board of her it will releive me from many very great Difficulties which I have now to struggle with, and give a much better appearance to our Affairs as it will enable us to operate with far more Vigor and Activity.

It is now a very long Time since we have had any Tidings of Mr. Adams. We have indeed been informed (tho not from himself) that he had opened a Loan for a Million of Florins: but we are much in the Dark as to the Success of it as well as many other Particulars relative to his Situation which would be very interesting.

September 7th. 1781.

Since writing the above Letter Colo. Laurens has come to this City from Boston at which Place he arrived in the Resolu with the two Store Ships under her Convoy after a Passage uncommonly tedious. It is certainly unnecessary to mention how great Pleasure we have received from this Occurrence.

Another equally pleasing is the Arrival of the Count de Grasse in Chesapeak Bay on the thirtieth of August with twenty eight Sail of the Line to wit one of one hundred and ten Guns three of eighty four Guns nineteen of Seventy four Guns four of sixty four Guns and one of fifty. The Count de Barras sailed from Rhode Island on the twenty fourth so that probably he has before this made a Junction with the Count de Grasse altho he had not on the thirty first of August— A Detachment of about seven thousand Men is on the Way to Virginia of which about two thousand five hundred were at the Head of Elk yesterday: As many more must have arrived there by this Evening and the Remainder to Morrow. There are landed from the Fleet three thousand Men and we are told these will receive an Addition of one thousand five hundred Marines besides the Army under the Command of the Marquis de la fayette which was before in Virginia and consists of about five thousand including the Militia. My Lord Cornwallis was entrenched at York in Virginia with five thousand Men. General Washington takes the Command of the Southern Army in Person. The Fleet under the Count de Grasse took on its way a Packet from Charlestown to Great Britain on Board of which was Lord Rawdon— From this Combination of Circumstances you will perceive that we have Reason to flatter ourselves with the Expectation of pleasing Occurrences.

With the greatest Respect I have the Honor to be Sir Your Excellency's most obedient and humble Servant

RM

To George Washington, 28 August 1781

Office of Finance Philadelphia august 28th 1781

Dear Sir

Your favour of the 27th from Chatham, has just been delivered me by Coll Miles, and in consequence, I have advised him to secure the assistance of the President & Council of this State, in case it should be necessary; but, as a preferable mode of procuring the Craft, I advise his engaging to pay them in a short time after the Service is performed and, if needfull, I shall join in this assurance, and finally see it performed. I directed the Commissary General, immediately on my return from Camp, to cause the deposite of three hundred Barrels of Flour, three hundred Barrels Salt meat, and twelve Hogsheads of Rum to be made at the Head of Elk; and

107

pointed out the means of obtaining them, For this purpose, he sent down a Deputy some days since; and I expect all will be ready there. I am much more apprehensive on the Score of Craft, both in Delaware & Chesapeak. I have written to the Quarter Master of Maryland & Delaware, Mr Donaldson Yates, to exert himself in procuring the Craft. I have written to the Governor, and to several of the most eminent merchants in Baltimore, to extend their assistance and influence in expediting this business. Foreseeing the necessity of Supplies from Maryland & Delaware, I have written in the most pressing Terms, to the Governors and Agents to have the Specific Supplies required of them by Congress in readiness for Delivery to my order, and now that your movements must be unfolded to them, I shall still more strongly shew the necessity and stimulate their exertions, by holding forth what is due to their own immediate Interest and Safety. But still I fear you will be disappointed, in some degree, as to the Shipping; and that I shall be compelled to make purchases of provisions, which if it happens must divert the money from those payments to the army that I wish to make. I have already advised your Excellency of the unhappy situation of money matters, and very much doubt if it will be possible to pay the Detachment a months pay as you wish, therefore it will be best not to raise in them any expectation of that kind. Should it come unexpectedly so much the better. I do not think it practicable to provide the Salt Provisions here, even if a disappointment happens in New England but have particularly recommended attention to the Article in Maryland, which is to furnish 10.500 barrels of Beef & Pork.

No news here yet of the Count De Grasse; but I have had occasion to lament, that too many People have for some days past seemed to know your Excellency's intended movements.

This City is filled with Strangers, so that Coll Miles cannot procure private Lodgings, and my Family being chiefly at Springetsbury, affords me the opportunity of appropriating my

House in Town to your Use. I believe we can accommodate your aids &c. with matrasses, but our Beds are chiefly in the Country, and as what I have cannot possibly be appropriated to a better use, I beg your Excellency will Consider and use my House and what it affords as your own. I have the honour to be Your devoted Servant

Robt Morris

To George Washington, 6 September 1781

Office of Finance 6th September 1781

Dear General

The bearer Mr Audibert will deliver you five hundred Guineas as for secreet Service Money according to the request made in your Letter of the 17th of August last from Dobbs's Ferry. I had directed Mr Audibert to bring with him the ballance which might remain of the 20.000 Dollars after paying the Troops, but upon Consideration I think it will be best if there be any Ballance that it should be paid to the Use of your Excellency's Table.

You will perceive by my Letter to Mr Audibert that he is directed to take your Order wherefore I am now to request that your Excellency will be pleased to order the Payment of this Ballance for the Purpose above mentioned and direct a proper Receipt to be given to the paymaster. I am respectfully Your Excellency's Most Obedient & humble Servant

Robt Morris

To George Washington, 6 September 1781

Office of Finance Sept. 6th 1781

Dr General

I had the Honor to send you two Letters this Morning by Major Clerkson. This will be delivered you by Mr Audibert the Paymaster and encloses No. 1 a Copy of my Letter to him & No. 2 a Copy of my Letter to the Count de Rochambeau.

As it was not in Contemplation to make any Payments to the Civil Staff of the Detachment so the Heads of the Departments have made their seperate Applications to me for Money and I shall let them have what may prudently be spared.

It is possible that the Sum of twenty thousand Dollars may be insufficient in which Case I am to request of your Excellency that you would make Application to the Count for the Deficiency and I will readily replace the Whole on the first of October. I am with the greatest Respect and sincerest Attachment your Excellency's most Obedient

Robt Morris

To George Washington, 6 September 1781

Chester 6 Septr 1781

Several Worthy People & particularly the Romish Priest and Mr Fitzsimmons have interested themselves in favour of a Criminal under Sentence of Death for Desertion, I dont know his name but he is in Philada Goal—your Excy is the best judge of propriety in such cases and I am Sensible of the impropriety of such applications but as I promised to speak to your Excy & took the opportunity I desired Colo. Smith to mention it & now repeat the matter that I may not have to accuse myself of Neglect. this is a

110

Young Man & may become a good Soldier hereafter, tomorrow is fixed for his Execution, therefore if mercy is extended the order shou'd be instantly sent. I ever am yr Excys Sincere & devoted Sevt

R. Morris

To George Washington, 6 September 1781

Chester 6 Sepr 1781

Dr General

Permit me most sincerely to congratulate you on the arrival of the french Fleet and to express my warmest Wishes for the Success of your future operations.

As soon as I arrive at Philadelphia I shall give Directions for the Deputy Paymaster to repair to the Head of Elk and make Payment of a Month's Pay in Specie to the Detachment [un]der the Command of Genl Lincoln. I wish the States had enabled me to [d]o more, but it is to be lamented that the Supinenness of the several Legislatures still leaves the Servants of the Public to struggle with unmerited Distresses. It shall however be a Part of my Business to rouse them into Exertion and I hope soon to see the army better paid than heretofore and I confide that your Excellency will with every other Public officer exert your Influence to aid me in this necessary Task. with the greatest Respect I have the Honor to be your Excellency's most obedt & humble Servt

Robt Morris

P.S. I shall send the 500 Guineas by the Pay Master, as they were left behind by yr Excy.

To George Washington, 10 September 1781

Office of Finance September 10th 1781

Dear Sir

The sole intent of the present is to acknowledge the receipt of your two Letters of the 7th Instant that which related to the Months pay you woud see was answered by the Steps previously taken but I am a good deal disappointed and put to inconvenience by the Money at Elk falling short of the object which obliges me to send Money thither that was absolutely necessary to fulfill my engagements here I must struggle thro these difficulties, but the doing so requires that attention and time which ought to be bestowed upon greater objects.

The letter respecting the Criminal was too late, the poor Fellow was gone. I am sorry for it, and remain Your Excellency's Most Obedient humble Servant

Robt Morris

To George Washington, 13 September 1781

Office of Finance September 13th 1781

Dear General

You mention'd to me in Conversation that the Bill I formerly remitted you on Messrs Richards & Co. of New London had not been paid, I must therefore request that you will give orders for its being returned to me.

Herein you will find the first bill of a Sett drawn by Mr Thomas Pleasants Junr yesterday at Ten days sight in my favour on David Ross Esqr. Commercial Agent of the State of Virginia for three hundred and twenty Pounds hard Money at the rate of six Shillings per Dollar equal to 1066 2/3rds Spanish Silver Dollars which the Drawer assures me will be punctually paid, and I have charged the same as a Supply for Your Excellency's Table.

Mr John May of Virginia will pay you thirty Silver Dollars for the same Sum advanced him here for which be pleased to grant him a draft on me and apply it to the same purpose. I ever am Your Excellency's Most Obedt & humble Servant

Robt Morris

To Benjamin Franklin, 14 September 1781

Office of Finance Philada. Septbr. 14th. 1781

Sir

I take the Liberty to enclose to you a Note of two Books of which I am to request that you will cause three compleat Setts to be purchased on the public Account and sent to me by three different Conveyances. I am very respectfully Sir your most Obedient & humble Servant

Robt Morris

To Benjamin Franklin, 14 October 1781

Philadelphia October 14th. 1781

Dear Sir

The Interuption given to the Progress of Learning, the Distresses which the several Seminaries in this Country, have undergone, the various lucrative Employments, to which Masters, and Tutors, have been invited, in the Progress of the present War; are Circumstances, which operate powerfully to the Disadvantage, of the present race of American Youth, and which have induced me, to take the Determination, of Educating my two Eldest Sons, Robert and Thomas, in Europe. The bearer of this Letter Mathew Ridley Esqr. with whom you are already acquainted, has kindly offered to take them over to France, and to see them placed at the Schools, which may be judged most proper for them; Geneva has the reputation of good Schools, able Masters, in every Branch of Education, and is strongly recommended also, on Account of the Sober, orderly, manners of the People, who strengthen by their Practice and Example, that rectitude of Morals, which Precept alone, might not sufficiently impress; on young Minds. Books and Travellers give this Account of Geneva, and Doctor Franklin, fixed my Faith, when he placed a favorite Grandson there, so that my Boys go over destined for that, as the Place of their residence, unless Circumstances should have arisen to render it ineligible; We are told that this little republic has lately been disturbed by some internal Convulsions, which obliged the Students to retire for Safety. Whether the Peace of the Place is again restored, I do not know. My Boys, will have the Honor of paying you their respects in Paris, and Mr. Ridley will beg leave to consult you, on the Propriety of placing them at Geneva, or any other more eligible Schools. It is my Intention, to give them a liberal Education, to open their Minds to every Science, and Channell of Knoledge, so that in future Times, they may choose for themselves their Walk through Life, upon Terms of Advantage equal to any; should they possess Genius, and Powers of Mind, to profit by that Foundation I wish to establish for them.

The veneration, in which I hold your Abilities, the respect I have for your Character, and the Esteem founded on Acquaintance, which I have for your Person, must plead my Excuse, for drawing your Attention, from more important Concerns, to the Affairs of two little helpless Boys in a Strange Country. I pray you to assist Mr. Ridley with your good Advice, respecting them, and that you will, if convenient recommend them to any Friend, so situated as to view their Conduct, and occasionally, to administer the Advice, Encouragement or reproof, which may be necessary. You are certain of my gratefull Thanks, and the Youngsters when ripened into Manhood, will feel the Weight of personal Obligations, joined to that Admiration, and Esteem, which the Virtues and Talents of the Patriot, minister & Philosopher must inspire. And when your Name is mentioned they shall be heard to say "That great and good Man, smiled on our infant Years, and encouraged us by his benign Influence, while we gained Strength, and aquired Knoledge, in a Country far distant from our native Shore, he was our Father, Protector and Friend." In short, my good Sir, I wish these Boys, to benefit by your Advice, but with as little Trouble to you as possible. When favorable Opportunities shall offer you will permit them to pay their respects, you have every Title to mine, and I shall always continue what I have long been, Your sincere Friend and Admirer as well as Your obliged and Obedient humble Servant

Robt Morris

To George Washington, 17 October 1781

Office of Finance Octr 17th 1781

Sir

I have had the Honor to receive your Excellency's two several Letters, of the twenty seventh of September, and first, Instant. The latter did not come to Hand untill nine oClock last Evening. I have this Morning directed the Purchase of a quantity of Rum, and lament that I cannot possibly arrive as soon as you will stand in Need of it. This must be attributed to the Delay of your Letter, which was truly unaccountable. I shall direct it to be forwarded with all possible Expedition.

The Bill in your Favor, on Richards & Co. of New London, was inclosed in your Letter of the first Instant. I am much obliged by your Promise to take Care of my Letter to Genl Greene, and pray you will accept my Thanks.

On the thirteenth of September, I had the Honor to remit your Excellency a Bill on David Ross Esqr. for the amount of one thousand & sixty six Dollars and two thirds. I shall be glad to be informed by your Excellency if this Bill has been duly honored, and also whether you have received thirty Dollars mentioned in my Letter of the thirteenth of September, to be paid to you by Mr John May of Virginia.

I shall at all Times be very happy to hear from your Excellency and it will give me the greatest Pleasure to render you every possible Aid. I sincerely wish that my abilities were equal to my Inclinations and as sincerely regret that I have little else besides Wishes to dispose of. I do not perceive in the State, a Desire to furnish Revenue, on the contrary there is a Degree of Torpor and Lukewarmness which nothing can justify. The very little Money which I can command is called for in a thousand different Ways, and must soon be exhausted. However your Excellency has Cares enough, and I will not trouble you with my Perplexities. With the greatest Esteem and Respect I am Your Excellency's most obedient and humble Servant

Robt Morris

To George Washington, 19 October 1781

Philada Octr 19th 1781

Dear Sir

Should an opportunity offer Mr Ridley will present before you my two Sons who have the ambition to pay their Compts. to you, before their departure for Europe, where they are now destined under the care and protection of that gentleman untill he can place them with their Tutors. I consider the step I have taken as advantageous to them, and also of some Public consequence, because if the example is followed and it becomes the practice to Educate American Youths in France, Habitual attachments will strengthen those ties of affection which in gratitude is due from this to that Country.

I have written to His Excy Count de Grasse excusing myself for depending on a passage on one of His Majesties Ships. Shou'd you have an opportunity of [adding] a Word on the Subject, it will procure to Mr Ridley & the Boys the favourable attention of the Commander they go with. I flatter myself with the fond hopes that these Boys may hereafter become usefull to their Country and that they will add to the Number of those who shall Publicly make repeated gratefull acknowledgments for the blessings of Liberty & Peace transmitted to them by means of those Noble, those Glorious Exertions of which your whole Conduct in this War affords one continued & unparalled Example. Your present operations must have become serious before this time and we begin here to feel, the full Force of that impatient expectation which is Natural on such an occasion. With Sincere attachments of the most ardent wishes for Your Success I ever am D Sir, Your devoted hble servt

RM

To John Jay, 19 October 1781

Philada. Octr. 19th 1781

My Dear Sir—

I believe Kitty Livingston has availed herself of this good Conveyance by Matthew Ridley Esqr. to write you very fully & of course she will have told you all the news both Domestick & Political— Mrs. Morris has also written to Mrs Jay & no doubt assures her of that Esteem & affection in which she holds both her and you. I need not tell you how Sincerely I join her in those Sentiments. You are often the Subject of our Conversations & we never Speak of you but with Pleasing Remembrance of past time— We anxiously look forward to those Hours when we may again enjoy your Company, but the keenest Wishes are checked when necessity prescribes Patience— I will therefore Quit this Subject and proceed to Inform you that some particular Circumstances have put me in Possession of Kitty's Picture taken by Mr. Du Simitier It was Intended for you and therefore you must permit me to present you with it— Whilst the Original is under my Roof—the Copy has less Value, or perhaps you might not have found me so Ready to part with it, Don't allow me the Merit of being Generous in this Instance, wherein I have an Opportunity of Obliging three Persons, for any one of whom I would Sacrifice my own Gratifications— Consequently I Resolve this Sacrifice into an Act of mere Selfishness— The Portrait goes by Mr Ridley who will send it to you by the first good Opportunity after his Arrival in France— My two Oldest Sons go with Mr. Ridley in Order to Receive their Educations in France— Many Considerations which it is needless to Enumerate, Induced me to this measure, which my Judgment approves, but which now that it is to be Carried into Execution Awakens all the Tender Feelings of a Father— Your and Mrs. Jays Sensibility will disclose the beloved Boys.

Mrs. Morris and myself when I tell you that these two good & well leave us to morrow—they are tractable good Boys I Hope they will make good Men, for that is Essential, Perhaps they may become Usefull to their Country which is very desirable, and if they have Genius and Judgement, the Education they will Receive may be the Foundation for them to become Learned or Great Men, but this is of most Consequence to themselves, Should it fall in your Way to Notice them I am sure you will do it— I expect they will be fixed at the Schools in Geneva—this parting Reminds me my Good Friend that we are but too much the Slaves of Ambition & Vanity to permit the Enjoyment of that happyness, which is in our Power. I need not part with my Children but.—

Excuse me from writing on Political Matters at this time, when I know that you have seen Major Franks & Received my Cypher, you shall hear from me officially on many Points— Chancellor Livingston is this day arrived to take Possession of his office, so that I hope you will in future be well informed of all things in the Publick Line, that can be of Use for you to know—and I flatter myself that your Situation will become far more eligible than it has been— *Governeur* is with me and a most usefull & able assistant he is— I hope our Joint Labours will in the end have the desired Effect. — We have mended the appearance of things very much, and are Regaining Publick Credit and Confidence by degrees, —& our Efforts are Seconded & Supported by the Several Legislatures as they ought— We need not fear the Utmost Efforts of our Enemies, because we will learn to Exert and Concenter our own Force.— With the most Sincere attachment & Esteem— I am My Dear Friend Your obed & hble Servt.

Robt Morris

To Benjamin Franklin (Two Letters), 27 November 1781

I.

Office of Finance 27th. November 1781

Sir

The Marquis de la fayette, who is about to sail for France, will have the Honor to deliver this Letter; and consistently with the Acts of Congress of the twenty third Instant I must request you to communicate it to him, and from Time to Time to take his Aid in the Prosecution of the Business which I must recommend to your particular Attention. The Affairs of my Department are of a Nature not to require Concealment, but even if that were not the Case, I have such perfect Confidence as well in the Prudence of the Marquis as in his Attachment to this Country, that the Acts of Congress out of the question I should feel a pleasure in making him acquainted with my Views and Wishes. Indeed I expect that his Zeal and Activity will go far in smoothing the Way towards the Accomplishment of those Objects which your Excellency will have to solicit.

In Order that you may be perfectly acquainted with the Situation of our Affairs, I shall previous to my Observations on the Supplies to be asked for the next Campaign, take some Notice of the Efforts I have made and am daily reiterating to obtain Supplies from the several States, upon the various Requisitions which Congress have already made; to operate a Settlement of past Accounts; and procure proper Funds for the public Debts. I shall also make some Remarks as to the prospect of future Supplies in this Country, and on those which have already been granted by the Court of France.

The Papers enclosed, and Numbered 1 to 8 inclusive, relate chiefly to the former Requisitions of Congress. You will observe Sir that by an Act of the twenty eighth of June last, I was directed to press a Compliance with those Requisitions and it is in Consequence thereof, that my circular Letter No. 1 of the sixth of July was written. The Demands of Congress were twofold, some for Specific Supplies of the Produce of the several States, the others for Money. It may be proper here to observe that the Manner of doing public Business had been such, that it was not meerly difficult, but absolutely impracticable, to state any Accounts in the clear satisfactory Manner which ought always to be wished even in private Life, but which in public Life is of the last Importance. I do not mention this to cast any Reflection or Aspersion, for the Evil resulted more from the want of Arrangement than the faults of any particular Men; but it is right to take Notice of the Circumstance, because in the Course of what I am about to write the Want of such Accounts cannot but appear. I shall say Nothing as to the ill Effects of demanding generally a Contribution of specified Articles. My Opinions on that Subject will appear from the enclosed Papers, and Experience has taught that such Contributions are no longer to be relied on. At the same Time I declare now, that in some Degree it must still take Place, for Reasons which will be mentioned at the proper Time.—

As the Letter last mentioned contains no state of the Accounts, I wrote on the 16th of July another whereof Number two is a Copy, containing the Cash Account of each State as extracted from the Treasury Books. A State however which I knew to be imperfect, for Causes not necessary to be repeated. On the twenty fifth of July I wrote another circular Letter, whereof Number 3 is a Copy, and in which was enclosed a State of the several Demands for specific Supplies. These were considerable, and I am of Opinion that a very great part of them still remains to be delivered at this day, but there have yet come to my Hands no Accounts by which to determine the Ballances. What is said as to the Settlement of Accounts in this Letter, will be honored with your Notice presently, you will now observe that I therein request Information as to the Revenue Laws which have been passed, the Mode of collecting Taxes, the Monies in their Treasuries, the various Appropriations of it, and the different Paper Currencies in the several States. To your Excellency it is unnecessary to observe that my Object was to obtain proper Materials on which to ground my future Expectations, and to form efficacious Systems of Revenue and Expenditures. I have the Mortification however to mention that no accurate or satisfactory Answers have been received to those questions, and when I tell you that I am not much deceived in my Expectations, you will readily form the proper Conclusions as to the relaxed Habit of Administration in this Country. I wish you to be fully possessed of our Situation, and that you may convey a clear Idea of it to the Court of Versailles. This will be useful to the common Cause. I trust that I need not remind you how advantageous it would be for us to know as fully the real Situation of France.

The low State of public Credit for the want of solid Funds to support it, had induced the United States in Congress to call for an Impost of five per Cent on all Goods imported and on all Prizes and Prize Goods, to be granted for the Payment of the principal and Interest of the Debts contracted or which might be contracted during the present War. Some of the States had complied with this Demand. The two more southern States were in such Disorder that a Compliance from them could not reasonably be expected, neither was it relied on as you doubtless have remarked on reading the Resolutions of the third of February upon that Subject, which must have reached you before this Day. On the twenty seventh of July therefore I wrote the Letter, whereof Number four is a Copy, to the deficient States of Massachusetts, Rhode Island, New York, Delaware, Maryland and North Carolina. I have the Pleasure to inform you that the States of New York, Delaware and North Carolina have since complied with the Demand of Congress, and I am well convinced that they will in this laudable Step be speedily followed by the other States. In the mean Time we must patiently wait the Event. Such Things require Time, and since we cannot command Obedience we must stay for the Assent of Conviction.—

On the sixth of August I wrote a Letter to the President of Congress enclosing those already mentioned. Number five is Copy of this Letter on which it is necessary to say nothing more than that it met with the Approbation of the several Members who have I believe written such Letters to their respective States as I desired—

My Letter of the fifteenth of September to the Governor of Massachusetts, of which Number six is Copy, was as your Excellency will perceive altho the Settlement of past Accounts is mentioned in it, written in Answer to his of the twenty third of August, in which he tells me that he will lay the Business of the Impost Law candidly before the Legislature, but thinks it will go heavily thro. I shall add nothing here to what is said in that Letter.

My Letter of the 28th. of September to the Assembly of Pennsylvania, of which Number 7. A is Copy, was written so particularly in Consequence of the Authorities they had confided by their Resolutions of which Number seven B is Copy. I wrote to you respecting these Resolutions, and my Plans founded on them, the twenty first of July, and I just mention here, by the bye, that this Plan has not been in any Degree executed, for Reasons not necessary to be at present enlarged upon. My Letter to the Assembly of Pennsilvania with the Enclosures refered to in it as Accounts Number 1. 2 & 3, and of which I send you Copies number seven C, D & E, will need no Explanation; unless it be to mention that this State had issued £100.000 secured with Interest on certain Lands near this City, which is now nearly paid by the Sales of those Lands, and £500.000 more not bearing Interest which was funded upon the Land Office, the Dues to which were estimated at a much larger Sum. I have sent this Letter as also my private Letter of the sixteenth of October to Governor Nelson, meerly that you may be well apprized of the incessant Attention which is paid here to call forth our own Resources. I might have added many other Letters to particular States on particular Occasions, but I dare say you will find this Letter sufficiently voluminous.—

Before I quit this Subject of the past Requisitions of Congress I must add that notwithstanding my pressing Instances very little hard Money has been obtained from the States, not more than 100.000 Dollars, during the whole of my Administration. There have indeed been drawn forth some considerable specific Supplies of Provisions. And there is on Hand a great Deal of Paper Money. From the former our Army have been principally maintained, and indeed there is a small advance made to the Count De Rochambeau which I mean to be in Part of your Promise mentioned in a former Letter, and here repeat to you my Determination to comply with it as speedily as my Convenience will possibly admit. As to the paper Money it is of no Use, altho it is necessary for evident Reasons to receive it in Taxes, but the Confidence of the People is so entirely lost that for the present no Bills of Credit whatever can be made Use of as Money. I hope that the Taxes laid and collecting in most of the States will bring in all this useless Load by the middle of next Summer, and I have some Expectation that the States of Massachusetts, Connecticutt, Pennsilvania and Delaware will be entirely Rid of it by the Spring. If I *could* buy any Thing with it I would not, untill the last Necessity, but it will buy Nothing so that it must be burnt as soon as it honestly can.—

The Picture I have already given of this Country will not be pleasing to you, Truth bids me add that it will admit of a higher coloring. But what else could be expected from us? A Revolution, a War, the Dissolution of Government, the creating of it anew, Cruelty Rapine and Devastation in the midst of our very Bowels, these Sir are Circumstances by no means favorable to Finance. The Wonder then is that we have done so much, that we have borne so much, and the candid World will add that we have dared so much. I could take up much of your Time in Recapitulating many lesser Matters which have tended to lessen the Exertions we have otherwise been capable of. The confused State of public Accounts, and the deplorable Situation of Credit for want of Funds to secure, or means to redeem the Debts for which the public Faith is pledged are however of such important Operation that I must not pass them over in Silence.

In the Enclosures number three and Number six your Excellency will have perceived that I have noticed the Effects which follow from the Want of a final Settlement of Accounts. Representations on the Subject of those Accounts, and also of Certificates given by public Officers in the Commissary's and Quarter Master's Departments for Articles taken from the People, had been made by some of the States to Congress. The Impost asked for by Congress was, as I have already observed, for the funding of our Debts. On the thirteenth of October, I wrote a Letter to the several Loan Officers of which number nine is Copy, in which I expressly prohibit the issuing of any more Loan Office Certificates. The Reason for this Order will appear more clearly from the latter Part of my circular Letter to the several Governors, of the nineteenth of October, of which number ten A is a Copy. The Papers Number eleven and twelve are all which I shall add on this Subject. Number eleven is, as you will observe, a Letter to Congress of the fifth Instant in Consequence of their Acts of the second, contained in the Paper marked number thirteen. That Letter enclosed another of the twenty eighth of August of which number twelve is a Copy. These Letters contain my Sentiments on the Subjects they relate to very fully, and it will be unnecessary to say any Thing in Explanation of them. I do hope and expect that some Methods will speedily be adopted by the United States in Congress assembled, for Settlement of the Public Accounts; as also to liquidate the several Certificates given by the Public Officers, and to provide Revenues for funding the public Debts. The last of these Objects must not however be urged with too much Rapidity. The Impost Law is not yet passed, and that is the first Step. When that shall have been taken, it will give Room for urging what farther may be necessary. In the mean Time there is a well grounded Expectation, that the Clamors of our Creditors will induce the several Legislatures to comply with the Requisitions of Congress upon that Subject.—

From what has been said, your Excellency will perceive that the Prospect of future Supplies from the several States, is by no means very brilliant. The Paper number thirteen contains the Act of Congress of the twenty ninth of October, calling for eight Million of Dollars, the Act of the second Instant, apportioning that Demand upon the several States, And the Act of the twelfth Instant repealing (in Consequence of my Letter of the fifth) a part of the Act of the second. My circular Letter of the seventeenth, enclosing those Acts to the Governors of the several States a Copy of which is contained in the Paper number fourteen, will close what I have to say on that Subject. But I must observe to you on my Letter of the fifth to the President of Congress, that altho it is strictly true that I had not seen the Estimates as mentioned in that Letter, yet it is equally true that untill the Business was nearly compleated I was supposed to have seen them, and when the contrary was suggested they would have been sent, from Congress, but that so few States were represented as that only the Number absolutely necessary to pass such Requisitions were then present, and some of the Representatives of those few were about to depart, wherefore it was waved. I have further to remark on the Estimates themselves, that they are made only for the feeding and paying of the Army. The Expence of recruiting that Army, of moving it from Place to Place, the Heavy Articles of Cloathing and Ordinance, with the Expence of the Hospitals, and the long Train which is comprehended under the Title of Contingencies, is totally unprovided for. Defective as it is, I have no Hope that it will be complied with. The great Arrearage of unfunded Debt, the cumbrous Load of useless Paper, the multiplied Mass of Certificates, the distracted Situation of the more Southern States, the Ravages which have been made in them, the total Loss of their Commerce, the real Want of Coin in many States, and the equal Want of System in all, these Sir are Circumstances which forbid the most sanguine Temper to expect a full Compliance. It shall be my Business, as it is my Duty, to get as much as I can; and for this Purpose I shall make Compositions where it is necessary, take Articles of Provisions in Lieu of Money, and the like. Still however I am convinced that I shall not get what is asked for, and indeed I do not expect any Part of it, before the middle of the next Campaign.—

I have said that I will make some Remarks on the Supplies already furnished by France. It is necessary to do this, as well because I am so unfortunate as to differ a little in Opinion on the Subject with the Minister of his most Christian Majesty here, as because the Demands we are to make on the Court for the next Year will much depend on the Compliances which have been and shall be made with the Grants for the present Year.—

It was a Point understood in Congress very early, that his most Christian Majesty would pay the Interest of certain Monies to be borrowed by Congress in America. Your Excellency knows better than any other Man what passed on that Subject, it would therefore be absurd in me to recapitulate it. Those Circumstances which rendered an express Stipulation improper then, have introduced much Delicacy into it now, and therefore I do not expect that the Court will recur to a formal Acknowlegement of what was then perhaps rather a personal than national Obligation. But I do expect that the Payment of that Interest will be provided for as heretofore, without considering the Monies appropriated to that Purpose as a Relief to us in carrying on the War. You will have seen Sir from the Course of my Letters, how much it is an Object with me to collect from ourselves the Revenues necessary to liquidate our Debts. There are a Variety of Reasons for it which I will not repeat, Among them however this is one that I wish to remove the Load from France to ourselves. It will in the End be the same Thing; because in Proportion as our Resources here are appropriated we must ask Help there, but it would be better that the People were taught to look at Home for the Basis of national Credit, because there alone it can be found. I should not have mentioned this Matter, but that you will find it noticed in the Correspondence between the Chevalier de la Luzerne and myself, of which Copies are enclosed.

Shortly after the arrival of Monsieur Gerrard, it was understood that France would supply us with the Cloathing and warlike Stores which might be necessary, and therefore it was that Coll. Laurens when in France labored to prevent a Deduction from the Subsidy of six Millions, on Account of the Articles furnished to him. As I am perswaded that his Efforts were in Consequence of your Advice, and in Concert with you, I shall say nothing more upon that Subject, only to lament that the Court have differed from you in Opinion, and to acquiesce in their Determination, on the Principle that those who give have a Right to dispose of that which is given.

By a Note from the Count de Vergennes whereof Number fifteen is a Copy, I perceive that the Court granted the united States as a Gift six Millions, advanced you four Millions to pay the Bills which might be drawn on you, and became Security for a Loan of ten Millions, the Amount of which was to be advanced from the Royal Treasury in Case the Loan should fail of Success. The Expression as to this last Object is Strong namely *that his Majesty will see himself under the necessity of supplying the Deficiency,* altho in the former Part of the Note it is said, that he will supply it from his own Finances *as soon as possible*, an Expression which, while at the first Blush it marks an Earnestness of Affection, may be and in fact has been construed into a Kind of cautionary Provision. Your Excellency will also I doubt not observe what is there said of the appropriation of the Gift, the last two Millions whereof as is already observed we did not expect to find there.

Number sixteen is the Copy of an Account delivered by the Minister of France, in the Month of September, to a Committee of Congress which had been appointed to confer with him. There are striking Differences between this Account and the Note last mentioned. But from this Account it appears, by the Articles A 1. 2. and F, that it was the Design of the Court to make the Advances of the present Year distinct from all past Transactions; from whence this Conclusion at least will follow, that such of the Bills drawn by Congress either on yourself or on their Agents in Spain or Holland as you may have discharged before the Commencement of the present Year are not to be deducted from the Sums mentioned in the Count De Vergennes Note. Now that I am on this Subject I will observe to you Sir, that I have determined to prevent that circuitous Negotiation of Bills which had so much perplexed and distressed you, and have for that Reason stopped many of those already drawn as will presently appear. Another Observation to be made on this Account is, that no Notice is taken of the four Millions expressly mentioned in the Count de Vergenne's Note as granted to you for payment of Bills drawn by Congress. A third observation is, that the Articles marked B and the Article number 2. C. which together amount to the Sum of 6.686.109 *l.t.* are all charged as being expended to the Order of Coll. Laurens, but by the Count de Vergennes Letter to you of the eighth of June last it appears that Col. Laurens was to have had the Command of no other than the 6.000.000 *l.t.* given by the King. Indeed the Counts Note of the sixteenth of May shews the same Thing. The Letter of the eighth of June just mentioned shews clearly the Opinion of the Court on another Point of very great Importance, namely that the whole 10.000.000 *l.t.* to be advanced for the Loan are, as in Effect they ought to be, subject to the Disposition of the united States only. A fourth Observation is that the Articles A 3. B 2. and C 1. amounting to 4.300.000 *l.t.* were or were to have been in your Possession for Payment of Bills, if to this be added the 4.000.000 *l.t.* granted for that express purpose, of which no mention is made in the Account, it would follow that you would have 8.300.000 *l.t.* at your Disposal, and this leads me to consider the Amount of the Demands which would be made on you. These cannot be precisely ascertained, but the Paper number seventeen contains the best estimate in my Power. The first six Articles of this Estimate contain all the Bills which have been drawn upon you, excepting some Interest Bills which altho made out had not been delivered to the People before the first of April last. These Amount to 10.671.456 *l.t.* 13 *s.* 4 *d.* The Article Number seven is the whole Amount of Guilders drawn for, the far greater Part of which I have detained as you will perceive by the Article Number eight. The Ballance it is not possible to ascertain exactly in Livres because it must depend upon the Course of Exchange, but at two Livres for a Guilder the whole of the Bills actually negotiated on Holland will amount to 1.094.729 *l.t.* The Article Number nine is the Amount of Bills drawn on Spain, of which a considerable Part has been paid by Mr. Jay, and a Part somewhat more considerable is destroyed. These Parts are contained in the Articles ten and eleven. The Ballance (calculated at the Value of a Dollar in France which will I suppose be as much as it can cost) amounts to 1.077.218 *l.t.* So that the whole of those Bills which by any Means whatever could have come upon you for Payment, will be 12.843.403 *l.t.* 13 *s.* 4 *d.*, and from this Sum very considerable Deductions are to be made. The Article Number twelve, which is the first of them, contains the exact amount of the several Bills for Interest which were negotiated previously to the first of April last. It may be objected that these Bills will, many of them, be payable during the present year which indeed is true, and for that Reason I have added to the Bottom of the Account the Extent of one years Interest on Loan Office Certificates, and which is more than will I believe be presented.— The next Article Number thirteen, is for Bills which had been drawn on you and have been stopped by me. The Article Number fourteen is you will perceive for Bills which in all human Probability will have been paid during the last Year. The Certainty of this Transaction is doubtless with you, and what we are now upon is an Estimate not an Account. The remaining Articles speak clearly for themselves; wherefore I conceive myself well founded in making the Amount of Deductions in this Estimate 9.163.265 *l.t.* So that, after including one Years Interest as is already mentioned, the Total is 5.873.128 [*l.t.*] 13 *s.* 4 *d.* and from this there must be some Deductions because undoubtedly you have paid some of the Bills drawn on Spain and Holland before the first Day of January last. I have mentioned no Sum for this Purpose, but in Order to be within Bounds I will suppose it to be only 373.128 *l.t.* 13 *s.* 4 *d.* and then the Extent of the Bills payable by you in the Year 1781 will be five Millions and an half of Livres, and therefore the four Millions granted by the Court, and the Million and an half said to have been stopped by you in Holland, will apply to this Demand. As the last mentioned Sum appears by the Count De Vergennes Note to have been Part of that which was given by the Court, This State of the Matter will leave clear the 10.000.000 *l.t.* to have been loaned, and seems properly to consist with the Counts Note of the sixteenth of May, and his Letter to you of the eighth of June following. I have mentioned above, that in making the Deduction for Bills paid previous to the Year 1781 I meant to be within Bounds. It is proper to give a Reason why I supposed that Deduction to be so. I have already made one Remark on the Articles A 1. 2. and F in the Account officially communicated by the Minister of France in September last. From those Articles it appears at least that 3.000.000 Livres were advanced for the Payment of Bills last year. The Amount of the Interest Bills I have already Stated as being in the Extent 2.193.990 *l.t.* To this Sum must be added 144.000 *l.t.* due to Mr. Beaumarchais and the 125.000 *l.t.* deducted in the Estimates as having been drawn for by the Resolutions of the nineteenth of May 1780. These Sums together amount to 2.462.990 *l.t.*, to which I will add for Contingencies 137.010 *l.t.* more, making the whole Amount 2.600.000 *l.t.* Wherefore supposing the Grant of Monies to pay Bills for the Year 1780 to have been but 3.000.000 *l.t.*, and it appears evidently to have been at least that, there would have remained in your Hands a Ballance of 400.000 *l.t.* which is more than I have deducted from the Amount of my Estimate. On the whole then I conceive myself well grounded in the Opinion, that the whole Loan is still at our Disposal, and this Opinion is so well Supported by the Count de Vergennes Letter to you, that I might with great Propriety insist on that Point. The Letter therefore which I shall write with such Act of Congress as may be made in Consequence of yours of the eleventh of June, will proceed entirely upon that Supposition. I must however remark to you in this Place, that I by no means intend to insist rigidly with the Court on Points which may incommode them. We are neither in a Situation to do it, nor would it be proper even if we were. But while I say this I do not mean to preclude myself from such Observations as my Duty shall render necessary on any Transaction which has happened or which may happen hereafter.

I enclose you an account containing the Extent of what I conceive to have been the Appropriation of the Supplies above mentioned, which is Numbered thirty three, together with an Invoice from the Board of War Number thirty four, amounting to the Sum of 1.777.520 *l.t.* 10 *s.* and which I call 1.800.000 *l.t.*, from which it will appear that there must remain Subject to my Disposition the

Sum of four Millions at least, after replacing the Fayettes Cargo and purchasing the Articles mentioned in the Invoice.

I have had the Honor to mention to your Excellency that I have the Misfortune to differ in Opinion with the Minister of France, this is upon two Points namely the drawing of Bills by me, and the Amount of what may remain due by the Court. From the Correspondence between us, which is contained in the Papers from number eighteen to Number twenty nine inclusive, there will appear to have been some Warmth on the Occasion; but this rather arose from the Nature of the Transaction than any Thing else. I know not what Impression it may have left on his Mind, but for my own Part as I greatly respect him, so I sincerely feel for a Situation to which the Orders of his Court have reduced him, and altho the Language of his Letter of the twenty fourth of November, evidently intended for his Court, was so pointed as to force me into the Observation contained in mine of the twenty sixth, in my own Justification; yet I was almost as much wounded while writing, as he appeared to have been at the Reading of it. I am much inclined to believe that he wishes to place this Business substantially in the same Point of Light that I do. The whole Correspondence is enclosed, that you may be in Capacity to make any proper Observations which Occasion may dictate. Before I take up this Correspondence more particularly, I must detain you one Moment longer to mention the Facts which preceded it. Before my Acceptance of the Office which I now hold, the Chevalier de la Luzerne informed me that the Court had given Money to the United States with a Determination that it should be at the Disposal of General Washington, but that upon my Acceptance he would authorize me to draw for it. It was agreed between us that I should draw for 500.000 *l.t.* and so much be deposited to answer the Drafts, and by giving him Notice in Season a new Deposit of 500.000 *l.t.* should be made, and so on from Time to Time. Shortly afterwards I formed a Plan to get

Money from the Havannah, and on explaining it to the Chevalier he approved of it and in Consequence I drew a Bill on Messrs. Le Couteulx & Co. the 17th. July for 500.000 *l.t.*, but the Capture of the Trumbull Frigate prevented the negotiation of that Bill, which being then onboard of her intended for Havannah, was sunk with my Dispatches; and the Knowlege that Coll. Laurens was then on his Way with Specie, together with the Expectation of that which was to have been sent by the Way of Holland, prevented a Repetition of the Experiment upon Havannah at that time. It was previously to the second of July 1781, that the Chevalier agreed I should negotiate Bills for 1.500.000 *l.t.*, of which the 500.000 *l.t.* to have been Negotiated at the Havannah was a Part.—

Number 18 is my Letter of the second of July upon this Subject, which was the Day before Monsr. de la Luzerne went to Camp; and Number nineteen is Monsieur de Marbois Answer to it. My Reply of the fourth, number twenty, closes the Matter at that Time; and then it was understood on all Hands in the Manner I have just now mentioned, and which I have as you will perceive insisted on thro the whole of my Correspondence, and which was equally insisted on in a Variety of Conversations.

That Part of the Letter last mentioned which relates to the Effect of drawing Bills, together with the Letters of the second and third of August numbered twenty one and twenty two, need no Comment. They meerly serve to shew the Desire which animates the Servants of the United States to œconomize the Resources of France. I am not disposed to criminate, but it is right that I should inform you of my Opinion, which is that the french Troops in this Country have cost much more than was necessary, if my Information is not extremely erroneous. I have now in Contemplation Plans for feeding them more cheaply, and I think the french Ration ought not to cost more than half a Livre, at least not much more if so much. The Officers who now return to Europe can best answer whether it has formerly exceeded that Amount, and the Court must know how much has been lost on the Negotiation of their Bills. While on this Subject it is my Duty to add, that the Minister of France here has demonstrated the most earnest Desire to introduce Oeconomy in the Expenditures of the Army, and that the Readiness shewn by Monsieur de Rochambeau and other General Officers to aid in it demand Acknowlegements.

On the twenty fourth of September the Chevalier wrote me a note of which Number twenty three is Copy. This you will observe was after the Receipt of those Letters in Consequence of which he, among other Things, communicated the Account on which I have already had the Honor of making some Remarks. This Letter, while it assigns Reasons for continuing my Drafts, shews clearly that the Chevalier had communicated his Instructions to stop them; which was done not only to me but also to the Committee. But I confess that I was very far from considering those Instructions as absolute. I concluded that a Line of Discretion had been then left to the Minister, and indeed his answer to my Letter confirmed me in that Opinion. This answer is of the twenty sixth and is numbered twenty five. He does indeed say that, *it is impossible to depart from the precise Instructions received on that Subject and authorise my Drafts to the amount of 2.500.000.* but he immediately goes on to permit an Addition of 298.981 *l.t.* 15 *s.* 4 *d.* Wherefore it followed, either that those Instructions left him at Liberty to extend the Drafts, or that he was at Liberty to disregard the Instructions. I therefore did expect to have gone on to the Sum first agreed for. These Expectations were frequently mentioned in Conversation, and particularly so in that alluded to in mine of the twenty second Instant, marked number twenty six A. On the other Hand I must acknowlege, that he always mentioned his Instructions, but still so as to leave me under the original Impressions I had received. As this Letter of the twenty second takes Notice of another Matter, it is proper to mention here that the Chevalier had observed on a difference between the Account he delivered officially to the Committee of Congress, and the Note from the Count de Vergennes; but no pointed Conversation on this Subject had taken Place, he expecting further Information from his Court, and I hoping daily to hear from your Excellency, and being unwilling to raise a Question unnecessarily. The Reason why I did at last bring it forward is contained in my Letter, and therefore I shall say nothing about it. The Account sent in that Letter and marked number twenty six B, needs no Commentary altho it differs very widely from that marked thirty three. I shall only note that if the Sum of 686.109 *l.t.* be taken from that mentioned as advanced for Stores by Order of Coll. Laurens, so as to render that Article conformable to what is said in the Count de Vergennes Note, the same Sum must be added to the Ballance, by which Means placing the 1.500.000 *l.t.* to have been drawn for by me, in the Stead of that to have been sent out from Holland, the whole will stand as first above mentioned, leaving the Amount of the Loan untouched. In the Close of my Letter I mentiond a Determination to draw *on Account of the Ballance*, an Expression which appears to have been mistaken. The Reason of the Assertion will in some Degree appear from the Answer to it. I will add that altho I shall not risque the drawing of Bills while there is any Chance that they may return protested, I must nevertheless take Measures to obtain this Money for very evident Reasons, and it is with this View that I have drawn on you in Favor of Messrs. Le Couteulx & Co. for 1.000.000 Livres.—

The Paper numbered twenty seven contains a Copy of the Letter written on the twenty fourth Instant, in answer to that last mentioned. I shall not here notice the Difference between what we have said about the additional Million, as well because it is in Substance the same, as because I had not insisted on drawing for it. In like manner I shall say nothing about the Permission given me to extend my Drafts after the Orders to stop them brought by Coll. Laurens, but your Excellency will observe that the pointed Declaration that the Letter of the twenty sixth of September could not leave me the Shadow of a Hope &c (with what follows it) stands in such direct Opposition to the whole Tenor of my Letter, and to the real State of my Expectations, that to have submitted in Silence would have been tantamount to the acknowlegement of Falsehood. It is indeed easy to perceive that the Chevalier wrote this Letter to his Court, altho he directed it in the first Instance to me; and I concluded it to have been in Consequence of his last Dispatches which had not been received long before his Letter was written. The equivocal Use of the Expression *as soon as possible* will not escape you Sir, it shall meet no other remark from me than this, that I am convinced the Court will not apply it in the same Sense with the Chevalier. Neither the Dignity of the Prince, nor the Magnitude of the Occasion, will permit a Reliance on such Distinctions. The State of the Account made in this Letter I really do not see the Propriety of. It seems to have been in some Degree extracted from the Account furnished in September to the Committee of Congress, because if the Mistake of 6000 *l.t.* in the Castings of that Account be rectified, it will make the first Sum Total amount to 15.199.501 *l.t.*, from which deducting 10.000.000 (being the Amount of the Subsidy of 6.000.000 *l.t.* and Loan of 4) there will remain the first Article of that Account, namely 5.199.501 *l.t.* But if this be the Case, it is a little surprizing that the Chevalier should not have noticed a Deduction made in that very Account of the two first Articles, amounting to 3.416.000 *l.t.* which are it is there said, to be added to the Advances formerly made to the Congress. It is also somewhat extraordinary, that all these should be considered by the Chevalier as Advances made in the Month of September. For altho that Account was rendered in September, yet 4.694.392 *l.t.* are expressly mentioned as being to be furnished. I shall dwell no longer but I must repeat notwithstanding the 137 polite Manner in which the Assertion has been contradicted, that my Operations have received a very severe as well as a very material Check from Stopping my Drafts, not so much on Account of the Value of the 300.000 *l.t.*, as because while they were negotiating I should have undoubtedly received those Advices from you which would have enabled me to go on in the same Line. I had brought the Exchange up very nearly to Par, and should soon have Sold at 17 *d.* this Money for a Livre or 8/6 for a Crown which is worth here at the Extent but 8/4, this would therefore have been two per Cent advance with a Saving of Time Freight & Insurance, and altho a very large Sum could not have been negotiated during the Winter, perhaps not more than 1.500.000 *l.t.*, yet that would have enabled me to go on making the Preparations for an early and vigorous Campaign, and kept every Thing in Train till some Money could either have been shipt from Europe, or so Negotiated as to be sent hither from Havannah. I will take no Notice of what is said in the Letter now before us as to the Error of 6.000 *l.t.* because you must at once perceive how little it was an Object of Conversation, and how easy to be remedied by any Clerk without waiting either Orders or Instructions from the Court, and because you must also perceive the material Omission of 4.000.000 which cannot be overlooked let the Calculations be combined as they may. I have not however the less Concern about it, because so rigid an Adherence to so palpable an Error leads me to fear a Design which the generous Conduct of the King will not permit me to suspect. Having already given my Sentiments as to the Interest of Loan Office Certificates, I will not now repeat them. As to the replacing the Marquis de la fayette's Cargo, it is a Matter which I will not seriously contend about, because altho there will not be Use for all the Articles, there certainly will for many of them, and therefore I hardly think a Representation on that Score necessary, because there is no Use of multiplying disagreeable Considerations: but by the way I must observe that it is a little extraordinary this Cargo should have been replaced (out of the

Loan to have been opened &ca.) at your Request, while at the same Request Money could not be obtained to pay the Bills drawn by Order of Congress, as appears from your Letter and that from the Count de Vergennes which is enclosed in it. The Idea of making Advances for any individual State from the Funds of the United States, must never be admitted by any Servant of Congress. It will be quite Time enough to do that when they shall have Complied with the several Requisitions made upon them, and when they shall have entrusted these Subaltern Negotiations to the Ministers whom Congress have appointed. Such Advances stand on a very different Ground indeed from those made for purchasing a like Cargo to that of the la fayette, and it cannot be expected that they should be passed to the Account of Congress. Besides this the Successes to the Southward have rendered Succors of that Sort unnecessary. What has already been said will render Observations on the Letters of the twenty sixth Instant marked twenty eight and twenty nine unnecessary.

On the whole Matter I have to request your Excellency's Exertions to have this Matter settled as soon as possible, and that you will cause the whole of what remains to be paid over to Messrs. le Couteulx & Co., sending me Notice thereof by every Opportunity that I may attend to the Disposition of it. I mean nevertheless that a Reservation should be made of what is necessary to purchase the Articles mentioned in the enclosed Invoice of the Board of War. I wish you to have as little trouble as possible in this Business, and therefore I am to request you to employ the honorable Mr. Barclay our Consul General and Mr. Mathew Ridley in this Business. They are both Gentlemen of Knowlege and Integrity and I doubt not will perform it with Expedition and Oeconomy. Your Excellency will also be pleased to take Arrangements with the Minister of Marine; and give your consequent Orders to those Gentlemen, so that all Articles of every Sort and Kind which are the Property of the United States and now in Europe may come under safe Convoy to this Port. The marquis, who is charged with the General's Instructions on military Subjects, will assist in combining Matters so as to accomplish these Objects. I confide Sir that your Wisdom and his Vivacity will produce the most beneficial Consequences. Let me add, while I mention the Depositing all which remains due to us with Messrs. Le Couteulx & Co., that I wish you in Conformity to the Act of Congress enclosed whereof number thirty five is Copy to pay the Sum of 42.189 *l.t.* ... Livres therein mentioned with the Interest to Mr. William Lee. Let me also mention my Desire that you would retain 2.200.000 *l.t.* to pay Interest Bills drawn from the first of September to the first of April next, I will take such arrangements as will save you the Trouble of doing this Business in future, and I mention it here altho the Money will come more properly under the Head of Supplies to be asked from the Court for the ensuing Year.

The Declarations that no more pecuniary Aid will be afforded to us, is I know very clear and explicit, but I trust that these Declarations will not be adhered to. The Interest Bills as I have just now observed will amount to about 2.200.000 *l.t.*, You have to pay Mr. Beaumarchais 2.544.000 *l.t.*, and the Cloathing and Stores necessary will amount to 4.000.000; besides all this We must have Money, so that it will become necessary to obtain at least twelve Millions. When I mention this Sum I take the lowest, and I do it from my sincere Desire not to burthen the Finances of France with American Demands, but I think such clear Reasons can be assigned for it as must produce Conviction.

The Paper number thirty contains my Letter to the Chevalier, of the third Instant, upon this Subject. You will have observed that my circular Letter of the nineteenth of October which was enclosed in this of the third Instant, is so formed as to lower the Expectations of the several States, and accordingly the Account sent with it is framed from the erroneous one before mentioned, and the four Millions are totally omitted. The Languor of the

States had been so fostered by their teeming Expectations from France, that it became my Duty to prevent if possible the ill Effects of it. But on the other Hand a circular Letter could not but be public, and it necessarily contained such Matter as must stand in the Way of procuring a proper Settlement of past Accounts with the Court, or obtaining future Supplies from them. I therefore communicated that Letter to the Minister, and as he very naturally asked a Copy, I took the first Opportunity after the many necessary Copies could be made out, to send it with mine of the third Instant. This contains, as you will perceive, some short Reasons why we want, and why France should grant, pecuniary Assistance. The Answer to it of the fourth Instant is contained in Number thirty one, and my Reply of the sixth Number thirty two closes the Correspondence on that Subject. This last was meerly intended to take off from the Force of those Observations as to the King's Wisdom and Integrity, which had rather more of republican Simplicity than courtly Elegance. As my Letter of the third was not intended to convince the Minister, that being unnecessary as I am perswaded the Conviction was already produced, but to prevent any improper Conclusions from my circular Letter, so it was unnecessary to make any particular Reply to his Observations; because after all a paper Argument in Philadelphia can have but very little Influence at Versailles, and as the Chevalier observes very properly in one of his Letters, the Instructions from his Court must necessarily form the Basis of his Opinions. The proper and useful Mode therefore of convincing him, is by stimulating them. Knowing as I do the great Force and Compass of your Talents, I should not presume to add one Word of Remark on the Chevallier's Letter if I were not convinced that, as it is written for the Court, so it will be necessary to oppose it in some Degree by a Knowlege of Facts which may not lie within your immediate View. He takes it for granted that the People will make extraordinary Efforts in Consequence of their Successes, and I will readily admit that they have the Ability, and ought to have the Inclination; but they must differ much from former Experiences if they really do exert themselves. I will admit that their Rulers ought to urge them into Activity, but it must be remembered that those Rulers are themselves of the People, that their Ideas and Views are limited, and that they act like the People, rather from Feeling than from Reflection. I speak here of the several Legislatures, for I must repeat again and again that our general System has not yet grown into that Form and Vigor which can communicate the Impulses of a Sovereign Mind to the remotest Members of subjected Power. I will admit that a Monarch could on so brilliant a Success call into Action all which his Kingdom possessed of Strength and Resources, but America is not under Monarchial Government. I will admit further that if the Object of the War was Conquest instead of Security, every Victory would give new Animation to all the Members of our Republican Confederacy; but this War is not carried on for Conquest. While it rages in any Quarter it makes Food for itself. The Inroads of the Enemy create Opposition. An Application is then made immediately to the Feelings of the People, but when the Inroad ceases, when the Enemy retires, the Storm subsides, each Man returns to his domestic Pursuits and Employments, and thinks no more of the Scenes which had just passed before him. It is true that this is only changing the Field of Battle, but America is so extensive that a Shock given at one Extremity is lost, before it reaches the other. This true Picture of our Country, while it demonstrates the Impracticability of subjugating it, explains the Reasons why our Exertions have always disappointed both our Friends and our Enemies. If then, as the Fact is, the meer Change of Position at the Option of the Foe can so lull our People to rest, how much more are we to expect that it will follow from the Capture of a considerable Part of his Force.— To reason rightly on the late Events we must admit the Ability to make greater Exertions, and then seek the Means of calling them forth. This Sir can only be accomplished by pecuniary Aid. The Chevalier observes that the Kings Obligations to us have been exceeded. This is but a narrow Idea. If the King is engaged to support the War untill our Independence is established, his simple Object of Enquiry will be how that can be most speedily and cheaply accomplished. It is certain that America ought to do every Thing in her power, and you may assure the Court that Congress and the Servants of Congress are sensible of their Duty, and determined to comply with it. But it is in Vain to think of breaking the Bounds of Possibility, and equally vain to think of Changing the Nature of Man. Let me add that there is little Propriety in reproaching Americans with Faults inseperable from Humanity. Besides this, the Exertions of our Country have really been very great, and as soon as more Consistency shall have been put in the Administration, they will again be great; but this is the Period of weakness between the convulsive Labors of Enthusiasm, and the sound and regular Operations of Order and Government. There is in the End of the Chevalier's Letter a Hint with Relation to our Commerce, which altho it does not immediately apply to the present Purpose, must not pass unnoticed. That an indirect Commerce has taken Place with England is true, and that France has in a great Measure been the Cause of it is equally true. Men will naturally buy where they can obtain Things most cheaply. The prime Cost of Goods, tho a great Object in Time of Peace, is not equally so in Time of War. The Freight, the Insurance are then so high, that a small Difference of Danger or Convenience will counterballance a great Difference of Price. When France by subscribing to the principles of the armed Neutrallity gave her Enemy the Means of bringing her Manufactures in Safety to our Neighbourhood,4 she tempted our Merchants to buy those Manufactures. She added the motives of Interest to the Force of Habit, and ought not therefore to be surprized that such cogent Principles have had Effect. One Mode remained, that of convoying the Trade between France and America, and that Mode has been neglected. I am happy however to observe that this

British Commerce is dwindling very fast. The War with Holland has given it one deadly Blow, and if our Privateers are once more freed from the Shackles too hastily imposed upon them, I cannot doubt but that the Trade of this Country will flow directly to France, as indeed it ought to do.

And now Sir before I close this Letter, let me make one farther Observation with Respect to the future Supplies from his Majesty. To solicit them is considered as asking for Assistance in a War whose Object is of the last Importance to us. This is the Point of View in which I have placed it, and in which I am desirous that it should stand; but there is another Method of looking at it. And altho Delicacy will forbid us so to present it, yet you may depend that there are many who have taught themselves to reason about it in a different Way from what you or I would wish. Whether Britain will acknowlege our Independence, is a Question which is to be answered only with some Modifications. If in Consequence of such an Acknowlegement we would forego our Connection with France, there is no manner of Doubt but she would make it immediately. This would on our Part be wrong, and therefore it ought not to be done; but Sir when this great Object shall be presented on the one Side, and the Weight of new and great Taxes be felt on the other, with all their ancient Prejudices and Predilections in aid, will there not be some Men who for the Shades of Ease will quit the Paths of Virtue?—

With the most Sincere Wishes for your Health and Prosperity and that you may speedily enjoy the exalted Pleasure of seeing your Country possessed of Peace Liberty & Safety with the grateful Reflections that your Exertions have principally contributed to it let me assure you of that Esteem & Respect with which I am your Excellency's most obedient & humble Servant

Robt Morris

To Benjamin Franklin, 3 December 1781

Office of Finance 3d Decr. 1781

Sir

I was yesterday morning favoured with yours of the twelfth of September, inclosing third copies of your two Letters of the twenty sixth of July, also a copy of Count de Vergennes Letter to you of the twenty third of August. I find by these Letters that the Idea I had entertained as to the advances made by the Court, was not so favourable as the truth, & that the ten Million Livres (or five Million Florins) to be borrowed in Holland will be over and above those advances. How much pleasure I recieve from that circumstance you will easily concieve. It is an additional pleasure that the Labor of adjusting the matters mentioned in mine of the twenty seventh of November, will be saved to you.

I am much surprized to find so large purchases made on account of the United States in Holland. If every thing else were equal, the generous conduct of France towards us is such that I cannot but think every possible preference ought to be given to the Manufacturers of that Nation. But there is in my opinion very essential preferences of a different kind. The Position of Amsterdam is unfavorable, in a war with England, to a Commerce with this Country. France also can (and I suppose will) give Convoy to the Articles procured there. But I will dwell no longer on this subject, for I trust that nothing of the kind will happen hereafter.

Should the Loan be obtained, you will be so kind Sir as to deposit one Million Florins with Mr. Grand, to whom I will pray you to deliver the inclosed Letter. I shall in consequence not draw upon you for a Million Livres in favour of Messrs. Le Couteulx & Co., as I intended, and in like manner I beg leave to revoke what I have said on the subject of paying all Ballances into their hands in my

145

Letter of the twenty seventh last; one Million of Florins you will also be pleased to deposit with the house of Grand at Amsterdam, sending me the precise address of both so that I can direct my Bills properly to them. Nearly one Million will be necessary to pay for the Invoice sent in my letter of the twenty seventh last; the remaining two Millions I wish may be Shipped from France in Gold in proper vessels of War, which I dare say will readily be provided by Monsr: de Castres.

I percieve you have not written to Congress on the subjects mentioned in the Count de Vergennes Letter, of the twenty third of August, which I am glad of. The more an opinion prevails here that we must succor ourselves, the more we shall do it; and therefore I shall not communicate what you have said for the present, but as the best acknowlegment I shall endeavour to further the operations against our Common Enemy, and draw forth all our resources for an early and vigorous Campaign. The splendid and important success which has crowned the combined Arms in Virginia, is I hope only an earnest of what is to be done next year. These are the returns which we will make to the King for the aid he so generously affords, and I have a very particular satisfaction in assuring you, that throughout this Country a strong attachment to the French Nation is daily taking place of that Blind partiallity once felt for every thing that had the name of English. Let me add for your use, a piece of Mercantile information lately communicated to me from unquestionable authority. The demand for french goods to this Country has raised the price there from twenty to thirty per Cent, the importations have reduced the prices here near twenty per Cent, and the Exchange you already know has been raised considerably.

I shall say nothing to you in this Letter on the subject of future Supplies, further than what is contained in mine of the twenty seventh last, because I feel a Conviction that you will obtain such as may be necessary. I will only repeat what I have often said, let them be early.— I enclose a Letter to Mr. Fleury which you shall either deliver or not as may best answer your purposes.

I hope often to have the pleasure of hearing from you, and I pray you to believe me with very great truth Dr. Sir Your Excellency's most obedient & humble Servant

Robt Morris

P.S. You have enclosed the Copy of An Act of Congress passed in Consequence of one of your letters on the Subject it relates to.

To Benjamin Franklin, 4 December 1781

Office of Finance 4th. Decemr. 1781

Sir

I observe that in your Letter of the twelfth of September you say you beleive those Bills of Mr. Ross's must go back protested. This I am convinced proceeds from a Mistake with respect to that Transaction. It is true that the Resolution for delivering those Bills to Mr. Ross was passed in June, but the Bills had been drawn long previous to that Date, and were part of those which I presume [*you*] to have been regularly advised of. At any Rate they are included in the State I have made and enclosed in my Letter of the twenty seventh of last Month, and therefore as you will I think see your Way clearly thro all which are contained in that State, I will hope that those of Mr. Ross's will be paid. You will perceive by my Letter to Mr. Grand that I am making him another Payment as also to Mr. Bingham. Both of them are greatly in Advance for the United States and Justice requires that their Situation be alleviated. The Sum directed to be paid on Account of Mr. Holker is in Part of Cloathing purchased here for our Troops Thanks to the bad Management in Holland.

With Sincere Esteem & Respect I am Sir your most obedient & humble Servant

Robt Morris

To Benjamin Franklin, 5 December 1781

Office of Finance 5th. Decem. 1781—

Sir,

The Bearer of this Letter the Baron de Frey will shew you a Certificate for five hundred Dollars signed by Joseph Nourse Esqr. Register of the Treasury of the United States and issued by Virtue of a Warrant of this Day from me. This Money is on Interest at six per Cent from the fifth of December and is the Balance still due after a partial Payment. Should it be perfectly convenient to you it will be [a] great Favor to him and agreable to me that this five hundred Dollars be paid to Baron de Frey taking his receipt in full of all Demands against the United States on the Back of the Certificate with three Copies signed by him and sending them by different Opportunities. I mention five hundred Dollars without noticing the Interest, because in Case of Payment by you the Transaction will be substantially as if I had given him here a Bill of Exchange. With all possible respect I have the Honor to be Sir your most obedient and humble Servant

R M

To Benjamin Franklin, 2 January 1782

Office of Finance 2. January 1782

Sir,

The Bearer of this Letter Capt. Archibald McCallister has been an Officer of Merit in the Army of the United States; And I am sorry to add that unlucky Circumstances has made him a Sufferer in the service of his Country. The loss of his Health obliges him to make a Voyage to France and upon the Settlement of his Accounts a balance of four hundred spanish silver Dollars and seventy four ninetieths of a Dollar has been found due to him. The State of the Treasury did not permit the payment of this balance, therefore it is put on Interest at six per Cent from the twenty sixth Day of December last. Now Sir as this Gentleman is going to France he is apprehensive of wanting Money there and I give him this Letter as the Ground on which he may make an Application to you for the whole or Part, at the same Time I assure him that it is uncertain whether you will be able to releive him. If the Monies at your Command will enable you to do it consistently I wish it may be done and in that Case you will be pleased to transmit me Copies of his Certificate and the receipts you take thereon for the Payments you make to him in Order that I may have them duly entered in the Treasury Books.

I have the Honor to be Sir your most obedient & humble Servant

RM

To Benjamin Franklin, 7 January 1782

Office of Finance 7th. January 1782

Dear Sir,

This Letter is to go by the French Frigate Hermione. Mr. le Comte de la Touche Captain of that Frigate is now here and will go in a Day or two to the Head of Elk where his Ship lies and sail thence for France stopping in his Way down the Chesapeak to receive the Dispatches of the Comte de Rochambeau.

This fair Opportunity induces me to send Duplicates of my several Letters of the twenty seventh November third December and fourth December last as well as to add in this to what is contained in them. I have not since they were written received a single Line from you nor indeed have we heard any thing here from the Court so that we remain in Uncertainty as to our pecuniary Dependence. And this is the more distressing as the Time rapidly approaches when I must draw Bills either with or without advise from you and therefore I must pray you to prepare for them if I should be compelled to do it with this Assurance nevertheless that as my Drafts will be delayed to the last Moment so they will be as moderate as I can contrive to make them.

I enclose to you Copies of my Letters of the third Instant to the different States on the Impost Law which as you will perceive has not been agreed to by Massachusetts Rhode Island and Maryland. The States of South Carolina and Georgia were not called upon but I have transmitted the requisition to them now that they are in a Situation to pass Laws by the meeting of their Legislatures which has by this Time taken Place.

I also enclose you a Plan for adjusting the public Accounts which I have laid before Congress in Consequence of their Order upon that Subject. It has not yet been adopted because there are now present so few members that it is with Difficulty they can get thro their Business, the Confederation requiring seven States to agree on most Questions. Whether this Plan will be adopted I really do not know but I incline to think that in Substance it will. I send it for your Information and you will observe that it proceeds upon Principles already laid before Congress altho from Circumstances I have found it useful in some Degree to vary the Form. Among those Circumstances you will Count as one the superior Cheapness both as to Time and Money which attends the Transaction of Business by one Man in Preference of three. As also the greater Simplicity in bringing all the Expence until the first of this Month into one general Account. Let me observe to you Sir that the very many different ways of doing Business which have been adopted subject us to great Difficulties and the Republic must of Necessity be put to considerable and unnecessary Expence to do Justice and to satisfy Demands which if not well founded are at least too specious to neglect the Clamors which arise from leaving them unsettled. But I will not enter into a Detail of Circumstances which as inseperable Attendants of a great Revolution you must be well apprized of.

In Consequence of the Power vested in me by the Act of Congress of the second of November and in Order to facilitate the Payment of Taxes in the States of North and South Carolina and Georgia which States by the Operations of the War have been greatly deprived of the Means, I devised a Plan which will need no other Explanation than what is contained in the enclosed Copies of my Letters on the Subject to the Governors of those States and to General Greene commanding the Army in that Quarter. Whether this Plan will take Effect I know not, nor whether if it does take Effect it will produce the beneficial Consequences I wish for; but I am not without Hopes and Time alone can discover whether they are well founded. This at least is certain that those States cannot pay in Coin as they have not Coin to pay. I send it [so] you may see we neglect no Opportunity of calling forth the Resources of this Country: and that when we ask Help it is not because we are unwilling to help ourselves.

After my Dispatches by the Alliance had been sent away & when it was too late to write to you by her the Minister of France informed me that in Consequence of my Letter to him he had written to his Court praying that the Cargo of the Ship Marquis de la fayette might not be replaced. Your Excellency will perceive by my Letters to you that I had taken my Arrangements in Subordination to those which I presumed to have been taken by the Court and therefore having expected from the Chevalier de la Luzernes Letters that the Fayette's Cargo would be replaced I have built upon that and shall expect that it will be done. I must pray you therefore to explain the Matter to his Majesty's Ministers in this clear Way.

That I would rather the Money had been deposited with Mr. Grand subject to my Order than invested by the Court in the Purchase of Arms Cloathing and Ammunition for the United States because I could then have taken Measures for the Disposition of that Money more advantageous to their Interest but as I found the Court were already engaged in replacing it I have formed all my other Plans upon the Supposition that it will be done and of Consequence shall expect it. It is for that Reason that I do not send you a List of the precise Articles we shall want and which would necessarily exclude many of those which were intended by the Fayette because I do not think it proper by any Means to countervail the Operations of the Court and thro them into Embarrassments as to past Transactions. In future our Requests will be simplified and the Instructions which may be given so clear as to prevent Misunderstanding.

And now Sir let me congratulate you on the Establishment of the Bank of the United States or according to the Stile of it the national Bank of America which opens and does Business this Day. I expect to derive great Advantage from it, and that the Commerce of this Country will lie under great Obligations to an Institution long wanted among us. Several of the shares are yet in the Hands of the Public so that if you chuse to become interested or any of your Friends it can be done without Difficulty.

I pray to hear from you as often and as particularly as your Convenience will admit and intreat you to believe that I am with the greatest Veneration and Respect Dear Sir your Excellency's most obedient Servant

R M

To the President of Congress, 15 January 1782

Office of Finance 15 January 1782

Sir

Finding by the Act of the United States in Congress of the seventh Instant that I am Instructed to prepare and report a Table of Rates at which the different Species of foreign Coins most likely to circulate within the United States shall be received at the Treasury I have been induced again to turn my Attention to an Object which has employed my Thoughts very frequently and which would have been long since submitted to Congress had I not been prevented by other Business and much delayed by those Things relating to this Business which depended upon others. I shall now pray Leave to deliver my Sentiments somewhat at large on this Subject.

The United States labor under many Inconveniences and even Disadvantages which may at present be remedied but which if suffered to continue would become incurable and lead to pernicious Consequences. It is very fortunate for us that the Weights and Measures used throughout America are the same. Experience has shewn in other Countries that the Efforts of the

Legislator to Change Weights and Measures altho fully seconded by the more enlightened Part of the Community have been so strongly opposed by the popular Habits and Prejudices that Ages have elapsed without producing the desired Effect. I repeat therefore that it is happy for us to have throughout the Union the same Ideas of a Mile and an Inch a Hogshead and a Quart, a Pound an Ounce. So far our commercial Dealings are simplified and brought down to the level of every Capacity. With respect to our Money the Case is very widely different. The Ideas annexed to a Pound a Shilling and a Penny are almost as various as the States themselves. Calculations are therefore as necessary for our inland Commerce as upon foreign Exchanges and the commonest Things become intricate where Money has any thing to do with them. A Farmer in New hampshire for Instance can readily form an Idea of a Bushell of Wheat in South Carolina weighing sixty Pounds and placed at one hundred Miles from Charlestown but if he were told that in such Situation it is worth twenty one Shillings and eight Pence, he would be obliged to make many Enquiries and form some Calculations before he could know that this Sum meant in general what he would call four Shillings. And even then he would have to enquire what Kind of Coin that four Shillings was paid in before he could estimate it in his own Mind according to the Ideas of Money which he had imbibed. Difficulties of this Sort do not occur to Farmers alone, they are perplexing to most Men and troublesome to all. It is however a fortunate Circumstance that Money is so much in the Power of the Sovereign as that he can easily lead the People into new Ideas of it and even if that were not the Case yet the loose State in which our Currency has been for some Years past has opened the Way for receiving any Impressions on that Subject. As we are now shaking off the Inconveniencies of a depreciating Medium the present Moment seems to be that in which a general Currency can best be established so as that in a few Months the same Names of Money

154

will mean the same Things in the several Parts of the United States.

Another Inconvenience which admits of the same easy Remedy and which would indeed be cured by the very same Act is the Want of a legal Tender. This is as necessary for the Purposes of Jurisprudence as a general Currency is for those of Commerce. For altho there is great Impropriety not to say Injustice in compelling a Man to receive a Part of his Debt in discharge of the whole yet it is both Just and proper that the Law should protect the honest Debtor who is willing to pay against the vexatious Suits of an Oppressive Creditor who refuses to receive the full Value.

The Nature Value and Use of Money have always occasioned strong Temptations to the Commission of Fraud and of Consequence the Practice of counterfeiting is coeval with that of Coining. No Government can Guard its Subjects entirely against the wicked Ingenuity which has been exercised in this respect. But it has always been the Object of every wise Government to take all the Precautions against it which are within the Compass of human Ability. These Precautions will be most effectual where the Coins are few and simple because they by that Means become familiar to all Ranks and Degrees of Men but where the Coins are so numerous that the Knowlege of them is a kind of Science the lower Order of Citizens are constantly injured by those who carry on the Business of debasing sweating clipping counterfeiting and the like. It is therefore to be lamented that we have so many different Coins in the United States.

It is not necessary to mention what is in every Body's Mouth that the precious Metals were first used as Bullion and that the Inconvenience of weighing and the Difficulty of Assaying introduced the Practice of Coining in Order that the weight and fineness might be known at the first View and of Consequence the Value be instantly ascertained. It is equally unnecessary to observe that the great Privilege of declaring this Value by particular Marks has among all Nations been vested exclusively in the Sovereign. A Trust so important could not indeed be vested any where else because the Danger of abusing it was too great. And History informs us that Sovereigns themselves have not on this Occasion behaved with that Integrity which was alike due to their Subjects and to themselves to the Interests of their People and to their own personal Glory. Experience has already told us that the advantage of Gold as a Coin is in this Country very considerably diminished for every distinct Piece must be weighed before it can be safely received. Both Gold and Silver Coins are indeed preferable, in one respect to common Bullion that the Standard is presumed to be just and consequently they are received without the Delays and Expences of assaying. It must however be remembered that they are all foreign Coins and of Course we are not only exposed to the Tricks of Individuals but should it suit the Interest or Convenience of any Sovereign to make base Money for us there is Nothing to prevent it. If for Instance the King of England or any of his Birmingham Artists should coin Guineas worth but sixteen shillings Sterling our Citizens would readily and freely receive them at twenty one Shillings Sterling. It is my Duty to mention to Congress Information I have received that Guineas of base Metal are coined at Birmingham so well as to escape any common Attention. Now there can be no Doubt but that every such Guinea received here would be a national Loss to us of an English Crown. How much we suffer in this Way at present it is impossible to estimate.

What I have already had the Honor to observe contains some of the reasons why it appears to me highly necessary that an American Coin should be adopted without Delay and to these Reasons it may be added that there is a want of small Money for the common Occasions of Trade and that it is more felt by our Soldiery than any other Persons. For the little Pay which they do receive being either in Gold or at best in Dollars the Sutlers and others with whom they have Dealings continually take the Advantage of their want of Change and rate the Prices of their Goods accordingly.

Shortly after my Appointment finding that there was a considerable Quantity of public Copper at Boston I ordered it round to this Place. It has safely arrived and will when coined amount to a considerable Sum. The necessary Machinery of a Mint can be easily made and there are Persons who can perform the whole Business. I must pray leave therefore to submit to Congress some few more particular remarks on this Subject as introductory to a Plan for an American Coin.

Altho most Nations have coined Copper yet that Metal is so impure that it has never been considered as constituting the Money Standard. This is affixed to the two precious Metals because they alone will admit of having their intrinsic Value precisely ascertained. But Nations differ very much in the relation they have established between Gold and Silver. In some European Countries an Ounce of pure Gold passes for fifteen Ounces of pure Silver. In others for fourteen. In China it passes for much less. The Standard therefore which is affixed to both Metals is in Reality affixed to neither. In England Gold is to Silver nearly in the Proportion of one to fifteen and in France nearly of one to fourteen. If a Man carries fourteen ounces of Gold from France to England he receives two hundred and ten Ounces of Silver which in France purchase fifteen ounces of Gold so that he gains on that Exchange one ounce of Gold. In like Manner he who carries from England fourteen Ounces of Silver to France receives one Ounce of Gold which in England purchases fifteen Ounces of Silver wherefore he gains on that Exchange one Ounce of Silver. If it be then supposed that the Coins of these two Countries were alike pure it must follow that in a short Time all the gold Coin of full Weight would be in England and all the silver Coin of full weight in France. But the light Silver circulating in England and the light Gold in France the real Standard of Coin in each would be different from the legal and seek a Medium of fourteen and an half of Silver for one of Gold altho the legal Standard might still be in the one Place fifteen and in the other fourteen.

The Demand which Commerce might make for any one of the precious Metals in Preference of the other would vary this real Standard from Time to Time and in every Payment a Man would get more or less of real Value for his Debt according as he were paid in the Coin of greater or lesser Value in relation to the real Standard. If for Instance the Debt were contracted when the Silver was to Gold as one to fifteen and paid when as one to fourteen; if the Debt were paid in Silver he would gain one thirtieth and if in Gold he would loose one thirtieth. In England the Money Standard is rather affixed to Gold than to Silver because all Payments are made in the former and in France it is rather affixed to Silver than to Gold.

Arguments are unnecessary to shew that the Scale by which every thing is to be measured ought to be as fixed as the Nature of Things will permit of. Since therefore a Money Standard affixed to both the precious Metals will not give this certain Scale it is better to make use of one only. Gold is more valuable than Silver and so far must have the Preference but it is from that very Circumstance the more exposed to fraudulent Practices. Its Value rendering it more portable is an Advantage. But it is an Advantage which Paper possesses in a much greater Degree and of Consequence the commercial Nation of England has had recourse to Paper for the Purposes of it's Trade altho the Mass of circulating Coin is Gold. It will always be in our Power to carry a Paper Circulation to every proper Extent. There can be no doubt therefore that our Money Standard ought to be affixed to Silver.

But Silver is liable like every Thing else to a Change of Value, if there is a Demand for it, to export, the Value will rise, if the Contrary it will fall, and so far it cannot be considered as a fixed Measure of Value. Before this Objection be considered it will be proper to make a few reflextions on another Part of the present Subject but in this Place I remark that if the Objection cannot be removed we must not suffer it to preponderate because it weighs alike against every other Metal.

To Coin Money is a certain Expence and of Course it is an Expence which must be borne by the People. In England the Coin when melted will sell as Bullion for just as much as its Weight in other Coin. The Expence of Coinage is paid by the Crown and of Course it is raised by Taxes from the People. In France the Coinage instead of being expensive yields a Profit. The Price given for Metal at the Mint is about eight Pr. Cent less than the same Quantity will yield when coined at the french Standard. Both of these Methods are liable to Objections. When Commerce demands an Exportation of Bullion from England the Coin of the Kingdom goes out in common with others; this increases of Course the National Expence of Coinage. Laws to prevent the Exportation or Importation of any Thing so valuable as Money are always Nugatory because they always *can* be eluded and therefore when private Interest requires they always *will* be eluded. That the Guineas of England therefore are not continually going away is to be attributed to the extraordinary Value affixed to Gold which has been just mentioned and which banishes silver continually. In France the People are not liable to this Inconvenience because their Money passing for more than its Value in Bullion, Bullion will always be exported in Preference of Coin. But for the same Reason there is always a strong Temptation to imitate their Coin and send it for the Purchase of their Commodities. It would be both impossible and unnecessary to distinguish the True from the false because both would be of equal intrinsic Value. The Place at which they were struck would be indifferent to the Receiver, of Consequence the foreigner who made french Coin would gain by his Trade and the french Nation would loose proportionately.

The Money paid for Coining or the Coinage of France has however this Advantage that the Money is a Standard which does not fluctuate with the Price of Bullion. This Coinage is as has been said about eight Pr. Cent. When Bullion is below ninety two it is carried to the Mint when above ninety two to the Broker or Silver Smith. The Coin still continues fixed nor will it bear Exportation until Bullion rises to an hundred when the french Coin would be as liable to Exportation as the English. In that Case it would be exported on one Hand, while on the other no more would have been coined for a considerable Period because to make the eight Pr. Cent Coinage it is necessary that the Mint Price should be ninety two. The Coin therefore could not long be exported if at all but would soon resume it's Value. The Price of Bullion must float between ninety two and an hundred while the Coin would preserve its fixed Quality as Money.

Hence then it appears proper that the Price of Coining should be defrayed by the Coinage because first it is natural and proper that the Price should be paid when the Benefit is received and that the Citizen in Return for the Advantage of being ascertained in the Value of the Medium of Commerce by the Sovereign should pay for ascertaining it just as that he should pay for the fashion of the Plate he uses or the Construction of the Cart he employs. Secondly it is right that Money should acquire a Value, as Money distinct from that which it Possesses as a Commodity in Order that it should be a fixed Rule whereby to Measure the Value of all other Things and thirdly it is wise to prevent the Exportation of the Coin which would involve an unnecessary national Expence and also to prevent the Imitation of it abroad so as to create a national Loss: For both which Purposes it is proper that the Coinage should only defray the Expence without making any considerable Profit. The

Laws usual in all Countries with respect to the Money will then fully operate the Effect intended.

In Order that a Coin may be perfectly intelligible to the whole People it must have some Affinity to the former Currency. This therefore will be requisite in the present Case. The Purposes of Commerce require that the lowest divisible Point of Money or what is more properly called the Money Unit should be very small because by that Means Price can be brought in the smallest Things to bear a Proportion to the Value. And altho it is not absolutely necessary yet it is very desirable that Money should be increased in a decimal Ratio because by that Means all Calculations of Interest Exchange Insurance and the like are rendered much more simple and accurate and of Course more within the Power of the great Mass of People. Wherever such Things require much Labor Time and Reflection the greater Number who do not know are made the Dupes of the lesser Number who do.

The various Coins which have circulated in America have undergone different Changes in their Value so that there is hardly any which can be considered as a general Standard unless it be spanish Dollars. These pass in Georgia at five Shillings in North Carolina and New York at eight Shillings in Virginia and the four Eastern states at six Shillings in all the other States except South Carolina at seven Shillings and six Pence and in South Carolina at thirty two Shillings and six Pence: The Money Unit of a new Coin to agree without a Fraction with all these different Values of a Dollar except the last will be the fourteen hundred and fortieth Part of a Dollar equal to the sixteen hundreth Part of a Crown. Of these Units twenty four will be a Penny of Georgia, fifteen will be a Penny of North Carolina, or New York, twenty will be a Penny of Virginia and the four Eastern States sixteen will be a Penny of all the other States except South Carolina and forty eight will be thirteen Pence of South Carolina.

It has been already observed that to have the Money Unit very small is advantageous to Commerce but there is no Necessity that this Money Unit be exactly represented in Coin it is sufficient that its Value be precisely known. On the present Occasion two Copper Coins will be proper the one of eight Units and the other of five. These may be called an eight and a five two of the former will make a Penny Proclamation or Pennsylvania Money and three a Penny Georgia Money, of the latter three will make a Penny York Money and four a Penny lawful or Virginia Money. The Money Unit will be equal to a quarter of a Grain of fine Silver in coined Money. Proceeding thence in a decimal Ratio one hundred would be the lowest Silver Coin and might be called a Cent. It would contain twenty five Grains of fine Silver to which may be added two Grains of Copper and the whole would weigh one Penny Weight three Grains. Five of these would make a Quint or five hundred Units weighing five Penny Weight fifteen Grains and ten would make a Mark or one thousand Units weighing Seven Penny weight six Grains.

If the Mint Price of fine Silver be established at 22,237. Units per Pound. This being coined would be four Times 5,760 Grains or 23,040 Units. The difference is 803. Units and therefore the Coinage is 803 on 23,040 or somewhat more than 3 48/100 P. Cent, which would be about the Expence attending it. A Dollar contains by the best Assays which I have been able to get about 373 Grains of fine Silver and that at the Mint Price would be 1,440 Units. In like Manner if Crowns contain from 414. to 415 Grains of fine Silver they would at the Mint Price be worth 1600 Units.

When such a Coin shall have been established the Value of all others would be easily ascertained because Nothing more would be necessary than to have them assayed at the Mint. The Advantage of Possessing legal Money in Preference of any other would induce People to carry foreign Coin to the Mint until a sufficiency were struck for the circulating Medium. The remainder of the foreign Silver together with the Gold should be left entirely to the Operations of Commerce as Bullion. In the present Moment it is by no Means of such Consequence to establish the relative Value of different Coins as to provide a Standard of our own by which in future to estimate them. If the Value were now sought they must all be estimated in Dollars because Dollars are called for in the several requisitions of Congress. Without noticing the Preference thus given to one foreign Coin over another it is sufficient to observe that if a greater Alloy should be introduced by the Spanish Government into their Dollars our interior regulations as to Money would be overturned and certainly we have no Security that this will not happen. There is not any great Inconvenience from leaving Matters on their present footing until they can be remedied by the Operations of a Mint for it is not to be supposed that all the Money raised by Taxes in a State is to be brought out of it. I expect that there will be very little Occasion to transport money from Place to Place. It is much easier to negotiate than to carry it and if any Species of Money is generally received within a State at the same Rate in which it is paid in Taxes there will be no Difficulty in expending it at its Value. Whenever Money shall be struck by Authority of the United States then indeed it will be proper to receive in Taxes no other Coin.

If Congress are of Opinion with me that it will be proper to Coin Money I will immediately obey their Orders and establish a Mint. And I think I can say with Safety that no better Moment could be chosen for the Purpose than the present. Neither will any thing have a greater tendency to restore public Credit for altho it is possible that the new Money will at first be received with Diffidence by some Yet when it has been fairly assayed it will gain full Confidence from all; and the Advantage of holding the only Money which can Pay Debts or Discharge Taxes will soon give it the Preference over all and indeed banish all other from

Circulation. Whereas fixing a Relation of Value now on whatever Principles attempted might give Offence to the Power whose Coin should in any Instance be reduced from its present numerary Value among us.

These Sentiments are submitted with all possible Deference to the United States in Congress Assembled in Expectation of their further Instructions on the Subject.

With great respect, I have the honor to be, Sir, Your most obedient, And humble servant,

Robt. Morris

To Benjamin Franklin, 22 January 1782

Office of Finance 22d. January 1782

Sir

I send enclosed herewith the Copy of a Certificate the original whereof was transmitted to me by Monsr. de la Tombe Consul General of France from Boston after the unloading of the Transports which arrived at that Post with the Stores shipped on them by Order of Colo. Laurens. The original I shall keep and not knowing with whom the Accounts of Freight is to be settled nor by whom to be paid, I only take this precaution of sending Copies to you, in Order that you may know the Times of discharge should the Business pass through your Hands or any other Person by your Appointment.

I have the Honor to remain your Excellency's most obedient and humble Servant

RM

To George Washington, 23 January 1782

Office of Finance 23d Jany 1782

Sir

Captain Hutchins in a Letter of the twenty Second Instant, inclosed to me a copy of his letter to your Excellency of the fourteenth, and of your answer of the Sixteenth. I have had a conference on the Subject of these letters with the Minister of War, and afterwards with Captain Hutchins. General Lincoln tells me that a Map of South Carolina has already been taken at great expence and with great accuracy, which will Serve General Greene for all the Purposes he may want, and that as he concieves the Geographer cannot be Sufficiently covered and Protected in Georgia, there will be little or no use for his presence to the Southward. These however are matters which I do not pretend to judge of.

It will require a considerable Sum of money to fit out Captain Hutchins and while he remains in Philadelphia his Salary is going on without producing any advantage to the Public from his Labors. He tells me that if he is permitted to engage as one of the Commissioners for running the Pennsilvania line he will forego his Salary, while employed in that business. At the same time General Lincoln is of opinion that he may be usefully employed in chusing ground for a Post in the vicinage of Fort Pitt which while he is employed by Pennsilvania can be effected with little or no additional expence.

Should your Excellency on the whole be of opinion that it is better to permit Captain Hutchins to accept the offer made him by this State I will thank you to be informed of it, that if it is not in your power to grant such permission an application may be made on the subject to Congress. With great Respect I have the honor to be Sir Your Excellency's most obedient & humble Servant

Robt Morris

To George Washington, 26 January 1782

Office of Finance 26th January 1782

Sir,

As Provision is now made for Cloathing and feeding the Soldiery and for the Subsistence Money of the Officers, it is proper that some method be adopted to provide the latter with Cloathing also. This must be done out of their Pay, and therefore, the regular mode would be by an advance of Pay, but unfortunately the State of the Treasury will not admit of such advance, and even if it would, they could not at Camp procure the Articles which they may stand in need of. To remedy as much as possible these Inconveniencies I propose, that a Number of Promissory Notes be struck off in the following Form.

I, John Pierce Pay Master Genl promise to pay to [   ] or Bearer, on the first Day of [   ] next the sum of [   ] at my Office in Philadelphia, from Funds to be furnished me by the Superintendant of the Finances of the United States, for that Purpose. I propose that the latter Blank be filled up by the Pay Master Genl with sums equal to two Months Pay of the several Officers, who may be with the different Corps, or at the several Posts, and signed by him. And I propose, that the former Blank be filled up by the Deputy Pay Master with the Name, Rank, Regiment &c. of the Officer, and then that he countersign it. I will take care that the Pay Master be provided with Funds for Payment of these Notes punctually; and to minister more fully to their Convenience, I have agreed with a Gentlemn to supply Goods to the Officers, such as they may want, and to take the Notes in Payment. I have the Pleasure to add, that I expect these Goods will be supplied at Camp, as Cheap as they can be bought for Cash in this City.

Should your Excellency approve of this Plan I will immediately cause it to be carried into Execution. I have the Honor to be Sir Your Excellency's Most Obedient & humble Servant

Robt Morris

To George Washington, 26 January 1782

Office of Finance January the 26th 1782

Sir,

I take this earliest Opportunity of acknowleging your Excellency's Letter of the twenty fifth, which I received last Evening, and in which you request me to have ready my Letters to the Officers you are sending to the Eastern States, so as that they may go by the next Post. I would willingly comply with your Excellency's Desire most literally, but I have rather wished to transmit my Sentiments to you, that you may send them to the Gentlemen, either in the whole or in Part, as you shall think it proper, and with such Observations as may occur to you.

Recruiting the Army is certainly of Importance and ought therefore to be urged upon the several States, but should it be necessary to expend Money for that Purpose, it must not be considered as a Part of the Quota called for by Congress for the Service of the current Year. I shall make an Application on this Subject to Congress and endeavor to have certain Principles established by which, those States who exert themselves to bring their Quota of Troops early into the Field may have full Justice done them, and those States which are negligent be charged in Proportion to that Negligence. I mention these Things Sir, to obviate Mistakes which might be productive of very evil

167

Consequences. You, who being on the Spot and knowing my Situation and arrangements are better informed than any Person, how necessary it is that the money called for from the several States be punctually paid, without any Deduction whatever. You are I am sure convinced, that if my measures are obstructed your own Designs must prove abortive. And therefore you will I am persuaded take Care to prevent an Application of those Funds to the recruiting Service, which are necessary to the Support and operation of those who are already enlisted. But as it may obviate those Doubts which are too apt to start in the minds of such Gentlemen as compose the respective Legislatures, I repeat to your Excellency my Assurance, that I will exert myself to have full Justice done to the States, who may bring their proportion of men into the Field at an early Period.

Should you send Officers who are now with the Army I expect, that they will be able to give full Information from what they have seen of the Benefits, which result from the present mode of administration. And I am sure, that you are fully convinced of the superior Cheapness with which Supplies are obtained from what they were formerly. In Order then, that the Army may be well and cheaply maintained it is necessary that the States grant money.

In considering the Situation of the Army and comparing the Wants with the means of satisfying them, it became necessary for me to arrange those Wants, so that the relief in my Power might be properly extended. Feeding the Army appeared to be an Object of the first necessity; Cloathing them was almost if not altogether as indispensible. After feeding and Cloathing them the Equipment for Service demands Attention, under which Head must be classed the Arms, Ammunition, Military Stores, Tents, Camp Equipage, and in short the whole of the Quarter Masters Department. To the Equipment for Service succeeds the Attention which is to be paid to the Sick and wounded, an Object in which Justice and Humanity combine most forcilbly together. The Pay of the Army must of necessity be placed last in this List: But tho' last, it is by no means last in my mode of contemplating it. Your Excellency knows so well my Solicitude on this Subject, that it is unnecessary to mention it here. But I should ill deserve, the [high] Trust reposed in me if I permitted any Consideration to divert me from that Line which Reason points out as my Duty to walk in.

The Officers you may employ on the present Occasion will I am sure, be men of good Sense and Candor. They will therefore judge properly of my Reasonings and give them their due Weight to others. I may perhaps have misarranged the wants of our Army, but I think not, it is however proper to observe, that under the Head of Cloathing I comprehend, those Means for Cloathing the Officers which, I have now in contemplation, and had the Honor of mentioning to your Excellency. If I am right in my Ideas, as to what is the proper Mode of applying the public money, then every prudent Officer will instead of urging the States to grant a little money for the Purpose of paying them, urge the Grant of so much, as will support and equip the Army, and still leave a Sufficiency for the Pay. To increase the means of Payment by retrenching every other Expenditure is my constant Object; to increase the means of Payment by grant of money the States alone are competent to. I hope therefore, that the Gentlemen you employ will join me in urging such Grants, with all their Force and Abilities.

It is from the same Conviction which you feel of the Advantages which must result to our Country from an early and vigorous Campaign, that I have spent money and stretched my Credit to the utmost Extent which I dare, in Order that you might take the Field at an early Hour and in a respectable manner. I have confided in the States, and the Consequences of being deceived will be such, that it is better you should conceive than I describe them. If they do not grant the Sums called for by Congress, I cannot give that Aid to your Operations which I know to be indespensibly necessary. But if they do grant me those Sums, I pledge myself to support you fully in All your Views, and you shall then have the Pleasure of seeing your brave Troops as regularly paid as they are now fed, and then knowing them to be well appointed and in all respects fit for Service you will be enabled to accomplish those Plans for the Defence and Salvation of our Country which be nearest your Heart. That this may be speedily the Case is the most fervent wish of Your Excellency's Most Obt and humble Servant

Robt Morris

To United States Congress, 10 February 1782

Philadelphia 10 Feby 1782

The Subscribers, taking into Consideration the important Situation of Affairs in the present Moment, and the Propriety & even Necessity of informing the People and rousing them into Action; considering also the Abilities of Mr Thomas Paine as a Writer, and that he has been of considerable Utility to the common Cause by several of his Publications. They have agreed that it will be much for the Interest of the united States that Mr Paine be engaged in their Service for the Purposes abovementioned. They have therefore agreed, that Mr Payne be offered a Salary of eight hundred Dollars per Annum, and that the same be paid him by the Secretary of foreign Affairs. The Salary to commence from this Day and to be paid by the Secretary of foreign Affairs, out of Monies to be allowed by the Superintendant of Finance for secret Services. The Subscribers being of Opinion that a Salary publickly and avowedly given for the above Purpose would injure the Effect of Mr Paine's Publications, and subject him to injurious personal Reflections.

Robt Morris

Rob. R. Livingston

Go: Washington

To Alexander Hamilton, 12 February 1782

Philadelphia, February 12, 1782. Sends the several receivers an "Advertisement respecting the Receivers of Continental Taxes," which states: "And whereas it is not only necessary that some precise mode be adopted for managing the public Business in this respect, but also that the same be publickly known, so that all Persons concerned therein may have due notice thereof I have therefore established the following rules in that Behalf, for the Receivers who have been or shall be by me appointed."

To George Washington, 20 March 1782

Office of Finance March 20th 1782

Sir

In consequence of Colo. Tilghman's letter of the 18th I granted a warrant on the Treasury for one thousand dollars for the purposes therein mentioned, and as he intimates that your Excellency would wish to know how you are to be supplied with money in future, whether from me or from the military chest. I should certainly refer you to the latter were I sure of a regular supply to it—I think however that the best mode for supplying your household expence will be by means of my orders on Mr Swanwick of this place. They are drawn payable to the bearer at sight, and as I shall cause them to be received for the continental taxes in all the states they will procure money wherever your excellency may happen to be. If you approve this I will send four Thousand dollars or more if you think necessary; and as you will only part with them when the course of expenditure requires, it prevents an advance of money from the Treasury until they come round for payment. I have the honour to be—your Excellency's Most Obt Hble St

R. Morris

To Benjamin Franklin, 22 March 1782

Office of Finance Philada March the 22d. 1782

Sir

The Bearer of this Letter Monsieur le Baron d'Arndt will shew you a Certificate for Two Thousand Nine hundred & Ninety Seven Dollrs. & 37/90ths signed by Joseph Nourse Esquire Register of the Treasury of the United States and issued by Virtue of a Warrant this Day from me. This Money is on Interest at six per Cent from the Eighteenth Inst. and is the Ballance still due after a partial Payment, Should it be perfectly convenient to you it will be a great Favor to him and agreable to me that this Balance be paid to Monsieur le Baron d'Arndt taking his Receipt in full of all Demands against the United States on the Back of the Certificate with three Copies thereof signed by him and sending them by different Opportunities. I mention the Balance as it stands in the Certificate without noticing the Interest because in Case of Payment by you the Transaction will be substantially as if I had given him here a Bill of Exchange.

I have the honor to be sir Your most Obedient & most hble Servant

Robt Morris

PS On the final adjustment of the Baron's Acct I find the balance larger than was expected, therefore it is probable that a partial Payment from You may answer his purpose, the Receipts to be indorsed on the Certificate & Copies transmitted as already mentioned.

R M

To Benjamin Franklin, 23 March 1782

Office of Finance, Philada. March 23d. 1782

Sir,

Applications being frequently made by the several Loan Officers for Orders to Renew Setts of Exchange in consequence of proof made to them by the Proprietors of Interest bills,that the first Second, third and fourth bills have been lost and destroyed, or by Accident prevented from reaching the Persons to whom they were Remitted, and as it is but just in such Instances to Renew the Same, I have Caused a Number of Bills to be Struck of the same denomination and in the same Stile, Manner and Tenor except that they are fifth, sixth seventh and eighth Bills and when made use of will be filled up in the same Manner as the first four were and Issued from the Same office.

I give you this Notice that you may direct the Banker to pay due honor to any one of these bills in all instances where no One of the Sett Consisting of Eight, has before been paid and of course he will before such payment always Satisfy himself that none of the others have been honored. This general Advice will I think answer the purpose and render unnecessary particular advice with each Renewed Sett of Exchange.

I have the Honor to be Sir Your Excellency's Most Obedient and Humble Servant

Robt Morris

To George Washington, 3 April 1782

Office of Finance Philada 3d April 1782

Sir

I have received letters from Wm Duer Esqr. respecting a request made by Genl Heath for Magazines of Salt provisions to be provided at some of the Posts which Mr Duer is to supply, he alledges that the laying up such Magazines will create an expence & advance of Money beyond what he is bound to by the Contract, which I suppose may be the case, and if so it is but reasonable & Just that such extra Expence should be to the public. I am too distant & too little acquainted with the Posts, also with your intentions as to these Magazines to decide with propriety on the Allowances to be made the Contractor for the extra supplies or services which may be required. Therefore I enclose herewith Copies of Mr Duers Contract & of his letters on the subject, Your Excellency will determine the quantities of provision to be laid up in Magazines, if any are necessary, & the places where, and then commission some proper person to meet the Contractor & fix with him a reasonable compensation for the services he renders over & above the terms of his Contract, and the Act of your Commissioner shall be complied with. I am sure he will be properly impressed with the Necessity of Frugality in all our Affairs. I have the honor to be your Excellency's Most obedient & most humble servant

Robt Morris

To Benjamin Franklin, 8 April 1782

Office of Finance, April 8th., 1782

Sir,

Since my Letter of the twenty sixth ultimo, I have compleated the sale of the Bills on Mr. grand to the extent of the livres five hundred thousand proposed as you will perceive by the letters and lists sent under your cover for that gentleman. I was in hopes that this sum would have carried me thro' untill payments from some of the States on account of their first quarterly quota of the requisition of Congress for the service of the present year, should come to my relief, but unfortunately the delays which are almost unavoidable in the tedious forms of Business conducted by public Bodies of men in commonwealths have thrown back the collection of taxes so that I am left at the moment of preparation for a vigorous campaign without any other Resources than those which my own Credit and address is able to supply; and altho' I sold the Bills above mentioned at a high price yet you must be sensible that the sum produced is very smal compared to my wants. I have just perfected a contract for supplying our moveing Army with rations thro' out the present campaign at ten pence per ration which I think vastly cheap it is made with men who combine an interest and influence equal to the undertakeing and you may depend that it will be performed, as I wish you to be fully informed of everything that can be usefull for you to know or that tends to give satisfaction to the court. I will enclose herewith a copy of the contract and a copy of a circular letter written to the Several States on the ninth February last, The first will sheew that I am attentive to our expenditures and the latter, that I mean to excite such exertions as will relieve our alies from future demands altho' the immediate inference is to induce a compliance on their parts of those aids that have already been requested for the service of the present year. At any rate I expect that necessity will soon compell me to draw for another half million of livres, and perhaps the like sum after that, but sir, you may assure yourself and the Ministers of his most Christian majesty that I shall not exceed the aggregate of these sums without proper encouragement from you, as I expect that the Money which I shall raise upon the sale of those Bills will carry me forward untill the taxes from several of the states come to my aid. I will venture also to assure you that if reimbursement of the sums which I shall draw should be demanded toward the close of the Year I will repay them on your Drafts, let what will be the consequence my word is sacred, and the united States are at this moment supported by the belief that it is so, for you may depend that we are not less than fourhundd. thousd. Dollars advanced on the Credit of the Taxes for this Year; at which however I do not feel any uneasiness as our preparations for the Campaign are fast advanceing & the spirit of exertion in the Several Governments Is gaining ground so, that I see plainly I shall be tollerably well supported by a vigorous Collection of the Taxes which in the end will enable me to perform what I promise; at the same Time I cannot help observing that the sum asked of the Court for the Service of the current Year, Is not large, especially if it enables us to give permanancy to arrangements calculated to relieve France entirely from our importunities: I do not however promise that we shall entirely cease to ask aids, but I promise to do everything in my Power to prevent the necessity of such solicitations and again I repeat, that nothing will make me so happy as to see America in condition not only to defend herself but able to render essential service to her allies. This letter will prepare you for farther drafts, my next will advise of them unless some favourable supply of Money should turn up to prevent the necessity of that measure which I wish to avoid if possble.—

I am, Sir, your obedient humble Servant

Robt Morris

To Alexander Hamilton, 15 April 1782

Office of Finance [Philadelphia] 15th. April 1782

Sir,

As several of the Legislatures have passed the Laws for levying Money in their respective states in Order to pay their Quota's of the eight Million of Dollars required by Congress for the service of the United States this present year, without noticing that part of the Act of Congress of the second of November last which recommends "the passing of Acts directing the Collectors to pay the same to the Commissioner of the Loan Office or such other Person as shall be appointed by the Superintendant of Finance to receive the same within the State &ca." It hath become necessary to pass my Warrant on the executive or Treasurer of the State of Wherein you are appointed to receive the Taxes payable to the United States, for the first Quarterly Payment which fell due the first day of this Month, and accordingly you will herein find my Warrant of this date in your Favor for Dollars you will learn whether the Payment is to be made by Order of the executive Authority or by the State Treasurer and apply accordingly. It is not probable that this Warrant will be discharged at one Payment and should that be the Case you are to receive the Money or bank Notes from time to time in such Sums as you can obtain, granting a Receipt for every Sum you receive specifying the day on which the Payment is made and endorse a Copy thereof on the back of the Warrant, so that when the whole is discharged you may deliver up the said Warrant then taking back your several loose Receipts. And as I find all the States have been more backward in passing their Tax Bills than was expected when my general Instructions of the twelfth of February last to the several Receivers were published, I desire that you will commence your Monthly Publications of the Sums you receive on the first day of June next and it is also my Direction that you publish on that day and on the first day of every succeeding Month the Amount of what you have received during the preceeding Month or if no Payment is made that you declare in one of the Newspapers published in the state that you have not during that Month received any money for the use of the United States. Let your Publications be made in Terms that will make known the Facts without giving Offence; and I must request that you will constantly solicit such Payments as will give them a good face. Indeed I must suppose that the State in which you reside will be anxious on this Subject as their Reputation is so materially connected therewith.

I have found great Use and the United States have derived great benefit from certain Notes or Orders which I have drawn on Mr. John Swanwick of this City payable at Sight to the Bearer, a Number of these Notes are now in Circulation they are struck on a Copper plate, Numbered Letter'd, signed and directed in my own Hand writing, they are for twenty fifty or eighty Dollars. These Notes you are to receive as Money or if you receive Money exchange it for them in the same Manner as already directed with respect to Bank Notes. I shall address you from time to time as Occasion may require but being much employed you will continue to write to me such things as you may judge I ought to be informed of without expecting regular Answers to your Letters. I desire also that you will Cause all the Newspapers published in your State as also Political Pamphlets or Publications to be sent to me regularly by the Post.

I am Sir your most obedient and humble Servant

RM

To George Washington, 15 April 1782

Office of Finance April 15th 1782

Sir.

After a good deal of Trouble the Contract for the moving Army has been Compleated and the Issues under it are to Commence the first day of May next. The Gentlemen concerned in it were so long in agreeing on several points regarding each other, that at last they grew too Impatient to allow the Secretary at War Time sufficient to have the Contract drawn with that precision and Clearness which he intended, it will however be easily understood, and herewith I enclose a Copy for your Excellencys use and Information.

You will perceive that I am to appoint a person who is to decide on all disputes and Complaints that may arise on the Contract which differs from the Mode prescribed in the others. This alteration was made in Consequence of some of those Complaints and Observations which were forwarded by General Heath and I shall in due Time make the appointment. The Person so to be appointed must be perfectly Free and Independent of all Connection with the Army, or with the Contractors, so that his decisions may be truly Impartial; and I hope to find such a Person as will save your Excellency from all Trouble or Complaint on this Subject which I know must be very disagreeable and distressing to you.

The present Contractors are all Men of respectable Characters, and Combine such an Interest and Influence in the several States from whence the supplies are to be extracted, as will I believe enable them to fulfill their Contract to the Satisfaction of the Army, and so long as they do their part with Integrity, I am sure they will meet with your protection. I shall make it a point to do mine by them therefore they shall have no Excuse on that Score. It will however be a troublesome and hazardous Business, it is an absolutely necessary one, and if the officers of the Army wish to receive regular pay, they ought to Support and second all Systems which have public Oeconomy for their Object, as it is by that means, and by such means only, that America can be enabled to pay them as they ought to be paid, and which it is and shall be my constant Study to accomplish. With the greatest Respect and Esteem I have the honor to be Your Excellency's most Obedient & most humble Servant

Robt Morris

To Benjamin Franklin, 17 April 1782

Office of Finance, Philadelphia, April 17th., 1782

Sir,

In consequence of the communications made to me by his Excellency the Chevalier de La Luzerne since his return from Virga., I shall proceed to draw Bills upon Monsieur Grand to the Extent of Livs. five hund: thousd. monthly; so that Computing the Months of Jany., Feby., March, and Apl., I have now to draw for two Millions of Livs.; as I hope and expect that the Livres 500,000 already drawn may be provided for out of the ballance due on the dutch Loan. This Supply Comes most seasonably, and at a more leisure moment you will be charged with the proper Acknowledement to the Court. I must however repeat that the Sum requested for the service of this year, will be necessary to enable me to support the Campaign and perfect my arrangements; it will be my constant study to draw forth our own resources and lessen our demands on France, but these things require time. I find it will be advantageous to draw upon Holland and Cadiz as well as on Paris, and therefore I request that you will desire mr. Grand to give immediate Orders to Messieurs Fizeaux

Grand & Co. in Amsterdam, to honour any Bills I may draw on them, with directions to take their reimbursement on him, for account of the United States. He must also give similar Orders to Messieurs Harrison & Company of Cadiz, and I shall furnish Mr Grand with regular Advice of every Bill I draw, whether on himself or either of those housses; my Bills in the whole wil not exceed the sums to which I am limited, and the Commission those Houses charge will be paid by mr. Grand, I expect it will not exceed a half per Cent respecting which I shall write to them. I am induced to draw on those places because the sale of Bills will thereby be extended and the price better supported. I have the honour to be, your Excellency's most obedient & most humble Servant

Robt Morris

To George Washington, 22 April 1782

Office of Finance Philadelphia April 22d 1782

Sir

When Your Letter of the 28 Ultimo came to my Hands enclosing one from Mr John Logan the SubContracor, assigning the want of Money as the Cause of his not having been regular in the Supply of provisions to the Troops at Morris Town and Pumpton; I delivered the same to Messrs Francis and Slough the persons that contracted with me, they instantly acknowledged that so far from being kept in want of money, I had even made Advances beyond the Terms of the Contract, which was the Fact. They also declared that all the money they received was immediately delivered over to Logan and Co. Logan has since been here and acknowledges that the want of Money of which he complained, did not originate with me, nor indeed with his Principals, it rather appears to have been founded in his not understanding the Terms of the Contract;

Be that as it may I could not permit it to be supposed, that I had failed in any part of my Engagements with the Contractors, and he wrote me a Letter of which No. 1 is a Copy.

This Jersey Contract has been badly executed, and it appears to be oweing chiefly to the Inability of those to whom the Management is committed, when I called upon the Principals, they replyed that by the Contract the commanding Officer at the post had the remedy in his own Hands, and that if he had executed it, Logan and Thompson must have suffered the Damages, the latter say they have made Compensation to the Troops and thus the matter stands.

When the Contract for the moving Army was perfected Messrs Francis and Slough came to me with an original Letter of which No. 2 is a Copy. I told them that the Contract for the moving Army would not in my apprehension interfere with that for the posts in New Jersey, that the latter related to permanent posts, and the former to temporary Posts and to Troops in motion, that if there were no permanent Posts, they would not be called upon for any Issues, and that if your Excellency should think proper to continue those Posts at Morris Town, Pumpton, Trenton or Burlington, or to establish any other Posts in New Jersey, and fix at any or all of them stationary Troops, you would give them timely Notice to provide the Supplies; but that they would not be called upon to supply Troops that are not stationed at such Posts altho they should occasionally pass and repass—There may arise some Difficulties however in this affair, and therefore, I enclose herewith a Copy of their Contract to enable you to avoid them, by such Decisions as you think consistant with Justice. I believe Messrs Francis and Slough wish to be clear of this Contract, and their Subs as far as I can learn are rather sick of it notwithstanding their Letter; which was probably written with an Intention to obtain a premium to induce them to give it up. If this was the Design they are totally mistaken. because if my Construction of what is meant by Posts

182

be admitted, it is best for the public that they be held to it, as the rations are to be delivered cheaper than those to the moving Army.

Should your Excellency be of opinion that these two Contracts will interfere so that you cannot draw a clear Line of Distinction between the Issues to be made under them, we must relinquish that of New Jersey if they will agree to it, if not, I fancy your Decisions on all Disputes will satisfy them, or if that will not do I will enter into the necessary Arbitration with them. I have the Honor to be your Excellency's most obedient and most humble Servant

Robt Morris

To Alexander Hamilton, 2 May 1782

Office of Finance
Philda. May 2d. 1782

Sir

Mr. Charles Stewart late Commissary general of Issues has informed me ⟨that⟩ you are disposed to quit the military line for the purpose of ⟨en⟩tering into civil life. He at the same time induced me to believe ⟨that⟩ you would accept of the Office of Receiver of the continental taxes ⟨for⟩ the state of New York. The intention of this letter is to offer you that ⟨app⟩ointment. The duties of the Office will appear in a great degree from the publications made by me on this subject. In addition it will be necessary that you correspond with me frequently and give accurate accounts of whatever may be passing in your State which it may be necessary for this Office to be acquainted with. But this and other things of that sort will be more fully communicated after you shall have signifyed your acceptance of the Office. For the trouble of executing it I shall allow you one fourth pr Cent on the monies you receive. The amount of the quota called for from New

York for the current year is as you know three hundred and seventy three thousand, five hundred and ninety eight Dollars. I shall be glad to know your determination as soon as possible. I make to you no professions of my confidence and esteem because I hope ⟨they⟩ are unnecessary, but if they are, my wish that you would accept the Offer I make is the Strongest evidence I can give of them.

I pray you Sir to believe me very respectfully Your most Obedi⟨ent⟩ and Humble ⟨Servant⟩

Robt. Morris

To Benjamin Franklin, 17 May 1782

Office of Finance May 17th. 1782

Sir

In the Letter which I had the Honor to write to your Excellency on the seventeenth of last Month I mentioned the Communications of his Excellency the Minister of France here by which I was empowered to draw to the Amount of six Millions in monthly Installments of half a Million each. He has since informed me that no Monies will be paid by his Court except on my Drafts and in a Letter of the thirtieth April on the same Subject he says. "Il me paroit Monsieur, que vous pouvez regarder les Fonds des mois deja ècoulés comme ètant à votre Disposition; cependant comme on ne me le mande pas positivement, je desire que vous mettiez le Dr. Franklin en etat d'informer, quelques semaines d'avance, le Ministre des Finances du montant des Fonds d'ont il aura besoin. Il me paroit que cette Operation seroit simplifie a notre Egard, si vous tiriez sur M. le Dr. Franklin douze Lettres de Change que vous lui adresserez a lui meme et dont il touchera le montant aux Epoques indiques. Il s'arangera ensuite avec votre Correspondant pour le payement de vos traites particulieres."— It is in Consequence of this that I have drawn the Bills contained in the enclosed Letter to Mr. Grand which is left open for your Perusal— Your Excellency will be pleased to arrange this Matter with Mr. Grand so as best to answer the purposes intended.— You will also be pleased Sir to pay over to Mr. Grand on my Account such Monies belonging to the United States as may be in Europe distinct from those to be advanced by the Court for the current Year. I am extremely desirious of having a State of these Matters so as to know what Dependance can be made on the Funds which are at our Command. You would therefore confer upon me a very particular Obligation by transmitting the best state in your power. I mentioned to your Excellency in a former Letter that I would write to you on the Subject of your Salary more particularly than I then did but I have since spoken and written to Mr. Livingston with Relation to those Matters and he will I expect write to you and to all our foreign Ministers very fully— We have not yet heard any Thing of the Alliance and therefore conclude that she must have been delayed in Europe.— I hope this may have been the Case for if she sailed on the first of March according to my Orders she must have met with some unfortunate Accident.— I hope soon to hear from your Excellency indeed I perswade myself that in the very critical Situation of Affairs at present we cannot be long without receiving very important Intelligence.

I have the Honor to be with great Respect & Esteem Sir your Excellency's most obedient and humble Servant

Robt Morris

To Benjamin Franklin (Two Letters), 18 May 1782

I.

Office of Finance 18th May 1782

Sir.

I have left the enclosed Letter open for your Excellency's Perusal and am to request that you will be Pleased to apply to the Court and learn what Opportunities may Offer for making the Shippments of Money within directed. The Alliance was Spoken with twenty seven Days ago off the Banks of Newfoundland being then bound for this Port. If she has not changed her distination I have very little hopes of her arrival as there are now no less than seven Ships of the Enemy in our Bay. But I am not without hopes that she may arrive in Boston altho she must run the Gauntlet to do even that as there are two Ships one of them of fifty Guns now cruizing in Boston Bay— Indeed the Vigilance of the Enemies numerous Cruizers is so great and they are so much unchecked by any Apprehensions that it must be by a kind of Miracle if any Vessel escapes them—

I am with perfect Respect & Esteem Sir Your Excellencys Most Obedient and humble Servant

Robt Morris

P.S. Enclosed is a List of the Bills drawn on you in favor of Mr Grand—

II.

Office of Finance 18th. May 1782—

Sir.

I am to pray your Excellency to take Charge of the enclosed Letter to Messrs. le Couteulx and Co. You will remember Sir that the

Court by their Minister here empowered me to draw twelve hundred thousand Livres, I drew only for Eleven hundred and ninety five thousand Livres intending the Remainder to be in Part Payment of the Bankers Commissions and Charges. I have some Reason to believe the Court have only paid the Sum drawn for which your Excellency can know from Messrs le Couteulx. If they have paid no more I must request of you Sir, to procure the remaining five thousand Livres from the Court for Messr le Couteulx and I must farther pray you to inform Mr. Grand of the Result as I have given him eventual orders for Payment of their Account.

I have the Honor to be with perfect Esteem & Respect Sir Your most obedient and humble Servant.

Robt Morris

To Alexander Hamilton, 20 May 1782

Office of Finance [Philadelphia] 20 May 1782

Sir,

I have received your Letter of the fourth Instant and am very much obliged by the Attention shewn to the Subject of it. Your Sentiments on the Occasion I entirely approve and indeed before this reaches you will probably have seen that the Letter has been republished in one of the Philadelphia Papers. I should readily consent to the Publication of many others which I have written on the same Subject and am fearless of any Injury they can do us abroad. Foreigners are already acquainted with our Circumstances and so are our Enemy. The People are kept in Ignorance of their true Interests by those Men who having little Objects of their own in View are regardless of the general Cause.

I am Sir your most obedient and humble servant

RM.

To Benjamin Franklin, 29 May 1782

Office of Finance, 29th. May 1782—

Dr. Sir—

I do myself the Honor to enclose you Copies of two Acts of Congress one of the fifth of June, and the other of the eighteenth of June 1779 relating to the affairs of Mr: de beaumarchais. You will observe Sir that you was authorized to Pledge the faith of the United States to the Court of Versailles for obtaining money or Credit to honor the Drafts on you— There is a misteriousness in this Transaction arising from the very nature of it which will not admit of Explanation here, neither can you go fully into an Explanation with the Court. Mr. de beaumarchais certainly had not funds of his own to make such considerable Expenditures neither is there any reason to beleive that he had Credit. If the Court advanced money it must be a Secret. But there would be no Difficulty in giving an order in your favor for the Sum necessary to Pay those Bills and thereupon measures might be taken to obtain from him the Reimbursment of any Sums he might have received— Consequently there would be no Actual advance of money made as the whole might be managed by the Passing of proper Receipts from you to the Court from Mr de beaumarchais to you, and from the Court to him. I wish that you would Apply on this Subject, and get it adjusted. The diverting from a Loan for the Service of the Current Year, so considerable a Part as that due to Mr de beaumarchais will defeat the Object for which it was granted. It ought not therefore to be done if possible to be avoided.

I have the honor to be sir Your most Obedt & most humble Servant

Robt Morris

To Alexander Hamilton, 4 June 1782

Office of Finance [Philadelphia] 4th. June 1782

Sir

I have received your favor of the eighteenth of May. I am much obliged by the friendly Sentiments you express for me which be assured I shall retain a gratefull Sense of. I see with you that the Office I had the Pleasure of Offering will not be equal to what your own Abilities will gain in the Profession of the Law but I did intend that the whole Sum should have been paid altho the whole quota of the Taxes had not been collected by the state, consequently the object is greater than you supposed and the business might probably be effected without more attention than you could spare from your Studies, if so, I should still be happy in your acceptance and will leave the Matter open untill I have an Opportunity of hearing from you upon the Subject.

I pray you to believe that I am with unfained Esteem Your Most Obedient Servant

Robt. Morris

To George Washington, 4 June 1782

Office of Finance 4th June 1782

Sir

I have received your Excellency's Letter of the Seventeenth and twenty fifth of May with the Enclosure. I am much obliged by the Attention paid in your circular Letter to the Situation of my Department. I am very sorry to inform you that it is really deplorable. I with difficulty am enabled to perform my Engagements and am absolutely precluded from forming any new ones. I have therefore been under the very disagreeable Necessity of suffering the public Service to stand still in more Lines than one—I have been driven to the greatest Shifts and am at this moment unable to provide for the civil List.

I can easily suppose that military Men should murmer to find the Salaries of the civil List more punctually paid than their own. To enter into Arguments on this Occasion will be unnecessary, for I am perswaded that your Excellency must be of Opinion with me that without the civil List is paid neither civil nor military can exist at all.

I am very sorry to find so many Difficulties made about the Contract. The first which was formed and which the Officers now refer to was as you will remember much opposed and many Difficulties arose in the Execution. The Methods taken to obviate those Difficulties have produced many others and I am perswaded that if attending to the Reasons assigned by the Officers an Alteration should be made, conformably to them their Complaints would thereby be increased. If for Instance on the Principle that they are intitled to the Ration in kind, orders should issue that they draw those Rations or in case of not drawing receive no compensation this would leave them in the Mercy of the Contractor to allow so much as they may think proper for the Rations retained. And yet this would be a literal Performance of the Promise made in 1775.

I shall not enter into the various Causes of Complaint because that I expect the Minister of War will go to Camp for the Purpose of enquiring into them and I shall on my Part do every thing I can to facilitate his Measures—I am nevertheless perswaded that all the Obstacles might be more readily surmounted by a good Understanding between the Officers and Contractors than in any other Mode. As I am told that the old Commissary of Issues is now about to become the Issuing Contractor I expect that his knowledge of the Army will enable him to get over many

Difficulties which have formerly existed. If the Officers and Contractors understand each other they may easily square their Mode of doing Business with that which is prescribed for the public Convenience. For altho the Provisions be actually issued during every Day of the weak or Month it will be extremely easy to make a weekly or monthly Settlement and comprise all the Rations in one Order and Return, this by simplifying the Vouchers will facilitate the Adjustment of public Accounts.

I should have sent forward e'er this Moment the Intendant and had applied to General Cornell to accept that office but some Circumstances prevented him from going after he agreed that he would and this which only came to my Knowledge Yesterday has reduced me to the Necessity of seeking another and find it no easy Matter to fix on a proper Person for that important Station.

I pray you will be convinced that I have no Partiality or Prediliction in Favor of Mr Sands or of any other Person. If they are guilty of Fraud or Neglect of Duty I am not only willing but desirious that they should suffer. The Contract for West point of which I presume your Excellency has a copy from the War-Office will point out the Remedy where there is a Deficiency of Quantity or Quality in the Articles of a Ration. Besides this the Contractors all give Bond for the faithful Performance of their Contracts. That they have not laid up the Magazines required at West Point is an Omission for which they are answerable and I trust that General Lincoln will take the proper Measures to compel their Obedience or punish their Neglect.

I am well perswaded of your Excellency's Desire to promote the Success of those Measures I have taken because I am sure you are convinced that their Tendency and my Intentions are all directed to the public Good Indeed my dear Sir you will hardly be able to form an adequate Idea of the Earnestness with which I desire to relieve you from the Anxieties you must undergo. But when the several Gazetts Shall have announced the Sums received for this Year's Service, and I am well convinced that the whole did not on the first of June amount to twenty thousand Dollars, when it is recollected that our Expences at the Rate of near eight Millions annually are near twenty thousand Dollars pr day and when it is known that the Estimates on which the Demand was founded do not include many essential Branches among which the marine and foreign Affairs are to be numbered, surely it cannot be a Matter of Surprise that the Army are not paid. Surely the Blame is to fall on those from whose Negligence the Evil originates. But I will not give you the Pain of hearing me repeat Complaints which you know to be but too well founded. I pray you to believe that I am Sir with very great respect Your Excellency's most Obedient and Humble servant

Robt Morris

P.S. I have received yours of the 29th of May. The Notes for Mr Varrick did not go when I expected owing to a Mistake of Mr Swanwick's They are now sent in a Letter to Colo. Varrick by favor of Colo. Wadsworth.

To George Washington, 4 June 1782

Office of Finance 4th June 1782

Dear Sir

Since I wrote you in Cypher relating to the Loan in France I have received Letters from Doctor Franklin which made it proper to communicate the Matter to Congress. By those Letters and by Communications from the french Minister on the Part of his Court it appeared that Mr Franklin had already anticipated the whole of this Loan excepting the small Part which I have drawn for, so that we can count upon nothing from that Quarter towards the Relief of our Necessities. In Consequence of this and of other matters of the like Kind which I found myself compelled to lay before the United states in Congress they have appointed two Gentlemen of their Body to go to the Eastern and two others to the southern States. Messrs Root and Montgomery will I presume have been at Head Quarters before this Letter reaches you and will have explained to your Excellency more fully than I can do by writing the State of our Public Affairs. This Letter will go by Colo. Wadsworth and therefore I shall trust it as well as my other Letter of this Date without using our Cypher. I have the honor to be Your Excellencies Most Obedt & most hble servant

Robt Morris

To Benjamin Franklin, 10 June 1782

Office of Finance Philada. June 10th. 1782

Sir,

The Annexed is Copy of a Letter which was written to you on the 22d. March last by the Baron D'arndt who had the misfortune to be Captured and carried into New York, he is come out on Parole and informs me that he lost the original Letter wherefore I furnish him with a Copy and hereby Confirm the Contents.

I am Sir Your most obedient humble Servant.

Robt Morris

To George Washington, 12 June 1782

Office of Finance 12th-13 June 1782

Sir

I presume that General Lincoln will have made your Excellency acquainted with the Situation of Affairs here. It becomes my Duty to mention one Circumstance for your Determination which I will adhere to even tho it should contravene my own Opinion not only because I have a firm Reliance in your Judgement but because you are in a better Position to be well informed of the Facts. It is with great Pain I learn that the few Taxes raised by the State of New York instead of being applied in Discharge of their Quota are all appropriated to particular Purposes. My Information on this Subject may be ill founded but having applied to the Governor for the Laws of the State relative to Revenue which I have not received I am obliged to take it upon verbal Communications Supposing the Fact to be as stated I am inclined to think that at least the Levies raised by that State should not be fed at the continental Expence. The Expenditures on those Levies I cannot precisely ascertain but I believe it to be somewhere between five and Six thousand Dollars monthly. This Expence at a Moment when the Wheat and Flour collected in that State is as I am informed held up untill Money can be sent from hence to purchase it at a high Price appears to be improper. There may perhaps be good Reasons for it but it may also be considered as unnecessary Profusion. Your Excellency can best judge what ought to be done but you may rely on it that we can very ill afford any Expence in our present Situation. I have the Honor to be with great Respect and esteem Sir Your Excellency's most obedient and humble Servant

Robt Morris

June 13

Since writing the above of the twelfth I have received your Excellency's Letter of the eigth—To which I shall make no particular Answer at present having as I had the Honor to mention in a former Letter referred the whole of that Business to the secretary at War. I am &c.

R.M.

To George Washington, 21 June 1782

Office of Finance 21 June 1782

Sir.

I am informed that several of our Officer's have left behind them in New York considerable sums of money unpaid, which had been advanced to them while they were Prisoner's. The Humanity of those who have made such advances, as well as the Principles of Justice require that they shou'd be repaid, but there is another reason which has considerable weight on my Mind.

The Establishment of a credit among our Enemies by the punctual payment of such debts, will induce them again to make advances should the Chance of War place any of our unfortunate Officers in a Situation to render it necessary. I am therefore to request of your Excellency (should you agree with me in Opinion) that you would take measures to cause the Amount of those Debts to be particularly ascertained, In order that I may devise some means of discharging them as soon as the Scale of the Treasury will permit. I am Sir, your Excellency's most obedient & humble Servant

Robt Morris

To George Washington, 22 June 1782

Office of Finance June 22d 1782

Sir

I do myself the Honor to enclose to your Excellency the Copies of a Letter of the seventeenth Instant from some of the Contractors of the moving Army to me, and of my Answer of this Date—Your Excellency will perceive in their Letter a Doubt whether I will perform my Engagements held up as an Apology should they not perform theirs. They have no Reason to entertain, and less Right to express any such Doubts. When I entered into the Contract I promised payment by forming the Agreement, I think that making new Assurances is extremely unnecessary, and therefore I will not do it. This together with the general Stile of their Letter will account for the Brevity of mine. I am Sir with great Respect, Your Excellency's most obedient & humble Servant

Robt Morris

To Benjamin Franklin, 26 June 1782

Office of Finance 26. June 1782

Sir,

The Bearer of this Letter Doctor Texier late Surgeon of Count Pulaski's Legion will shew you a Certificate for two thousand one hundred and ten dollars signed by Joseph Nourse Esquire Register of the Treasury of the United States and issued by Virtue of a Warrant of the eighth day of January last from me. This Money is on Interest at six per Cent from the fifth of January 1782. and is the Balance still due after a partial Payment in Consequence of an Act of Congress of the twelfth of November, a Copy of which he will also shew you. Should it be perfectly convenient to you it will be a great Favor to him and agreable to me that this two thousand one hundred and ten Dollars be paid to Doctor Texier taking his Receipt in full of all Demands against the United States on the Back of the Certificate with three Copies thereof signed by him and sending them by different Opportunities. I mention two thousand one hundred and ten Dollars without noticing the Interest because in Case of Payment by you the Transaction will be substantially as if I had given him here a Bill of Exchange.

With all possible Respect I have the Honor to be Sir your most obedient and humble Servant

R M.

To George Washington, 29 June 1782

Office of Finance June 29th 1782

Dr Sir.

I have received your Favors of the eighth and sixteenth Instant the former enclosing Alterations proposed in the present Mode of Issues and the latter a Copy of your circular Letter to the States of the fourth of May. I pray you to accept my Thanks for these Communications. I consent to the Alterations mentioned and shall be very happy that Harmony be restored for I do assure you that let the Cause of Disputes be what it may I am extremely sorry to find that any exist. I am sorry also for the Character you have given of Mr Sands. I have too good an Opinion of your Penetration and Candor not to beleive in it. I find you have misunderstood that Part of my Letter which relates to the Complaints of the Officers— My Design was not to oppose any arrangement which might contribute to their Convenience, I only meant to shew that their Convenience having been consulted in the first Istance, The Mode had excited uneasiness, and that the Endeavor to remove that uneasiness having excited Complaint and Remonstrance the direct Compliance with the reasoning adopted by them would produce greater Hardship than that which was complained of. Hence follows the Inference which was on my Mind, that a spirit of Accomodation alone would place all Parties at their Ease and I supposed that the Interest of the Contractors on one Hand and the Convenience of the Army on the other would produce that accomodating Disposition in both. I am happy to find that Matters are now in a Train towards that desirable End and much lament that it has not sooner arrived. I shall close what I have to say upon this Subject by assuring you most confidentially that I will to the utmost of my Power do Justice and bring Relief to both Officers and Soldiers but as these Things can only be effected by exact Method and Oeconomy so I must pursue that Method and oeconomy as the only Means by which the desired releif can be obtained.

With Respect to the civil List I shall say but one or two Words. I know well the Connection which ties together all the public Servants, and I lament every Comparison which implies a Distinction between them. The civil List consists chiefly of Persons whose Salaries will do more than find them Food and cloathing. Many of them complain that with great Parsimony they cannot obtain even those Necessaries. The Difference then between them and the Army supposing the latter to get but four Months Pay out of twelve is that both would be alike subsisted and the Army would have an Arrearage of eight Months Pay to receive at a future Period but the civil List would have to receive nothing. I am my dear Sir Your's very Sincerely

Robt Morris

To Benjamin Franklin, 1 July 1782

Office of Finance 1 July 1782

Sir,

I have deferred until this Moment my Answers to your Letters of the fourth ninth and thirtieth of March in Expectation that I should have heard from you by the Marquis de la fayette. A Vessel now about to depart induces me to address you— I enclose an Act of Congress by which you are empowered to adjust the Public Accounts with the Court of France. I wish this may be done and the Amount transmitted hither that Arrangements may be taken for ascertaining the times and mode of Payment. You will at the same time observe that it is determined to appoint a Commissioner for Liquidating and finally adjusting the Accots. of the public Servants of Congress in Europe.

The Minister here in a Letter to me of the twenty fifth of May last gives the following State of Monies granted by France Viz: "These Advances have been made at the following Periods and are payable with Interest according to the Obligations and Acknowlegements of Mr Franklin

In	1778	3.000.000 *l.t.*
	1779	1.000.000
	1780	4,000.000
	1781	<u>10.000.000</u>
	Total—	18.000.000

From this Sum must be deducted the <u>6.000.000</u> gratuitous Subsidy of last Year

Remains	12.000,000

To this must be added—

1st The Produce of the Loan in Holland	10,000,000

2ly The Loan made by his Majesty for the <u>6.000.000</u> current Year

Capital of the Debt due to his Majesty by the 28.000.000 *l.t.*" United States

I think it right to send you this State on which I will make a few Observations. I could have wished that the whole of the Monies which the Court have furnished us had been what the greater Part is a *Loan*. I know that the united States will find no difficulty in making Payment and I take this Opportunity to give *you* an Assurance which is not meant for the Court that I will endeavor to provide *even now* the Means of Repayment by getting Laws passed to take Effect at a future Period or otherwise as shall be most convenient and agreeable to all Parties after the Amount is ascertained and the Times of Payment fixed. I wish it had *all* been a Loan because I do not think the Weight of the Debt would be so great as the Weight of an Obligation is generally found to be and the latter is of all others what I would least wish to labour under either in a public or private Capacity. A still further Reason with me is that there is less Pain in soliciting the *Aid* of a Loan when there is no Expectation that it is to be a Gift. Prompted by such Reasons I could be well content that the advances made previously to the Year 1778 were by some Means or other brought into this Account. By Mr Grands Accounts it appears that Messrs. Franklin, Deane and Lee paid him on the thirty first of January 1777. 500.000 *l.t.* on the twenty eighth of April other 500.000 *l.t.* on the fourth of June 1.000.000 *l.t.* on the third of July 500.000 *l.t.* and on the tenth of October other 500.000 *l.t.* Amounting in the whole to three Millions of Livres. I suppose that these Sums were received of Private Persons in like manner with those Supplies which were obtained thro' Mr de Beaumarchais and if so they will be payable in like Manner with those Supplies— I have in a former Letter estimated the Yearly Interest on Loan Office Certificates payable in France at 2.200.000 *l.t.* consequently taking in the Months intervening between September and March the Total Amount from September the tenth 1777 to March the first 1782 may be stated at 9.000.000 *l.t.* which is just one half the Supplies granted for the Years 1778. 1779 1780 and 1781. A Resolution now before Congress will I beleive direct that no more Bills be drawn for this Interest but Mr. Grand in his Letter of the fourth of March tells me he has paid £6.239.186 *l.t.* 13.4. in 16819 Bills from 11th February 1779. to 28th Jany 1782. His Accounts are now translating and when that is compleated I shall transmit them to the Treasury and I hope soon to have the Accounts of the Several Loan Officers in such a train of Settlement that all these Matters may finally be wound up.

Should the Court grant 6.000,000 *l.t.* more for the Service of the Current Year making 12.000.000 *l.t.* in the whole which to tell you the Truth I do expect then the Sum Total in five Years will be 40.000.000 *l.t.* or 8.000.000 *l.t.* annually. And when the Occasion of this Grant is considered the Magnitude of the Object and the Derangement of our Finances naturally to be expected in so great a Revolution I cannot think this Sum is by any Means very extraordinary. I beleive with you most perfectly in the good Dispositions of the Court but I must request you to urge those Dispositions into Effect. I consider the six Millions mentioned to me by the Minister here and afterwards in your Letters as being at my Disposal. The Taxes come in so slowly that I have been Compelled and must Continue to draw Bills but I shall avoid it as much as possible. In my Letters of the twenty third and twenty ninth of May of which I enclose Copies are Contained my

Sentiments as to Mr. de Beaumarchais Demand. Indeed if the Sums paid to him and others for Expenditures Previous to the Year 1778 and the Amount of the Interest Money of which the principal was also expended at that Time be deducted the remaining Sum will be considerably less than thirty Millions.

I must entreat of you Sir that all the Stores may be forwarded from Brest as soon as possible and I shall hope that the Court will take Measures to afford you the necessary Transports so as that they may come under proper Convoy. As to the Cargo of the Ship Marquis de la fayette it is true that some of it has arrived here thro' neutral Ports but it is equally true that Money was necessary to purchase it and that money is quite as scarce as any other Article. If however all the Cargo of that Ship was like some which I did procure the taking of her has been no great loss for the Cloathing was too small to go on Men's Backs. The Goods from Holland we still most anxiously expect Would to God that they had never been purchased— Mr. Gillon however is at Length arrived and I hope we shall have those Matters in which he was concerned brought to some kind of Settlement.

I have the Honor to be with perfect Esteem and Respect Sir your most obedient and humble Servant

Robt Morris

To Alexander Hamilton, 2 July 1782

Office of Finance [Philadelphia] 2 July 1782

Sir,

I yesterday received your Letter of the seventeenth of June and am very happy to find you have determined to accept the office I had the Pleasure of offering to you. I enclose the commission, Instructions &ca. together with a Bond for Performance of the

Duties which I must request you to fill up, execute with some sufficient Surety and transmit. The complaint you make of the System of taxation, in New York might I beleive very justly be extended, for tho' it may be more defective in some than in others it is I fear very far from perfect in any. I had already heard that no part of the Taxes were appropriated to continental Purposes, but I expect that the Legislature will when they meet make such appropriations as well as lay new and I hope Productive Taxes for the purposes of Paying what may remain of their quotas. It gives me a singular pleasure to find that you have yourself pointed out one of the principal objects of your appointment. You will find that it is specified in the Enclosure of the fifteenth of April. I do not conceive that any interview will be necessary, tho' I shall always be happy to see you when your Leisure and convenience will admit. In the mean time I must request you to exert your talents in forwarding with your Legislature the Views of Congress. Your former situation in the Army, the present situation of that very army, your connections in the state, your perfect knowledge of men and measures, and the abilities which heaven has blessed you with will give you, a fine opportunity to forward the public service by convincing the Legislature of the necessity of copious supplies, and by convincing all who have claims on the Justice of Congress that those claims exist only by that hard Necessity which arises from the Negligence of the States. When to this you shall super add the conviction that what remains of the War being only a War of Finance solid arrangements of Finance must necessarily terminate favorably not only to our Hopes, but even to Our Wishes, then Sir the Governments will be disposed to lay and the people to bear those Burthens which ⟨are⟩ necessary, and then the Utility of your office, and of the Officer ⟨wil⟩l be as manifest to other's as at present to me.

I am with perfect Respect Your most obedient & Humble Servant

Robt Morris

To Benjamin Franklin, 5 July 1782

Office of Finance 5th July 1782

Sir.

I enclose to you the form of an acknowledgement of our Debt to the Court of France which I desire you would Seal and execute, After having ascertained the Amount of the Debt, and that you will send Copies thereof thro the Office of foreign Affairs to Congress; as well as inform me of the Amount of the Debt and the Time of Settlement.

I have the Honor to be with great Respect Your most Obedient and humble Servant

Robt. Morris

To George Washington, 6 July 1782

Office of Finance July 6th 1782

Sir

I am to pray that your Excellency will cause the inclosed Letter containing Affidavits of the Plunder of Some Americans on Board a Flag by British Privateers to be transmitted. I am Sir Your Excellencys Most Obedient & humble servt

Robt Morris

To George Washington, 9 July 1782

Office of Finance 9th July 1782

Sir

I have received your Favor of the third Instant, and am obliged by your Attention to my Requests—I entirely approve your Excellencys Reasons for directing a Magazine at West Point—The Contractors will I believe exert themselves.

It is impossible for me to state the Trouble and Distress I undergo—This Morning the Southern Post brought me a Letter from the Reciever in Virginia, of which the following Clause is an Extract. "Our Assembly having postponed the Collection of one half the Land Tax (which was payable in Specie only) for three Months, and all the Appropriations of the Revenue for the Support of Government, being to be first provided for by the Treasurer; I fear it will be December or January next before any Thing will come to the Hands of the continental Receiver, and what may then be the Sum, it is not in my Power at this Time to give you the least Information, as it will depend upon a great many Contingencies which may, or may not happen"—With such gloomy Prospects as this Letter affords I am tied here to be baited by continual clamorous Demands, and for the Forfeiture of all which is desirable in Life, and which I hoped at this Moment to enjoy, I am to be paid by Invective—There is Scarce a Day passes in which I am not tempted to give back into the Hands of Congress the Power They have delegated, and lay down a Burthen which presses me to the Earth. Nothing prevents me, but a Knowledge of the Difficulties I am obliged to struggle under.

What may be the Success of my Efforts God only knows, but to leave my Post at present would I know be ruinous. This candid State of my Situation and feelings I give to your Bosom because you who have already felt and Suffered so much will be able to Sympathize with me. Believe me I pray you very Sincerely your's

Robt Morris

To Alexander Hamilton, 12 July 1782

Office of Finance [Philadelphia] 12 July 1782

Sir,

I inclose you the Copy of my circular Letter to the several States of the twenty fifth of July 1781. The Answers I have received have been very few and very short of the Objects so that I have not been able to Act as I wished for want of necessary Information. I must beg you to take the most speedy and effectual Means in your Power to enable me to form a proper Judgment on such of the Subjects referred to as the actual State of Things renders it important to know.

I am Sir your most obedient and humble Servant

RM

To Alexander Hamilton, 19 July 1782

Office of Finance [Philadelphia] 19th. July 1782

Sir,

I have found it necessary to draw Bills on Mr. Swanwick in favor of different People and payable at various Periods. These are Bills of Exchange in the common Form and must be negotiated by Indorsements. You will always receive them in like Manner with my other Notes or Bank Notes and remit them which you can do without cutting them as they will be paid only to the Indorsee.

I am Sir your most obedient Servant

RM.

To Alexander Hamilton, 22 July 1782

Office of Finance [Philadelphia] July 22nd. 1782

Sir

I have received your letter dated at Albany the 13th, Instant, as I can have no doubt but that your Efforts will be applyed to promote the Public Interests, I hope the Journey you propose to Poughkepsie may prove every way agreable to your Wishes.

I am Sir Your Most Obedient Servt.

Robt Morris

To George Washington, 5 August 1782

Office of Finance 5 Augst 1782

Dear Sir,

I received your Letter of the thirtieth of July late in the Evening of Friday the second Instant. The Ideas which in Conversation with you I endeavoured to impress were, that I should at all Events fulfil my Part of the Contracts entered into for feeding your Army, That I had constantly attended to the claims of the Contractors. That I should continue to do so, and that I beleived I had in many Instances been in Advance to them. On Saturday Morning I desired the comptroller to make out a State of these Accounts, which State I have received this Morning, and now enclose— Copies. Your Excellency will perceive from the State Number One, of the Accounts of the Contractors for West Point, that I have for a Considerable Part of the Time been Considerably in Advance to them, instead of their being one Month in advance to me. Besides which it is to be observed, that the Amount stated for Provisions, they received out of the public Stores is entirely as they themselves have Stated it, and that the Accounts not being as yet settled I ought not to have paid perhaps so much as I have done, because certainly there is no Way to secure the public Interest, but by with holding Money until Accounts be adjusted. And this Sir leads me to an Observation, which applies fully to the whole of this Business. When I contracted to pay monthly it was well understood, that I should pay what appeared to be due for the preceding Month. Now until the Account be settled at the Treasury, there is in Fact nothing due which I can take Notice of as such. Supposing the Accounts & Vouchers to be all kept and delivered with that Accuracy and Simplicity which they ought, it is probable that they would get settled in the Course of a Week. Supposing then the greatest Dispatch which can reasonably be expected in transmitting & settling the Accts paying and remitting the Money, &ca the Contractors could not have expected any thing else than to have been two Months in Advance. And if they do not keep and transmit their Accounts and Vouchers with due Regularity they ought to have expected a Still longer Detention, especially if I were disposed to comply only with the Letter of my agreements, But tho' I neither have done, nor will do any Thing, which could be construed into taking an undue advantage, I think myself not only justifiable, but I think and will contend, that it is my duty to take Care, that there be always such an arrearage, as will make the Public perfectly Safe. I do not examine Accounts, and therefore if I would take the meer assertion of any Man, or Set of Men, the Consequences might be most pernicious. With Respect to the Contractors for the Moving Army whose account is contained in the Enclosure number two, I confess that I was deficient, one Hundred Dollars, in the Payments for April & May, but when it is recollected, that the Advances stipulated for were under the Ideas then entertained, that the whole Army would take the Field on the first day of may, and expend (at the rate of only eighteen Thousand Rations per Day) sixty Thousand Dollars Monthly, and when it is further recollected, that nothing like this has happened, it will then appear, that I have more than complied with what they had any Right to expect, and that if they had prepared as they ought to have done, Funds equal to the Supply of between two and three Months Pay, nay, if they had prepared Funds equal to the expected Supply of only one Month, they have never yet been in a Situation when the Deficiences of the Public (had the Public been defective) could have injured the Army. And now Sir, if you examine the Account number two, you will see, that they have received quite as much, as they had any Right to expect previous to a Settlement of their Accounts, And indeed you will see by the enclosed note from Mr Swanwick, that they have received even more than is Stated in that account. But as these Various contractors have as I am informed lately joined Stocks & Contracts, I have made a Short State in the Paper Number three, of the Issues according to their Accounts, and of the Payments made from which it will appear, that there are not four thousand Dollars due for the Month of June and that if a Credit is given for Provisions, purchased of the State of Connecticut, the Public are at least four thousand Dollars in Advance. They say that there are forty thousand Dollars due for the Issues in July, but the Accounts are not yet even presented, notwithstanding which, I shall pay them a considerable Sum this Week.

I should not however do Justice, were I not to Observe that the Contractors for West Point have made considerable Advances for the Purpose of Cloathing the Officers, which Cloathing they were paid for in Notes of the Pay Master General due on the first of August—I owe them yet on those Notes between nineteen and twenty thousand Dollars—If I had asked Indulgence in the Situation to which the Demand for those Notes, and the Delays of the States had reduced me, I might, I think, have expected it, but I have asked none, & I am thoroughly perswaded, that the Contractors were intimidated by the Apprehension, that those Notes would break me, and thereby prevented from applying as they ought to have done, their own Money and Credit—I do myself the Honor to enclose Sir, the Copy of a Letter to me from the Comptroller, to which I will pray that your Excellency will enable me to make the proper Answer. With sincere Friendship & Esteem I am my Dear Sir Your most obedient & humble Servant

Robt Morris

To George Washington, 8 August 1782

Philada August 8th 1782

Dear Sir

Having occasion to Answer a letter lately received from a Mr Creeden in New York, I beg leave to trouble You with the care of sending it in by such opportunity as may first occur.

I am preparing Money for the Contractors their demands so immediately on the back of the Pay Master Generals Notes due the 1st Inst. press me closely. I am most truely Dear Sir Your affectionate hble servt

R. Morris

To George Washington, 9 August 1782

Office of Finance, 9th Augst 1782

Sir.

I had the Honor to receive your Excellency's Favor of the Fifth Instant, last Evening. I beg Leave to refer, for a State of Matters between the public & the Contractors, to mine of the Fifth Instant. I should long since have appointed the Officer you mention, could I have got a proper Person. I had applied to General Cornell, and he had (in a manner) undertaken, but afterwards declined. Colo. Tilgman will give your Excellency an Account of some Conversation, with him on the Subject. I wait to hear from you or him, or both, before I go into an Appointment. I pray you Sir, to beleive that I am, with the greatest Esteem & Respect Your Excellency's most Obedient & humble Servant

Robt Morris

To George Washington, 13 August 1782

Office of Finance 13th August 1782

Sir

The urgent Demands on me for Money oblige me to use a Thousand different Expedients—The bearer of this letter Mr Richd Wells is on his way to New York, He goes for the purpose of receiving a very considerable Sum of Money and will if Successful pay it to your Excellency to be held at my orders—I am therefore to request that he may have every Facility in going to New York and bringing the Money from thence, I will by another Opportunity mention to your Excellency the Disposition of a Party and the Remainder at a future Period—The Sum being uncertain I cannot give such pointed Directions as I could wish. I am to pray that your Excellency will receive whatever he may bring and sign Receipts therefor as for so much on Account of the United States to be held at my order. I am Sir, with great Respect Your Excellency's most Obedient and humble Servt

Robt Morris

To George Washington, 17 August 1782

Office of Finance 17th Augt 82

Sir

I found it necessary, in order to get money for alleviating my distress, to sell Bills which I knew were to be negociated thro' New York. The remittances coming in too slowly, induced my assent to a plan for bringing out the Specie. This was the money which I lately wrote to you about. I am &ca

Robt Morris

To George Washington, 20 August 1782

Office of Finance 20th August 1782

Sir,

The Contractor's Accounts both for West Point and the moving Army for the Month of July amount by their State to the Sum of Forty seven Thousand Dollars; of this I have already paid about Twenty five Thousand. I have taken Arrangements for Payment of Ten thousand at Morristown, and I am to request that from the Monies payable to your Excellency in the Manner I mentioned in a former Letter you would pay them Twelve thousand Dollars. These several Sums will amount to the whole of what is due to them, but I have not stopped here: I gave them in the middle of July Twenty Thousand Dollars in Orders on Mr Swanwick. In the Begining of August Ten thousand more, and now Twenty thousand more, making in the whole Fifty thousand Dollars. The Money for these Notes I doubt not they will readily obtain, and of Course I must be considered from that Time as so much in Advance for them. I hope therefore that we shall have no Complaints from that Quarter again. These Notes form an Anticipation of the Taxes, and it is not by any Means a considerable One, for with the Exception of some small Sums not worth mentioning, it consists of Forty five Thousand to the Quarter Master General, Twenty Thousand to Mr Langdon for the Ship America, and the Fifty Thousand just mentioned. I expect the Payment of them from New York and the States Eastward of it; and I hope that the greater part of this Money must be already collected from the People. I have given Colonel Charles Stewart Orders to the Amount of Three thousand five hundred Dollars, and I am to request that your Excellency would transmit to Mr Duer the Sum of Five thousand Dollars, and to me his Receipt for them. Whatever may remain in your Hands after paying the two Sums of Five and Twelve thousand Dollars, you will be so kind as to invest in the Purchase of my Orders on Mr Swanwick from such of the Persons already mentioned as you may think it most useful to possess of the Specie in that Way. I have the Honor to be Your Excellency's most obedient and most humble Servant

Robt Morris

To George Washington, 22 August 1782

Office of Finance 22d August 1782

Sir

I have directed Capt. John Green who is the Bearer of this Letter to carry in some Letters from the Captains of two flag Ships which have arrived from England (on board one of which he was a Passenger) enclosed in a Letter from me to Sir Guy Carleton. I am to request your Excellency would facilitate his going in and that he be permitted to stay untill he obtain the Answer which those Ships are now waiting for in this Port. I am Sir with great Respect your Excellency's Most Obedient & humble Servant

Robt Morris

To Alexander Hamilton, 28 August 1782

Office of Finance [Philadelphia] 28th, August 1782

Sir,

I have duly received your several Favors of the Twenty second & twenty Seventh of July, and tenth and thirteenth of August. My not answering them is owing to Causes which you will easily conceive; because you will easily conceive the Multiplicity of Objects to which I must turn my Attention. I am very sorry to learn that you can no longer continue in the Office of Receiver. It would have given me great Pleasure that you should have done so, because I am sure that you would have rendered very signal Services to the public Cause: This you will now do in another Line more important, as it is more extensive; and the Justness of your Sentiments on public Affairs induce my warm Wish that you may find a Place in Congress so agreeable as that you may be induced to continue in it.

I should readily have complied with your Wish as to a Successor, but there are many Reasons which have called my Attention to and fixed my Choice upon Doctor Tillotson. We will converse on this Subject when we meet. I am however very far from being unmindful of your Recommendations; and altho I cannot name the Citizen of any State to settle the Accounts of that particular State consistently with the general Line of Conduct I have laid down for myself; yet I shall do in other Respects what is in my Power. I have not hitherto been able to fix on a proper Commissioner for the State of New York. The Office is vacant for New Hampshire & Rhode Island. I enclose you a Copy of the Ordinance on the Subject, that you may know the Powers, Duties and Emoluments; and I have to request that you offer these Places to Colo. Malcolm and Mr. Lawrence. You will make the first offer including the Choice as your own Judgement may direct. Should the Gentlemen, or either of them accept, you will be so Kind as to give me early Notice. I will then immediately recommend them to the States respectively and on receiving their Approbation, the proper Instructions &c can be expedited.

I am sorry to learn that any Letter of mine should have given Offence, but I conclude that this Effect must follow from many Parts of my Writings and Conduct, because the steady Pursuit of what appears to be the true Line of Duty will necessarily cross the various oblique Views of Interest & Opinion. To offend is sometimes a Fault, always a Misfortune. The Letter in Question is, I suppose, under the date of the Eleventh of December, of which I inclose you a Copy. Let me at the same time assure you that in all your excellent Letter of the thirteenth Instant, I must esteem the Clause now in question because it contains that useful Information which is least common. I will make no Apologies for the Letter to any one because Apologies are rarely useful, and where the Intention has been good, they are to candid Minds unnecessary. Possessed of the Facts, you can guard against

Misrepresentation; and I have ever found that to be the most hostile Weapon which either my personal or political Enemies have been able to wield against me.

I have not *even yet* seen the Resolutions of your Legislature relative to an Extension of the Powers of Congress. I had supposed the same Reason for them which you have expressed. Indeed Power is generally such a darling Object with weak Minds that they must feel extreme Reluctance to bid it farewell; neither do I believe that any Thing will induce a general Consent to part with it, but a perfect Sense of absolute Necessity. This may arise from two Sources, the one of Reason and the other of Feeling; the former more safe and more uncertain; the latter always severe and often dangerous. It is, my dear Sir, in Circumstances like this, that a patriot Mind, seeking the great good of the Whole on enlightened Principles, can best be distinguished from those vulgar Souls whose narrow Opticks can see but the little Circle of selfish Concerns. Unhappily such Souls are but too common, and but too often fill the Seats of Dignity and Authority. A firm, wise, manly System of federal Government is what I once wished, what I now Hope, what I dare not expect, but what I will not despair of.

Your Description of the Mode of Collecting Taxes, contains an Epitome of the Follies which prevail from One End of the Continent to the Other. There is no End to the Absurdity of human Nature. Mankind seem to delight in Contrast & Paradox; for surely Nothing else could sanctify (during a Contest on the precise Point of being taxed by our own Consent) the arbitrary Police which on this Subject almost universally prevails. God grant you Success in your Views to amend it. Your Ideas on the Subject are perfectly correspondent to my own. As to your Doubt on the Mode of collecting it, I would wish to obviate it by the Observation that the farther off we can remove the Appointment of Collectors from popular Influence, the more effectual will be their Operations, and the more they conform to the Views of Congress the more effectually will they enable that Body to provide for general Defence. In political Life, the Creature will generally pay some Deference to ⟨the Creator. The⟩ having a double Set of Officers is indeed an Evil, but a good Thing is not always to be rejected because of that necessary Portion of Evil which in the Course of Things must be attached to it. Neither is this a necessary Evil, for with a proper federal Government, Army, Navy & Revenue the civil Administration might well be provided for by a Stamp Act, Roads by Turnpikes, and Navigation by Tolls.

The Account you give of the State is by no Means flattering, and the more true it appears, the more Concern it gives me. The Loan I hope will be compleated; and I wish the *whole* Amount of the Tax may be collected. The forage Plan I have disagreed to, and inclose for your Information the Copy of my Letter on that Subject to the Quarter Master General. I believe your State is exhausted, but perhaps even you consider it as being more so than it is. The Certificates which now form an useless load will (if the United States adopt, and the several States agree to a Plan now before Congress) become valuable Property: This will afford great Relief. The Scarcity of Money also may be immediately relieved, if the Love of popular favor would so far give Way to the Love of public Good as to inforce plentiful Taxation. The Necessity of having Money will always produce Money. The Desire of having it produces, you see, so much as is necessary to gratify the Desire of enjoying foreign Luxuries. Turn the Stream which now flows in the Channels of Commerce to those of Revenue, and the Business is compleated. Unfortunately for us this is an Operation which requires Fortitude, Perseverance, Virtue, and which cannot be effected by the weak or wicked Minds, who have only partial, private or interested Views.

When I consider the Exertions which the Country you possess has already made under striking Disadvantages and with astonishing

Prodigality of national wealth by pernicious Modes of applying it, I persuade myself that regular consistent Efforts would produce much ⟨more than you suppose.⟩

For your accurate, clear and comprehensive Descriptions of general and particular Characters, Sentiments and Opinions, accept my sincere Thanks and warm Approbation. They do equal Justice to your Talents both for Observation & Description.

Mr. Duer's Attention to the Business of his Contract is very pleasing to me and honorable to himself. I am sorry that he should loose by it, but to avoid this as much ⟨as possible I am determined to support him by liberal Advances so soon as it shall be in my Power to do it.

I pray you to believe me very sincerely your Friend and Servant

RM.

To Alexander Hamilton, 29 August 1782

Office of Finance [Philadelphia] 29. Augt. 1782

Sir,

I have for certain Reasons thought it expedient to issue no more Orders on Mr. Swanwick *payable at Sight* but destroy them as they are brought in. And as the larger Bills of Exchange mentioned in my Letter of the nineteenth of July last tho an excellent Mode of general Remittance will not by Reason of the Greatness of the Sums answer the Ends intended by the States in making my Notes receivable in Taxes, I have thought it alike useful to the Public and convenient to the People to issue Notes in the following Form. At sixty Days from the Date pay on Account of the United States   Dollars to or Bearer. These Notes are signed by me directed to Mr. Swanwick and are for Sums of one hundred, fifty, thirty and twenty Dollars each of them have in the Body of the Bill in Water Marks. *United States* and the Bills of one hundred Dollars have a Water Mark 1. & those of fifty 2. those of thirty 3 and those of twenty 4. You will receive them as Cash and when you have Cash you will give it for them in like Manner as for Bank Notes and that without any Regard whether they have any Time still to run or whether the sixty Days are expired.

I am Sir your most obedient Servant

RM

To George Washington, 29 August 1782

Office of Finance 29th August 1782

Sir,

I am to request your Excellency that out of the Sums which may come to your Hands in the Manner already mentioned, You will endeavour after making the Payments of which I informed you in a former Letter, to transmit three thousand Dollars more to Mr Duer at Albany. I am Sir with great Respect, Your Excellency's Most Obedient & Humble Servant

Robt Morris

To George Washington, 30 August 1782

Office of Finance 30. Aug. 1782

Sir,

My Letter of the twenty night which is enclosed I have written for two Reasons one that you may be informed and I may Hand justified in every Respect should the Event take Place the other which is the principal on that you may found a warm Application on it to the States—You will I hope keep <u>this</u> entirely to yourself. You will see that I have not entrusted a View of it to Secretary or to any of the Clerks—The Effect of you Application must depend on raising a very general Alarm. I have the Honor to be with great Esteem and Respect you Excelly most obedient & humble Servant

R.M.

To Alexander Hamilton, 6 September 1782

Office of Finance [Philadelphia] 6th. September 1782

Sir.

I have received your Favor dated at Albany on the 25th. of last Month, with the Enclosures. I am much obliged by your attention in the Business you allude to, and knowing that your abilities and Zeal to promote the public Good are equal to the most arduous Undertakings I have no doubt but your Endeavours will be successful.

I am Sir Your most obedient Servant

Robt Morris

To George Washington, 9 September 1782

Office of Finance Septr 9th 1782

Dear Sir

The dates of the enclosed Letters will shew you my extreme Reluctance to wound your mind with the Anxieties which distress my own.

At the time they were written I was sore pressed on every quarter, but a gleam of Hope broke in upon me and induced me to bear up still longer against the Torrent of demands which was rushing upon me. These would long since have overwhelmed me had I been supported <u>only</u> by the Revenues drawn from the States. At length however my other resources which are nearly exhausted have become useless by the total Stagnation of Trade oweing to the expectations of Peace. There is therefore no other dependance left but the Taxes, and unless these become immediately productive of Funds sufficient to feed our Troops, I need not describe the Consequences. Already I am in Arrear in spite of all my Efforts. I am determined however to continue those Efforts to the last moment, but at present I really know not which way to turn myself. With the most Sincere esteem I am My Dear Sir Your most obedient & most humble Servant

Robt Morris

To Alexander Hamilton, 12 September 1782

Office of Finance [Philadelphia] 12. Septem. 1782

Sir,

Enclosed you will find Copies of my Letters of the twenty-ninth and thirtieth of July to Congress. I know not what Determinations they may come to on these Subjects but I transmit the Letters that you may be possessed of the Matter, fully obviate Misrepresentations, and inculcate at proper Opportunities those Principles of national Integrity which are essential to our Safety.

I am Sir with Esteem your most obedient Servt.

RM

P.S. You will also find enclosed Acts of Congress of the fourth and tenth Instant.

To George Washington, 12 September 1782

Office of Finance 12th September 1782

Sir,

I have before me your Excellency's several Letters of the 23d of August, and 2d & 4th Instant. I have now the Pleasure to inform you that General Cornell has agreed to accept the Office of Inspector of the Contracts &c. for your Army, and will soon proceed on the Business of his Department. I hope you may find Relief from this Appointment, and that it may prove perfectly agreable to you. If Mr Skinner was in Town, I did not see him, but I have thought it best to send James Mullins to attend the Commissioners with the Accounts. He can act as a Clerk for them during the Meeting. My chief Reasons for sending him, are, that he made up the Accounts of Issues, as Clerk to the Commissary General, that he affords a safe Conveyance for the five hundred Dollars mentioned in your Excellency's Letter, and that he may perhaps prove useful to the Commissioners. I am entirely persuaded of the Propriety of such Instructions as your Excellency may think proper to give as to the Accounts. With perfect Respect I have the Honor to be Your most obedient & humble Servant

Robt Morris

To Alexander Hamilton, 17 September 1782

Office of Finance [Philadelphia] 17. Sepr. 1782

Sir,

I received by the Post your Favor of the seventh Instant. I have always suspected that the disorderly Manner of doing Business in many Parts of this Continent has enabled People to commit Frauds or what is the same thing as to the Public Loss covered their Ignorance Indolence and Extravagance. It is only by probing these Matters to the Bottom that the Extent of the Evil can be discovered and I shall be very happy that the Legislature step in with their Authority to the Aid of my Efforts. The Commissioner for settling the Accounts of your State shall be appointed as soon as a proper Person offers which no one has yet done. You have formed a proper Conception as to what were my Views in enquiring into the Rates of Depreciation which are now of but little Consequence indeed of none unless to know what Degree of real Taxation may be necessary to absorp the Remainder of that useless Paper Mass which has so long burthened all our Movements.

I am by no Means surprized at the Backwardness which you meet with from public Officers in rendering an Account of Supplies furnished to the Public. The several States and many of their public Officers have so long been in the Habit of boasting superior Exertions that what was at first Assumption has advanced along the Road of Belief to perfect Conviction. And the Delusion is now kept up by the Darkness in which it is inveloped. It is not impossible that somewhat both of Interest and Importance is concerned in leading the Public Officers to keep up the Mistery.

I am Sir your most obedient and humble Servant

RM.

To George Washington, 19 September 1782

Office of Finance 19th September 1782

Sir

I have received your Excellency's Letter of the eleventh Instant enclosing the Copy of a Letter from Colo. Varick. I enclose herein Notes to the amount of eight hundred Dollars for which I am to pray that your Excellency will take and transmit his Receipt as for so much received of Mr Swanwick for which he Colo. Varick is to be accountable. I am with Respect Your Excellency's most obedient & humble Servant

Robt Morris

To George Washington, 19 September 1782

Office of Finance 19th September 1782

Sir,

The Bearer of this Letter, Mr Ezekiel Cornell is appointed to be the Inspector of the Contracts for your Army. I have a perfect Reliance both on his Zeal & Integrity, and am persuaded that your Excellency may repose the utmost Confidence in him. I write this Letter to recommend him to your favorable Notice, and to pray that he may meet your Excellency's Aid in performing the Business committed to him. With perfect Respect I have the Honor to be Your Excellency's most obedient & humble Servant

Robt Morris

To John Adams, 25 September 1782

Office of Finance 25th September 1782

Sir

I do myself the Honor to enclose for your Perusal Acts of Congress of the twenty seventh of November and third of December 1781, and the fourteenth and twenty third Instant. In Consequence I have to request that all Bills hitherto drawn by Authority of Congress be paid, and the Accounts of those Transactions closed. After this is done, and I hope and beleive that while I am writing this Letter it may have been already accomplished, you will be freed from the Torment and Perplexity of attending to Money Matters. I am persuaded that this Consideration will be highly pleasing to you, as such Things must necessarily interfere with your more important Attentions.

I have long since requested the Secretary of foreign Affairs to desire you would appoint an Agent or Attorney here to receive and remit your Salary, which will be paid quarterly: in the mean Time it is paid to him for your Use. As to any contingent Expenses which may arise, I shall readily make the necessary Advances upon Mr Livingston's Application. These Arrangements will I hope be both useful and agreable to you.

I am, Sir, With perfect Respect Your Excellency's Most obedient & humble Servant

Robt Morris

To John Adams, 25 September 1782

Philadelphia September 25th: 1782

Sir

Your letter of the 22nd April has been delivered to me by Mr. Peter Paulus to whom I shall most chearfully Afford such advice or countenance as he may stand in need of. But it seems this Gentlemans wants are not confined to those Points, he applies to me for a Supply of Money to set up his Trade, I have explained that your desires in his favor do not extend to the advance of Money, and I am exposed by my Station to too many such Applications, they have indeed proved extreamly inconvenient and I am compelled to resist them all in my Power, it is probable that I shall be obliged to Number this Gentleman in the list of those whose Necessities encrease my advances.

I congratulate your Excellency most Sincerely on the event of the 19th April from which I hope and expect that our Country will derive essential benefits.

With great Respect and Esteem I have the Honor to be Your Excellencys most obedient & hble Servt:

Robt Morris

To Benjamin Franklin (Two Letters), 25 September 1782

I.

Office of Finance 25th September 1782

Sir

I do myself the Honor to enclose for your Perusal Acts of Congress of the twenty seventh of November and third of December 1781 and the fourteenth and twenty third Instant. In Consequence I have to request that all Bills hitherto drawn by Authority of Congress be paid and the Accounts of those Transactions closed. After this is done, and I hope and believe that while I am writing this Letter it may have been already accomplished you will be freed from the Torment and Perplexity of attending to Money Matters. I am persuaded that this Consideration will be highly pleasing to you as such Things must necessarily interfere with your more important Attentions.

I have long since requested the Secretary of foreign Affairs to desire you would appoint an Agent or Attorney here to receive and remit your Salary which will be paid Quarterly, in the mean Time it is paid to him for your Use. As to any contingent Expences which may arise I shall readily make the necessary Advances upon Mr. Livingston's Application. These Arrangements will I hope be both useful and agreable to you.

I am Sir with perfect Respect Your Excellency's most obedient & humble Servant

Robt Morris

II.

Office of Finance 25th. September 1782.

Sir

In my Letter of the 27th of November last I requested your Excellency to cause Purchases to be made of certain Articles contained in an Invoice exhibited to me from the War Office. The Difficulties which have hitherto attended every Purchase and Shipment of Goods on public Account and other Circumstances have determined me to obtain all future Supplies by Contracts here, and therefore I am to request that no future Purchases may be made. I have directed Mr. Barclay to send out whatever may have been already purchased on public Account.

With perfect Respect I have the Honor to be Sir Your most obedient & humble Servant

Robt Morris

To George Washington, 25 September 1782

Office of finance 25 Sepr 1782

Dear Sir

I have just now received your Letters of the twenty second Instant. The Doubt you are in with Respect to my Letters of the twenty ninth and thirtieth of August will be easily resolved on an Inspection of them. The Letter of the twenty ninth is of a Nature to be transmitted, if necessary, to the several States. That of the thirtieth explains my Reasons for writing the other, and the Paragraph you have extracted will be quite clear by inserting a Word Thus. "you will I hope keep this (Letter) entirely to yourself" &ca.

The necessity of your Writing to the States, as well as the Matter which you will have to mention must depend very much on the Conclusions which Genl Cornell shall come to with the Contractors or with Colo. Wadsworth. You will determine as you find best.

When I found that the Supplies of Money from the States would prove so very inadequate as they have done, I determined to check all other Expence and think only of feeding the Army. This Conduct I am now rigidly pursuing, and shall endeavor to accomplish the Object and to pay the Engagements I have already made without which my Credit (which has alone supported us hitherto) must be ruined.

We have lately had an Arrival here of Linnens which the Cloathier says are sufficient to make thirty thousand Shirts, but he is already so much indebted to the poor People who have worked for him and who are starving for want of their Wages, that he cannot procure Credit to get them made. Money I have none and even if he could run inDebt still further, it would only increase the Mischief for I see no Prospect of Payment, and the while People who live in Ease and even in Luxury avoid under various Pretexts the Payment of Taxes a great Portion of the Public Expence is borne by poor Women who earn their daily Bread by their daily Labor. I am Sir, your most obedient & humble Servant

Robt Morris

To John Adams, 27 September 1782

Office of Finance 27th Septem 1782

Sir

I do myself the Pleasure to congratulate you on the Success of your patriotic Labors in Holland. The general Tribute paid to your Abilities on this Occasion will so well dispense with the Addition of my feeble Voice that I shall spare your Delicacy the Pain of expressing my Sentiments.

The enclosed Resolutions and Copies of Letters will convey to you so fully the Views of Congress, and explain so clearly my Conceptions on the Subject, that very little need to be added. If the Application to France should fail of Success, which I cannot permit myself to believe, you will then have a new Opportunity of shewing the Influence you have acquired over the Minds of Men in the Country where you reside, and of exerting it in the Manner most beneficial to our Country.

Before I conclude this Letter I must congratulate your Excellency on the Success of the Loan you have already opened, and which I consider as being by this Time compleated.

With perfect Respect I have the Honor to be Sir Your Excellency's most obedient & humble Servant

Robt Morris

To Benjamin Franklin (Two Letters), 27 September 1782

I.

Office of Finance 27th Septemr. 1782

Sir,

I have the Honor to enclose the Copy of Acts of Congress of the fourteenth and twenty third Instant, together with the Copy of my Letter of the thirtieth of July covering the Estimates for the Year 1783. These Estimates are not yet finally decided on. By the Act of the fourteenth you are (as you perceive) instructed to communicate the Resolution for borrowing four Millions of Dollars to his most Christian Majesty,—and first to assure His Majesty of the high Sense which the United States in Congress assembled entertain of his Friendship and generous Exertions; secondly their Reliance on a Continuance of them; and thirdly the Necessity of applying to his Majesty on the present Occasion. From this, and even more particularly from the Act of the twenty third, you will see that it is the wish of Congress to obtain this Money from or by Means of the King. After the decisive Expressions contained in these Resolutions of the Sense of our Sovereign, I am sure that it is unnecessary for me to attempt any

Thing like Argument to induce your Exertions. I shall therefore rather confine myself to giving Information.

The grateful Sense of the King's Exertions which has so warmly impressed your Bosom, operates with undiminished Force upon Congress; and, what is of more Importance in a Country like ours, has the strongest Influence upon the whole Whig Interest of America. I have no Doubt but the King's Minister here has given his Court regular Information on this and every other Subject of equal Importance, and therefore any general Assurances on your Part will be complimentary and in some Degree superfluous. But there is a Kind of Knowledge not easily attainable by Foreigners in any Country, particularly on such a Matter as the present. It is not amiss therefore that I should convey it to you, and your good Sense will apply it in the most proper Manner. You (of all Men in the World) are not now to learn that the sower english Prejudice against every Thing french had taken deep Root in the Minds of America. It could not have been expected that this should be obliterated in a Moment: But by Degrees almost every Trace of it has been effaced. The Conduct of Britain has weaned us from our Attachments, and those very Attachments have been transferred in a great Measure to France. Whatever Remains of monarchical Disposition exist are disposing themselves fast to a Connection with the french Monarchy: For the british Adherents begin to feel the Pangs of a deep Despair; which must generate as deep Aversion. The british Army here felt the national Haughtiness encreased by the Contempt which as Englishmen they could not but feel for those who had combined against the Freedom of their own Country. Every Part of their Conduct therefore towards the Tories while they flattered themselves with Victory shewed how much they despised their American Friends. Now that a Reverse of Fortune has brought on a little Consideration, they find a total Seperation from this Country unavoidable: They must feel for the Fate of their Country; they must therefore hate, but they must respect us too, while their own Adherents are both detested and despised. Treated thus like common Prostitutes it is not in Human Nature so much to forgive as not to feel in Return. Since General Carleton's Arrival, or rather since the Change of Ministers, the British have shewn that their Intention is, if possible, to conciliate the Rulers of America, and by the Influence of a common Language and similar Laws, with the Force of ancient Habits and mutual Friendships not yet forgotten, not only to renew again the commercial Intercourse, but to substitute a new federal Connection to their ancient Sovereignty and Dominion.

The Assurance therefore which Congress has directed you to make must not be considered in the Number of those idle Compliments which are the common Currency or small Change of a Court. It is an Assurance important, because it is founded in Truth; and more important still, because it is dictated by the Affections of a whole People. If I may venture an Opinion still farther, it is principally important, because of the critical Situation of Things.— The sudden Change of Britain from Vengeance and War to Kindness and Conciliation, must have Effects, and those Effects, whether they be Contempt or Affection, will depend less perhaps on them than upon Others. It cannot be doubted that they will ring all the Changes upon their usual Theme of gallic Ambition. They will naturally insinuate the Idea that France will neglect us when we have served her Purposes, and it would be very strange if they did not find some Converts among that Class of People who would sacrifice to present Ease, every future Consideration. What I have said will I am confident put your Mind into the Train of Reflections which arise out of our Situation; and you will draw the proper Conclusions and make a proper Application of them.

Congress have directed you further to express to the King their Reliance on a Continuance of his Friendship and Exertions. I have no Doubt that a full Beleif of this Reliance will be easily inculcated. Indeed I rather apprehend that we shall be considered

232

as relying too much on France, or in other Words doing too little for ourselves. There can be no sort of Doubt that a mighty good Argument may be raised on the usual Position that the Nation which will not help itself does not merit the Aid of Others, and it would be easy to tell us that we must put our own Shoulders to the Wheel before we call upon Hercules. In short if the Application be refused or evaded, Nothing can be easier than to assign very good Reasons why it is done. But you have very justly remarked in one of your Letters that it is possible to get the better in Argument, and to get Nothing else. So it might be here. True Sagacity consists in making proper Distinctions, and true Wisdom in taking Determinations according to those Distinctions. Twenty Years hence when Time and Habit have settled and compleated the federal Constitution of America Congress will not think of relying on any other than that Being to whose Justice they appealed at the Commencement of their Opposition. But there is a Period in the Progress of Things, a Crisis between the Ardor of Enthusiasm and the Authority of Laws, when much Skill and Management are necessary to those who are charged with administering the Affairs of a Nation. I have already taken Occasion to observe that the present Moment is rendered particularly critical by the Conduct of the Enemy, and I would add here (if I dared even in Idea to seperate Congress from those they represent) that now above all other Times Congress must rely on the Exertions of their Ally. This Sentiment would open to his Majesty's Ministers many Reflections the least of which has a material Connection with the Interests of his Kingdom: But an Argument of no little Weight is that which applies itself directly to the Bosom of a young and generous Prince, who would be greatly wounded to see that Temple, dedicated to Humanity, which he has taken so much Pains to rear, fall at once into Ruins by a Remission of the last Cares which are requisite for giving Solidity to the Structure. I think I might add that there are some Occasions on which a good Heart is the best Counsellor.

The third Topic which Congress have directed you to dwell upon is the Necessity of their present Applications, and it is this which falls most particularly within my Department; for I doubt not that every Sentiment on the other Objects has been most forcibly inculcated by the Minister of Foreign Affairs. I might write Volumes on our Necessities and not convey to you so accurate an Idea as by the Relation of a single Fact which you may see in the Public News Papers. It is that the Requisitions of last October for eight Millions had produced on the first Day of this Month only One hundred and twenty five thousand Dollars. You are so perfectly a Master of every Thing which relates to Calculation that I need not state any Thing of our Expences. You know also what were our Resources beyond Taxation and therefore you have every Material for forming an accurate Idea of our Distresses. The Smallness of the Sum which has been paid will doubtless astonish you, and it is only by Conversation or a long History that you could see why it has been no greater. The People are undoubtedly able to pay, but they have easily persuaded themselves into a Conviction of their own Inability, and in a Government like ours the Beleif creates the Thing. The Modes of laying and levying Taxes are vicious in the Extreme: The Faults can be demonstrated, but would it not be a new Thing under the Sun that People should obey the Voice of Reason? Experience of the Evil is always a Preliminary to Amendment, and is frequently unable to effect it. Many who see the Right-road and approve of it, continue to follow the wrong road because it leads to Popularity. The Love of Popularity is our endemial Disease and can only be checked by a Change of Seasons. When the People have had dear Experience of the Consequences of not being taxed, they will probably work the proper Amendment; but our Necessities in the Interim are not the less severe. To tell America in such a Situation that she should reform her interior Administration would be very good Advice; but to neglect affording her Aid, and thereby to lose the capital Objects of the War, would be very bad Conduct. The Necessity of the present Application for Money arises from the Necessity of drawing by Degrees the Bands of Authority together, establishing the Power of Government over a People impatient of Control, and confirming the federal Union of the several States, by correcting Defects in the general Constitution. In a Word it arises from the Necessity of doing that infinite Variety of Things which are to be done in an infant Government placed in such delicate Circumstances that the People must be woed and won to do their Duty to themselves and pursue their own Interests. This Application also becomes the more necessary in order to obviate the Efforts of that british Faction which the Enemy are now attempting to excite among us. Hitherto indeed they have been unsuccessful unless perhaps with a very few Men who are under the Influence of disappointed Ambition; but much Care will be required when their Plans are brought to greater Maturity. The savage Inroads on our Frontiers have kept up the general Horror of Britain. The great Captures made on our Coasts have also rather enraged than Otherwise, tho such Captures have always the twofold Operation of making People wish for Peace as well as for Revenge. But when the Enemy shall quit our Coasts (and they have already stopped the Inroads of their savage Allies) if the People are urged at once to pay heavy unusual Taxes, it may draw forth and give weight to Arguments which the boldest Emissaries would not at present hazard the Use of.

I have already observed that Congress wish to obtain this Money either from or by Means of the King. The most cautious Prudence will justify us in confiding to the Wisdom of his Ministers the Portrait of our Situation. But it might not be very wise to explain to Others those Reasons for the Application which lie so deep in the Nature of Things as easily to escape superficial Observers. I shall enclose a Copy of this Letter to Mr. Adams, and you will find herein a Copy of what I say to him on the Subject.— I hope the Court will take such Measures as to render any Efforts on his Part unnecessary. But you and he must decide on what is best for your Country. I must trouble you still farther on this Subject with the Mention of what you will indeed collect from a cursory Reading of the Resolutions—that Congress have the strongest Reason for their Procedure when they direct your utmost Endeavors to effect this Loan, notwithstanding the Information contained in your Letters. If the War is to be carried on this Aid is indispensible, and when obtained will enable us to act powerfully in the Prosecution of it. If a Peace takes place it is still necessary, and as it is the last request which we shall then have Occasion to make I cannot think that it will be refused. In a Word, Sir, we must have it.— With perfect Respect I have the Honor to be, Sir, Your Excellency's most obedient & humble Servant

Robt Morris.

To Benjamin Franklin, 28 September 1782

Philadelphia. 28 Sept. 1782

Sir,

In my Letter of yesterday, I have dwelt on the resolutions of Congress, in the manner requir'd by my duty as their Servant. I will now add a few hints, as Your friend. Your Enemies industriously publish that your age & indolence have unabled you for your station, that a Sense of obligation to France Seals your lips when you should ask their aid, & that (whatever your friends may say to the contrary) both your connections & Influence at Court are extremely feeble. I need not tell you that Messieurs Lee & company are among the foremost who make these assertions, & many others not worth mention, I should not have given you the pain of reading even these but that (as you will see from the resolution of the twenty third instant) Congress have believed your grateful sensibilities might render you unwilling to apply with all that warmth which the sense of their Necessities convinces them is necessary. In addition to the general reflection how envy has pursued superior merit in all Ages, You will draw a farther consolation from this, that many who censure you are well disposed to cast like censure on France, & would fain describe her as acting only the part of self interest, without a wishe to render us effectual aid. You will I am sure attribute what I now say to a friendly desire of apprizing you of things useful for you to know, & you will so act, as to convince every man that your exertions are what I verily believe them to be.

I am Sir, Your most obedient Servant

Robt Morris

To Benjamin Franklin, 30 September 1782

Office of Finance 30th September 1782

Sir,

I have received and already acknowledged your Letters of the 9th January, two of the 28th January, those of the 30th January, 4th March 9th March and 30th March. The Acknowledgement of the three last was by mine of the first of July. I am now to acknowledge yours of the eighth of April and twenty fifth of June. I have written to you since the Ninth of March (which you acknowledge the Receipt of in yours of the twenty fifth of June) on the twenty second and twenty third of March, on the seventeenth of April, on the seventeeth, and twice on the eighteenth and twenty third of May, also on the twenty ninth of May, twenty sixth of June, first and fifth of July.

It is in some Respects fortunate that our Stores were not shipped, because, as you observe, they might have been taken; but I hope they are now on the Way, for if they are to lie in France at a heavy

Expence of Storage &c while we suffer for the Want, it will be even worse than if they were taken. You will find by the Letters which are to go with this, that Mr. Barclay is prohibited from making any more Purchases on Account of the United States. I confess that I disapprove of those he has made: for the Purchase of unnecessary Things, *because they are cheap*, appears to be a very great Extravagance. We want Money as much as any Thing else, and the World must form a strange Idea of our Management, if, while we are begging to borrow, we leave vast Magazines of Cloathing to rot at Brest, and purchase Others to be shipped from Holland. I have said Nothing on this Subject to Mr. Barclay, because the Thing, having been done, could not be undone, and because the pointed Resolutions of Congress on the Subject will prevent any more such Operations. What I have now said however will, I hope, lead you to urge on him the Necessity of making immediate Shipments of all the Stores in Europe. A Merchant does not sustain the total Loss of his Goods by their Detention, but the Public do. The Service of the Year must be accomplished within the Year by such Means as the Year affords. The Detention of our Goods has obliged me to purchase Cloathing and other Articles at a great Expence, while those very Things were lying about at different Places in Europe. I am sure that any Demand made for Money on our Part must appear extraordinary, while we shew so great Negligence of the Property we possess. The Funds, therefore, which were obtained for the Year 1781, are not only rendered useless during that Year, but so far pernicious as that the Disposition of them will naturally influence a Dimunition of the Grants made for the Year 1782.

You mention in yours of the twenty fifth of June, that you would send enclosed the Account of the Replacing of the Fayette's Cargo, if it could be copied in Season. As it did not arrive, I shall expect it by the next Opportunity.

238

I have received Mr. Grand's Accounts, which are not stated in the Manner I wish; and in Consequence I have written to him by this Opportunity to alter them. I have desired him to give your Account Credit for every Livre received previous to the current Year, including therein the Loan of 10.000.000 *l.t.* in Holland, tho a Part of it may not have been received until this Year. I have desired him to debit your Account for every Expenditure made by your Order, which will include all your Acceptances of Bills &c, and of Course Mr. De Beaumarchais' Bills, if they shall have been paid. Finally, I have desired him to carry the Balance of your Account to mine, in which he is to credit all Monies received for the current Year: for Instance the six Millions (and the other six, if they are obtained) together with such Monies as may come to his Hands from the Loan opened for the United States by Messrs Willink Stapherst &c.—

I did expect to have had some Kind of Adjustment made by this Time of Captain Gillon's Affair, but Congress referred much of it to a Committee with whom it has long slept; but I have informed Mr. Gillon that I must have a Settlement, and at present I wait a little for the Determination of Congress.—

You mention to me that the Interest on the 10,000.000 *l.t.* Dutch Loan is payable at Paris annually on the fifth of November at four per Cent. I must request you to send me the particular Details on this Subject, such as who it is payable to, and by whom, that I may make proper Arrangements for a punctual Performance, so as not to incur unnecessary Expence. I presume that the first Year's Interest may be discharged before this reaches you; but at any Rate I enclose a Letter to Mr. Grand, to prevent any ill Consequences which might arise from a Deficiency of Payment.

I informed you in mine of the first of July, that Congress had resolved to appoint a Commissioner to settle the public Accounts in Europe: This is not done, but they have reconsidered and committed the Resolution. Where the Thing will end I do not know. I think however that eventually they must send over some Person for the Purpose.

The Appearances of Peace have been materially disserviceable to us here, and general Cautions on the Subject from Europe, and the most pointed Applications from the public Officers, will not prevent that Lethargy which the very Name of Peace extends thro' all the States. I hope Measures will be taken by our public Ministers in Europe to prevent the People from falling into the Snares which the Enemy has laid. Undue Security in Opinion is generally very hurtful in Effect; and I dread the Consequences of it here if the War is to be carried on, which is not improbable.

I am, Sir, Your most obedient & humble Servant,

Robt Morris

To Benjamin Franklin, 1 October 1782

Office of Finance 1st October 1782—

Sir,—

In my Letter of the twenty seventh of September last I express my Wish "that the Court of Spain should give Orders for the Shipment of a Million of Dollars at the Havanna free of Duties, and *to be convoyed by One or more Ships of the Line* to an American Port, &c." Upon farther Reflection I am induced to believe that the Court of Spain will not readily go into the whole of this Arrangement; for altho they may & probably will agree to so much of it as will procure them an Equivalent in France for the Million Dollars to be shipped from the Havanna, yet there are Reasons to doubt whether they will convoy the Washington hither. I wish you therefore (should you meet with Difficulties in that Quarter) to apply to the Court for such Convoy. I wish it may consist of a Ship of the Line, because none but Frigates will cruize on this Coast during the Winter, and therefore One Ship of the Line will afford more Protection than two or three Frigates. However this will depend entirely on the Convenience or Inconvenience which may attend the Business. I shall communicate both this Letter and that of the twenty seventh to the Chevalier de la Luzerne, on whose Representations I rely much, as well for procuring the Aid asked for, as for accomplishing the necessary Arrangements after it is procured.

I am, Sir, Your most obedient & humble Servant

Robt Morris

To Alexander Hamilton, 5 October 1782

Office of Finance [Philadelphia] 5th October 1782

Sir,

I have now before me your Letters of the fourteenth and twenty first of last Month. I am sorry to find that you are less sanguine in your pecuniary Expectations than the Governor appears to be, for I have always found that the worst forebodings on this Subject are the truest. You will find at the Bottom of this Letter a List of all those which I have hitherto received from you. I think they have all been already acknowledged, but lest they should not, you will see in One Moment by the List whether any have miscarried.

I am not surprized to find that the Contractors apply with their Paper in the first Instance to the Receiver and Collectors: This I expected, because much of that Paper is not fit for other Purposes. Some of it however which is payable to the Bearer is calculated for circulation, which you observe is not so general as otherwise it might have been; by Reason of the Largeness of the

Sums expressed in the Notes. Mr. Duer's Letters contain the same Sentiment.

In issuing this Paper one principal View was to facilitate the Payment of Taxes by obviating the too general (tho unjust) Complaint of the Want of a circulating Medium. In substituting Paper to Specie the first Obstacle to be encountered was the total Diffidence which had arisen from the late Profusion of it. Had a considerable Quantity been thrown into the Hands of that Class of the People whose Ideas on the Subject of Money are more the Offspring of Habit than of Reason, it must have depreciated. That this Apprehension was just is clear from this Fact, that the Paper I first issued, and the Bank Paper which came out after it, did depreciate from ten to fifteen per Cent in the Eastern States not withstanding all the Precautions which were used. If I had not taken immediate Measures to create a Demand for it on the Spot, and to stop Issues to that Quarter it's Credit would have been totally lost for a Time, and not easily restored; besides that, the Quantities which were pouring in from thence would have done Mischief here. Confidence is a Plant of very slow Growth, and our political Situation is not too favorable to it. I am therefore very unwilling to hazard the Germ of a Credit which will in its greater Maturity become very useful. If my Notes circulate only among mercantile People, I do not regret it, but rather wish that the Circulation may for the present be confined to them and to the wealthier Members of other Professions. It is Nothing but the greater Convenience which will induce People to prefer any Kind of Paper to the precious Metals, and this Convenience is principally felt in large Sums. Whenever the Shop Keepers in general discover that my Paper will answer as a Remittance to the principal Ports, and will be readily exchanged by the Receivers, they will as readily exchange it for other People. When the People in general find that the Shop Keepers receive it freely, they will begin to look after it, and not before: For you must know that whatever fine plausible Speeches may be made on this Subject, the Farmers will not give full Credit to Money merely because it will pay Taxes, for that is an Object they are not very violently devoted to; but that Money which goes freely at the Store and the Tavern, will be sought after as greedily as those Things which the Store and the Tavern contain. Still, however, your Objection remains good, that the Traffickings in which the greater Part of the Community engage do not require Sums so large as Twenty Dollars. This I shall readily acknowledge; but you will observe that there is infinitely less Danger that large Notes, which go only thro the Hands of intelligent People, will be counterfeited than small ones, which come to the Possession of illiterate Men. When public Credit is firmly established, the little Shocks it receives from the Counterfeitors of Paper Money do not lead to material Consequences; but in the present ticklish State of Things there is just Ground of Apprehension. Besides this, the Value of Paper will depend much upon the Interchanges of it for Specie, and these will not take place when there is a Circulation of small Paper. Lastly, I have to observe, that until more Reliance can be placed on the Revenues required, I dare not issue any very considerable Amount of this Paper, lest I should be run upon for more than I could answer, and as the Circulation of what I dare issue by increasing the general Mass, enables People (so far as it goes) more easily to get hold of other Money, it consequently produces in its Degree that Object of facilitating Taxation which I had in View.

I am, Sir, Your most obedient & Humbl Servant

Robt Morris

To Alexander Hamilton, 5 October 1782

Office of Finance [Philadelphia] 5 Octo: 1782

Sir

I enclose you the Copy of an Act of the first Instant with the Copy of my Circular Letter to the Governors inclosing it. You will consider this Act as an Additional Evidence of the firm Determination of our Sovereign to persevere in those Systems which they have adopted. I recommend this Act to your serious and vigilant Attention in all its Parts. It is a mighty fashionable Thing to declaim on the Virtue and sufferings of the Army and it is a very common Thing for these very Declaimers to evade by one Artifice or another the Payment of those Taxes which alone can remove every Source of Complaint. Now Sir it is a matter of perfect Indifference by what Subterfuge this Evasion is effected whether by voting against Taxes or what is more usual agreeing to them in the first Instance but taking Care in the second to provide no competent Means to compel a Collection which cunning Device leaves the Army at last as a Kind of Pensionary upon the voluntary Contributions of good Whigs and suffers those of a different Complection to skulk and skreen themselves entirely from the Weight and Inconvenience. I am far from desiring to involve in general and indiscriminate Censure all the Advocates for wrong Measures. I know that much of it may be attributed to an Ignorance which exists both from the Want of proper Means and Materials of Instruction and from the Defect of Experience. But the Evil exists and you must labor assiduo[u]sly for the Remedy.

I am Sir your most obedient and humble Servant

RM

To Alexander Hamilton, 5 October 1782

Office of Finance [Philadelphia] 5 Octo: 1782

Sir

I enclose you the Copy of an Act of the first Instant with the Copy of my Circular Letter to the Governors inclosing it. You will consider this Act as an Additional Evidence of the firm Determination of our Sovereign to persevere in those Systems which they have adopted. I recommend this Act to your serious and vigilant Attention in all its Parts. It is a mighty fashionable Thing to declaim on the Virtue and sufferings of the Army and it is a very common Thing for these very Declaimers to evade by one Artifice or another the Payment of those Taxes which alone can remove every Source of Complaint. Now Sir it is a matter of perfect Indifference by what Subterfuge this Evasion is effected whether by voting against Taxes or what is more usual agreeing to them in the first Instance but taking Care in the second to provide no competent Means to compel a Collection which cunning Device leaves the Army at last as a Kind of Pensionary upon the voluntary Contributions of good Whigs and suffers those of a different Complection to skulk and skreen themselves entirely from the Weight and Inconvenience. I am far from desiring to involve in general and indiscriminate Censure all the Advocates for wrong Measures. I know that much of it may be attributed to an Ignorance which exists both from the Want of proper Means and Materials of Instruction and from the Defect of Experience. But the Evil exists and you must labor assiduo[u]sly for the Remedy.

I am Sir your most obedient and humble Servant

RM

To Benjamin Franklin, 5 October 1782

Office of Finance 5th. October 1782

Sir

I have the Pleasure to enclose you the Copy of an Act of Congress of the ninth of September last. I shall make no Comments on this Act which as it relieves you from farther Trouble and Anxiety on the Subject it relates to will I am sure be agreable.

I am Sir Your Excellency's most obedient & humble Servant

Robt Morris

To Alexander Hamilton, 5 October 1782

Office of Finance [Philadelphia] 5 Octo: 1782

Sir

I enclose you the Copy of an Act of the first Instant with the Copy of my Circular Letter to the Governors inclosing it. You will consider this Act as an Additional Evidence of the firm Determination of our Sovereign to persevere in those Systems which they have adopted. I recommend this Act to your serious and vigilant Attention in all its Parts. It is a mighty fashionable Thing to declaim on the Virtue and sufferings of the Army and it is a very common Thing for these very Declaimers to evade by one Artifice or another the Payment of those Taxes which alone can remove every Source of Complaint. Now Sir it is a matter of perfect Indifference by what Subterfuge this Evasion is effected whether by voting against Taxes or what is more usual agreeing to them in the first Instance but taking Care in the second to provide no competent Means to compel a Collection which cunning Device leaves the Army at last as a Kind of Pensionary upon the voluntary Contributions of good Whigs and suffers those of a different Complection to skulk and skreen themselves entirely from the Weight and Inconvenience. I am far from desiring to involve in general and indiscriminate Censure all the Advocates for wrong Measures. I know that much of it may be attributed to an Ignorance which exists both from the Want of proper Means and Materials of Instruction and from the Defect of Experience. But the Evil exists and you must labor assiduo[u]sly for the Remedy.

I am Sir your most obedient and humble Servant

RM

To Benjamin Franklin, 5 October 1782

Office of Finance 5th. October 1782

Sir

I have the Pleasure to enclose you the Copy of an Act of Congress of the ninth of September last. I shall make no Comments on this Act which as it relieves you from farther Trouble and Anxiety on the Subject it relates to will I am sure be agreable.

I am Sir Your Excellency's most obedient & humble Servant

Robt Morris

To George Washington, 5 October 1782

Office of Finance 5th October 1782

Sir

I do myself the Honor to enclose with an Act of Congress of the first Instant my two circular Letters of this Date, one to the several

Governors, and the other to the Receivers. I think it my Duty to communicate to you this Act that you may have an Opportunity at every convenient Season to shew the military Servants of the Country that their Sovereign is attentive to their just Claims. I have added Copies of my Letters that you may apprize any such Officers of Influence and Discretion as may be about to pass from your Army to the Legislatures, of the whole of what has passed on this Subject so that the Views and Efforts of all the public Servants being directed to the same Object may produce the desired Success. I am Sir Your most obedient & humble Servant

Robt Morris

To Benjamin Franklin (Three Letters), 7 October 1782

I.

Marine Office 7th. October 1782.—

Sir

This Letter will be delivered to you by Joshua Barney Esqr. a Lieutenant in the Navy of the United States, and now commanding the Packet Ship Washington. This young Gentleman is an Active, gallant Officer, who has already behaved very well on many Occasions, and I recommend him to your particular Notice and Attention from the Conviction that his Conduct will do Honor to those by whom he is patronized and introduced.

I am Sir Your most obedient & humble Servant

Robt Morris

II.

Office of Finance 7th. October 1782.

Sir

Captain Barney having been detained until this Day and it being probable that he will not arrive in Europe so early as I expected I am very doubtful whether it would be proper to send him to the Havanna but think it would be better he should return immediately hither because it is likely that the Negotiation I proposed will consume more time than he can spare. His Ship is small but she sails remarkably well and will therefore give us a good Chance of being well informed of the Situation of our Affairs. If there is likely to be any Delay or Difficulty in the Havanna Plan it will be best that you endeavor to obtain the Shipment of a considerable Sum in Europe on Board some of the King's frigates. At any Rate we must have Money and I think you may venture fifty thousand Crowns by this Vessel. You will see that Capt. Barney is put under your Directions and is to wait your Instructions but I must at the same time inform you that Congress have directed his Ship to be purchased and sent to France among other Things for the Purpose of obtaining a better Communication with their Servants and more frequent and accurate Intelligence from Europe you will see therefore the Propriety of dispatching her as speedily as possible and I think we may probably fall upon ways & Means to afford you frequent Opportunities of writing with a great Chance of Security.

I am Sir your most obedient and humble Servant

Robt Morris

III.

Office of Finance 7th October 1782

Dear Sir

In a Letter of the second Instant which I have just now received from the Head Quarters of the American Army is the following

Paragraph— In short, my dear Sir, the Want of Money gives rise to so many complaints and uneaseinesses, that without a portion of it, I fear the infection will spread from Officer to Soldier. It is most vexatious to see the parade of the states upon every occasion; They declare in the most pompous manner that they will never make peace but upon their own terms, and yet call upon them for the support of the war, and you may as well call upon the dead. If they persist in their present accursed system, I do not see but they must accept Peace upon any terms.

I am Sir your most obedient Servant

Robt Morris

P.S. I would have sent the whole Letter from which this is extracted but I have not time to put it in Cypher

To Alexander Hamilton, 15 October 1782

Office of Finance [Philadelphia] 15 Octo: 1782

Sir,

On perusing the Advertizement enclosed herewith you will see the Propriety of its having a general Circulation throughout the United States. I therefore request you will cause it to be published in the several News Papers that are printed in your State.

I am Sir Your most obedient & humble Servant

RM.

To George Washington, 15 October 1782

Office of Finance 15th-16 October 1782

Sir

I have received your Letters of the second, third and seventh Instant. There is no Man in America more heartily disposed than I am to remove from the Army and from all others who have Claims on the Public every just Ground of Complaint. But with the Means in my Power, how is it possible? I have been obliged to submit to Cancelling one Contract and forming another at one third advance on the former Price, for the Want of a meer Trifle compared with what we had a Right to expect. I am in advance on Credit to an Amount which you can scarcely form an Idea of altho I have declined every Expenditure not indispensible. That Part of the late arrival of Cloathing which is unfit for Soldiers Use is now Selling to pay off Debts contracted by the Cloathing Department during my Administration. Among these Debts are twelve thousand Dollars for needle Work done by People in extreme Indigence. The Cloathing which arrived fit for Officers wear was inadequate to the Purpose of Cloathing them all. The Division must have created Confusion and raised Disputes. If this had not been the Case still it would have been liable to the Inconveniences attending partial Payments and we should have been justly Reproached for having broken repeated Promises that no such Payments should take Place. Congress have done all in their Power to procure Money for the Army. My own Efforts I shall not dwell upon. If Money is obtained that will produce Satisfaction. I am sure that nothing else will. My Credit has already been on the Brink of Ruin. If that goes all is gone, but if it can be preserved there will in the last necessity be some Chance of making advances on Credit to the Army as well as to others. Thus Sir you will see that I look forwards as far as my distressed Situation will admit; but after all if the States cannot be prevailed on to make greater Exertions it is difficult to foresee where the Thing is to terminate.

I have this Day commissioned Major Turner as a Marine Commissary of Prisoners, and I trust he will soon be in Capacity to prevent your Excellency from any farther Trouble on that Subject. I am Sir with sincere Respect & Esteem Your most obedient & humble Servant

Robt Morris

To Alexander Hamilton, 16 October 1782

Office of Finance [Philadelphia] 16 Octo: 1782

Sir,

I am indebted for two of your Favors, one of which is without date, the other of the fifth Instant enclosing the Account of your Receipts to that Time. I am sorry the Propositions I made did not suit Colo. Malcolm and Mr. Lawrence. I am pleased that you approve the Plans for restoring public Credit and wish they had been adopted, as I conceive the substituting a mere temporary Expedient is dangerous. I am happy to find that the public Creditors are organizing themselves, their Numbers and Influence joined to the Justness of their Cause must prevail if they persevere. The Proceedings of the Committee on Taxation are just what are to be expected on such Occasions.

The Establishment of solid Systems require Time and Industry and the Bulk of Mankind are so attached to their particular Interests, that they are seldom persuaded to extend their Efforts in favor of general Regulations, untill Experience convinces them of their Necessity. I hope the People of America will feel that Conviction before it be too late.

and remain Sir, your most obedient and humble Servant

RM.

To George Washington, 16 October 1782

Office of finance 16 Octr 1782

Sir

I have, for some time past, anticipated the reflection which you have made, on the situation of the Army. I know that some Money is necessary, and my efforts to obtain it, both at home and abroad, have been unceasing. I am now about to purchase a vessel, and send a person on board of her to the Havanah, for the purpose of vending Bills of Exchange to the amount of half a million dollars. I have issued orders to the Alliance Frigate, to go thither inquest of it and take the proper measures for payment of the Bills in Europe. This plan was adopted, from a conviction that a considerable sum would be wanted about the close of the Year, and my experience that Bills could not be sold to the amount. Your letters confirm me in my ideas of its propriety. If I succeed, a part of the Money shall be applied as pay. If the plan should fail, the Army will not be the only persons who will have reason to lament the failure. This matter I mention to you sir, in confidence, as well because I will not raise hopes which may prove abortive, as because it is necessary the profoundest secrecy should be observed lest the Enemy should prevent the execution of it. You observe in your letter, that a peace is necessary; But if I were to hazard an opinion on the subject, it would be, that War is more likely than peace to produce funds for the public debts, increase of authority to Congress, and vigor to the administration as well of the union as of its component parts. These things all appear necessary to our future prosperity—safety and happiness. Beleive me I pray you with sincere Esteem your most obedient and humble Servant

Robt Morris

To Alexander Hamilton, 23 October 1782

Office of Finance [Philadelphia] 23rd. October 1782

Sir

I have received your favors of the 9th. and 12th. Instant with the account of your Receipts to the latter Date.

As the purposes for which Mr Brown is employed will not admit of his passing through Albany, I shall consider of some arrangement for making Remittances from thence; of which you shall be seasonably Informed. Your Letter for General Green shall be forwarded. I shall soon have Occasion to write you Respecting the appointment of Doctor Tillotson and his acceptance which I am prevented, by much business, from doing by this Post.

I am Sir Your most Obedient & most humble Servant

Robt Morris

To Benjamin Franklin, 27 October 1782

Office of Finance 27th October 1782

Sir

I do myself the Honor to enclose the Copy of a Paper transmitted to me by the Governor of Virginia. The Cloathing there mentioned is a Part of those Supplies for the State of Virginia which the Court of France have charged to the United States. You will recollect the Discussions on this Subject. It is with a sincere Desire to remove every disagreeable Trace of them that I have agreed to a Proposition made me by the Governor of Virginia in his Letter dated in Council Chamber the twenty third of September last of which the following is an Extract—

"The Regulations you have entered into for Cloathing the continental Army will render useless to the State a quantity of Necessaries now in France furnished by his most christian Majesty, as the Terms we have them on (which I have before transmitted to you) are such as will make the Payment easy to the United States we shall be obliged to you to take them off our Hands, and take the Debt so far as they go on the States. You have a Copy of the Invoice inclosed by which you will see that they will be useful and necessary for the Army which will I hope induce you to oblige the State." The Enclosure referred to is that above mentioned—

I make no Doubt that the Court will chuse to consider the whole of these Supplies as advanced on the Credit of the United States, and therefore there is so much the less Objection to taking a Part of the Goods. As for the Remainder I think it better for Congress to adjust the Matter with Virginia than to plague the Kings Ministers with Altercations about it.—

I am Sir Your most obedient & humble Servant

Robt Morris

To Alexander Hamilton, 28 October 1782

Office of Finance [Philadelphia] 28th October 1782

Sir,

I have received your Favor dated at Albany on the 19th Instant with the Enclosures. What you say of your Prospect with Respect to the Receipt of Money for Taxes, is as you may easily suppose very unpleasing. I hope it will soon assume a different

Appearance. Unless Something more be done by the States, many very dangerous as well as disagreable Consequences are to be apprehended.

With sincere Esteem I am Sir Your most obedient Servant

Robt Morris

To George Washington, 30 November 1782

Office of Finance 30th November 1782

Sir,

I do myself the Honor to enclose to your Excellency the Copy of a Letter addressed to me on the twenty second Instant as Agent of Marine, by the Commissary of Marine Prisoners, Major Turner. From this Letter two Points arise for Consideration. 1st whether it would be prudent to send in a very large Quantity of Wood, apply a Part to the Comfort of our Prisoners, and the Remainder to be sold for the Purpose of procuring Cloathing &c. And 2dly whether it would be prudent to agree with the Enemy on a Tariff of Money for the Exchange of Seamen. On these Points I wish to have your Sentiments fully. I would observe however that it is my own Opinion even if such Measures should be adopted in any Degree that it be under considerable Limitations. Thus if Wood be sent in, I think it should be purchased to the Eastward and sent in by Flag Vessels un[der] proper Precautions to prevent any illicit Commerce, and that the Quantity should be such as meerly to reimburse by the Sales of it the Cost and charges and to place the Sums in New York which may be necessary to purchase the Cloathing and Necessaries for the Prisoners, and to redeem them, should the second Point be adopted. In like Manner if that Point be adopted, that it should be in such cautious Manner as to exclude the Idea of a similar Tariff for Land Prisoners. I have the Honor to be Sir Your Excellency's most obedient humble Servant

Robt Morris

To George Washington, 3 December 1782

Marine Office December 3rd 1782

Sir

Captain Turner Commissary of Marine Prisoners informs me that he has made two written Applications to Mr Skinner the late Commissary General of Prisoners for a general Return and every official Paper respecting his Department, and has very good Reason to beleive that one if not both of his Letters have been received.

To these Applications he says no Answer has been received, and that Mr Skinner considers himself as accountable only to your Excellency. The Papers which Captain Turner has applied for are important towards the Arrangement of his Department, and therefore I am induced to request your Excellency would direct Mr Skinner to render a faithful Account of Transactions in the Marine part of his Appointment, and deliver up without Reserve all Official Papers respecting it whether in his own Hands or those of His Deputies.

If Lieutt Colo. Smith should have in his Possession any Papers which respect Marine Prisoners I should be glad to have these also transmitted to the Commissary's Office here. With the highest Respect & Regard I have the Honor to be Sir Your Excellency's most obedient & humble Servant

Robt Morris

To George Washington, 17 December 1782

Office of Finance 17th December 1782

Sir

I do myself the Honor to enclose to your Excellency the Copy of a System for Issuing Provisions and Hospital Stores entered into with the Secretary at War. As he is now on his Way to Head Quarters I shall take the Liberty to refer your Excellency to him for those Observations which I should otherwise have written. I am Sir Your Excellency's most obedient & humble Servant

Robt Morris

To George Washington, 19 December 1782

Office of Finance 19th December 1782

Sir.

I have now the Honor to enclose to your Excellency the Copy of a Contract entered into by Messrs Duer & Parker with me for supplying Rations within the States of New York and New Jersey during the Year 1783.

In the Letter which your Excellency did me the Honor to write [o]n the thirty first of October last was contained sundry Observations for which I again beg Leave to return you my Thanks. I hope and believe that these Gentlemen will act in such a Manner as to attract your Excellency's Esteem, and instead of endeavoring to screen themselves by the Letter, where to the true Spirit of their Contract. I have however drawn the Agreement in such Form as will I hope obviate most if not all of the Inconveniences which you were formerly subjected to.

The sixth Article contains the provisionary Clause against Provisions of bad Quality, and altho it does not entirely come up to your Excellency's Ideas will I trust prove effectual. No Contractors would have put themselves so entirely into the Power of an Inspector as to let him name the Prices of Articles furnished by them. This Caprice or a Fit of ill Humor might, they say, prove ruinous, and as they have no Voice in the Nomination, their Property would be exposed beyond what any Prudence would justify, and therefore beyond what the Public have a Right to require. In the present Form your Excellency will observe that the Inspector has a Right to reject the Article entirely, and oblige them to paying Money, which may always be done without much inconvenience to the Troops, except for the Articles of Bread and Flesh which would prove so heavy a Loss as to prevent them from attempting to furnish bad Articles in future. And as to the Bread and Beef, if the Inspector should in one Instance procure a Supply at their Expence I am persuaded they would for similar Reasons never risque a second.

The seventh Article is of a general Nature for the most extensive Purposes, and will therefore readily comprehend within it any Articles of salted Provisions or hard Bread which you may think proper to have lept on Hand, as well as any additional Magazine which you may cause to be laid up at West Point.

You will observe Sir, that to obviate the Artifices which might be used with Respect to the smaller Parts of the Ration, it is provided that the Contractors shall issue no due-Bills, but either provide the Article or pay the Money. This is, I beleive, the most effectual Check, for they must, if compelled to adhere to it, either provide the Articles themselves of a good Quality, or be three Months in Advance for a considerable Sum of Money without any Compensation.

The Vinegar will, I hope, be furnished good, but I have agreed with Mr Duer that he need not furnish any before the Month of June. The Reason is this—he assures me that good Vinegar cannot, until then, be procured, and that the Money may be employed more for the Benefit of the Troops in some other Way—Beleiving this to be the Case, and being convinced that the Article is of most Importance during the hot Season, I gave my Consent. And altho this forms no written Agreement, yet I must intreat of your Excellency to countenance such Arrangements as may carry the Substance and Spirit of it into Effect, for the mutual Conveniences of all the Parties concerned, and I persuade myself the Contractors will endeavor to render it as agreable as possible.

I will add while I am upon this Subject that by the present Regulation for Officers Subsistence they will have somewhat more than the Ration Price for every Ration where they are, and much more when within the Bounds of some other Contracts. This Circumstance, without being very expensive to the United States, will, I imagine, contribute much to their Convenience. I have warmly recommended it to the Contractors to be upon Terms of Friendship with the Army, and I flatter myself with the Hope that all Things may harmonize as to promote those Plans of Oeconomy which must always form one Part of the Remedy for all Grievances arising from the Want of Money. The other Part, and now indeed the principal Part, which is an Increase of Revenue, depends on the States. The Defect in this Branch lies principally at present in the Defects of their Modes of Collection. The Remedies which have been and those which may be proposed, will, I am sure, be warmly seconded by your Excellency, and I trust they will meet the Support of every well Wisher to our Cause. A Cause which I think can never be crowned with Success until it shall be supported by doing Justice to all who have exerted themselves in its Support. With perfect Respect and Esteem I have the Honor to be Sir Your Excellency's most obedient & humble Servant

Robt Morris

To George Washington, 26 December 1782

Philadelphia 26th Decr 1782

Sir,

I do myself the Honor to enclose to you a Bill of Exchange for fifty Guineas drawn by Doctor Smith upon yourself together with a Letter which I presume advises of it. Conceiving that a small Remittance might not be useless to your Family I have indorsed it accordingly and of Course it will be chargable in the Public Books to your Household. When the Subsistence Notes go up I shall direct a Sum to be also paid for the use of your Family which will answer for any Dealings you may have with Contractors and perhaps this may prove to yourself as well as to your officers a matter of great Convenience in general Cases. I have the Honor to be with perfect Respect your Excellency's most obedient & humble Servant.

Robt Morris

To George Washington, 27 December 1782

Office of Finance 27 Decemr 1782

Sir

I am duly honored with your Excellency's Favor of the seventeenth Instant. Previous to the Receipt of it Admiral Digby had transmitted the polite Application of which a Copy is enclosed. In Answer to it I wrote a Letter of which a Copy is also enclosed and which I think Consists with your Excellency's Sentiments. As this Letter involved Engagements which were of an extensive Nature whether considered in a pecuniary or political Point of Light I thought it best to submit it to Congress, more especially as it militated in some Degree with their Resolutions. To avoid the tedious Discussions which might have attended any Resolution as well as to leave it on the Basis of a mere ministerial Act in which the Sovereign Authority might not be compromised in any supposable Case, I desired the President to read it and take the Sentiments of Congress without a formal Minute that so their Approbation or Disapprobation might be verbally expressed. This was done and the Letter was approved. What may be it's Fate with the Enemy I know not but hope it may prove agreeable to our Wishes. With perfect Respect & Esteem I have the Honor to be Sir your Excellency's most obedient & humble Servant

Robt Morris

To George Washington, 31 December 1782

Office of Finance 31st Decr 1782

Sir,

I have received your Excellency's favors of the twenty first and twenty fifth Instant. Colo. Tilghman had already mentioned the Cannon which Mr Billings engraved and I assured him I would pay for it. This assurance I beg Leave to repeat and to add that if your Excellency will be pleased to draw on me in his favor the Bill shall be duly honored. In such Case I wish the Service may be specified in the Bill so that the Warrant grounded on it may at once be carried to the proper account.

I presume Sir that the Quarter Master General who is by this time at Head Quarters will have taken the necessary arrangements for obtaining the Forage required. With perfect Respect & Esteem I have the Honor to be Sir your Excellency's most obedient & humble Servant

Robt Morris,

To Benjamin Franklin, 2 January 1783

Office of Finance 2 January. 1783

Sir,

—Circular—

The Bearer of this Letter is the Chevalier de Chattelleux who sets off to Morrow Morning, for France. There are many Things which I am desirous of communicating to you but which I have not now sufficient Time to commit to Paper and still less to put in Cypher. I have therefore entered very much into the Detail of our Situation with Genl. Chattelleux and requested him to communicate to you the Result. His attentive Observation in this Country will also enable him to place before you a more complete State of it than could easily be written as he will be able to Answer Questions which might not even suggest themselves to me.

I am Sir with sincere Respect and Esteem Your most obedient and humble Servant

RM

To Benjamin Franklin, 3 January 1783

Office of Finance 3rd. January 1783

Sir

I do myself the Honor to enclose to your Excellency under flying Seal a Letter to Mr Grand which I pray you to peruse. To what is said in that Letter I need add but little. The Bill to Messrs. Wadsworth and Carter is in Payment of what our Army have eaten during the last two Months and an half, and you will see by the Correspondence on that Subject which will be transmitted in my next Letter what a Situation I was drawn to. Be assured my dear Sir that nothing but extreme Necessity shall induce me to distress you but be also assured that unless a considerable Sum of Money is obtained for us in Europe we are inevitably ruined and that too whether a Peace takes Place or not for we must keep our Army together and we must prepare for war or we do Justice neither to ourselves nor our Allies. The Expence therefore is inevitable and I have no means of defraying it but the Sales of Bills. I shall write you more particularly as soon as my Leisure will admit and only repeat for the Present once more that money is indispensible.

I am Sir With Esteem and affection Your most obedient & humble Servant.

Robt Morris

To Benjamin Franklin, 11 January 1783

Office of Finance 11th. January 1783

Sir

On the ninth Instant, from an Investigation of Mr. Grands Accounts, then lately received, I found that after making due Allowance for Loan Office Bills &ca. which might still come upon him, my Drafts (and those which I have directed) would exceed, by Something more than six Millions (exclusive of the Interest payable by him in November on the Dutch Loan) any Funds which he could be possessed of. It appeared also by indirect Information so late as in the Month of September, that the Loan opened by Mr. Adams had not produced above three Millions, so that unless he had met with further Success, there would be a Deficiency of three Millions. Had the Court granted us twelve Millions in the first Instance, Had Mr. Adams' Loan produced six Millions, had Mr de Beaumarchais Bills been provided for, without Recurrence to the American Banker, or finally had the heavy Deduction made by those Bills been replaced, this disagreeable Thing would not have happened. Presuming that the Loan of the last Year was exclusively at my Disposition, I drew during the Year to the Amount of it, and I am convinced that all my Bills, and those drawn by my Authority will have been paid. Rely on it, that as I told you in a former Letter, I have acted under the Influence of dire Necessity, and this you will be convinced of by a few out of many Circumstances. Enclosed you have a general State of the public Account, until the end of 1781: On which you will observe, that the Army was fed principally (tho scantily) by the specific Supplies called for at different previous Periods; and that there remained in the Treasury near three hundred thousand Dollars, being Part of the Money which Colo. Laurens brought with him from France. I also enclose you the Copy of a Letter written to Congress, on the twenty first of October, and of its several Enclosures whch. will need no Commentary, or if it did, I would only add that I have been obliged to sell part of the Goods which arrived here from Holland, in Order to raise so much Money as would save my sinking Credit from Destruction. I would go into a Detail of the various Measures pursued to stimulate the Exertions of the States, but to do this with Accuracy would be to give a tedious History of my whole Administration. Whatever Expedient could suggest itself which might have that desirable Effect, I have tried: and I do assure you that when I look back at the Scenes I have passed thro, they strike my own Mind with Astonishment. As soon as I can get the Accounts made up, I will transmit you the Total of our Expenditures, but to transmit, or even relate, our Hazards and Difficulties would be impossible.

Even at this Moment I am making farther Exertions to bring our unwieldy System into Form, and Ward off impending Evils, but what the Success may be Heaven knows. Imagine the Situation of a Man who is to direct the Finances of a Country, almost without Revenue (for such you will perceive this to be) surrounded by Creditors whose Distresses, while they encrease their Clamors, render it more difficult to appease them. An Army ready to disband or Mutiny. A Government whose sole Authority consists in the Power of framing Recommendations. Surely it is not necessary to add any Colouring to such a Piece, and yet Truth would justify more than Fancy could paint. The Settlement of Accounts, long and intricate beyond Comprehension, becomes next to impossible, from the Want of that Authority which is on the Verge of Annihilation from those Confusions which nothing can disipate except the complete Settlement of Accounts, and an honest Provision for Payment.

Upon Discovering the Situation of our Affairs, in the manner already mentioned, I laid them before Congress. You will know the Result. The Secretary of foreign Affairs will doubtless transmit their Act, to which I must add this farther Communication, that I expect my Bills will amot. to a Million, within a Month from this Date. There are Cases where Nothing worse can be apprehended from a Measure, than what would inevitably happen without it, and our present Position is one of them. An immediate Command of Money is alike necessary to our present Existence and future Prospects. In Europe, when this Letter arrives, you will know decidedly whether we are to expect Peace or War, but in America we must prepare for the latter; for by so doing we may forward

Negotiations for Peace, and at the worst will only have incurred some additional Expence whereas by neglecting it, we risk the Chance of being taken unawares, and paying very dearly the Penalties of Neglect.

But Sir, notwithstanding these Reasons and many others which will justify every Counsel and every Act (however irregular in other Respects) I would not draw one more Bill, and I would boldly hazard every Consequence of the Omission, if I were not persuaded that they would be paid. On this Occasion your Sovereign will expect your most vigorous Exertions, and your Country will, I trust, be indebted to you in a Degree for her political Existence.

I am Sir your most obedient and humble Servant

Robt Morris

To Benjamin Franklin, 13 January 1783

Office of Finance 13th January 1783

Dear Sir

I have received, in Addition to those already acknowledged, your Letters of the twelfth of August, twenty sixth of September, and fourteenth of October. I should therefore, regularly, have received two Copies of the Contract entered into on the sixteenth of July between you and the Count de Vergennes; but I suppose it has been omitted, thro' Mistake, in both the Letters which refer to it. I lament this the more, as no one Copy of it has yet arrived, and consequently the Congress cannot do what I am perswaded they would, on the Occasion. But altho' they (from this Circumstance) do not make Professions, yet as far as I know the Sentiments of that Body, they are penetrated with Gratitude. And you hazard Nothing in making to the King the fullest Assurances of their

Desire to repay the Obligations they have received, and gratify their Affection for his Person and Family, by Services and Benefits. You will oblige me much if (together with the Contract in Question) you will send a State of the farmers-generals Account, and of the Agreement with them.

You tell me that the Losses in the West Indies prevent you from obtaining farther Aid. It is therefore to Us a double Loss. As to the Caution you give me about my Banker, you will find that before the Receipt of Mr. Grand's Accounts, I had valued on him beyond his Funds. I have this Day entered into an Explanation with the Minister on that Subject, and I inclose you the Copy of my Letter, as also of another Paper deliverd him which may be worth your Attention. In my Turn, I rely on your Promise of Exertion to pay my Drafts. If one Bill should be protested, I could no longer serve the United States.

With Respect to the Apprehension you express as to my Bills, I do not perceive the Matter in the same Point of Light with you. The Lists of my Bills are transmitted to Mr. Grand, by various Opportunities, and *they* will check any which might be forged or altered.

I shall take due Notice of what you say about your Salary, and will enclose the Bills to you, the Amount will depend on the Course of Exchange: during the War you will be a Gainer, and after the Peace you may perhaps loose some Trifle but not much, because Remittances might then be made in Specie should the Exchange be extravagantly high. You will readily perceive, that altho the Fluctuations of Exchange are in themselves of very little Consequence to the Individuals who may be connected with Government, they become Important at the Treasury, partly from the Number of Payments and consequent Amount, but more so because they would introduce a Degree of Intricacy and Perplexity in the public Accounts, which are generally either the Effect or the

Cause of Fraud and Peculation. Besides, there is no other Way of adjusting Salaries than by a Payment of so much at the Treasury, unless by rating them in the Currency of every different Country, as Livres, Dollars Guilders, Rubles &c. The late Mode of rating them, in Pounds Sterling, required a double Exchange. For Instance, the Number of Livres to be given in Payment of one hundred Pounds Sterling, at Paris, on any given Day, depends on the then Rate of Exchange between Paris and London, and the Value of those Livres here, depends on the Exchange between Paris and Philada.

I pray you, Sir, to accept my sincere Thanks for the kind Interest you take in the Success of my Administration. The only Return which I can make to your Goodness, is by assuring you that all my Measures shall be honestly directed towards the good of that Cause which you have so long, so faithfully, and so honorably served.

I am with the Sincerest Respect & Esteem Sir Your most obedient & humble Servant

Robt Morris

To John Adams, 19 January 1783

Office of Finance 19th. Jany 1783—

Sir

Altho' I have not yet been honored with any Letters from your Excellency I cannot omit the Occasion of Writing which offers itself by Mr Jefferson. Having already congratulated you on the Acknowlegement of our Independence by the States General, and on the rapid Successes of your Labors equally splendid and useful. I hope when this Letter shall have reached your Hands I may have the additional Cause of Congratulation that the Loan you have opened in Holland shall have been compleated, this is a Circumstance of great Importance to our Country and most particularly so to the Department which I have the Honor to fill— Whatever may be the Success of it whether general or partial I pray your Excellency to favor me by every Conveyance with every minute Detail which can tend to form my Judgment or enlighten my Mind. For the more perfect Security of our Correspondence, I do myself the Honor to enclose the Counterpart of a Cypher to the Use of which you will soon become familiarized and I hope you will be convinced that any Confidence with which you may honor me shall be safely reposed and usefully employed for the public Benefit—

I have the Honor to be / with perfect Respect / Sir / your Excellency's / most Obedient / & / humble Servant

Robt Morris

To Benjamin Franklin, 19 January 1783

Office of Finance 19th. Janry. 1783

Sir,

His Excellency the Governor and the Honorable the Delagates of Virginia have applied to me for my Assistance in obtaining from France certain Arms and Ammunition said to have been furnished by the Court for that State according to an Agreement entered into between Mr. Harrison a special Agent appointed by the Legislature and Monsr. de la luzerne the King's Minister. These Articles wheresoever they may be deposited are (according to my Informants) in the Care and Custody and Subject to the Direction of Mr. Thomas Barclay the Consul General of the United States who is also the agent of the State of Virginia in France. I have accordingly written to the Consul directing him to cause those

Goods to be shipped along with those belonging to the United States and at the repeated Instance of those Gentlemen I am now to address your Excellency upon the same Subject. Going upon the Supposition that the Arms &c. may still be in Europe I take the Liberty to mention that if the War continues the necessity of a Convoy necessarily continuing with it Monsr. de Ville Brun who has long been in the Chesapeak and is well acquainted with the Coast would not only feel himself happy in being charged with that Business but has even assured me that he would gladly take them on Board of his own Ship and at the same Time act as Convoy to the Trade which might be bound to the Chesapeak. Your Excellency will undoubtedly obtain every Information which may be useful on this Subject and your Zeal and Talents will prompt and direct to what is best. I can only add that I shall be happy if you can render any Service on this occasion to the State of Virginia and shall esteem as a Favor the Efforts which you may make—

Before I close this Letter it is well to observe that I have received another Copy of your Letter of the twenty sixth of September in which I find a Copy of the agreement entered into between you and Monsr. de Vergenes.

I have the Honor to be Sir Your most obedient & humble Servant

Robt Morris

To George Washington, 20 January 1783

Office of Finance 20th Janry 1783

Sir,

I have the Honor to enclose to your Excellency the Copy of a Letter of this Date to the PayMaster General which I will intreat you to communicate to the acting Contractor that the use of the

Notes may be facilitated to such of the officers as shall wish to receive them. I do expect from a Conversation I have had with the Committee of Officers now here that the Officers of your Army will render this Arrangement With Respect to the Soldiers and themselves their own Act, and I shall direct the Suspension of the Business for some little time so as to give Room for their Operations as otherwise it might have an ill appearance to make Payment in the manner proposed however in itself eligible proper and indeed necessary. I have the Honor to be with perfect Respect Sir, Your Excellency's most obedient & humble Servant

Robt Morris

To George Washington, 21 January 1783

Office of finance 21 Jany 1783

Sir,

I have received your Excellency's favors of the Sixth and Eight Instant. I have directed the Commissary of arine Prisoners to appoint a proper Agent at Dobb's Ferry and I hope for your Excellency's advice to him on that Occasion which he will be desired to apply for. Without wishing to incur the Blame of too great Suspicion I take the Liberty to suggest (as an additional Reason for Caution) that monies intended for commercial Pursuits might be transmitted under the Idea of relieving Prisoners. Mr Skinner has never yet communicated his Returns or accounts.

It was with very great Pleasure, Sir, that I paid the money you desired, to Mr Adam, and I beg you to believe that I shall at all Times be happy to facilitate your Views. At present the negociation happens (by good Luck) to minister alike to your Convenience and mine. I am very sorry that you did not make an earlier mention to me of your Demands for Secret Service. I would have anticipated your views had it not escaped my attention for be the Distresses of my Department what they may, this is of too much Importance ever to be neglected. I think it is best in future that a solid Arrangement should be taken and for this Purpose I will give Directions to the Paymaster General always to keep some money in his hands of his Deputy to answer your Drafts for Contingencies and Secret Service. I have, as you will see, taken methods to put the Deputy in Cash; and then your Excellency will be relieved from any farther care than the due application. I am however to pray for the Sake of Regularity in accounts that your Excellency in the Warrants would be so kind as to specify the particular Service when on the contingent account and draw in favor of one of your Family on account of secret Services mentioning that it is for secret Service. I shall direct Mr Swanwick to endorse the Bills on you in favor of Mr Adams to the Paymaster General whose Deputy will receive for your Excellency the Amount.

The Reason why it was determined to Issue sixteen Rations to fifteen Soldiers is this, Congress (as the Secretary at War informed me) had long Since made that allowance for the Women & Children and I (knowing how much a certain Expence is preferable to an uncertain one) very readily adopted it. But our Idea is, that the Rations actually drawn in a Regiment should be divided according to the number of Women & Children actually existing in the several companies. If there are a lesser proportion than the Allowance, the Surplus may be disposed of as they please. If there be a greater Proportion they must be dismissed or provided for from some other Source. Thus the Rations being only issuable to non Commissioned & privates an addition of one fifteenth to the Inspectorate Returns will shew the Amount drawn and a variance as to any Corps will require Examination and Explanation. I have the Honor to be With sincere Esteem & Respect Sir, Your Excellency's Most Obedient & humble Servant

Robt Morris

To George Washington, 20 January 1783

Office of Finance 20th Janry 1783

Sir,

I have the Honor to enclose to your Excellency the Copy of a Letter of this Date to the PayMaster General which I will intreat you to communicate to the acting Contractor that the use of the Notes may be facilitated to such of the officers as shall wish to receive them. I do expect from a Conversation I have had with the Committee of Officers now here that the Officers of your Army will render this Arrangement With Respect to the Soldiers and themselves their own Act, and I shall direct the Suspension of the Business for some little time so as to give Room for their Operations as otherwise it might have an ill appearance to make Payment in the manner proposed however in itself eligible proper and indeed necessary. I have the Honor to be with perfect Respect Sir, Your Excellency's most obedient & humble Servant

Robt Morris

To George Washington, 21 January 1783

Office of finance 21 Jany 1783

Sir,

I have received your Excellency's favors of the Sixth and Eight Instant. I have directed the Commissary of arine Prisoners to appoint a proper Agent at Dobb's Ferry and I hope for your Excellency's advice to him on that Occasion which he will be desired to apply for. Without wishing to incur the Blame of too great Suspicion I take the Liberty to suggest (as an additional Reason for Caution) that monies intended for commercial Pursuits might be transmitted under the Idea of relieving Prisoners. Mr Skinner has never yet communicated his Returns or accounts.

It was with very great Pleasure, Sir, that I paid the money you desired, to Mr Adam, and I beg you to believe that I shall at all Times be happy to facilitate your Views. At present the negociation happens (by good Luck) to minister alike to your Convenience and mine. I am very sorry that you did not make an earlier mention to me of your Demands for Secret Service. I would have anticipated your views had it not escaped my attention for be the Distresses of my Department what they may, this is of too much Importance ever to be neglected. I think it is best in future that a solid Arrangement should be taken and for this Purpose I will give Directions to the Paymaster General always to keep some money in his hands of his Deputy to answer your Drafts for Contingencies and Secret Service. I have, as you will see, taken methods to put the Deputy in Cash; and then your Excellency will be relieved from any farther care than the due application. I am however to pray for the Sake of Regularity in accounts that your Excellency in the Warrants would be so kind as to specify the particular Service when on the contingent account and draw in favor of one of your Family on account of secret Services mentioning that it is for secret Service. I shall direct Mr Swanwick to endorse the Bills on you in favor of Mr Adams to the Paymaster General whose Deputy will receive for your Excellency the Amount.

The Reason why it was determined to Issue sixteen Rations to fifteen Soldiers is this, Congress (as the Secretary at War informed me) had long Since made that allowance for the Women & Children and I (knowing how much a certain Expence is preferable to an uncertain one) very readily adopted it. But our Idea is, that the Rations actually drawn in a Regiment should be divided according to the number of Women & Children actually existing in the several companies. If there are a lesser proportion than the Allowance, the Surplus may be disposed of as they please. If there be a greater Proportion they must be dismissed or provided for from some other Source. Thus the Rations being only issuable to non Commissioned & privates an addition of one fifteenth to the Inspectorate Returns will shew the Amount drawn and a variance as to any Corps will require Examination and Explanation. I have the Honor to be With sincere Esteem & Respect Sir, Your Excellency's Most Obedient & humble Servant

Robt Morris

To George Washington, 5 February 1783

Office of Finance 5th February 1783

Dear Sir

I have received your Letter of the twenty ninth of last Month which gave me much Pain as the Subject of it appears to have affected your Mind in a Manner very distant from my Apprehensions. I myself never saw any Resolution of Congress limiting the Number of Rations to Women &c. but took it up on the Suggestion of the Secretary at War as the proper Standard when we were seeking for a Standard. I know not how far any Abuses had in that Respect prevailed. With your Consent I knew there could be none. It was however represented to me that the Drafts of Rations for Women under some of the Contracts were enormous. In a general System therefore it became necessary to establish a certain Rule. The Uncertainty of Drafts made by Officers, had destroyed that Clearness and Precision which is essential in the Settlement of Accounts. To obviate that Mischief the Subsistence was devised. There remained only the Differences as to the Number of Women and Children. When I have fully explained my Conceptions on the Subject you will clearly see that neither the Secretary at War nor myself had the most remote Idea of interfering in your Administration. Taking it for granted that there was such a Resolution as that mentioned it would follow that the Number allowed was either equal to the Number existing or greater or less. If equal there could be no Doubts. If greater it was to be presumed that the Officers would appropriate the Surplus to some Decorations of the Corps or other like Objects. If less the first Question which could arise would be whether the Number ought not to be reduced. And if not the second would be how should the Surplus be provided for. To this last the Answer is clear. The Commander in Chief or Commanding General is indubitably empowered to dispose of the public Property in Cases where the good of the Service requires it. A special Order would therefore be given to the Contractors for issuing fifty additional Rations per Day, or more if necessary to any particular Corps. This Order would support the Contractors Accounts and obtain the Provisions wanted. The Accounts for the several Corps would all remain Simple and clear as before, and the only Inconvenience would be the Surplus, drawn by some Corps. On this Subject I must observe 1st. That tho' this Inconvenience be real with Respect to the Corps under your Excellencys immediate Command it is not so perceptible elsewhere, and in many Instances the general Rule will remedy an improper Excess. 2ly. That this general Rule for our own Troops will apply to the Case of british Prisoners of War who have Herds of Women with them. And 3ly. That the great Advantages which result from reducing every kind of Charge to an absolute Certainty so that a perfect Clearness may obtain in all public Accounts is sufficient to overbalance much greater Inconveniencies.

I again repeat my dear Sir that as there was not in my own Mind so I am perswaded there was not in General Lincoln's the most distant Idea of Interference in the Line of your Department. An hundred different Occasions may arise in which it will be necessary for you to dispose of public Money, Provisions and Stores and I hope you will never hesitate on such Occasions at giving the proper Warrants.

You know our Situation and therefore I am sure you will never incur undue Expence and the kind Assurances you have given of Support to my Arrangements would have quieted any Doubts on that Subject if I had been capable of harboring them. With most sincere Esteem I am my dear Sir your most obedient humble Servant

Robt Morris

To George Washington, 17 February 1783

Office of Finance 17th February 1783

Sir,

By a Mistake it happened that the last Post did not carry my Acknowlegement of your Excellency's Letter of the fourth Instant. I am very sorry to find that the Officer who conducted hither the Prisoners met with any Difficulties on the score of Provisions. The Contractor for New York and New Jersey being at Head Quarters I could wish your Excellency to direct such Arrangmements as may in future be necessary so as that Provision be Issued at proper Posts on due notice. I have not thought of the Places, but suppose that Trenton and Morris Town will be two. At any such places the Contractors should have an Agent bound on due Notice to make the necessary Issues. With perfect Respect I have the honor to be Sir Your Excellency's Most Obedient and Humble Servt

Robt Morris

To George Washington, 27 February 1783

Office of Finance 27th February 1783

Sir

I do myself the Honor to enclose in the Paper Number one the Copy of a Letter to the President of Congress which was written on the twenty fourth of last Month. I should have transmitted it to you on the next Day but contrary to my Expectations Congress enjoined Secrecy—I yesterday wrote the Letter of which Number two is a Copy and in Consequence of it I am this Instant informed that the Injunction of Secrecy is taken off. I seize therefore the earliest Moment to give you the Information.

I do assure you Sir that Nothing would have induced me to take this Step but a painful Conviction that the Situation of those to whom the Public are indebted is desperate. I beleive sincerely that a great Majority of the Members of Congress wish to do Justice But I as sincerely beleive that they will not adopt the necessary Measures because they are afraid of offending their States. From my Soul I pity the Army, and you my dear Sir in particular, who must see and feel for their Distresses without the Power of releiving them. I did flatter myself that I should have been able to present them that Justice to which they are entitled, and in the mean Time I labored to made their Situation as tolerable as Circumstances would permit. For the Assistance which you have Kindly afforded me, I pray you to accept my Thanks, and be assured that I shall ever retain for it the most grateful Emotions. My Thanks are due also to all our Officers, for I know that unwearied Pains have been taken to give them disagreeable Impressions: I am therefore doubly Indebted for the just Sentiments which, amid so many Misrepresentations, they have constantly entertained. I hope my Successor will be more fortunate than I have been, and that our glorious Revolution may be crowned with those Acts of Justice, without which the greatest human Glory is but the Shadow of a Shade. I am with sincere Esteem & Respect Sir your most obedient & humble Servant

Robt Morris

To George Washington, 3 March 1783

Office of Finance 3d March 1783

Sir,

I received last Evening your Excellency's Letter of the twenty Sixth of Febry with the Enclosures. I am extreemely happy to find that the present Contract is conducted in an agreeable Manner. The Expectation that it would be so, rendered me less solicitous about filling the office of Inspector (which I had offered to Brigr General Williams) hoping thereby to save to the Public that Expence. Should your Excellency be of opinion that such an appointment is necessary I will endeavor to fill it leaving Mr Wikoff in the mean Time to do the duties which you have directed.

I observe from your Excellency's Letter to Mr Sands that after an Infraction of your order by him when an apprehension was expressed, that confounding the Issues of the two Contracts might perplex the accounts, he declared that the matter was perfectly understood, and agreed upon between him and me. Lest this assurance should be construed more extensively than Truth will authorize, I must trouble your Excellency with a State of the Fact—When it was conceived most for the good of the Service, that the Contracts should be joined, it was agreed that all the Rations should be charged at ten Pence, that your Excellency should determine which of the Troops should draw under the West Point Contract, and that a half-Penny per Ration should be deducted from such Issues. I am with Esteem & Respect Sir your Excellency's most obedient & humble Servant

Robt Morris

To George Washington, 25 March 1783

Office of Finance 25th March 1783

Dear Sir

I have now before me your several Letters of the tenth twelfth and twentieth Instant. I heartily wish it were in my Power to undertake for an Additional Months Pay to the Army but the State of the Finances will by no Means admit of it. The Plan proposed by Mr Parker is otherwise unexceptionable and if any fortunate Change of Affairs will enable me to do more I shall readily go into the Measures recommended.

I am very sorry that you should be put to the Trouble of the Application contained in yours of the twentieth—In future I wish you to draw for your Household from the contingent Fund. The Paymaster can easily cause a proper Account to be raised for the Purpose and it will go with other Details to the Pay Office so as to raise the necessary Applications for Money without giving you any farther trouble than to grant Warrants as it may be wanted. The Paymaster is already gone on to Camp so that if your Excellency will communicate to him this Arrangement he can take the necessary subordinate Measures.

The kind Sentiments contained in your Letter of the tenth demand my grateful Acknowlegements. When I was compelled to resign I made the express Exception of one Case that proper Funds should be provided and the implied Exception of another Case that offensive War should be carried on against us. Happily the latter Case has not arrived but instead of it our Ardent Wishes for Peace have been realized. May Heaven grant to all our Councils the Wisdom to improve this Event for the Honor and Advantage of our Country. With the most sincere Esteem I am my dear Sir your most obedient Servant

Robt Morris

To Alexander Hamilton, Theodorick Bland, Thomas FitzSimons, Samuel Osgood, and Richard Peters, 14 April 1783

Office of Finance [Philadelphia] 14 April 1783

Gentlemen

Since the Conference I had the Honor to hold with you the ninth Instant, my Mind has been continually occupied on the important Subject to which it relates. My Feelings are strongly excited by what I wish for the Public and what I apprehend both for them and for myself. The two Points which relate to my Department are the Settlement of Accounts and Advance of Pay. With respect to the first it is now going on in a satisfactory Manner and will be as speedily accomplished as can reasonably be expected. The Arrangements taken on that Subject are of such a Nature that I conceive the disbanding of the Army need not be delayed until the Settlement is compleated because the proper Officers may be kept together altho the Men be dismissed. The Amount of three Months Pay, which is stated by the General to be *indispensible*, is according to the Estimates, seven hundred and fifty thousand Dollars. From what I have already Stated to Congress it will appear that Reliance for a great Part of this Sum must be on the Sales of public Property and the Taxes. Neither of these Sources can produce much immediately and from the latter there is but little Hope at all unless Something can be done to stimulate the Exertions of the States. The Receipts being regularly published spare me the Necessity of disagreeable Observations on that Topick. To supply so large a Sum as is required is utterly impracticable or indeed to obtain any very considerable Part. The most therefore which can be done is to risk a large Paper Anticipation. This is an Operation of great Delicacy and it is essential to the Success of it that my Credit should be staked for the Redemption. Do not suppose Gentlemen that this Declaration is dictated by Vanity. It becomes my Duty to mention the Truth. I had rather it had fallen from any other Person and I had [– – –] rather it did not exist. In issuing my Notes to the required Amount it would be n⟨ecessary that⟩ I should give an express Assurance of Payment: And in so doing I should ⟨be answerable⟩ personally for about half a Million when I leave this Office and depe⟨nd on the arrange⟩ments of those who come after to save me from Ruin. I am willing ⟨to risk as much⟩ for this Country as any Man in America but it cannot be expected tha⟨t I would place⟩ myself in so desperate a Situation. To render the Arrangements which ⟨the plan would⟩ require effectual in an official Point of View would be a Work of Time ⟨and the end⟩ of my official Existence is nearly arrived. Disbanding the Army in a Manner Satisfactory to them and to the Country is doubtless desirable and altho extremely difficult yet is I beleive practicable. I shall be very ready at all Times Gentlemen to give my advice and Assistance to those who may be charged with that delicate and perilous Undertaking and I would go as far to effect it myself as any reasonable Man could require. But tho I would sacrifice much of my Property yet I cannot risk my Reputation as a Man of Integrity nor expose myself to absolute Ruin.

I am Gentlemen with perfect Respect your most obedient and humble Servant

Robt Morris

To Alexander Hamilton, 16 April 1783

Office of Finance [Philadelphia] 16. April 1783

Sir,

I have been duly honored with the Receipt of your favor of the fifteenth Instant. I accepted the Marine Agency simply with a View to save the Expence of the Department but whenever a marine is to be established a previous Point would be (in my Opinion) to nominate a Minister of Marine and let his first Work be the forming of those Plans and Systems which when adopted by Congress he would have to execute. For my own Part were my Abilities equal to this Task my Leizure would not permit the Attempt.

With Respect to the Finances I am of Opinion that as we cannot increase our Revenue we must do all we can to lessen our Expenditures and that therefore we should take off every Expence not absolutely necessary as soon as possible.

On the Subject of the Coin I hope soon to make a Communication to Congress which if approved of by them will compleat that Business.

I am Sir with very sincere Esteem and Respect—your most obedient and humble Servant

RM.

To Benjamin Franklin, 29 April 1783

Philada. April 29th. 1783

Dear Sir

When an Officer who has distinguished himself by a Series of Brave Actions in the defence of american Liberty wishes to be introduced to you, whose time & Labours have been exhausted in the same cause, it would be unjust to him to you and to myself not to afford him the opportunity of payg you his respects.

This introduction is in favour of Colo. Maths. Ogden of the New Jersey Brigade whose testimonial from the Commander in Chief justifies what I have said, and I am confident you will not only countenance & advise, but also befriend him in any matters wherein you can with propriety become usefull to a deserving Young Gentleman.

With perfect respect & sincere regard, I am Dr sir Your Affectionate hble Servt

Robt Morris

To John Adams, 12 May 1783

Office of Finance 12th. May 1783—

Sir,

The Bills drawn by Congress in their necessities press very heavily upon me; and one of the greatest among many Evils attending them is the Confusion in which they have involved the Affairs of my Department— I have never yet been able to learn how many of these Bills have been paid nor how many remain due neither am I without my fears that some of them have received double Payment.—

To bring at Length some little Degree of order into this Chaos, after waiting till now for fuller Light and Information I write on the Subject to Mr Barclay who will have the Honor to deliver this Letter and I send him a Copy of the enclosed Account. I have directed him to consult with your Excellency and obtain an Account of the Bills which have been paid and to transmit me an account of those and of such as remain due and to take Measures with you for Payment of the latter so as to prevent double Payment which I seriously apprehend. The enclosed Account will inform you that the Bills which are gone forward drawn on Mr Lawrens and yourself amount to seven hundred and fifty three thousand, three hundred, and sixty four Guilders and two thirds—

Let me intreat you Sir to forward these Views as much as possible for you will I am sure be sensible how necessary it is for me to know the exact State of our pecuniary Affairs, lest on the one Hand I should risque the public Credit by an excess of Drafts, or on the other leave their Monies unemployed while they experience severe Distress from the want—

I am Sir / with perfect Respect / Your Excellency's / most obedient / & / humble Servant

Robt Morris

To Benjamin Franklin, 12 May 1783

Office of Finance 12th May 1783

Sir

The Bills drawn by Congress in their Necessities press very heavily upon me, and one of the greatest among many Evils attending them is the Confusion in which they have involved the Affairs of my Department. I have never yet been able to learn how many of these Bills have been paid nor how many remain due neither am I without my fears that some of them have received double Payment.

To bring at length some little Degree of Order into this Chaos, after waiting till now for fuller Light and Information I write on the Subject to Mr. Adams and Mr. Jay and send Mr. Barclay to whom I also write a Copy of the enclosed Accounts directing him to Consult with your Excellency and with them to transmit me an Account of the Bills paid and of those remaining due and to take Measures for preventing double Payments. The enclosed Accounts will inform you that of the Bills drawn for Interest and those for carrying on the current Service which have gone forward thro the Loan Offices amount the first to one Million six hundred and eighty four thousand two hundred and seventy eight Dollars equal to eight Million four hundred and twenty one thousand three hundred and ninety Livres and the second to two hundred and eighty six thousand seven hundred and thirty three and one third Dollars equal to one Million four hundred and thirty three thousand six hundred and sixty six Livres six Sous and eight deniers.

Let me intreat you Sir to forward these Views as much as possible for you will, I am sure, be Sensible how necessary it is for me to know the exact State of our pecuniary Affairs lest on the one Hand I should risque the public Credit by an Excess of Drafts or on the other leave their Monies unemployed while they experience severe distress from the Want. I am Sir with perfect Respect your Excellency's most obedient and humble Servant

Robt Morris

To Alexander Hamilton, Richard Peters, and Nathaniel Gorham, 15 May 1783

Office of Finance [Philadelphia] 15th. May 1783

Gentlemen

In Consequence of the Conversation which passed between us this Morning I shall give you the best information in my Power as to the State of my Department and the Resources I can command.

You have in the enclosed Paper Number one an Account of Receipts and Expenditures from the Commencement of the Year to the End of the last Month by which it appears that there is an Advance on Credit to the Amount of near six hundred thousand Dollars exclusive of what may appear in Mr. Swanwicks Accounts for the Month of April. A large Sum is also due on Genl. Green's Drafts and the Contractors are to be paid in this Month for the Supplies of January last. At the End of this Month therefore that Anticipation must necessarily be much increased. As will appear from the slightest Reflection after what is to be said of our Resources.

These are either foreign or domestic. As to the first I enclose the Copy of the last Letter I have received from Mr. Grand and I have to add to what is contained in that Letter that the Day it was received my Drafts on him over and above those mentioned in it amounted to Three million and forty thousand two hundred and seventy eight Livres and six deniers. I have directed therefore Mr. Barclay to pay over to Mr. Grand any Monies which may be in his Possession and I have directed Messrs. Willink &ca. of Amsterdam to do the same after deducting what may be necessary to pay the Interest of their Loan falling due the first of June next. But as I have no Accounts how much has been borrowed since the End of January and as all which had been borrowed before was disposed of I cannot determine how far they can come in Aid of

Mr. Grand neither can I tell until the Receipt of his Accounts what Aid he may stand in need of. In these Circumstances I am obliged to leave about eighteen hundred thousand Livres (which remain of a Sum placed in the Hands of Messrs. Le Couteulx for answering Drafts intended thro Havanna to answer any Deficiency of other Funds to pay my Drafts on Mr. Grand. These then Gentlemen are all the foreign Resources except what the french Court may advance on the late Resolutions of Congress and you will see by the enclosed Translation of a Letter from the Minister of france what little Hope is to be entertained from that Quarter.

Our domestic Resources are twofold first certain Goods and other Property such as Horses Waggons &ca. These latter will produce very little and the former are (by the Peace) very much reduced in Value and from the nature of the Goods themselves they are chiefly unsaleable. Very little Reliance therefore can be placed on this first Dependance. The Amount I cannot possibly ascertain for I do not yet know (and cannot until the opening of them now in Hand shall be compleated) the Kinds Quality and Situation. Some are damaged those which were deemed most Saleable have been tried at Vendue and went under the first Cost and much the greater Part will certainly not sell at a fourth of their Value.

The only Remaining Resource is in the Taxes and what they may amount to, it is impossible to tell. But you have enclosed an Account of what they yielded the four first Months of this Year and you will see from thence that if all Expence had ceased on the first day of this Month the Anticipations already made would not have been absorbed by the same Rate of Taxation in eight Months more.

Now then Gentlemen you will please to consider that if your Army is kept together they will consume as much in one Month as the Taxes will produce in two and Probably much more. To make them three Months Pay will require I suppose at least six hundred thousand Dollars and every Day they continue in the Field lessens the Practicability of sending them Home satisfied. The Anticipations of Revenue are threefold two of which appear as to their Effects in the public Accounts and one very considerable one tho it produces great Relief is not seen. It consists in the Drawing of Bills on me for the public Service by different Persons and at different Usances. I imagine that these Amount at the present Moment to one hundred thousand Dollars. The other Anticipations consist in Loans from the Bank or the issuing of my own Notes. As to the first of these it is limited in its Nature by the Capital of the Bank which being small will not admit of great Deductions and it depends much upon Circumstances whether the Bank will go to the Extent which they may go. If they find the Revenues increasing and the Expences diminishing they will; otherwise they certainly will not. As to the Notes I issue (and which form the greater Part of my Anticipations) these have also a certain Limit to exceed which would be fatal. I must not so extend that Circulation as that I shall be unable to pay them when presented for that would totally destroy their Credit and of Course their Utility.

Now Gentlemen if any Thing of this Sort should take place before the Army are disbanded you will see at once that they could be fed no longer and must of Course disband themselves. I will not dwell on the Consequences but I will draw one clear Conclusion which you have doubtless by this time anticipated viz. that unless they are disbanded immediately the Means of paying them even with Paper will be gone. And this Sentiment I have not only delivered to you but to a former Committee as well as to many individual Members of Congress.

But Gentlemen when I speak of disbanding the Army I beg to be understood as meaning to reserve a sufficient Garrison for West Point. And on this Subject I pray to be indulged in a View of our Political and military Situation as far as relates to this capital

Object of my Department. And first as to our political Situation I conceive that we are at Peace. It is true that the definitive Treaty is not that we know of compleated but it is equally true that all the other beligerent Powers have been disarming for months past and I presume they are at least as well acquainted with the State of things as we are. To express Doubts of the Sincerity of Britain on this Subject is I know a fashionable but in my Opinion a very foolish Language. We have the best Evidence of their Sincerity which the Nature of Things will admit for we know they are unable to carry on the War and we see & feel that they are passing every Act and doing everything in their Power to conciliate our Affections. Expressions of Doubts as to their Sincerity if intended to foster Enmity against them will fail of the Effect and produce the direct Contrary for every Body will soon learn to consider them as unjustly suspected and their Ministers will take Care to inculcate and enforce the Sentiment.

As to our military Situation some of the Troops in the Southern States have already mutinied the principal Part of them are ordered away and since the floridas are ceded to Spain it follows that those Troops which may remain in the Southern States will have to operate against the Spaniards if they operate at all. So that every Man except those under the Generals immediate Command and the little Garrison of fort Pitt are in fact disbanded to every Purpose but that of Expence.

The Prisoners are some of them going and the rest gone into New York so that in a few Days the Enemy will be able to do every Thing which they could do if the greater Part of our Army were gone Home. For they could not take West Point if it is properly Garrisoned and they could ravage the Country in spite of our Army when theirs shall be all collected.

Our Situation therefore seems to be this. We are keeping up an Army at a great Expence and very much against their Inclinations for a meer Punctilio and by that Means incapacitating ourselves from Performing what they begin to consider as a kind of Engagement taken with them. I shall detain you no longer on this Subject but must repeat one Observation which is that unless the far greater Part of our Expences be immediately curtailed the Object Congress had in View by their Resolutions of the second Instant cannot possibly be accomplished.

I have the Honor to be Gentlemen your most obedient and humble Servant

Robt. Morris

To Benjamin Franklin (Two Letters), 26 May 1783

I.

Office of Finance 26th: May 1783

Sir

By the enclosed Acts of the twenty eighth of April and second of May with the Copy of my Letter to Congress of the third of May you will perceive that I am to Continue somewhat longer in the Superintendance of our Finances. Be assured Sir, that nothing but a clear View of our Distresses could have induced my Consent. I must at the same time acknowledge that the Distresses we experience arise from our own Misconduct. If the Resources of this Country were drawn forth they would be amply sufficient, but this is not the Case. Congress have not Authority equal to the Object, and their Influence is greatly lessened by their evident Incapacity to do Justice. This is but a melancholy Introduction to the Request contained in the Act of the second Instant. But I shall not be guilty of Falsehood nor will I intentionally Deceive you or put you in the Necessity of deceiving others. My Official Situation compels me to do things which I would certainly avoid under any other Circumstances. Nothing should Induce me in my private Character to make such Applications for Money, as I am obliged to in my Public Character. I know and feel that you must be in a disagreeable Situation on this Subject. I can anticipate the Answers to all your Requests. And I know you may be asked for Payment when you ask for Loans. Yet Sir I must desire you to repeat your Applications. My only Hope arises from the Belief that as the Kings Expences are much lessened he may be able to comply with his gracious Intentions towards America. And the only Inducement I can Offer is the Assurance that the Taxes already called for shall be appropriated as fast as other indispensible Services will admit to the Replacement of what the Court may advance.

Our Situation is shortly this. The Army expect a Payment which will amount to about seven hundred thousand Dollars. I am already above half a Million Dollars in Advance of our Resources by Paper Anticipation. I must increase this Anticipation immediately to pay Monies due on the Contracts for feeding our Army and I must make them the expected Payment by Notes to be discharged at a distant Day. Now Sir if these Notes are not satisfied when they become due, the little Credit which remains to this Country must fall and the little Authority dependent on it must fall too. Under such Circumstances it is that your are to ask Aid for the United States. If it can be obtained I shall consider the obligation as being in some degree personal to my self and I shall certainly exert my self for the Repayment. You will be so kind Sir as to Ship on Board the Washington eighteen hundred thousand Livres, but if the Loan be not obtained I must intreat you will give me the earliest possible Information of the Refusal.

I shall communicate this Letter to the Minister of his Most Christian Majesty and request him to write to Mr. de Vergennes on the Subject of it.

Beleive me I pray With sincere & respectful Esteem & Regard Your Excellency's Most obedient & Humble Servt.

Robt Morris

P.S. You have enclosed the Copy of a Letter which was sent with this to Monsr. de La Luzerne

II.

Office of Finance 26th: May 1783

Sir

I have now before me your Letters of the fourteenth and twenty third of December which are the last I have received. Enclosed you have a Letter from me to the Minister of France, with his Answer of the fourteenth of March on the Subject of the Delay which happened in transmitting his Dispatches. You will see by these that Lieutenant Barney was not to blame.

Your Bills in Favor of Monsr: de Lauzun have not yet appeared or they should have been duly honoured. That Gentleman has since left the Country and therefore it is possible that the Bill may not come.

The Reflections you make as well on the Nature of Public Credit as on the Inattention of the several States, are just and unanswerable but in what Country of the World shall we find a Nation willing to Tax themselves. The Language of Panegyric has held forth the English as such a Nation, but certainly if our Legislatures were subject to like Influence with theirs we might preserve the Form, but we should already have lost the Substance of Freedom. Time, Reason, Argument and above all that kind of Conviction which arises from feeling are necessary to the Establishment of our Revenues and the Consolidation of our Union. Both of these appear to me essential to our public Happiness, but our Ideas (as you well know) are frequently the

Result rather of habit than Reflection so that Numbers who might think justly upon these Subjects have been early estranged from the Modes and Means of considering them properly.

I am in the Hourly Wish and Expectation of hearing from You and sincerely hope that it may be soon.

Beleive me I pray with Esteem and Respect Your Excellency's Most obedient & Humble Servant

Robt Morris

To Benjamin Franklin from, 27 May 1783

Office of Finance 27th. May 1783

Sir

It was my earnest Desire from the first Moment when it was known that the Troops of his most Christian Majesty were intended for this Continent to promote his Service and forward the Views and Interests of his faithful Servants— It would appear like an empty Boast to say that I was early and frequently useful to them nor would I hint any thing of that kind or of the improper Returns I have met with. My present Object is meerly to possess you of facts as far as they relate to the Kings Service. Shortly after the Commencement of my Administration I proposed supplying the Kings Troops by Contract but found Obstacles were raised and objections were made by such as I was induced to suppose were interested in opposing œconomical Arrangements and therefore I desisted— Very slight enquiry will determine whether the Expences of this Army have been Moderate or excessive— The enclosed Letter from me to the Intendant will explain one Transaction— I shall add to it only that the Intendant having refused to pay, a Suit was commenced against Mr. DeMars by Solomons the Broker for all the Bills which he sold to DeMars and to Debrassine. On the Trial it appeared not only that Mr. Debrassine was employed by Mr. De Mars in public and private Business but that the Monies obtained by Sale of all those Bills of Exchange were applied to private Purposes— The Jury were but a few Minutes out of Court and brought in their Verdict for the Principal Interest &ca. Indeed had the Intendant thought proper to enquire into the facts stated in my Letter to him I have no Doubt but that they and others of equal Importance would have appeared— Enclosed you have the Copy of a Letter which has fallen into my Hands and which will shew you Something of the Business which has been transacted by the French Administration— The original of this Letter is now in my Hands and can (at any Time) be delivered if necessary to the Minister or Consul of France here—

I am to request Sir that you will have a Conference on the Subject of this Letter with General de Chattelleux. That Gentleman always appeared to me extremely Zealous and attentive to the King's Interest, desirous of introducing Œconomy and opposed to Plans which entailed a profuse Expence— Should you after a Consultation with him think it would at all conduce to the Kings Interests I shall be glad that you would bring the Matter regularly before his Ministers who will I perswade myself cause the proper Investigations by which means the Crown will be better served on Subsequent Occasions.

With perfect Respect I have the Honor to be Sir Your Excellency's most obedient & humble Servant

Robt Morris

To George Washington, 29 May 1783

Office of Finance 29th May 1783

Dear Sir

I am now to acknowlege the Receipt of your Excellency's Letter of the Eighth Instant. I have not answered it sooner because until now it has not been in my Power to answer it satisfactorily.

By some designing Men my Resignation of Office (grounded on a clear Conviction that unless Something were done to Support public Credit very pernicious Consequences would follow) was miscontrued. It was represented as a factious Desire to raise civil Commotions. It was said that the Army were to be employed as the Instruments to promote flagitious interested Views. These Insinuations found Admittance to Minds which should forever have been shut against them. We now rest on the Event to determine whether a sincere Regard to public Justice and public Interest or a sinister Respect to my own private Emolument were the influential Motives of my Conduct. I am a very mistaken Man if Time and Experience shall not demonstrate that the Interests of the Army and of the public Creditors are given up. But I mention these Things only to you and in Confidence for it shall not again be supposed that I am the Leader of Sedition.

Having done what was in my Power to establish those Plans which appeared necessary for doing Justice to all and affording Relief to our Army in particular I have acquitted what was the first and greatest duty. When it appeared that other Modes were to be pursued I would gladly have departed in Peace but it has been thought that my further Agency was necessary to procure for the Army that Species of Releif which they seem to desire—The factious designing Man who was to have lighted up the flames of Mutiny and Sedition has undertaken a most arduous and perilous Business to save this Country from those Convulsions which by

Negligence had hazarded. This became a duty when the first duty to Justice was performed And this shall be performed also.

It is now above a Month since the Committee conferred with us on that Subject and I then told them no Payment could be made to the Army but by Means of a Paper Anticipation and unless our Expenditures were immediately and considerably reduced even that could not be done—Our Expenditures have nevertheless been continued and our Revenues lessens, the States growing daily more and more rem[iss] in their Collections—The Consequence is that I cannot make Payments in the manner first intended—The Notes issued for this Purpose would have been payable at two four and six Months from the date but at present they will all be at six Months and even that will soon become impracticable unless our Expences be immediately curtailed.

I shall cause such Notes to be issued for three Months Pay to the Army and I must entreat Sir that every Influence be used with the States to absorb them together with my other Engagements by Taxation. The present Collections are most shameful and afford but sad Prospect to all those who are dependant upon them.

I hope my dear Sir that the State of public Affairs will soon permit you to lay down the Cares of your painful Office—I should two days have been liberated from mine if a desire to free you from our Embarrassments and procure some little Releif to your Army had not induced a Continuance of them—But it must always be remembered that this Continuance is distinct from every Ideal which may be connected with the Plans for funding our public Debts. As I do not approve of so I cannot be responsible for them. Neither will I involve myself in endless Details which must terminate in Disappointment. With great Respect I have the Honor to be Sir your Excellency's most obedient and humble Servant

Robt Morris

To Benjamin Franklin, 30 May 1783

Philadelphia 30th. May 1783

Dear Sir

I have received your private Letter of the twenty third of December. When I informed you of what was said by your Enemies I did not mean to insinuate any Doubt of your Exertions in my own mind. With Respect to your Resignation I personally lament it, and more so on the Part of the United States. But I shall readily agree that you will more consult your own Ease and Happiness by abandoning public Life and it will be almost impossible to add to your Reputation. I cannot however take a Part in procuring your Dismission for this would be an Injury to the Public. In whatever Situation and Character Believe me always with sincere Esteem & Respect Your Most Obedient & humble Servant

Robt Morris

To John Jay, 31 May 1783

Philada. May 31st—1783—

Dear Sir

I have none of your Letters to answer; the receipt of those which you formerly honored me with afforded me very great satisfaction, which I mention as an inducement for you to write more. We are told that your Health is injured and that you have been traveling to try whether change of air and Exercise will restore it. Wishes rarely produce any effect but I cannot restrain mine, they are offered with sincerity for the restoration and continuance of Good Health, and for the perpetual Happiness of you and yours. Governeur Morris heard a few days since that you are going back to Spain, and telling this a little abruptly to Kitty Livingston affected her Spirits so much that she has not recovered herself perfectly to this hour, that worthy Girl is most truly Her Sisters and your *Friend*.

Governeur is , Start deletion,, End, very sincerely attached to you I know it for I know him thoroughly, he is this Morning set off for New York and will be gone about a Fortnight— He leaves me encumbered with more difficulties than any one man ought to encounter. I have made an effort to get clear of this troublesome and dangerous Office but as yet I am not permitted to retire. on the Contrary I must of necessity encrease my Engagements to a degree that renders it entirely uncertain when I shall have it in my Power to see them discharged. If you can obtain me aid, for Heavens sake, or rather for the sake of ^our^ Country, do it—

The Blessings of Peace flow in upon us Spontaneosly but it requires the full exercise of more Virtue and good Sense than has yet appeared in our Councils to secure the Continuance of them— Providence has been Wonderfully kind and if Faith is acceptable in Heaven, we must be favourites as we place our whole Trust in Providence and do nothing for ourselves. You will Learn from the Public Prints, the Journals of Congress, the Letters of Mr Livingston &c. every thing worth knowing and as I can ill spare my own Time I will not take up yours with repetitions. Congress Complain that they do not hear often enough from any of their Ministers abroad.— I am most sincerely Dr: Sir Your affectionate Friend & obedient Servant

Robt. Morris

To George Washington, 5 June 1783

Office of Finance June 5 1783

Sir

I have just received your Letter of the third Instant. Nothing would please me better than to comply instantly with your Wishes. The Paper on which the Notes are to be Printed came from the Paper Mill on Saturday Evening, on Monday Morning the Printer was employed, and to Morrow Morning he is to send the first Parcel of Notes. I am then to sign them and fast as that can be done they shall be sent forward to the Paymaster General in Parcels; I am determined to devote my whole Time to the expeditious Accomplishment of this Business, and you will be the best Judge whether to detain the Troops a little while longer or not. I have the Honor to be your Excellency's most obedient and very humble Servant

Robt Morris

To John Jay, 26 July 1783

Philada. July. 26th. 1783

Dear Sir

Mr. Darby & Mr. Grigby have severally delivered your introductory letters of the 8th of April and I flatter my self that they will think themselves obliged to you. they are very deserving young Gentln. & make an agreable addition to our Circle of Society, this how ever will be of short duration as their own pursuits will very soon seperate us. Mr & Mrs. Carter, & Col. Wadsworth will soon add to the American Circle in Paris; they are too well known to Mrs. Jay & yourself to need recommendation from me. Kitty Livingston has left us about a Month. She is at

Elizabeth Town and very well and I am told all the Family are so — Mrs Morris always thinks & speaks of Mrs Jay & yourself, through that Medium of esteem & respect which You never fail to impress so strongly on Your Friends & Acquaintance.

My situation as a Public Man is distressing. I am Cursed with that worst of all political Sins, Poverty. My engagements & Anticipations for the Public amount to a Million of Dollars—it racks my utmost invention to keep pace with the demands, but hitherto I have been able to preserve that Credit which kept our affairs alive untill you had the opportunity of Concluding a Glorious Peace, and now a little exertion on the part of the States would enable me to make payment & quit the , Start deletion,, End, Service with reputation, the want of that exertion may ruin the Public Credit and involve the Country in New Convulsions. I hope my Dear Friend that you and our other Ministers, will be able to procure me some further assistance from France & Holland, it is as important at this as it has been at any other Period, but less will do. Our Government is yet too Weak, bad Men have too much sway, there are evils afloat which can only be avoided or cured by wise & honest measures, assisted by the lenient hand of time. I am ever, my Dr Sir Your Affectionate hble Servt.

Robt. Morris

To George Washington, 12 August 1783

Office of Finance 12th Augt 1783

Sir

I have received your Excellency's favor of the Sixth Instant—I am always happy to hear from you altho I confess that every new Demand for Money makes me Shudder. Your Recommendations will always meet my utmost attention because I am perswaded that you have equally with me the Desire to husband and to enlarge our Resources—Your perfect Knowlege of our political and military Situation must decide on the Measures to be pursued and I am perswaded that your Advice to Congress on these Subjects will be equally directed to the Safety the Honor and the Interest of the United States—With very sincere Esteem I have the Honor to be Sir your Excellency's most obedient & humble Servant

Robt Morris

To George Washington, 20 August 1783

Office of Finance 20th Augt 1783

Dear Sir

I have received your Letter of the thirteenth of August from Newburgh—The Business mentioned in it does by no means fall within my Cognizance but is purely in your own Discretion. You may indeed by the Exhibition of your account at the Treasury bring it under my notice but this is exactly what I would advise you not to do because as the Ballance would in that Case be certified among the old Debts I could only direct it to be placed on Interest—If on the contrary you direct Payment of the amount from the Pay Chest, which I conceive you have a Right to do, then on the Exhibition of your accounts they will stand completely ballanced—I mention this for two Reasons, first because I wish to facilitate your Views, and secondly because I think that Congress have made you the sole Judge as to the Extent and manner of your Expence and that it is my Duty to enable the Paymaster to answer your Drafts. I am Sir with very sincere Esteem your most obedient & humble Servant

Robt Morris

To George Washington, 2 September 1783

Office of Finance 2nd Septr 1783

Sir

I received your Excellency's favors of the twenty fifth and thirtieth of last Month the latter was by far the more agreable for I confess to you Sir that I beheld the attempt to Garrison the Western Posts with Pain and went into so much of it as concerns my Department with infinite Reluctance. I perswade myself that the only effectual means of getting a good American Establishment of any Kind is to be so long without it that a Sense of the want shall stimulate the States into the means of forming it—At present all we can do is to close the past Scene if possible with Reputation. I am very sincerely your Excellency's most obedient & humble Servant

Robt Morris

To George Washington, 5 September 1783

Philada Septr 5th 1783

Dear Sir

Mrs Morris & myself accept most chearfully, the polite & Friendly invitation with which Mrs Washington & you are pleased to honor us, it is our intention to pay you a visit in a short time unless Congress should prevent it by removing themselves & You to this City previous to our journey.

One part of our business at Prince Town is to entreat in person that our House may be Your's whenever business or any occasion whatever shall bring you to this City, We have room enough & I persuade myself that Mrs Washington & yourself are perfectly Convinced how happy we shall be in the enjoyment of your Company Mr G. Morris will deliver this and to him I beg leave to refer your Excelly for such information as you may wish from this quarter. Mrs Washinton & you will accept our best wishes & Compliments, and in the expectation of soon taking you by the hand. I remain Dear Sir Your most Obedient & humble Servant

Robt Morris

To George Washington, 10 September 1783

Office of Finance 10th Septr 1783

Sir

I have received your Excellency's Letter of the thirty first of last Month enclosing a Copy of that of the eighteenth from Colo. Varick. I know do myself the Honor to enclose Notes for eighteen hundred Dollars and am to request that when this Service shall have been compleated Colo. Varick will be directed to transmit his Accounts with proper Vouchers that they may be passed at the Treasury. With perfect Respect I have the Honor to be Sir Your Excellency's most Obedient and Humble Servant

Robt Morris

To Benjamin Franklin, 17 September 1783

Philada Septr. 17th. 1783

Dear Sir

You have above an extract of a letter from the Honble Mr. Jefferson, to me by which you will perceive that he wants one of your late invented Machines for Copying Writings, he desires me to write to England but if I am not much mistaken France is the place. You however will know where his order can be best executed, and give orders accordingly, shou'd it be shipped from France Messrs LeCouteulx & Co will supply the Money to pay Cost on my acct. If you think it best to order it from London Messrs Herries & Company of that place will pay for it, or in either case if it will suit you to draw on Mr. Jefferson or me payable in America for the Cost the bill shall be punctually acquitted. You will excuse this trouble it is occasioned by the opinion which I entertain, that this is the most likely way to have our Friend Jefferson well Served. With sincere Attachment I ever am Dear Sir Your most Obedient & Most humble servant

Robt Morris

To John Adams, 20 September 1783

Office of Finance 20 September 1783

Sir

I have been duly honored with your Excellency's favors of the fifth tenth and eleventh of July— I have taken the Liberty to make some Extracts from the two latter which are transmitted in a Letter to the Governor of Massachusetts Copy whereof is enclosed— Permit me Sir to give my feeble Approbation and Applause to those Sentiments of Wisdom and Integrity which are as happily expressed as they are forcibly conceived.— The Necessity of strengthening our Confederation providing for our Debts and forming some fœderal Constitution begins to be most seriously felt; But unfortunately for America the narrow and illiberal Prejudices of some have taken such deep Root that it must be difficult and may prove impracticable to remove them.

I agree with you Sir in Opinion that the late Peace was not all Circumstances considered a bad one for England. It is undoubtedly a Peace equally glorious to, and necessary for

America. All Ranks of Men in this Country feel as well as perceive the Benefits of it; and the Fault-Finders (for such Men there always will be) are borne down by the general Torrent of Applause—

I was happy to learn by the Washington Packet that you intended a short Trip to Amsterdam for the Purpose of urging on the Loan. I hope you may have met with the Success due to your Zeal and Abilities, I shall ask no greater—

with perfect Respect / I have the Honor to be / Sir / your Excellency's / most obedient / and / humble Servant

Robt Morris

To Benjamin Franklin, 30 September 1783

Office of Finance 30 Septem: 1783

Sir,

I am to acknowlege the Receipt of your Favors of the seventh of March and twenty seventh of July. For both of them accept my Thanks. You express an Apprehension lest the Union between France and America should be diminished by Accounts from your Side of the Water. This Apprehension does you equal Honor as a Statesman and as a Man. Every Principle which ought to actuate the Councils of a Nation requires from us an affectionate Conduct towards France and I very sincerely lament those Misapprehensions which have indisposed some worthy Men towards that Nation whose Treasure and Blood have been so freely expended for us. I believe the Truth with respect to some to be this. A warm Attachment to America has prevented them from making due Allowances in those Cases where there Country was concerned. Under certain Prepossession it was natural for them to think that the french Ministry might do more for us, and it was quite as natural for the Ministers to think that we ought to have done more for ourselves. The Moment of Treaty with England was of Course the Moment of Profession with english Ministers. I fear that the Impressions made by these were for a little while rather more deep than was quite necessary. But the same Love of America which had raised such strong Irritability where her Interests were concerned, will of Course stimulate it to an equal Degree when those Interests are assailed from another Quarter. I think I may venture to assure you that the Esteem of this Country for France is not diminished and that the late Representations have not been so unfavorable as you fear.

Our Commerce is flowing very fast towards Great Britain and that from Causes which must for ever influence the commercial Part of Society. Some Articles are furnished by Britain cheaper many as cheap and all on a long Credit. Her Merchants are attentive and punctual. In her Ports our Vessels always meet with Dispatch. I say Nothing of Language and Manners because I do not think they influence so strongly on Commerce as many People suppose but what is of no little Importance is that the English having formed our Taste are more in a Capacity to gratify that Taste by the Nature and fashion of their Manufactures. There is another Circumstance also which must not be forgotten. The great Demand for french Manufactures during the War increased the Price of many and some Time will be required before it can by a fair Competition be discovered which of the two Countries france or England can supply us cheapest. The Delays in the public Bills is a further Circumstance which militates (a momentary Obstacle) against the Trade with France. I must therefore mention to you also a Matter which is of great Effect. Until we can navigate the Mediteranean in Safety we cannot trade in our own Bottoms with the Ports of france or Spain which are on that Sea. And we certainly will not Trade there in foreign Bottoms because we do not find the same Convenience and Advantage in so doing as in our own Vessels.

Unless indeed it be on Board of English Ships. This may be a disagreable Fact but it is not the less a Fact. I beleive that Informations are transmitted from hence to the Court which they ought not to rely on. Their Servants doubtless do their Duty in transmitting such Informations but I am perswaded that they are themselves not well informed. Indeed it is quite natural that Men should mistake when they examine and treat of a Subject with which they are unacquainted. And it cannot well be supposed that political Characters are competent to decide on the Advantages and Disadvantages of allowing to or witholding from us a share in the carrying Trade— On this Subject I will make a further Observation and you may rely on it that I speak to you with Candor and Sincerity not with a View to making any Impressions on the Court. You may communicate or withold what I say and they may or may not apply it to their own Purposes. If any thing will totally ruin the Commerce of England with this Country it is her blind Attachment to her Navigation Act. This Act which never was the real Foundation of her naval Superiority may and perhaps will be the Cause of its Destruction. If france possesses commercial Wisdom she will take Care not to imitate the Conduct of her Rival. The West India Islands can be supplied twenty per Cent cheaper in american than in french or british Bottoms I will not trouble you with the Reasons but you may rely on the Fact. The Price of the Produce of any Country must materially depend on the Cheapness of Subsistence. The Price at which that Produce can be vended abroad must depend on the Facility of Conveyance. Now admitting for a Moment (which by the bye is not true) that France might by Something like a british Navigation Act, increase her Ships and her Seamen these Things would necessarily follow. 1st. Her Islands would be less wealthy and therefore less able to consume and pay for her Manufactures 2ly. The Produce of those Islands would be less cheap and therefore less able to sustain the weight of Duties and support a Competition in foreign Markets. 3ly. The Commerce with this Country would be greatly lessened because that every American Ship which finds herself in a french or english or other Port will naturally seek a freight there rather than go elswhere to look for it because in many Commodities the Difference of Price in different Parts will not compensate the Time and Cost of going from Place to Place to look after them. To these Principal Reasons might be added many others of lesser weight tho not of little Influence such as the probable Increase of commercial Intercourse by increasing the Connections and Acquaintances of Individuals. To this and to every Thing else which can be said on the Subject by an American I know there is one short Answer always ready. viz: That we seek to encrease our own Wealth. So far from denying that this is among my Motives I place it as the foremost and (setting aside that Gratitude which I feel for France) I do not scruple to declare that a Regard to the Interests of America is with Respect to all Nations of the World my political Compass. But the different Nations of Europe should consider that in Proportion to the Wealth of this Country will be her Ability to pay for those Commodities which all of them are pressing us to buy.

The People of this Country still continue as remiss as ever in the Payment of Taxes. Much of this (as you justly observe) arises from the Difficulties of Collection. But those Difficulties are much owing to an ignorance of proper Modes and an Unwillingness to adopt them. In short tho all are content to acknowlege that there is a certain Burthen of Taxation which ought to be borne Yet each is desirous of Shifting it off of his own Shoulders on those of his Neighbors. Time will I hope produce a Remedy to the Evils under which we labor but it may also increase them.

Your Applications to the Court for Aid are certainly well calculated to obtain it, but I am not much surprized at your ill Success indeed I should have been much surprized if you had been more fortunate— Of all Men I was placed in the Situation to take a deep Concern in the Event but I cannot disapprove of the Refusal for we certainly ought to do more for ourselves before we ask the Aid of others— Copies of your Letters to the Court were laid before Congress and also the Copy of the new Contract. I will enclose with this a further Copy of the Ratification of the old if I can obtain it in Season from Princeton where the Congress now are.

I have written also on the Subject of the Debt due to the farmer's general and should Congress give me any Orders about it I shall attend carefully to the Execution. The Conduct they have maintained with regard to us has been generous and will demand a Return of Gratitude as well as of Justice. This I hope my Countrymen will always be disposed to Pay. I shall take some proper Opportunity of writing to the farmer's General but will wait a while to Know what may be the Determination of Congress on their Affairs.

It gives me much Pleasure to find that by the proposed Establishment of Packetts we shall shortly be in Condition to maintain more regular and connected Correspondence for altho I shall not myself be much longer in public Office I feel for those who are or will be charged with the Affairs of our Country both at Home and abroad.— It will naturally occur however that a good Cypher must be made use of not unfrequently when Dispatches are trusted to foreigners. They have no Regard either to Propriety or even Decency where Letters are concerned.

With very sincere Esteem and Respect I am Sir your Excellency's most obedient and humble Servant

RM.

To Benjamin Franklin, 2 October 1783

Philada. October 2d. 1783

Dear Sir

This Letter will either be delivered or forwarded to you by a most Worthy Gentn. Nathl. Gorham Esqr. of Boston for whose Public & private Character I have the highest respect, This Gentn has served as Member & Speaker of the Massachusetts assembly. & lately he had a pretty long Campaigne in Congress where I had that opportunity of knowing the integrity of his Conduct & the Soundness of his judgement that did not fail to inspire me with Strong personal Attachment it is probable that he will make some proposals to the Court for supplying their Marine with Masts & Spars & in this business he is associated with Thos. Russell & Wm Burgess Esqrs of Boston and John Langdon Esqr of Portsmouth in New Hampshire all Gentn of that Character & Solidity which ought to give Weight to what they offer.

They were kind enough to invite me to join them, but not suiting my situation & Views I declined it, I am however equally desirous of promoting their Interest and hope what I have Said may procure them your favourable aid. I will engage the Chevr La Luzerne to write in their favour. You always have my best Wishes for I am very Sincerely Dear Sir Your Affectionate Friend & Obedt. humble servt.

Robt Morris

To George Washington, 10 October 1783

Office of Finance 10th Octr 1783

Dear Sir

I have received your favor of the third Instant and am very much disposed to go into the measure you mention but for evident Reasons I cannot do it. You my dear Sir undoubtedly may and as the Paymaster is bound to answer your Drafts the money can be by your order put into the Hands of one of your Aids or of your Secretary and paid to these people as Compensation for voluntary extra Service without involving a Precedent as it would do in coming directly from this Office. I am Sir with sincere Esteem your most obedient & humble Servant

Robt Morris

To George Washington, 15 October 1783

Philada October 15th 1783

Dear Sir

I am sorry to find that the delay of my long intended visit to Prince Town has been attended with inconvenience to you. but those delays were unavoidable being generally occasioned by want of money which could only be raised whilst I was present here, each Week I proposed to Set out the ensuing one, but still fresh demands arose, to keep me fixed to this Spot I have now some expectation of Seeing you here as intimations have reached us, of the probability of Congress removing to this City, I wait the Certainty of this event & then shall determine whether to send forward Your Wine, it is a parcell that was Sent in by Mr Boudfield of Bourdeaux & paid for by the United States.

I have caused the Depy Pay Master to be supplied with four Thousand Dollrs for Your use of which 1500 have been paid to Mrs Washington & the rest I suppose sent forward to Yourself & your own Warrants will Cover the payment. I most sincerely wish to See you here but if Congress do not adjourn to this place Mrs Morris & myself will still pay you a visit if possible being most truely Dr Sir Your Affectionate humble servt

Robt Morris

To John Adams, 23 October 1783

Office of Finance 23. October 1783

Sir

I do myself the Honor to enclose the Copy of a Letter which I have just written to Mess$^{rs.}$ Wilhelm and Jan Willink, Nicolaas and Jacob Van Staphorst, De la Lande and Finje. This Letter will fully explain to your Excellency the Means I have adopted to bring our Funds into the most speedy Operation. Should the Plan meet your Approbation (which I hope may be the Case) I shall then rely on the Exertion of the great Influence you have so deservedly acquired for carrying it into Effect It will I am sure be as pleasing to you as it can be to me to find that the Disposition of our Country is turning fast towards those Measures of public Justice which can alone render her great and respected. Permit me to participate in the Satisfaction you must feel from Knowing that the honorable Sentiments so well inculcated in your Letters have greatly influenced in promoting that useful Disposition.—

I am Sir with unfeigned Esteem & Respect / your most obedient / and / hum^l Servant

Rm.—

To Benjamin Franklin, 4 November 1783

Office of Finance 4th. Novr. 1783

Sir,

I do myself the Honor to enclose another Copy of the Ratification of Congress to the Contract with the french Court of the sixteenth of July 1782 which is dated the twenty second Day of January last also the Ratification of the Contract of the twenty fifth of February last which is dated on the last Day of October— These Pieces will go by the Washington Packet and I hope that you may receive them safely and soon.

I am Sir Your most Obedient and Humble Servant

Robt Morris

To John Adams, 5 November 1783

Office of Finance 5th: Novr. 1783

Sir

I am honored with your Excellency's favor, of the twenty eighth of July, from Amsterdam; for which I pray you to accept my Acknowlegements. I am perfectly in Sentiment with you, that it is best to avoid Governmental Interference in the Affair of our Loan. If there were no other Reason, I should not like the Demand of grateful Acknowlegement which would be erected on that Foundation. We hear enough already of our National Obligations, and I most heartily wish, for my own Part, that we could at once acquit them all, even to the uttermost farthing; for I seriously beleive that both Nations and Individuals, generally, prove better friends when no Obligations can be charged, nor Acknowlegements and Retributions claimed on either Side.—

I am also very strongly in Opinion with you that Remittances from this Country would greatly uphold our Credit in Europe, for in Mercantile Life nothing vivify's Credit like Punctuality and Plentiousness of Remittance. The Plan you propose to obtain them, might also be attended with some good Consequences, but there are Impediments in the Way of it's Success, which it would be tedious to Detail, and which indeed you could not be so perfectly Master of without being on the Spot. I shall not therefore go into that Matter at present, and the more especially as we have now good Hopes that the Plan of Congress will be adopted by the States— Last Evening, I received advice that Massachusetts had acceded; and I have a double Pleasure in announcing this to you, as they certainly would not have come in but for the Sentiments contained in your Letters. Let me then, my dear Sir, most heartily congratulate you on those virtuous Emotions which must swell your Bosom at the Reflection that you have been the able, the useful, and (what is above all other Things) the honest Servant of a Republic indebted to you in a great Degree for her first Efforts at independent Existence— That you may long live to enjoy these pleasing Reflections which flow from the Memory of an Active and beneficial Exercise of Time and Talents, is the sincere Wish of / Your most Obedient / and / Humble Servant

Robt Morris

To George Washington, 26 November 1783

Office of Finance 26th Novr 1783

Sir

I have been honored with the Receipt of your Excellencys Letter of the 18th Inst. and in Consequence shall send this to the City of New York which I hope and expect is now in our possession. It is unnecessary to assure you Sir how pleasing it would be, to comply with the Wishes of the Officers now in Service, as expressed in their Memorial of the 17th Inst. because I am sure both you and they must be convinced of my disposition to render Justice to every part of the Army, but alas, Sir the good Will, is all which I have in my power. The means of Making payment is not. on the Contrary I am constantly involved in Scenes of Distress to keep pace with those engagements which I have already taken for the Subsistance and Pay which the Army have heretofore received. Those Engagements which I dreaded at the Time were taken under Various Considerations. The Relief of the Army then to be discharged, Your Excellency's earnest desire—The Orders of Congress and in particular the Urgency of the Committee appointed to treat with me on that Subject, and my own desire to render service to the Army, these were amongst the Motives which induced me to Hazard an Anticipation of a Million of Dollars on the Public Account. My Solicitude to fulfill those Engagements is extreme, but my Calls for help are disregarded, and under such Circumstances it cannot be expected that I shall make new Engagements, and there is not any Money in the Treasury. I lament the situation of the Officers and am truly sorry that the States are so inattentive to the Finances of the Union. I have the Honor to be, your Excellency's most obedient and Humble Servant

Robt Morris

To John Jay, 27 November 1783

Philadelphia November 27th 1783

My Dear Sir,

I Congratulate you on the signing of the Definitive Treaty and on the evacuation of New York which took place on Tuesday our Friend Gouverneur Morris is there he has been gone about 18 Days and I expect him back very soon. he will then give you the

Detail and inform you of such things as you may wish to know respecting any of your particular Friends.—

I agree with the Sentiments expressed in your letter of the 12th September Treaties of Commerce are dangerous rather than other wise, and if all Governments were to agree that Commerce should be as free as Air I believe they would then place it on the most advantageous footing for every Country & for all mankind; The restrictions which Great Britain is aiming at will in the end work for our Good, if we can work good out of any thing; which in the present State of things seems doubtful If Great Britain persists in refusing admittance to our Ships in their Islands, they will probably have great cause to repent for I shall not be surprized to see a general Prohibition to the admittance of theirs into our Ports, and if such a measure is once adopted they may find it very difficult to obtain any alteration and in that Case, the advantages of carrying will be much against them. Should the court of France pursue the same Policy we shall fall in with the Dutch & probably have more Connections in Commerce with them.

I have received the prints of the Rise & fall of the *Balloon* Pray cannot they contrive to send Passengers with a Man to steer the course, so as to make them the means of conveyance for Dispatches from one Country to another or must they only be sent for intelligence to the Moon & Clouds.—

Congress are now collecting at annapolis but I think will not make a House untill towards the end of next week, Gen Mifflin accepts the presidents chair

We are dismissing the remains of our Army and getting rid of expence so that I hope to see the end of my engagements before next May, but I doubt whether it will be in my power to observe that punctuality in performing them which I wish and have constantly aimed at.—

I rejoice at the encrease of your family because I consider it as an increase of happiness to Mrs. Jay & yourself Mrs. Morris and myself beg to be affectionately remembered to her, Our Boys and their Tutor Monsr. Basseville have given us great satisfaction by their last letters and I think they are in a good way.—

I am sending some Ships to China in order to encourage others in the adventurous pursuits of Commerce and I wish to see a foundation laid for an American Navy. I am Dr Sir Your Affectionate Friend & Humble Servant,

Robt. Morris

To Benjamin Franklin, 17 January 1784

Philada January 17th. 1784

Sir

Colo Harmar the Bearer of this Letter is just arrived from Annapolis charged with the Definitive Treaty Ratified by Congress with which he is to proceed for Paris in order to deliver the same to the Ministers who negotiated the Treaty, that the Ratifications may be exchanged— Congress have directed me to supply Colo Harmar with Money to defray his Necessary Expences, In Consequence of this Order I have advanced him Two Hundred Spanish Dollars here and now write to Mr. Grand Requesting that he may Supply such farther sum as you shall agree may be proper & necessary for the above purpose— I suppose His Excellency the President of Congress has Recommended Colo Harmar to your Notice— He has been a brave and deserving officer which alone will procure him your favorable Attention.

I am Your Excellencys Most obedt & very humble servt.

Robt Morris   319

To Benjamin Franklin, 12 February 1784

Office of Finance 12th. Febry. 1784—

Dr: Sir,

Three Days ago, I received in a Letter of the first of December from Messrs. Wilhelm and Jan Willink Nicolaas and Jacob Van Staphorst De la Lande and Finje at Amsterdam a Copy of their Letter to you of the thirtieth of November. Enclosed you have Copy of my answer of this Date. I flatter myself that you will not have suffered the public Credit to be ruined for Want of an Engagement to the Amount of so small a Sum as might be necessary to avoid the Danger to which it was exposed, and I wait in the Anxious Expectation of hearing from you what Arrangements have been taken on this Subject, as I wish to conform my Measures to them. If contrary to my Expectations, some unforeseen Causes should have induced you to decline that so necessary Engagement I hope this Letter may arrive in Season and induce you to do it. You will observe that a Copy of this Letter is transmitted to the Houses in Amsterdam, but I have not sent Copy of the enclosed Letters to Mr. Grand and Mr. Barclay which are left open for your Perusal. I have not Time now to go particularly into the Estimation of their Accounts, but I am almost perswaded that there is (between them) and ought to be in the Hands of the former (before this Time) about half a Million Livres belonging to the United States. But in the present Exigency I shall not reckon on this Sum, nor on the second Expedition of five hundred Hogsheads of Tobacco which are, I presume, before this Hour arrived at Amsterdam. I shall calculate on a Deficiency of five hundred thousand Guilders, and prepare Remittance as fast as proper Articles can be purchased to that Amount; because the Surplus may be well disposed of to answer the Interest of the Dutch Loan which falls due in June next. If therefore you can adopt any Measures by which, in circuitous Negotiations, the

Time of Payment can be prolonged you may rely on the Arrival of such Remittances in the Months of June and July, at farthest, as shall fully answer the Sums which may then fall due, and as I have told the Gentlemen in Amsterdam the Advices which I may receive will govern the Direction of those Remittances. I shall give immediate Orders for the Purchase of one thousand Hogsheads of Tobacco, and as that Amount is compleated I shall extend it according as Circumstances may require. The Season has been so intemperate that the Navigation of the Chesapeak is to this Hour shut up by the Ice, but that cannot last much longer, and therefore I have good Hopes that some capital Shippments may depart before the first of April; and, should the Urgency of the Case require it, I can draw at long Sight on the Consignees, and transmit the Bills, which will enable a farther Negotiation if necessary. The Means of making Remittances are now, thank God, in my Power; for the Amount of Taxes exceeds that of the Expenditures, which last are reduced almost to Nothing, and as the Revival of Commerce must encrease the Means of paying Taxes, I have no other Solicitude for the Event than what arises from the Want of Time to make due Arrangements. This Want I perswade myself you will remedy, if you have not already provided against it. And you may rely that any Engagements you may think it necessary to take, shall be most punctually complied with by me—

With Unfeigned Esteem and Respect I have the Honor to be Your Excellency's most obedient & humble Servant

Robt Morris

P.S. Since writing the above it occurs to me, that there is (particularly on the present Occasion) a Propriety in transmitting to you the best Account in my Power of the Situation of things, as to the Funding of our public Debt. I say the best in *my Power,* for I know not what is done Southward of Virginia, No Mail having come from thence in upwards of six weeks; by Reason of the

Inclemency of the Weather, which greatly impedes our Intelligence from every Quarter. New Hampshire, Massachusetts, New Jersey, Pennsylvania, Delaware, Maryland, and Virginia have adopted the Plan recommended by Congress. I am assured that New York & Connecticutt will adopt it very speedily; and I am told (on good Authority) that Rhode Island will come in so soon as the Example of the other States is communicated. It is in Consequence of my Conviction that the Plan will soon be agreed to by all, that I have published an Advertisement of the Ninth Instant Copy whereof is enclosed—

To Benjamin Franklin, 13 February 1784

Office of Finance 13th. Febry. 1784—

Dr. Sir,

I have written to you, under Yesterday's Date, on a very interesting Subject; and I will now add Something farther which I did not chuse to place in that Letter, as a Copy of it is transmitted to the Houses in Holland. And first I will give you an Account of my Situation, as accurately as possible, in order that (seeing the whole State of my Engagements, and the means of fulfilling them) you may rest at Ease under the Operation I have requested, and which I must now most strongly Urge and intreat you to engage in.

My present actual Engagements are threefold Viz. 1st. General Engagements for the public Service not yet Satisfied, including therein the Notes issued by me which remain in Circulation. 2ly. My Bills of Exchange unpaid. And 3ly. My Debts to the National Bank.

The first of these it is difficult to ascertain with Exactness For I take into the Account all Payments to be made for past Services and the like, and I set against it sundry Sums to be received and the public Goods which are yet to arrive. It cannot be expected therefore that any great Precision will take Place in this Estimate but from the clearest Insight I have, the Amount is rather under than over one hundred thousand Dollars.

The Second Stands thus. I drew for a Million of Guilders of which calculating to the Extent, not more than one half remains unprovided for, as I have observed in My Letter of Yesterday. This half may be considered as of the Value of two hundred thousand Dollars. Besides this Sum, I have drawn three Bills of two hundred and fifty thousand Guilders each, and one of one hundred thousand Guilders, for which I have received three hundred and forty thousand Dollars; but as I have agreed that those Bills shall not be protested they are not to be carried to the Account of Bills of Exchange.

My Debt to the National Bank is the above Sum of three hundred and forty thousand Dollars obtained from them by Discounting Notes received for the Bills of Exchange and which Notes they will continue on Interest, untill taken up by my Payments here, or by Monies raised on the Drafts of the Parties who gave them, should My Bills be eventually paid in Europe.

In this Calculation you will perceive that I make no mention of any Monies which I suppose to be in the Hands of Mr. Grand, because (for the greater Certainty) I will on the present Occasion consider them as equal to answer for Contingencies only. And on the other Hand, I will not calculate the Interest to arise on Monies borrowed in Europe, because altho that object may be Stated as of the Value of from one hundred and fifty to two hundred thousand Dollars, yet to answer it I place 1st. the general System for funding the public Debts, and 2ly. Whatever small Sums may arise on the Dutch Loan, supposing it to have no Success worth counting on for other Purposes.—

Hence therefore we will state the Account as of the first of the present Month thus

Balance due for past Services . . . . Dollars 100.000
. . .

Due for Bills of Exchange drawn 200.000
. . . .

Due to the national Bank 340.000
. . . .

640.000

Add for Contingencies 10.000
. . . .

Dollars—
650.000.

We come now to the Means of making Payment, after rejecting all Hope of any material Aid from the Dutch Loan. And they are as follows— The Taxes for the last four Months, ending the thirty first of January, amounting to somewhat more than two hundred thousand Dollars. Towards these Taxes, the States of Delaware, North Carolina and Georgia have as yet paid Nothing, neither is there any Thing paid by the State of South Carolina within the Account of those Months. The States of New Hampshire Connecticutt New York Maryland and Virginia have paid very little, in Proportion to their present Ability, and the other four States will all by the Extention of Peace and Commerce, be in better Circumstances for Revenue than they were before.

From the States of New York Maryland Virginia and South Carolina, I expect to derive very considerable Releif; particularly from the first, by a proposed Sale of confiscated Lands. However,

I shall (after deducting from the probable Increase of the Revenue, so much as may pay the current Expenditures) calculate the Surplus, and the proposed Sales of Lands, as amounting to no more than two hundred and fifty thousand Dollars, by the End of next September. This, then will place the Sum unprovided for at the amount of four hundred thousand Dollars and the Fund to pay it at fifty thousand Dollars per Month— That Fund will discharge the first Article above mentioned, by the End of March, And the next Thing to be provided for is the two hundred thousand, to answer Bills of Exchange drawn. The intended Provision for that Object is as follows, I shall borrow immediately one hundred thousand Dollars of the Bank, and direct Purchases of Tobacco and Rice partly with Cash, partly on Credit and partly by Bills drawn on me. By this Means, I can with that one hundred thousand Dollars, have the Purchases made in all March and April, so that the Shippments to the required Amount of two hundred thousand Dollars will take Place Some in March, some in April, and all of them I hope by the End of May. The Taxes during April and May, will pay the Purchases on Credit, and the Bills drawn on me; and the Taxes in June and July, will pay the hundred thousand Dollars due to the Bank. By the End of September therefore I may calculate on a full Discharge of all these Debts.

If the Loan should meet with Success, my Releif will be more speedy; but you will see, Sir, from this Detail, what is most important to you, Viz that the Funds will be placed in Europe during the Months of June and July, to pay the half Million of Guilders which I desire you provide for. I suppose the Mode of circuitous Negotiations to be very familiar with your Bankers, but I would hint at the following as practicable. Suppose the Houses in Amsterdam to draw in the Month of March on Mr. Grand at sixty Days Sight. Mr. Grand might in May draw on a good House in London for his full Reimbursement and the House in London might (in like Manner) reimburse on Messrs. Le Couteulx & Co:, by which Time the Remittances would arrive. Or the Time might be still farther extended, if the House in London should reimburse on Messrs. Wilhelm and Jan Willink, and they on Messrs. Le Couteulx.— Or the last Bills might perhaps be drawn on Mr. Grand instead of Messrs. Le Couteulx. However, supposing that the Credit of those Gentlemen might be useful, I have requested them to aid your Operations, should you think proper to ask their Aid.

And now my dear Sir, let me before I close this Letter, entreat of you most earnestly, that the public Credit just begining to revive, be not totally lost for Want of an Effort which is but Nothing in Comparison with what we have already experienced, and passed thro, with Success.—

With very sincere Esteem & Respect I am Your most obedt. & humble Servant

Robt Morris

To George Washington, 14 February 1784

Philadelphia 14th February 1784

Dear Sir

In acknowledging your Letters of the fourth & tenth of last month I must pray you to accept my Thanks for the Expressions of Kindness Contained in them. Mr Wright has promised that your Portrait should speedily be Compleated, but hitherto his Promise is unperformed. Whenever it shall be received I will obey your Orders in the Disposition of it. Your Accounts with the Explanation of them, were handed (in the usual Course) to the Comptroller of the Treasury, and I have issued a Warrant for the Amount of his Certificate being Eight hundred and Fifty Seven Dollars and Fifty Two Ninetieths. This Warrant is enclosed for you to put your name on the back of it and in the mean time Governor Clinton is informed that he may draw for the Amount and that his Bills shall be answered. Mrs Morris joins me in presenting our warmest Respects to yourself and Mrs Washington, and I pray you to beleive that with every Sentiment of Friendship & regard I am Your most obedient Very humble servt

Robt Morris

To Thomas Jefferson, 25 February 1784

Office of Finance 25th. Febry. 1784

Sir

Your Letter of the first Instant reached me but a few days since and I seize the earliest Moment in my Power of replying to it. I shall reply also in this Letter to that with which I was favored from the honorable Mr. Williamson, and pray both of him and of the Committee that they will excuse it, assuring them that it proceeds from a desire of collecting all I have to say on the Subject under one Point of View.

It was and is my opinion and has frequently been expressed that the Calls of Congress should be confined to the arrears of former Requisitions so long as it can be possible out of such Means to defray the current Expenditures. And altho it has been necessary to comprize a Part of the Expenditures of 1782 and 1783 within that Debt for the Interest whereof permanent Funds have been required I thought it my Duty to oppose any Relinquishment of the existing Requisitions. I will not repeat the Reasons because the grand Committee appear to be of the same opinion. It was evident that if those Requisitions should produce more than the current Expenditure the Surplus could easily be applied towards discharging a Part of the Debt which arose during the Year 1782 and 1783.

Enclosed Sir you will find the required account of Taxes received to the End of the last Year. But since that Period there have been further Receipts and I must observe that among these are some small Sums collected in New Jersey and Pennsylvania on the Requisitions for 1783 but these are nevertheless carried (in the Treasury Books) to account of the unsatisfied Requisitions of 1782. Confining myself to round Numbers because I presume the Committee would rather receive Information materially right in Season than wait for greater Accuracy at the Expence of Moments every one of which must be precious, I take Leave to mention that the Arrearages on the Requisitions of 1782 and 1783 exceed eight Millions and that one of those eight Millions would pay the unfunded Expenditures from the End of 1781 to the Commencement of the current Year by which Term of *unfunded Expenditures* used for want of a better, I mean such Part of the public Debt as arose in that Year and which not having been carried to the Account of the Public Debt but remaining due on my Official Engagements and Anticipations must still be provided for out of the Requisitions. There will remain therefore at best seven Millions for the Service of this Year and Payment of a Part of the former Debt should the Collections be so rapid as to pay off the required Million beyond the immediate Expences which I confess there is but too little Reason to expect. It will however be useful that pressing applications be made to the States to compleat their Quotas under those Requisitions for if only One hundred thousand Dollars were employed in Payment of our funded Debt before January next, in addition to the Provision for paying the Interest, we might then consider the Independence of our Country as firmly established. I shall dwell no longer [on] this Subject which will I am sure be better matured by the Committee than by any of my Reflections. But I am bound to mention Sir that (from the

Slowness and Smallness of the Collections) our Finances are in a more critical Situation than you can easily conceive: Such, that I dare not leave this Place altho I am very desirous of paying my Respects to Congress at Annapolis.

As to the Vote of September 1782 requiring One million two hundred thousand Dollars for Payment of Interest on Loan Office Certificates &c. I have no official Information of what has been done by the States. Some among them have I believe directed the Issue of a certain other Kind of Certificate for Payment of that Interest, but as the Acts do not conform to the Resolution of Congress I cannot know what Conduct the Loan Officers have pursued. It is much to be lamented that the States individually are not sensible how necessary it is to conform to general Regulations. On every Occasion some local Convenience is consulted and a Deviation made which appears to be of little Consequence to the general System and which [is] nevertheless important; and becomes injurious to the very State by which it was made. The Idea of an Officer dependent only on Congress amenable only to them and consequently obedient only to Orders derived from their Authority is disagreable to each State and carries with it the Air of Restraint. Every such Officer therefore finds a Weight of Public Opinion to contend with. But how, in a Continent so extensive, can that Simplicity of Administration which is essential to Order and Œconomy, be introduced; unless such Officers are not only tolerated but aided by the legislative and executive Authorities? I will pursue these Ideas no farther for the present, because I think the Opportunity will arrive in which the Subject must be considered with more diffused Attention.

Enclosed (Sir) I have the Honor to transmit an Account of the Civil Establishment of the United States together with an Account of contingent Expences of the several Offices. Neither of these is as complete as could be wished tho as perfect as they can at present be made. You will doubtless observe that all the Offices are not completely filled and that all the contingent Expences are not brought into the Account. Among the latter Omissions is the contingent Expence of our foreign Ministers which will I am perswaded be far from inconsiderable.

I have thought it proper also to transmit to the Committee an Estimate of the Sums at which our Civil Establishment might be fixed; and on this Estimate I make the following general Observations. 1st That the Articles of Contingencies therein mentioned are carried out on Conjecture and therefore the Sum Total may be somewhat more or less according to Circumstances. 2ly That the Numbers Titles and Salaries of the several Officers being entirely in the Disposition of Congress they will add to or diminish from them as they may think proper wherefore the Totals will doubtless be different from what I have Stated and 3ly. That a very considerable Part of this Expence being occasioned by the old Accounts will cease of itself when those Accounts are settled.

I proceed then to observe more particularly on the Expences of the Presidents Household (I) That the present Mode is certainly objectionable as I have frequently had Occasion to observe and which I now repeat with the more Freedom as Nothing which can be said will bear the least personal Application. My Reasons are 1st. No Person not accountable to the United States should be invested with the Right of drawing at Will on the Public Treasury. 2ly. Every Expenditure ought as far as the Reason and Nature of Things will permit to be ascertained with Precision. 3ly. A fixed Salary being annexed to the Office of President of Congress he will be more effectually Master of his own Household and in Consequence a greater Order and Œconomy may reasonably be expected. On the Expences of the Office of Secretary of Congress (II) I shall say nothing. The Expences, the Duties and the Cares are so immediately under the Eye of Congress themselves that it would be Presumption. But I would observe that to the Account of the Contingencies of this Office ought to be carried the Expence not only of Office Rent Stationary &c. But also Fuel for Congress, Printing of the Journals, Expresses sent by Congress and the like.

The Chaplains of Congress receive at present at the Rate of four hundred Dollars each. If the Office be necessary it ought to be so supported as that the Officers may be entirely attached to Congress and accompany them in their Changes or fix at their permanent Place of Residence which ever of these Modes shall eventually be adopted. I have ventured to state their Salaries at one thousand Dollars each perhaps. I am still under the proper Sum. On the Expence of the Court of Appeals (IV) I can say Nothing because I know not whether the Continuance of it be necessary. But I should suppose that if three Gentlemen well versed in the Law of Nations were from the Tenure of their Offices to be always with Congress (so as to be consulted and employed when the public Service might require it) Such an Establishment would be continued if the Expence did not exceed the Utility.

When all our Accounts shall be settled our Debts either paid or properly funded and Things reduced to a Peace Establishment the Expences of the Office of Finance (V) may perhaps be reduced about two thousand Dollars by taking away the Salaries of the Assistant and one Clerk and adding somewhat to that of the Secretary. Under the present Circumstances I do not think the Number of the Officers can be lessened. The Salary of the Superintendant has often been mentioned as very high. This is a Subject on which I can speak with great Plainness and, but for the disagreable Situation of Things above mentioned, I should speak also without any personal Reference. I humbly conceive that the Object of Congress is what it certainly ought to be an enlightened Œconomy. On the Powers of the Office I will say Nothing here because it would be misplaced. The Expences of it are and ought to be great. Untill we can create new Beings we must take Mankind as they are and not only so but we must take them as they are in our own Country. Now it is evident that a certain

Degree of Splendor is necessary to those who are clothed with the higher Offices of the United States. I will venture to say that without it those Officers do not perform one of the Duties which they owe to their Masters. And I can say also from Experience that the Salary of six thousand Dollars does not exceed the Expence of that Office. I speak for my Successor or rather for my Country. Neither the Powers nor the Emoluments of the Office have sufficient Charms to keep me in it one Hour after I can quit it with Consistence and I did Hope that Period would have arived during the next Month. Perhaps it may. If a Man of Fortune chuses to run the Course of Vanity or ambition he will naturally wish the Salaries of Office to be low because it must reduce the Number of honest Competitors. I say honest Competitors because that those who would make a Property of public Trusts will always be indifferent as to the amount of Salary seeing that with such Men it forms the smallest pecuniary Consideration. When a liberal Salary enables a Man not rich to live in a Stile of Splendor without impairing his private Fortune the Show he makes and the Respect attached to him really belong to the Country he serves and are among the necessary Trappings of her Dignity. Now it has always appeared to me that true Œconomy consists in putting proper Men in proper Places; to which Purpose proper Salaries are a previous Requisite. Here I shall pause because the Reflection occurs to my Mind that perhaps this with many other Propositions equally true will never be duly felt untill an opposed Conduct shall lead to disagreable Conviction. If indeed it were my object to enforce this Point I should go no further than the past Experience of Congress and perhaps there might be Room for some Argument on the actual State of the Office of foreign Affairs. The Expences of that Office (VII) as well as of the War Office (VI) require only a Reference to what has been just mentioned. The Expences of the Treasury Office (VIII) cannot be curtailed for before the present Business can be lessened that of our Debt must come forward and there must be some Persons to manage it altho the great Machinery at present employed will be unnecessary.

For Reasons of evident Propriety I say Nothing on the Establishment of our foreign Servants (IX) only recommending that as little as possible be left to the article of Contingencies. Because if on the one Hand it be just to compensate extraordinary and unexpected Expences for the public Service It is proper on the other Hand to reduce within the closest Limits of Certainty which the nature of things can permit the amount of those Burthens which the People must bear. And it ought to be remembered that Contingencies are generally speaking a Kind of Expences which tho justified by necessity are unprovided for by express appropriation and which therefore ought as much as possible to be avoided.

The last article is Expences on Collection of the Revenue (XI) and it is much to be lamented that this is so heavy Not indeed the Sum proposed in the Estimate which is trifling but it will be found on Examination that the Expence of collecting Taxes in this Country is greater than in almost any other—a serious Misfortune and which would certainly be provided against if the Officers of the Collection were nominated by Authority of the United States because then those Principles of Suspicion which have already done so much and spoken so loudly would soon fix upon a Grievance at present overlooked because it forms Part of a System favorable to withholding instead of collecting Taxes. It has already been observed that Officers of the Nature of the Receivers are necessary in several States; it is here repeated and Experience will prove it. At the same Time the Committee will please to take Notice that the Loan Officers are not included in the Estimate the Reason of which is that they can answer no Purpose but the Expence of the appointment and the complicating of a System which ought to be simplified. An Officer whose Duty it is to urge Collections may do good if he performs that Duty but when it is a question of paying Means may be adopted which will be more effectual, less expensive and infinitely less liable to fraud. Not to mention that these means may be such as to avoid long and intricate Accounts. In fact (And I hope Sir you will excuse the Observation) there seems to have existed a Solicitude how to spend Money conveniently and easily but little Care how to obtain it speedily and effectually. The Sums I have proposed as fixed Salaries for these Officers may at first Sight appear large but if the Office is to be at all useful it must be in the Hands of a good Man who can devote to it his whole Time and attention and who will neither by his private Distresses nor by the Scantiness of his Stipend be prompted to betray his Trust or abuse the Confidence reposed in him.

Before I close this letter I will take the Liberty farther to mention to the Committee as a principal means of avoiding many Disagreable Discussions relative to the present Object that the Establishment of a Mint and due Regulations of the Post Office would soon supply the Funds necessary to defray the Expences of our civil Establishment. The former of these is entirely in the Power of Congress and I should suppose that the States could have no reasonable Objection to leave the Revenue which might arise from the second to the Disposition of Congress for that Purpose.

I pray your Excuse Sir for troubling you with so long a letter which I will not add to by making Apologies, But assure you of the Respect with which I have the Honor to be Your most obedient & humble Servant,

Robt Morris

To Thomas Jefferson, 8 April 1784

Office of Finance 8th. April. 1784

Sir

I have received the Letter which you did me the Honor to write, on the thirtieth of last Month, for which I pray you to accept my Thanks. The Circular Letter, Copy of which you enclosed, has my entire Approbation; and I pray leave to assure the honorable Committee, that while I am favored with the firm support of Congress I shall not shrink from the Difficulties however great with which we are threatened.

The Idea of applying to the Banks for Aid, is in itself a good one, but the present Moment is unfavorable. The Establishment of so many Banks, instead of aiding Credit and facilitating Operations, will for some time to come have a contrary Effect, and it is not without great Difficulty that they will each collect a Capital sufficient to support its own Operations. The struggle to get such Capital places these Institutions in a degree of Opposition to each other injurious to them all. Without going more minutely into that part of the Subject, I take the Liberty to observe farther that as we had no Mint established when the Treaty of Peace took place, and consequently no proper Regulations of our Coin, a great part of it was immediately exported, and the Country being now laden with foreign Goods and having little means of Payment with produce, still farther Exportations of Coin will take place; especially if by the Return of the Public Bills so great an Additional remittance becomes necessary. I shall leave all observations upon this Matter to the good Sense of the Committee, and proceed to mention, farther, that if the Abilities of the several Banks were ever so great, we cannot rely much on their Inclinations unless their respective Directors could clearly see a Prospect of speedy reimbursement from the Taxes. It is therefore a Matter of much Delicacy to make any Proposals to them on the part of Government, for which, and for other evident Reasons, I pray leave to suggest the Propriety of leaving all such Negotiations to the Superintendant of Finance. That Officer has already sufficient Powers to do every thing except granting Premiums for the Loans proposed, and with respect to them, I am clearly of Opinion that none ought to be given. But if, in the last Necessity, that Step should be unavoidable, he may then Apply for Authority. This I conceive to be better than vesting him before hand with such an extensive Power: For the Committee will be pleased to observe, that as the Laws of the several States have fixed the Rate of Interest, Premiums on Loans, which in their effect [ra]ise the rate of Interest, would be exceptionable as well as odious. It is true that the Situation of Affairs is very disagreable, but it is better to bear up and struggle hard against present Difficulties, than lay the Foundation of future Evils. With perfect Respect, I have the Honor to be Sir, Your most obedient & Humble Servant,

Robt Morris

To Thomas Jefferson, 29 April 1784

Office of Finance 29th: April 1784

Sir

Upon the receipt of your Favor of the ninth Instant I made application to the Quarter Master General to whom I find that you had also written. That Gentleman (in Consequence of my Application) Yesterday transmitted the Copy of his Answer to you, which contains a full Account of the whole transaction. But to explain some Parts of it I beg leave to observe that the Payments made for the Teams of New Jersey were as follows, First, *"the Assistance"* mentioned as given by me to Colo. Neilson was an Order to the Loan Officer of New Jersey to comply with a Warrant granted on him by Congress in Favor of Colo. Neilson for Money of the New Emissions. This had been suspended in Consequence of a subsequent Warrant by Congress in favor of the Pay Master General. But that Paper having become useless to the Pay Office I gave the Order above mentioned. The subsequent Payment of two thousand four hundred Dollars on Application of the Quarter Master General was from Monies granted by the Court of France *for the service of 1781*. But these were so far inadequate to that service as to leave many Things unpaid for which yet remain due.

I beg leave further to remark that the rule mentioned in the begining of my Letter of the second of September was founded on the Stipulations made with Congress when I entered into Office. But setting that Matter aside; it is evident that if Congress should themselves direct an appropriation of the Requisitions for 1782, to the Discharge of Debts which accrued in 1781 before all the Debts of 1782 (among which is that heavy one to the Army) are paid it would raise a great Clamor. And the measure would indeed be of so questionable a Nature as that it might be difficult to find good Reasons by which to defend it. How little those requisitions could bear a Deduction at the present Moment is too clear and need not be repeated.

With perfect respect I have the Honor to be Sir, Your most obedient & Humble Servant,

Robt Morris

To Thomas Jefferson, 1 May 1784

Office of Finance 1 May 1784

Sir

I have received your favor of the twenty sixth Instant for which I pray you to accept my Thanks. Enclosed you have the Copy of my

Letter of the fifteenth of January 1782. to Congress and also Mr. Governeur Morris's Letter to Mr. Helmly of the thirtieth of April 1783. I will add to these such Observations as have occurred on your Notes which agreably to your Desire are herewith returned.

I agree with you as to your Idea of a Money Unit in the first and second Points but to the third must submit an Alteration. Premising however that in this Letter I shall adopt the Term *Unit* in the Sense in which you have used it viz: as the largest Silver Coin instead of that Sense in which it is applied in my Letter viz. as the lowest fractional Money of Account not represented precisely by any Coin, similar in this Respect to the Portugueze Rea. I think then the third Proposition would stand best in this Way *That its Parts be so correspondent to the present Money of Account as to be of easy Adoption to the People.*

I take it to be a self Evident Proposition that any Coin may be Circulated at a Rate nearly proportioned to it's intrinsic Worth and in that Point of View it is unimportant what the Size or Standard shall be. But the present Object is to go farther and adopt such a Coin as shall become exclusively the circulating Medium and a new Money of Account. It is true that Dollars form our general Circulation but they are not any where the Money of Account. No Merchants Books are kept in Dollars few if any Purchases are made at a Rate specified in Dollars and Parts of Dollars. Let it be supposed then that a Dollar be taken as the *Unit* and divided into an hundred Parts and that a Merchant desirous of adopting the New Coin should balance his Books to open them in it. Let it be a Merchant of Boston and let the first Sum he wants to reduce be £365. this would be expressed thus in the new Coin 1216.66 ⅔. His first Essay therefore would oblige him to combine both Vulgar and decimal fractions. If the same Essay be made on the Books of any other Merchant it would be attended with the same Effect. It is therefore of little Avail that the unit be nearly or even exactly of the Value of known Coins unless it's Parts correspond with the present Money of Account.

In this Letter you will find enclosed my original Letter to Congress of the twenty third of April 1783. together with the Specimens of a Coin there mentioned. These you will be so kind as to deliver to the Secretary of Congress after you have done with them and as the Reasoning on such Subjects is facilitated by a Reference to visible Objects let us take the largest of those Silver Coins as the Money *Unit* divisible into a thousand Parts each containing ¼ of a Grain of pure Silver. Here then we have a Piece of Money of convenient Size containing 250 grains of pure Silver, and worth about two thirds of a Dollar viz: 4/2 Virginia Money. The smallest Copper Piece is worth one Farthing Virginia Money and £ 365. is expressed thus 1752. Suppose we add 6.d. ¼ it will then stand 1752.125. Trials upon other Currencies will shew that all Sums can be brought to agree not only *nearly* but *exactly* to this unless in a very few Cases indeed where 1/15 of the small Copper Piece must be rejected. The Objection you State against this Coin is that the Unit is divided into 1000 Parts whereas you would divide a Unit one third larger into no more than 100 Parts but we must consider that the 1/100 of a Dollar is not sufficiently small to be rejected in any Matter of Accot. and that when the Poor are Purchasers or Venders it does not admit of the Divisibility necessary for their Affairs. The Rea of Portugal is 1/800 of a Dollar and is not found to make any Difficulty in Calculations or Entries but on the contrary to occasion much Convenience. Names are of little Consequence but they are not quite indifferent. Suppose that we call the largest Piece a Dollar the smallest a Shilling and that the Shilling be divisible into an hundred Pence. If a Gold Coin be struck it may be made equal to five Dollars and it's value about that of a Pistole. This might be called a Pound and would be exactly 20/10 of the Currency of New Hampshire Massachusetts Rhodes Island Connecticut and Virginia. In point of Size I believe that these Pieces of Money would be convenient and I do not think it of small Consequence that the lowest fractional Part be a Quantity of pure Silver equal to an established Weight because in considering foreign Exchanges we can by that Means always bring the Money of Account of foreign Nations to an exact analogy with our own.

On the whole there are but two Points in which we differ the first is as to the Value of the lowest fractional Part of the Money Unit for we agree that it should proceed from thence upwards in a decimal Ratio. The second is as to the Proportion which Gold should bear to Silver. I wish this to be rather too small than too large because I think the Bank Paper may supply the Place of Gold and not of Silver. If therefore we give more for Silver and less for Gold the Gold will be exported and the Silver will stay. To this I add that our direct Means of importing Bullion is Gold from Lisbon and not Silver from the Spanish Territories because the latter will probably continue to be shut against us and we know by Experience that Silver was exported to England in Preference to Gold while our legal Proportion was the same as theirs because theirs being too high Silver always was worth more at Market than the Mint Price. To shew that this continues to be the Case I will observe that the lowest Price Current of Dollars yet received from England is for old Dollars 63/9 and for new Dollars 62/6. per Pound, altho neither of them are so fine as the Sterling Standard which according to Law is worth but 62/. Hence you will see that the *actual* is below the *legal* Proportion and the fixing of the legal Proportion so high is the Cause why all but light Silver is banished from Circulation. If the Piece of five Dollars were made to contain 84 Grains of pure Gold and seven of Alloy this would establish a Proportion of 1. to 14. 87/42 and would be attended with this Advantage that the Piece would weigh exactly three Pennyweight nineteen Grains, without any fractions of a Grain either in the pure [gold or in the] Alloy. The Quantity of Alloy in the Silver is not material to the Value but if it be sufficiently hard all Alloy beyond that Point renders it more liable to Imitation by a baser Composition. Let the Plan be what it may I think it would be advantageous to make the different Pieces of Money consist of Weights represented by a Number of Pennyweights or Grains without Fractions and also to have in each Piece an integral Number of Grains of pure Metal.

I do not think it will be necessary to cause Assays of the different Coins to be made because I have already a Work more perfect in its Kind than any Assays we can have made. It is the Production of a Person employed by the french Court for the Purpose and the only Difficulty in the Application of it consists in the Difference between their Weights and ours. This however is easily surmounted by Approximation. I should suppose that Congress might adopt (before their Adjournment) a Plan for the Coinage and certainly it is an Object which merits immediate Attention. So far from being attached to the Plan which I have held out I am ready to confess that the Subject is not so familiar as I could wish and that I am not for that Reason competent to a decisive Judgment. All which I can pretend to is a general Sketch to be matured by the Wisdom of Congress but I wish that it may meet their speedy Determination.

There is one Point on which you have not said any Thing but which appears to be of Importance viz: how the Expence is to be defrayed. Supposing you to be with me in Opinion that it ought to be by what is called *Coinage* I would hint that the Price to be given for fine Silver or *Mint Price* should be established and if you make a Golden Coin that of Gold also. If the Mint Price of an Ounce of fine Gold be fixed at 28. Dollars this at the Rate of 84. Grains for 5 Dollars would when coined amount to 28.571. being a little more than two per Cent Difference.

I must intreat your Excuse for the Crudeness of this hasty Production which is not so attentively digested as it might have been because I am unwilling to delay it.

With very sincere Esteem I am Sir Your most obedient and huml. Servant,

R M

To George Washington, 15 June 1784

Philada June 15th 1784

Dear Sir

Having no Intention of entering again into the details of Mercantile Business, on the receipt of your Letter of the 2d Inst. I applied to those with whom I am Connected here, but found no Vacancy in their Counting Houses. And as I had announced to Congress my determination to quit the office of Finance during their recess, I had in Consequence of an Arrangement which I hinted to you when here, determined to establish a House of Business at New York. This is now fixed under the management of Mr Wm Constable & Mr John Rucker, two Gentlemen that have been regularly bred to business, are capable, active and Industrious; they have both had much Experience in Commerce, and their Honor and Integrity is unquestionable. Mr Rucker is going to Europe immediately, Mr Constable whom I think is personally known to you, sets down at New York and is now about to enter on the execution of his Business to him therefore I communicated your Letter and herewith you have a Copy of his Letter to me Containing the Terms on which he is willing to admit your Nephew into the Counting House. He wishes for a speedy Answer as many others will be applying the moment the House is publickly announced. As to the Terms I have nothing to say. With respect to the place I can only say that if one of my Sons was old enough I should embrace the opp[ortunit]y of placing him. Your letter was immediately sent to Genl Armand who only left this place for Baltimore (where he is to embark) yesterday—My Ice House is about 18 feet deep and 16 Square, the bottom is a Coarse Gravell & the Water which drains from the Ice soaks into it as fast as the Ice melts, this prevents the necessity of a Drain which if the bottom was a Clay or Stiff Loom would be necessary and for this reason the side of a Hill is preferred generally for digging an Ice House, as if needful a drain can easily be cut from the bottom of it, through the side of the Hill to let the Water run out. The Walls of my Ice House are built of Stone without Mortar (which is called a Dry Wall) untill within a foot and a half of the Surface of the Earth when Mortar was used from thence to the Surface to make the top more binding and Solid—When this wall was brought up even with the Surface of the Earth I stopped there and then dug the foundation for another Wall two foot back from the first, and about two feet deep, this done the foundation was laid so as to enclose the whole of the Walls built on the inside of the Hole where the Ice is put and on this foundation is built the Walls which appear above ground and in mine they are about ten foot high, On these the Roof is fixed, these Walls are very thick, built of Stone and Mortar, afterwards rough Cast on the outside. I nailed a Cieling of Boards under the Roof flat from Wall to Wall, and filled all the Space between that Cieling and the Shingling of the Roof with Straw, so that the Heat of the Sun Cannot possibly have any Effect.

In the Bottom of the Ice House I placed some Blocks of Wood about two foot long and on these I laid a plat form of Common fence Rails Close enough to hold the Ice & open enough to let the Water pass through; thus the Ice lays two foot from the gravel and of Course gives room for the Water to soak away gradually without being in contact with the Ice, which if it was for any time

343

would waste it amazingly. The upper Floor is laid on Joists placed across the top of the Inner wall and for greater security I nailed a Cieling under those Joists and filled the Space between the Cieling & Floor with Straw.

The Door for entering this Ice House from the north, a Trap Door is made in the middle of the Floor through which the Ice is put in and taken out—I find it best to fill with Ice which as it is put in should be broke into small peices and pounded down with heavy Clubs or Battons such as Pavers use, if well beat it will after a while consolidate into one solid mass, and require to be cut out with a Chizell or Axe—I tryed Snow one year and lost it in June— The Ice keeps untill October or November and I beleive if the Hole was larger so as ⟨to ho⟩ld more it would keep untill Christmass, the closer it is packed the bett⟨er i⟩t keeps & I beleive if the Walls were lined with Straw between the Ice a⟨n⟩d stone it would preserve it much, the melting begins next the Walls and Continues round the Edge of the Body of Ice throughout the Season.2 Mrs Morris joins me in our best Compliments to Mrs Washington & yourself and I beg to return Mrs Washington my thanks for her kind present which will be very useful to me next winter. I am Dear Sir Your most Obedt hble servt

Robt Morris

To John Adams, 16 June 1784

Office of Finance 16 June 1784

Dr Sir,

I have not any Letters from your Excellency which are unanswered except those of the twenty first of May and fourteenth of September in the last Year both of which arrived very long after their Dates. I have learnt from the Gentlemen to whom the

Management of the Loan in Holland was committed the various good and ill Success which they have met with. And now that I am about to leave this Office let me return to your Excellency my sincere Thanks for the Assistance which has at different Times been derived from the Exertion of your Industry and Talents. I pray you also to beleive that when in private Life I shall continue to feel that Esteem and Respect with which I have the Honor to be— / Sir / your Excellency's / most obedient / & / humble Servant

Robt Morris

To Benjamin Franklin, 30 September 1784

Office of Finance 30th. Septr. 1784—

Dear Sir

This is rather a late Day to acknowlege your Favors of the twenty fifth of December, and fifteenth of June last, but I have always intended in my Acknowlegement of them to close our public Correspondence, and I have always been disappointed in my Expectation of being able speedily to quit this Office. That Period however, so ardently desired, is at Length nearly arrived, and while I look back at Cares and Dangers past, I feel an encreased Emotion of Joy by a Comparison with future Hopes and Expectations. But I cannot review the past Scene without strong Feelings of Gratitude and Respect for the able and active Efforts you have made to support the Finances of this Country. I would to God that your just Sentiments on Property and Taxation were as fully felt, as they must be clearly understood in America: but Time is necessary to mellow the Judgment of a Country, as of a Man; happy indeed shall We be if it produce that Effect among us.— I am much obliged by your Explanation of Mr. Chaumont's Accounts; and Accounts lodged at the Treasury which is the most proper Place for both. If any Insinuations have been made injurious to you upon your Connection with Chaumont they have not reached me, and I am perswaded that none such can make any Impressions which ought to give you Pain.—

I have not remitted Bills for Salaries of the foreign Ministers because the Resolutions of Congress having varied, and Mr. Grand having informed me that he should pay them, I have left it as an Account unsettled to be arranged by Mr. Barclay, and as I cannot Doubt that the Attachments will have been taken off, and as I have given Mr. Grand a Credit on the Commissioners of the Loan in Holland for four hundred thousand Livres, and directed Messrs. Le Couteulx to pay over to him a Balance in their Hands, I have no Doubt that he will be in Cash for the Purpose. I agree with you that a Fund ought to be set apart for Contingencies; and had I continued and been supported in Administration, such a Fund should certainly have been provided. I am at the same Time an Enemy to contingent Accounts, and therefore I should have urged the Ascertainment of every Allowance as far as possible, thereby curtailing the Account of Contingencies; but after all it cannot be annihilated. Congress have hitherto made no Determination on this Subject. Indeed it is very difficult, and even almost disreputable, for them to make Arrangements of Expenditure, while the Means of Expenditure are so shamefully withheld by their Constituents. These Things however will mend; at least I hope so.—

I have already said that I expected the Attachments laid on the public Goods would be discharged. Your Letter to the Count De Vergennes on that Subject is perfect, and if that Minister did not immediately obtain a Compliance with your Request, I presume that it must have been occasioned by some Circumstances purely domestic, which we in this Country cannot guess at, for certainly Nothing can be more astonishing than to find a Subject countenanced in arresting the Property of a Sovereign Power in this enlightened Age, and in the Country which of all others has been most eminent for a sacred Regard to the Rights of Nations.—

From your last Letters to your Friends I find that your Return to this Country is somewhat doubtful I am therefore disappointed in one of the great Pleasures which I had promised myself. But Sir in whatever Country you may be and whether in public or in private Life, be assured of my warmest and most respectful Esteem, and that my best Wishes for your Happiness shall be cloathed with the utmost Efforts in my Power to promote it on every proper Occasion, for I am with sincere Regard your Excellency's most obedient and Humble Servant

Robt Morris

To George Washington, 1 January 1785

Philadelphia January 1st 178[5]

Dear Sir

The Gentlemen who will have the honor to deliver you this Letter are from the West Indias they were Recommended to me by an old acquaintance and I find them very Genteel agreable Men. The Brilliancy of your Character attracts the attention of the World, they cannot pass to the Southward without gratifying their Wishes by an interview with the first Man of the Age and I am sure they will meet a kind reception.

May the present Year be as propitious to you as the last was, and may you long live to enjoy a succession of them is the sincere Wish of Dear Sir Your most obedient & very humble Servant

Robt Morris

To George Washington, 17 April 1785

Philadelphia April 17th 1785

Dear Sir

I received in due time the Letter you were so obliging as to write me of the 1st February and am quite ashamed that I should have suffered so long a period to elapse, without acknowledging its Receipt, but this was owing to my having delivered it to some of my Friends for their Perusal who detained it longer than I expected, and have only now, returned it to me.

The Extent of inland Navigation therein pointed out is amazing indeed, and if brought to perfection cannot but be productive of the greatest advantage to the neighbouring Country, and indeed to all America. I think Alexandria must in that case, become a very flourishing City, where such an Establishment as you mention, I have no doubt would meet with very great Success, but for my own part I have no Intention at present to form other Connections in a Commercial Line than those I already hold. I shall make it a point to promote the undertaking by every means in my Power and particularly by recommending my Friends to become adventurers and shall subscribe some Shares for my Children, who, if the Plan succeeds will reap the Benefit thereof at a future day.

Be assured Sir, that I am sensible of the pure & disinterested motives which have induced you to take the trouble of giving me the very useful Information contained in your Letter—I know that none others can enter your mind, and I request you will accept my warmest acknowledgements.

Mrs Morris and the Family are well and join me in affe. Regards to Mrs Washington and yourself. With Sentiments of the most perfect Attachment I am Dear Sir Your most obedient & humble Servant

Robt Morris

P.S. I yesterday took the liberty to give Mr Pine, an Historical & portrait painter of some Eminence, a line of Introduction. He is drawing some interesting parts of our History and your Portrait is indispensably necessary to his Werks.

To John Jay, 19 May 1785

Philada. May 19th. 1785

Dear Sir

On my return here I find your obliging letter of the 13th. which arrived during my absence. I was unfortunate in not having the pleasure to meet you either at Elizabeth Town or at New York, and it vexed me much that I could not perform a promise made to Mrs. Jay, but I was detained by business untill there was danger of losing my passage in the Waggons from Paulus Hook to Elizabeth Town, therefore when the business was finished, I was obliged to push off without calling for Mrs Jay's letter, and after all, I lost the passage & was obliged to hire the Ferry Boat to carry us to Eliza. Town point I saw Kitty the next morning, well & in good Spirits and passed the Evening with the Governor at Trenton.

Our Ship from China does tollerably well for the Concerned & she has opened new objects to all America A Mandarine, Signs a pass port for all European Ships directed to the Commanders of Two of the Emperors Forts on the River of Canton, nearly in the following Words, "Permit this *Barbarian* Boat to pass She has Guns & Men, consequently can do the Emperour no harm" If the Government of America could concentre the Force of the Country in any one point when occasion required, I think our *Mandarin's* might grant similar pass ports to the rest of the World—I beg my Compliments to the Ladies & am with warm attachment Dr Sir Your obedt & hble Servant

Robt Morris

To George Washington, 28 January 1786

Philad[elphi]a Jany 28th 1786

Dear Sir

I did intend to save you the trouble of sending up the ten Dollars advanced to Jno. Fairfax on your Account & for that purpose took his draft on you for that Sum & remitted it to Messrs Josiah Watson & Co. from whom I have received it back at my own request & herein transmit the same with a receipt on it.

Whatever belongs to, or is connected with you, will ever meet attention from me. Mrs Morris joins me in thanks to Mrs Washington & yourself with assurances of the Warmest reciprocal good wishes for hers & your Health & happiness. I am with sincere attachmt Dear Sir Your most obedt Servt

Robt Morris

To George Washington, 26 April 1786

Philad[elphi]a April 26th 1786

Dear Sir

I am happy to confirm what Mr Dalby will have informed you off, the Successfull Issue of his Suit respecting his Slave, could any interference on my part have been usefull, your letter would have commanded it, indeed I had done him before what little service I could when his Petition was before the Assembly from a perfect Conviction both of the Injustice and impolicy of the treatment he had met with. The Society which attacked him tread on popular ground, and as their Views are disinterested as to themselves, and *sometimes* very laudable as to the objects of their Compassion, it is not a very pleasant thing to Attack them & this consideration deters Mr Dalby from seeking redress at Law for the Expense & trouble they have occasioned, altho I think he would meet a just determination in our Courts of Law. We are happy to hear that Mrs Washington & you are well, Mrs Morris is at present occupied in carefull attention to our youngest Son in the Small pox which is now out, & very fircely. She joins me in praying Mrs Washington & you to accept our best wishes for the long Continuance of your Health & happiness. Poor Tilghman, you my Dear Sir have lost in him a most faithfull and Valuable Friend, He was to me the same I esteemed him, very, very, much, and I lament the loss of him exceedingly. I am with sincere attachment Dear Sir Your most Obedient humble Servant

Robt Morris

To George Washington, 23 April 1787

Philad[elphi]a April 23d 1787

Dear Sir

The Public Papers have announced Your consent to serve as a Member of the Convention to be held in this City. this is what I ardently wished for & I am truely rejoiced at it—I was only restrained from writing to you by Motives of delicacy, thinking that your own judgement rather than the perswasion of Friends ought to determine. I hope Mrs Washington will come with you & Mrs Morris joins me in requesting that you will on your arrival come to our House & make it your Home during your Stay in this City. We will give You as little trouble as possible and endeavour to make it agreable, it will be a charming season for Travelling, and Mrs Washington as well as yourself will find benefit from the

Journey Change of Air &c. As I hope soon for the pleasure of seeing you I will only add that you must not refuse our request & the honor you confer by acceptance shall ever be considered as a great favour.

Our New Bishop brought the enclosed letter from England, He desired me to forward it & to present his most respectfull Compts. I am Dear Sir Your most obedt & humble Servant

Robt Morris

To George Washington, 25 October 1787

Philad[elphi]a Octr 25th 1787

Dear Sir

That you may not think me guilty of Neglect, I acknowledge the receipt of your obliging letter of the 14th Inst. by Post, but that by the Charming Polly is not yet arrived, when it comes to hand I shall have the pleasure of addressing you again. Mr G. Morris went to New York to stay Nine days, he has been gone near five Weeks & I wait his return before I can finally decide whether I can set out for Virginia or Not.

We rejoiced much to hear of your safe arrival at Home having been made very uneasy by the report of the accident at the Head of Elk If you read our News Papers you see much altercation about the proposed Constitution the oponents are not Numerous altho they fill the News Papers every day.

Mrs Morris & myself are much obliged by your & Mrs Washington good wishes We can truely say they are reciprocal & I am with great Sincerity Dear Sir Your most Obedient humble Servant

Robt Morris

To George Washington, 29 April 1788

Richmond April 29th 1788

Dear Sir

My detention here having been so much longer than expected, the Season in which Mrs Morris promised a Visit to Mount Vernon being come, and my Sons being arrived at Philada these circumstances induced me to propose the journey to which she very readily consents. I am therefore sending up my Servants & Horses to bring down Mrs & Miss Morris attended by my Sons Robert & Thomas, all of them being ambitious to pay their respects to that character which they so much admire. You see my Dear Sir the Liberty I take & the trouble I am about to bring on your Household by such a Host of Strangers but I shall shew my confidence that it will give you pleasure to receive them by declining to make any appology. Mrs Morris in her last letter mentioned that you had desired her to lay by for Mrs Washington, some Cambrick Book Muslins & she believes some large Book Muslin Handkerchiefs, out of Capt. Bells Cargo from the East Indies, will you be good enough to give John a note of the particulars Mrs Washington wishes to have & Mrs Morris will bring them with her—I pray my best respects to Mrs Washington & to assure her that the same Considerations determine me not to make an appology to her for the trouble She is likely to have with so large a part of my Family, especially as I hope they will render their Company very agreable & pleasing to that of Mount Vernon. With the most sincere esteem I am Dear Sir Your most obedient & humble Servant

Robt Morris

To George Washington, 18 May 1788

Richmond May 18th 1788

Dear Sir

The enclosed letter will probably deprive you of the Company of your guests sooner than you expected, & my partiality for them leads me to believe you will feel a disapointment in that event.

But by way of attonement we must pass a few days with you on our return. The business which has detained me so long being now in such train that I cannot leave it, and my presence for a Couple of Weeks longer likely either to finish it entirely, or so near as to render further attention unnecessary I determine to ⟨sort⟩ it out at all events. My anxiety to see my Family after so ⟨unexpectedly⟩ long absence, is surely excusable & I have desired Mrs Morris to come on, the journey is not long and they may make it easy by coming Thursday to Mr Fitzhughs, on Friday to the Bowling Green (where if I can I will meet them that Evening) & the next day here. They will have an opportunity of seeing more of this Country & of making some valuable acquaintances and can pass their time very agreably untill I am ready to return. Mr G. Morris joins in my request to be remembered most respectfully to Mrs Washington as also in the assurance of the esteem & regard with which I have the honor to profess myself Dr Sir Your most obedient & humble Servant

Robt Morris

To George Washington, 26 May 1788

Richmond May 26th 1788

Dear Sir,

I had the pleasure to meet Mrs Morris & my Children at the Bowling Green about two oClock on Friday & have since Conducted them safe to this place. We reserve our Acknowledgements for Mrs Washington & your kind Attentions untill they can be made in person as I hope it will not be long before we shall have the pleasure of waiting on you again at Mount Vernon—The letters Enclosed herewith were brought by Mrs Morris under a Sealed Cover directed to me on the supposition of my being with you. The French letter is from a meer *aventurier* who took me in for 100 Dollrs & has now put me to an expense of 50/ for Postage from Charles Town. these Circumstances will guard you against his importunities.

Mr Pollock's request you will be best able to judge of. He wishes me to solicit for him what I would not ask for myself. With perfect esteem & regard I remain Dear Sir Your obliged & obedient humble Servant

Robt Morris

To George Washington, 3 July 1788

Richmond July 3d 1788

Sir

Capt. Stephen Gregory the bearer of these lines being called by business to Dumfries, cannot think of returning from thence without gratifying his earnest desire of paying his respects to Genl Washington, a gratification which he is very ambitious to obtain on proper terms, but which his modesty forbad him to seek without an introduction. Excuse me therefore my Good Sir for presenting to you, a Gentleman that has Served with Reputation as a Lieutenant in our late Infant Navy under Capt. Barry & others and who since the Peace has Commanded a Ship of mine & so Conducted himself as to induce me to give favourable testimony to his merit. With great respect I have the honor to be Dear Sir Your most obliged & obedient humble servt

Robt Morris

To George Washington, 6 April 1789

New York April 6th 1789

Dear sir

This will be delivered by Mr Charles Thompson, who has the honour to be charged with the Public Dispatches which announce your Election to the first Office in the American Empire—Permit me on this occasion to congratulate your Excellency, not on the appointment to Office, for your honors and happiness were compleat without it, but upon this unequivical proof of the gratitude of Millions whose sense of your services and virtues is fully manifested by their unanimous Suffrage.

May you, Sir, long continue an instrument in the hands of Providence to dispense happiness to the People who have received Liberty at your hands, and may they ever continue equally sensible of, and grateful for, your Services. You have an arduous task to perform, in which you will have a right to call forth all the assistance which your Friends & the Friends of their Country, can supply—As one of this description I pray you to beleive that every exertion I am capable of will ever be devoted to your aid in the noble attempt to establish an energetic Government for the United States, beleiving as I do that such a Government is absolutely necessary to perpetuate the Liberties, promote the Interests, and secure the happiness of this People. I conclude that the unanimous voice of America is irresistable and that you will soon set out on your journy for this City. Mrs Washington I hope, will accompany you, and as Philadelphia is in the route, Mrs Morris joins me in the request that you will honour us with your company during your stay in that City. And as the journy will be fatiguing, we hope you will make it a resting place of some days, when probably you may think it adviseable to proceed from thence to New York some time before Mrs Washington, in order to get through the first forms of etiquette, and in order to make the necessary arrangements of your Household, in that case Mrs Morris prays that Mrs Washington will gratify her wishes by remaining with us untill all things are ready for her reception here, and she will then have the pleasure to accompany her to New York. Assuring myself of your compliance with these requests, I remain with the highest Respect and sincerest Attachment Dear Sir Your most obedient & obliged hble servant

Robt Morris

To John Jay, 20 April 1789

Philada. April 20th. 1789

Dear Sir

I delivered your letter to Genl Washington at Chester where I met him, and soon found that very prudential considerations had determined him against the Acceptance of the Invitations of his Friends, He gave much such reasons as indeed My own mind had Suggested before, and I acquiesced, so that He lodged at the City Tavern and I understand that Mr Osgoods House is prepared for his Reception at New York. Your letter however gave pleasure & the writing of it was not lost Labour, I expect soon to have the pleasure of paying my Respects to Mrs. Jay & yourself personally being always Dear Sir Your Obedt hble Servt

Robt Morris

To Alexander Hamilton, 13 November 1789

Philadelphia Novemr 13th. 1789

Dear sir

I had the pleasure to receive your favor of the 6th Instant, and should have replyed to the Contents by the last Mail, had not other Engagements prevented it. I always understood that if the Bank stock was to be replaced, I was to pay the Dividends, but as Interest must be allowed on the amount of the Warrants deposited, during the time that payment is delayed, I also understood that the payments to be made on those Warrants would be admitted as satisfactory in point of time both in replacing the Stock and discharging the dividends, therefore I made no other provision for this object. I do not know how productive the Impost may prove in other ports, but I am told it will exceed all expectation here, and consequently I expect that you will soon find yourself possessed of the means to discharge these Warrants, when the Dividends may be retained and the Stock replaced, but if you require payment of the Dividend sooner I will comply with your desire. Since my return to this City I could have disposed of some shares of Bank stock with little, if any loss, and I am from a full consideration of the matter, enclined to purchase the remainder of Mr Churchs Shares. My object is to obtain a Convenience to myself without suffering any loss, or exposing Mr Church or you to any disappointment. I therefore propose to your Consideration as follows.

I will take the whole of his Shares at par—Those which I have already received with the Dividends to be paid for out of the Deposited Warrants and securities now in your hands, and the sooner you can make that payment the better for all Parties.

The Shares now in your possession I will only call for as I can dispose of them, taking ten shares at a time, for the amount of which I will deposit in your hands Continental securities, say Loan office Certificates, Nourses Certificates, Final settlements, Facilities &ca. to the full value of the Shares as called for, computing the Certificates or Securities at the Market price, and these to remain in your hands untill I pay for the shares; for this payment, I ask as long time as you can give me, say twelve or Eighteen Months or longer if you please and I will pay the Bank Dividends on those Shares punctually as the Bank does, until the Cost is discharged. By this mode Mr Church will sell his stock, at the full value, without any charge of Commission Brokerage &ca. He will untill it is paid for be on the same footing as if no Sale had been made and ample Security will be in your hands, for you must be sensible, that the Value of these securities will rise as we proceed in making provision for discharging the annual Interest on them. It will not do to force the sale of Shares or it must be done at considerable Discount, but by the close attention I shall pay to this object I shall find means to place them gradually without loss, and by the time to be fixed for my Payments to you, I shall have the means of doing it with Convenience, but should any disappointments occur, then the deposited securities shall be sold rather than Mr Church shall suffer any disappointment; this however you may depend I will take care to prevent by my Payments.

I think this proposition rests upon such a solid Basis that it must meet your approbation, and if so, I will immediately send forward my note for four thousand Dollars, accompanied by a Sufficient Value of the Securities as a Deposit for that amount and you will send in return Ten Shares with a power for making the Transfer & by letter agree that I am to have the whole as fast as I make the deposits, for you must not be at liberty to part with any of them to others, or my Plan may be defeated by Competition in the sale.

I hope to hear from you soon in reply and that you will agree to this plan as it is calculated to serve all concerned & particularly

Dear sir Your most obedient & humble Servant

Robt Morris

To Alexander Hamilton, 4 April 1790

Philada. April 4th. 1790

Dear Sir

Mr B. Livingston delivered your favour of the 30th. ulto. on Thursday which He has made the needfull inquiries and is perfectly satisfied as to the Value & Title of my Ten Alley Estate.

But your letter to me and instructions to him have raised two difficulties which I did not expect. You require the payment to be made in London, nothing of this kind was mentioned that I recollect. My proposition was to pay £100 Stg for each share in twelve Months, and it was my expectation to make that payment here, because if I engage to pay in London the Credit would only be nine or Ten, instead of Twelve Months as I must so much sooner purchase bills to make the remittance. If however you prefer to have the payment made in London fix it for fifteen Months from the day the Stock is assigned & I agree. The other matter is respecting the forty Shares which having been included in our agreement, I had in Consequence of the liberation of my Certificates taken measures for obtaining some More Money in order to pay more of my debts whilst the Exchange is so favourable. If therefore I mortgage my Ten alley Estate for a part only of the purchase & leave the Certificates pledged for the redemption of the other part, you will unnecessarily do me a prejudice which I am sure you would not wish to do, I say unnecessarily, because the Estate is an Ample Security for the whole & would sell for much more at any Moment. I hope therefore that your answer will remove these two obstacles & we will perfect the business at once. Last night I had an opportunity to Speak to some of the Directors of the Bank. They promised that your wishes should be complied with and I believe Mr Fitzsimmons who goes for N York in the Morning will be authorized to assure you of it. With great regard

I remain Dr Sir Your most obedt & humble Servant

Robt Morris

To Thomas Jefferson, 25 November 1793

New Brunswick Novr 25th: 1793

Sir

On the evening of the 16th. instant I was honoured with yours of the 13th. enclosing the petition of Benjamin Freeman in behalf of his son Clarkson Freeman, and signifying the Presidents instructions thereon.

In complyance therewith I beg leave to inform

That Doctor Clarkson Freeman was apprehended (with difficulty and danger to the officer, as I understood,) in the beginning of March 1791 on a charge of being concerned with several others in counterfeiting a public security of the United States, and of uttering the same, knowing it to be so forged and a counterfeit, and was committed to the gaol of Essex county wherein he was apprehended.

He was removed by Habeas Corpus to the Circuit court of the United States held at Trenton for New Jersey District in April 1791, where he was indicted for forging, and uttering, knowing to be forged a public security of the United States purporting to be a final settlement. The District Attorney not bringing him to trial, and he appearing to be charged in Essex county on a process in a civil suit out of the Supreme court of the State, towards the close of the court on motion of the District Attorney he was remanded on his indictment to the gaol of Essex County there to be safely kept untill discharged by due course of Law. From thence he made his escape about the middle of the following August and is reported to have gone to Canada. I think I have heard that the Gaoler had unsuccessfully pursued him thither; The Gaoler, by his escape in the civil suit, being liable for a very considerable sum.

From the several depositions that I saw Clarkson Freeman appeared to be one of the most active and mischevous, in this State, of a gang of villains who, by forging and uttering counterfeit certificates, in a short time defrauded eight or nine of the inhabitants of certificates to the amount of upwards of seven thousand dollars.

He appeared to be about twenty four years of age and his demeanor in court indicated him impudent, hardened and incorrigible, which was corroborated by almost every account I heard of his behaviour at and after the time he was apprehended. He was reported not to want abillities nor knowledge in his profession equal to his standing; to have acquired by marriage something considerable for a low bred man, and to have been before guilty of many little thefts, for some of which he was early expelled the Medical society of this State.

I do not know of any person apprehended on his testimony, nor was there any such confined in this District after the rising of the court at which he was indicted. Amasa Parker was the only person then in custody, or since apprehended, besides Clarkson Freeman and Henry Smith, against whom an indictment was found. Smith had been previously pardoned, and Parker was in custody on a civil suit a long time before C: Freeman was taken, and was committed as a criminal on the testimony of the said Henry Smith, one of the gang, who was taken up in Philadelphia and there made a confession before, or about the time C. Freeman was taken.

The only considerations that I have knowledge of under which C: Freeman can set up any pretence for a pardon, are

1st. An engagement of Abraham Ogden Esquire Attorney for the United States in this District, the copy of which transmitted to me is as follows.

"Memorandum

"Clarkson Freeman being confined in goal at Newark Essex county State of New Jersey upon a warrant issued by John Chetwood Esquire one of the Justices of the Supreme court of the State of New Jersey against him the said Clarkson for counterfeiting the public securities of the United States or uttering counterfeit public securities of the United States knowing them to be counterfeit; He the said Clarkson sent for me as the Attorney of the United States for the district of New Jersey in order to make a voluntary confession of his guilt in the premises Whereupon in the presence of his Counsel Elisha Boudinot Esqr. I informed him, that I had it not in my power to give him any assurance of pardon in consequence of his proposed confession— nor would I give him any such assurance if it was in my power. But if he thought it prudent to make an unconditional voluntary confession that I would transmit that confession to the Chief

Justice of the United States with the most favourable representation of the circumstances attending such confession. At the same time I informed him that the charge against him affected his life. It was understood nevertheless by his attorney aforesaid and me that the confession aforesaid would not be made use of to work the conviction of the said Clarkson if the Government of the United States refused or neglected to make use of the said Clarkson as a witness against his accomplices or others whom he accused.

Newark 7th. March 1791.

Signed Abrm: Ogden Atty. &c."

2d. He made a confession, which by a letter from Mr. Ogden to me of the 21st: March 1791, he had not then signed.

3d. He was introduced by the District Atty. as a Witness to the Grand Jury while they were investigating the forgeries and frauds of himself and his accomplices, and also to the Court on the trial of Amasa Parker on an indictment, as one of the accomplices in that villany.

Amasa Parker was acquitted on that indictment through defect of proof.

In the room of the old doctrine of approvement, which was attended with difficulty, and perhaps unnecessary danger to the approver and is now out of use; A practice has prevaild in cases of extensive combinations of villany, that where an accomplice makes a true and full disclosure as well as of his own guilt as of the guilt of all concerned with him, which is accepted by the court, and he is thereupon admitted a witness, and, if required, testifies accordingly both to the grand jury and in court on the trial of his accomplices, and appears on the whole to act a fair and candid part—The Court will generally recommend him to Government for a pardon, will defer his trial, and even bail him, although indicted, to give him an opportunity of obtaining it.

Against C: Freemans pretensions on these grounds are

- 1st. That there was no need of his confession: Henry Smith, one of the gang, having by his confession made a pretty full disclosure, thereupon received a pardon from the President, and been detained as a witness if necessary. But Henry Smiths confession does not appear to have reached the District Attorney untill the 20th: of August 1791.

- 2d. The District Attorney had no authority to engage a pardon to C: Freeman, or make any contract with him that would equitably entitle him thereto without the consent of the Court, which does not appear to have been given. Although this may be considered a legal objection, yet it would lose much of its weight in an equitable view, if it appeared that C: Freeman, through the confidence he reposed in the district Attorneys power to engage a pardon, had been deceived into a full disclosure that would have worked his own conviction—As it would be unworthy the dignity of Government to take advantage of the mistake of its own officer, and a confession so obtained, if it did not opperate his pardon, would not be suffered by the court to be used against him on his trial: But this from the face of the contract appears not to be the case; Nor is the part of his confession which I have seen a full disclosure of his guilt, but rather an artful evasion thereof and an extenuation of his conduct.

- 3d. His want of candour in procrastinating the signing his confession from the seventh untill on, or after the twenty first of August, a delay sufficient to have given notice to his unapprehended accomplices to make their escape, and none of them, that I have heard of, were afterwards taken.

- 4th: The want of truth and candour in his confession and subsequent testimony; which appeared by comparing them with parts of Henry Smiths confession and evidence corroborated by testimony from Witnesses of undoubted credit, And I understood that the grand jury on examining him considered his answers so false and evasive that they entirely rejected his testimony.

- 5th. His fresh crime in breaking gaol and escaping; whereby he violated the spirit of the contract with the District Attorney on his part, and excluded himself from any benefit under the above mentioned Usage; as he thereby deprived Government of the power of using his testimony against his accomplices, in case it was deemed expedient to do so. The pretence of unnecessary confinement set forth in the petition is no palliation of this; as, if he had an equitable claim to a pardon on the foregoing considerations, or any other, the court on application would have bailed him, that he might with more ease and effect have solicited it. Previous to his examination on the trial of Amasa Parker he was questioned by the prisoners counsel touching his interestedness, and thereon declared, under oath, that he was not an evidence on condition of a pardon, and that he had no promise of a pardon from any body.

Add to this a circumstance, which, although it ought not to weigh if he was equitably entitled to a pardon, yet is worthy of consideration where that equity does not exist, or is forfieted by the act of the party; to wit, That some of the grand jury and other respectable inhabitants attending the court expressed dissatisfaction that C: Freeman was not tried, the public opinion

366

appeared to be much against him, and he was viewed by the people in general with abhorrence.

Moreover, some of the persons defrauded are men who stand fair in the public estimation; One of them, in addition to the loss of three thousand dollars, I understood was criminally proceeded against for selling one of the counterfiet certificates before he discovered the fraud. C: Freeman was the immediate perpetrator of the fraud on most of them. It would unnecessarily outrage the feelings of these men and their friends to learn that Government had pardoned an offender so base and detestable in their eyes.

However strongly the feelings of humanity may plead for saving the forfiet life of a fellow creature, whose death is not necessary for an example, or for the public safety: Or where the circumstances are such that the public forget the criminal in commiseration of the man—In my opinion, nothing short of strict justice, political necessity, or a litteral performance of contract should opperate to pardon and restore from a state of voluntary banishment to the community with the rights and privileges of a citizen a person so young and so depraved, so hardened and senseless of shame, so prone to and capacitated for mischief, and so odious in the public estimation as Clarkson Freeman appeared to be.

The foregoing contains every information that my memory, or a careful examination of my papers enables me to give relative to the object of the Presidents inquiry, with such observations as have occurred to me to have opperation respecting the pardon petitioned for. I have been the more minute as I supposed Mr. Ogden must have had more powerful motives for defering C: Freemans trial than I am fully informed of. I have understood there were some communications between Judge Duane and Mr. Ogden respecting him, the object of which I do not recollect to have fully heard. Having no oppertunity of personally acquiring information from Mr. Ogden, I forwarded to him a copy of the Petition, Signifyed the Presidents desire thereon, and requested his information of such facts as I had not an opportunity to be informed of. I have waited several days for an answer but yet have none. If I receive any I will forward it. With great respect I am Sir Your very humble Servant

Robt Morris

To Thomas Jefferson, 8 December 1793

New Brunswick Decr. 8th. 1793

Sir

On the fifth instant I received the enclosed from the Attorney of the United States for this District, and forward it for the Presidents further information of the case of Clarkson Freeman.

It appears from it that a pardon to him is already filled up, and resting in Mr. Ogdens hands. The opperation of it, under all the circumstances, will necessarily become a question before the Court, if he should ever be apprehended.

From the evidence that came to my knowledge, I did not consider Clarkson Freeman a necessary, or proper selection for the purposes mentioned by Mr. Ogden, and I should now doubt the policy of promulgating the existence of the pardon, least it should induce him to return within the jurisdiction of the United States; leaving which, I should have advised to have been made a condition of a pardon under any circumstances to so finished a villain. With the greatest respect I am Sir Your very humble Servt.

Robt Morris

To George Washington, 9 June 1794

Philada June 9th 1794

Dear Sir

The multiplicity of my engagements did not hinder me from Considering in conjunction with Mr Greenleaf the Contents of your letter of the 26th of last Month, altho those engagements occupied me too much to admit of an earlier reply.

We viewed and considered the proposition you were pleased to make, several times, and finally came to the conclusion, that due regard to our own interests would not admit of our acquiescence, The price or value being fixed so high in our estimation as not to admit of that reward for the use of our resources, which many other objects now offer. I return therefore all the Papers herewith & also a Copy of the Great Kanahwa & other Survey's. I am sorry that we cannot be the purchasers, the price so far exceeding our expectations puts it out of our power to make an offer I must however in justice observe that Your prices are such as may probably be obtained by selling the property in detail but even in that way there could be no chance of our obtaining the Compensation which a variety of other pursuits offer to us. With the most perfect Esteem & respect I am Dr sir Your obedt hble servt

Robt Morris

To Alexander Hamilton, 31 March 1795

Philada. 31st. March 1795

Dear Sir

I have before me your Friendly & Polite letter of the 18th. inst. and without making any professions, I shall only give you the assurance that every future opportunity of Social intercourse or agreeable business that may offer between you & me or your Family & mine will on my part be Seized with Avidity and I have not the smallest doubt of the continuance of that Friendship & Harmony that has hitherto Subsisted. I am obliged by the manner in which you have proposed the payment of Mr Church's Money with which I shall comply by placing in your hands good Acceptances or Notes payable by the time you mention, but this will require a little previous Arrangement on my part. You shall pretty soon hear from me again with the paper.

Mrs Morris & my Daughters desire to be remembered with affection to Mrs Hamilton whose Friendship they Value and with sincere regard

I remain Dear Sir Your obliged & Obedt humble Servant

Robt. Morris

To John B. Church, 28 May 1795

John B. Church Esqr (London)

Dear Sir

On the third of this month I received your letter of the 20th Feby and since a Copy of it. The bargain which my son made with you for the deferred Debt was an unpleasant transaction to me, but it was always my determination to comply with it, and with this view I had determined to make you a Consignment of a number of Shares in a plan which I have formed for the Sale Improvement and Settlement of Six million Acres of Land. I spoke to Colo Hamilton on this Subject some months ago and he promised me a letter to you respecting this plan, but in his and my hurry it was omitted at the time of his departure from hence. I shall now however carry my intentions into effect by sending you 750

Shares in the North American Land Compy which you will receive enclosed herewith—That is, the Certificates for the same together with Six printed Copies of the Plan by which you will perceive that these Shares are each of the Value of 100 Mexican Dollars and they must not be disposed of for less, but on the Contrary they should now produce considerably more because One Years Int will be paid on the 31st decemr next & because we are progressing in this business of the Company. None of the Parties can sell these shares for less than 100 Dollars being under Bond to each other & to all the Share holders not to part with them at less than that price under a penalty of $100,000. I would propose therefore that you ask such an additional price as will compensate your Trouble in disposg of them (by way of Commission). I have been led into this measure by the assurances that Robert (who is absent at present) has given me that you would readily undertake any thing of this kind upon being allowed a proper Commission, for that you had told him so, with an assurance that it would be pleasing to you if you could render me a service, consequently I place implicit confidence in your doing this business. Some of these Shares have already been sent to England & Holland for sale and directions were given to Messrs Bird Savage & Bird to have the plan reprinted in London, so that you can learn from them and from William Temple Franklin Esqr what success they have met with in the sale of what has been committed to them, and if needful you can get more of the Printed Plans from the former if they have had them reprinted. Whether the above named Gentlemen have or have not succeeded in the Sale of their Shares I expect you will; because I suppose you to be better connected with Persons likely to purchase and as I conceive this plan to be the best that ever was formed in this Country for the benefit of all Parties I will take up some of your time by giving you some of my reasons for thinking so well of it....

… As you make Sale of these Shares, you will be good enough to lay out the Money in the purchase of deferred debt to the Amount which you are to receive from me, and I pray your Attention to have the purchase made on the cheapest terms possible. Any Surplus that arises you will advise me of with authority to draw for the Same. I will send a Copy of this letter to Colo Hamilton & request that after reading he will forward it to you….

Robt. Morris

To Thomas Jefferson, 1 June 1795

Philada June 1. 1795

Dear Sir

I am much at a loss for an Apology to you but if the truth will form one you shall have it. When I received your letter of the 19th. of Febry. I determined not to answer untill I should go out to the Hills and enquire of Mr. Crouch about the Sheep. Your letter was laid by untill this could be done. My Constant Avocations put off the Walk to the Hills untill from Continual Employment the thing slipt out of my mind. At length I came across your letter again and then, ashamed of the neglect, away I went to the Hills; Crouch was not at home and nobody there that could give me a satisfactory Account, I mentioned the subject to Mrs. Morris who reminded me frequently and every time she did so, a second visit to the Hills was determined on. At length I saw Crouch who did not give me that satisfactory account which I expect. He says the Original imported Ram is dead but he has left a Successor which the Old Man thinks came from the imported Spanish Yew, but his memory being treacherous he cannot say positively that it is so. He firmly beleives it and from the appearance of the Animal I beleive so too. The Original imported Yew is alive but he thinks she is past breeding, there is one or two others which he beleives to be of the genuine Breed from the Spanish Ram and Yew but he cannot be positive. This Account of the spanish Family of Sheep mortified me on your Account exceedingly and cooled the Ardour I had felt in the desire of complying with your Wishes by assisting to give Virginia the opportunity of raising fine Wool—however the matter now stands as I have stated and if you think the pursuit still worthy of your Attention I will send round to Richmond any order of those above mentioned—that is, the Ram and Old Yew with the Young that are supposed to be genuine. Tell me to whose Care I shall address them at Richmond, or if you prefer to send for them they shall be delivered at once to whoever brings your Order. My time and attention has been and is too much engrossed by other Objects, or what you formerly said respecting these Sheep would have induced me to preserve and raise the Breed. As to trusting to others there is no getting proper attention to be paid without the Masters Eye or Interference, as you will observe in the case of Crouch whom I urged on the Subject. As I think my apology for neglecting to answer your letter in due time makes but an awkard figure, and as I feel, so I think it best to plead Guilty, and throw myself upon Mercy for forgiveness and to entitle myself to merciful Consideration I can truly say that the Crime has arisen not from intention or want of Respect, but from too much employment and engagement, beside, I suffer severe punishment every time the Recollection occurs. My Regard and friendship for you is your Avenger, therefore you must forgive as I cannot.

I have no doubt of the enjoyments you find in Retirement. You are a philosopher as well as a practicall Planter. These pursuits will occupy body and mind and when that is the case happiness is generally attendant. With respect to yourself, to retire was to act wisely, but as your Retirement regards the United States, the Public have to lament the loss of Abilities and Talents which have been eminently useful and which no doubt would have Continued to be so as the prime and vigour of life still remains. I think however that it is not improbable that you will again be drawn forth into public life. I have Retired from Public service and will never resume it, and I am trying to clear myself of a vast load of private business, in Order to enjoy if I can what will remain of life when my Work is accomplished in quiet and Calm. Mr. Jay is just arrived from England at New York and I suppose we shall soon know the sense of our Government upon the Treaty he has made with Britain. The Continuance of Neutrality and preservation of peace are great Objects and the most desirable to this Country which I hope will never be engaged in War. With my best Wishes for the Continuance of that Tranquility which you now enjoy I Remain in the utmost Sincerity and Truth Dear Sir Yr friend & obt hb St

RM

To Alexander Hamilton, 18 July 1795

Philada July 18th. 1795

Dear Sir

I desired Mr. Constable to pay you $2000 & promised to remit him a bill for this Amot. By his letter just recd I find it was inconvenient for him to pay as he wants Money himself. You will find herein bills for five hundred pounds Stg they are perfectly good as Mr Cazenove will tell you & you can readily get the Money for them. I charge you $2333.33 being 175 ₱ Ct and the exchge in New York is at least equal. I will answer your letters soon but I am hurried & much engaged.

Yours Sincerely

Robt Morris

To Alexander Hamilton, 20 July 1795

Philada July 20th. 1795

Dear Sir

I wrote you on Saturday & enclosed good Bills of Exchange for £500 Stg which I hope will be agreable. In your letter of the 7th of July you tell me that a letter from Mr Church makes it necessary you should open a negotiation with me respecting the deferred debt without waiting the Issue of those measures which I had taken in regard to that affair, and you have no objection to receive an offer of Lands. I own 50,000 acres of Land in Washington County State of Pensylvania, situated about 25 to 27 Miles from Pittsburg & 15 from the County Town of Washington; on this Land I have built a good Farm House, a Mill & a Number of Out Houses a Farm Fenced & tenanted about 200 Acres of Meadow cleared; perhaps you might have seen or heard of this place during the late insurrection; it is called properly Morrisville but commonly, Ryerson's place. Mr Ryerson was my Agent in forming the settlement which Cost much Money. For three Successive years the Indians committed depredations on us, and I gave up the pursuit. The two last years 1794 & 1795 they have not troubled those parts and Washington County is now so full of inhabitants that I think they never will again. You know that Country; it is broken & hilly, but the Land is rich & produces luxuriantly even on the tops of the Hills. There are already settlements all round my Lands besides those on them. The Cultivated Lands in that County sell from four to Twelve Dollrs. p Acre the Uncultivated from one to three Dollrs p Acre according to quality, situation and Circumstances. I reckon my Lands there to be Worth Two Dollrs or upwards at the present time and that they will rise considerably every year. If you approve of these Lands for Mr. Church I am willing to sell them payable in the defered Debt as far as it will go

375

and the rest as may be fixed between us, or so much of the Lands may be sold as will absorb the deferred Debt.

I am Dear Sir Your Obedt hble servt

Robt Morris

PS If the Mississippi becomes a free Navigation & inevitably it must the value of these Lands will thereby be very greatly enhanced.

To Alexander Hamilton, 8 October 1795

Phila 8 Octo. 1795

Dear Sir

I have received your letter of the 6th at a moment when I am extreamly hurried in preparing letters Papers &ca. &ca. for the Dispatch of my Son in Law James Marshall Esqr for Europe. My Daughter goes with him and they expect to Sail on Sunday. I must therefore pray your Excuse untill they are gone when I will take up the Subject of your letter I expect to your satisfaction notwithstanding the pressure of the times.

Yrs.
RM

To Alexander Hamilton, 16 November 1795

Phila Novr 16. 1795

Dear Sir

I have a Negotiation in hand which will probably enable me to transfer to Mr Church the Deferred Debt which my Son agreed to pay him. Before I can speak positively a Correspondence which is opened with Boston must ripen, and I expect that the intercourse of a few Posts will reduce the matter to a certainty one way or other. I have $140,000 Deferred Debt deposited with the Treasurer of Massachusetts and my present Object is to redeem it by a payment in Money or other Paper.

I am Yrs
RM

To George Washington, 7 December 1795

Philada Decemr 7th 1795

Dear Sir

My Strong desire to give an agreable Answer to your Note of the 3d inst. restrained me from doing it sooner. I am not in possession of Money at present, nor can it be obtained in any way but upon Usurious Loans, However repugnant such Loans are to my interest & feelings, I have made offers that are held under Consideration at present, which if accepted will put it in my power to remit the Sum asked by the Commrs for the City of Washington, and if attained I shall instantly do it. I am Dr Sir Your most obed. Servt

Robt Morris

To Alexander Hamilton, 18 December 1795

Philada December 18. 1795

Dear Sir

Your friendly letter of the 14th came to hand on the 16th. It should have been answered yesterday, but my engagements did not permit. I wrote to you on the 16th of Novemr last mentioning a Negotiation opened with Boston in consequence of which I expected to redeem $140,000 Deferred Debt which I have pledged there. This Negotiation was opened under the auspices of Mr Swan, but I begin to think now that like many other things which look promising in the Outsett, it will go off in Air. I shall therefore gladly acquiesce with the proposition contained in your letter of the 14 Inst. My Estate called Morrisville formerly the Delaware Works, is worth upwards of Three hundred thousand Dollars. A person proposing to buy it two years ago proposed two hundred and fifty thousand as the price, and I have since then added Several Improvements and valuable buildings and shall continue doing so, because I persevere in my desire of having a Manufactoring Town there. I have already borrowed upon the Security of this Estate the Amot of about One hundred thousand Dollars for which it is mortgaged. I propose to give to you or to Mr Church as you please a Mortgage upon the same Estate for the Amot of his Claim with my Bond payable as you mention with Interest annually—if the Deferred Debt is changed into Money, or for the stock say one hundred thousand Dollars deferred Debt if that is to remain the Claim. If it is to be changed to a Money Debt the price must be fixed I suppose according to the price of the day, & then the Bond will carry Interest from the date. I am ready to fix it either way and agreeably to what you shall think right. The Security now proposed I consider as ample, even for a much larger sum than will be charged upon it after Mr Churchs is added to the other. Besides that it is ample it is also a Saleable property. There are not less than 17 Farms and the Land (about 3000 acres) has lately risen from £ 10 & £ 12. to above £ 15 p Acre through that neighborhood. I have in all about sixty Houses Three ferries, two Fisheries, Grist Mill, Brewery, Bake House, slitting & Rolling Mill, Fulling Mill, snuff Mill saw Mill, Quarry &ca. It is one of those lively Estates that brings in a Regular annual Income which is constantly increasing. My son Robert lives there and I think it the first Estate and the best for a Gentlemans Residence of any in America. In short I expect to double its present value in the Course of a few years. I observe you seem to think it may be necessary for me to justify my Conduct if I give you Security. I have no such Idea, I want time and nothing but time to pay every farthing that I owe in the World, and I have Property that will do that and leave to myself and family enough to Satisfy Ambition, if they should be ambitious, or Avarice should they be avaricious. I did not know that you had become uneasy on this Subject but I suppose the Stories that are propagated have made you so, and I am not surprized at it. I want Ready Money sadly, but it is not want of property—property however will not command Ready Money at this time without great sacrifices. I do not like to sacrifice if I can help it, because I have worked hard to get what I have, and I will fight a good Battle to keep it. Another year will probably produce the Change in my situation which I wish & altho' you give me five Years to pay Mr Church I will do it sooner if sooner it shall be convenient.

I am Dr Sir Yours &ca

RM

P.S. If you agree I will have a Mortgage drafted & send it for your Inspection.

To Alexander Hamilton, 6 March 1796

Phila 6 March 1796

Dear Sir

I am glad to see by your line of yesterday that you had got safe home. I am at present in treaty for the Sale of some Lands of Pennsa & perhaps some of the Tracts I proposed to you may be included in the sale. If they are, others shall be Substituted & you may rely that I will not lose a day unnecessarily in preparing & transmitting the Mortgages, but instead of putting the whole into one Mortgage I think it will be best to put one parcel of contiguous Tracts into one Mortgage & another in another & so on—then if any one of those Parcels should be sold, I can pay or exchange the Security without affecting the others.

You omitted to Return the Copy of Mr Greenleafs Deed for the Washington Lotts. The Original is gone to be recorded & I have no other Copy, therefore I request you to send it to me. I am very busy but you shall soon hear again from

Yrs
RM

To Alexander Hamilton, 14 March 1796

Phila 14 March 1796

Dear Sir

Agreeably to my promise I enclose herewith a List of the Lands which I propose to mortgage to you as Security for the debt due to Mr Church and I think the value more than Sufficient. For some of these Lands the Patents are issued, for some they are not issued, but the Patents are only considered as Evidence of Title, because when Warrants of Survey are granted the money is paid & a return of the Survey upon the Warrants vests the absolute Fee Simple Title in the Warantee who conveys by Deed Poll to whom he pleases. These Deeds Poll are commonly assigned from one person to another & he that holds them is always entitled to the Land and has the right to take out the patents when he pleases and it is only done *when he pleases*, so that many of the Oldest Estates in Pennsylvania are held to this day without having taken out the Patents. In all decisions in the Courts of Law such Titles have been recognized and confirmed. I have mentioned this matter that you may know every thing respecting the business and at the same time that every Objection may be Removed. I have given Orders for taking out the Patents which is a work of some time owing to the quantity of Business in the Land Office and the slow mode of doing it. In your last letter you supposed that Lands in the preferable Situations might be sold to the Injury or impairing of the Security offered. This was never intended by me, because if any of the Tracks proposed to be mortgaged should be sold either before or after the mortgage takes effect my intention is to substitute other property to your entire Satisfaction otherwise I could not think of making such sales. I believe the Lands standing in my name in the state of new york near Chemung or near the Pennsa Line as marked on DeWitts New Map are now worth about 2 of York Curry P Acre, and I expect soon to be in a Situation to sell the whole, that is about 38000 Acres. If you incline to buy Lands for Mr Church perhaps we may agree for those or some others, so as to discharge this debt with advantage to Mr Church, & in the mean time I am ready to execute the Mortgage as soon as you please.

I am Dr Sir Yrs &c.

To Alexander Hamilton, 27 April 1796

Philada. April 27th 1796

Dr. Sir

Your letter without date arrived within this half hour & in consequence I run down to Mr Lewis from whom I am just returned he says he has written you two letters, the last of them this morning & it was sent to the Post Office before I got there. If Mr Lewis does me justice he will tell you that I called on him more than once with a strong desire to finish the business. I am mortified not a little to see your extreme anxiety & at the same time acknowledge that it is my duty to relieve you from it. I make it a point of honor to do so, and would now offer you as good a security in this City as that you gave up, but I perceive the existing judgements would lead you to object. I will therefore send you a Mortgage upon one hundred thousand acres of the Genesee Land adjoining that which I am now selling at 1 of your Curry ⅌ Acre in order to discharge the Mortgage to Colo. Walker. Mr Saml. Ogden will go over to New York in order to finish that business perhaps you can assist him in it. If that Mortgage is cleared away there is no other & the land I would not sell for less than two Dollr ⅌ Acre were it not to pay that cursed Mortgage. I must however stipulate with you that if at any time I should wish to change the security, you will allow me to do it upon giving one equally satisfactory. I wish also to know whether I should give the Bonds for 100,000 Drs deferred debt, or if to be commuted to Money at what rate shall it be done or how will you settle the Acct. I will have the Mortgage drawn up immediately after hearing from you unless you choose to send me the draft of one & point out the formalities. Must Mrs Morris be a party, as there is no income arising from uncultivated Lands I suppose it is not necessary. You may rely you shall not have cause in any event to change your opinion of my honor or integrity if that opinion has been what I believe it always has been.

I am Dr. Sir Y. O. h. S.

RM

To Alexander Hamilton, 10 May 1796

Philada. May 10th. 1796

Dear Sir

Your letter dated April 9th. but which was written yesterday, I presume, came to hand this Morning and I have since the receipt of it and of one from Colo Ogden seen Colo Walker who tells me that he left power with you to adjust with the latter the business of the Mortgage formerly granted by me to Colo W. Smith on behalf of Mr Pulteney &c., therefore I presume it has been settled in some way or other. Colo Ogden has sent me a Copy of the Articles of agreement made by him on my behalf with Othniel Taylor & Asa Danforth for the Sale of 50000 Acres of Land, and in order to have the affair compleatly finished, I proposed to Colo Walker that I would Convey the said 50,000 Acres to him and assign to him the above mentioned Contract which binds the parties to pay $57,500 and interest at the times therein mentioned. My debt to Mr. Pulteney for which the Mortgage was given is about fifty thousand Dollrs of Six ⅌ Ct Stock now Worth about 17/4 in the pound, but that I would Commute it into Money at 20/ or par, and Colo Walker to pay the bale of the Account, & enter Satisfaction on the Mortgage discharging me of the demand. It appears to me that this is necessary in order to give Value to the Mortgage I am to make to you and I have thus explained myself lest Colo Walker might misunderstand or not Recollect clearly my proposition. I think it is fair, honorable and generous such as will be approved by the principal, and therefore I expect that you will advise his Concurrence. I will have the Mortgage to you immediately drawn and the form you prescribe Shall be duly observed. I expect however to hear from you & Col Walker in answer to this letter, as I consider my hands to be tied up by the Chancery Suit, untill the Mortgage is discharged.

I am Dr Sir RM

To Alexander Hamilton, 17 May 1796

Phila May 17. 1796

Dear sir

When you received the Bond & Mortgage Deed transmitted herewith which are dated the 16 Instant you will perceive that there has been all the sincerity in my Professions which you could expect. I have from you experienced that degree of Confidence which consisted with my Character and I have been gratified thereby but the extreme solicitude that has lately appeared on your part leads me to suppose that Mr Churchs letters or the Common Reports have impaired that Confidence. You probably dread the Effects of the Judgements you have heard of but you need not, I have provided for them and so I shall continue to do whenever it becomes indispensible. I would never Suffer a Judgement to come against me, if I was alone in the business, but as I am now situated I cannot prevent it untill such time as solid relief shall arise from the abundant Property which I possess. I will seek the means of clearing away the Mortgage to Colo Smith and I am sure the Principals in that Business would never have treated me as the Attorneys have done. Were I to act agreeably to my feelings a very different letter would be written by me to Mr Church than that which you will find inclosed herein & that such a letter is not written you may truly ascribe to yourself because I respect and esteem you. Be so kind to transmit with this letter your Advice of our new Arrangement & desire him to transfer the North American Land Company Shares agreeably to my request. You did not leave with me the Deed of Conveyance of the 20290 Acres of Land but I still have the Patents & will either send them to you or deliver them to any Person you please. I am Sincerely

Yrs
RM

To John B. Church, 17 May 1796

Phila May 17. 1796

Sir

Colo Hamilton transmitted to me your letter of the 20 Febry last, wherein you complain that I had done wrong & treated you unfriendly "in having prevailed upon him to cancel the Mortgage I had given him on an Estate in Philadelphia, when the Agreemt was expressly made with my Son that the Mortgage should remain as Security to you untill the deferred stock was delivered in discharge of the Contract made with him." Be pleased to attend to the following state of Facts and your *astonishment* will probably cease & your Opinion become more favorable. The Origin of my Debt to you was a purchase of 100 Shares of Bank stock at £100 Stg ℔ Share which gave you a profit of £16.13.4 Currency upon each Share. I then sold to Colo Hamilton 20290 Acres of Land at 7/6 Curry ℔ acre which at the Par of Exchange amounted to £4565..5.. Stg and was to go according to his Agreement with me in part payment of the said Bank stock & for the Balance I gave a Bill on my Son in your favor being for £5434..15 Stg. The 20290 Acres of Land sold to Colo Hamilton for your Account will now sell for thrice what I got for it and before he or I knew of the Agreement which took place between you and my Son, the Mortgage on the Philadelphia Estate was cancelled. I proposed & urged this being done because the sale of Lands paid nearly half the Debt due to you & because I had then good reason to expect that my Son to pay the Bill drawn upon him; & Colo Hamilton having the same Idea, was disposed to accomodate me, especially as I promised him to give a new Security for the Amot of the bill in case my Son could not pay it or if from any cause whatever the said Bill should not be paid. My Son finding after the failure of J. Warder & Co it would be inconvenient for him to pay that Bill and that the receipt of money from you for the Cost of the 20290 Acres of Land which I had sold to Colo Hamilton for you would be convenient to my Affairs in his hands, agreed with you to receive the Money for that Purchase & to commute the Original Debt contracted for 100 shares of Bank stock of the value of $40,000 Mexican to $100,000 of Deferred debt payable in February 1795 for which you demand $75000 Mexican with Interest of Six ₽ Cent ₽ Annum. Now sir, you will be good enough to attend to the Circumstance that the Mortgage was cancelled before Colo Hamilton or myself knew of the Agreement made by my Son Robert with you, consequently there was no violation of Faith or Friendship on my part nor any Neglect of Duty on the part of Colo Hamilton, who had obtained for you a real property of more Value than your stock, and my bill for £5434..15 Stg for which I was liable and had promised him a new security if necessary. My Promises I hold Sacred and I am always willing to fulfill them. I have therefore given to Colo Hamilton my Bond for $81679. 44/100 payable in five Years from the 1st January last with six p Cent interest annually and an ample Security by Mortgage of Lands for the Payment of this Debt. I hope therefor that you will find cause to be Satisfied both with Colo Hamilton and myself, and in order to shew that your Money has not been unproductive I beg leave to submit to your Consideration the enclosed statemt, which I think ought to Satisfy any reasonable person.

You have threatened me with a Public sale of my North American Land Company Shares, which were entrusted to you by me in the expectation that they would on the terms of that Trust, have produced the discharge of my Debt, and it seems to me that the Act of transferring these Shares to your name ought to have convinced you that I never wished or designed you to be insecure. I disclaim any fears or Apprehensions from threats, and I will not use any, but as Colo Hamilton will advise you of our new arrangement and of the Security I have given, I must again request that you will transfer the 750 Shares in the North American Land

Company to James Marshall Esqre or execute a power for him to transfer the same, being the shares which I had transferred to your name. Should Mrs. Church still remain in England, I pray you to present Mrs. Morris's and my thanks for her kind Attention to our Daughter and that you will also accept the Same yourself. Should she be on her Passage to this Country as it is said she is, we will thank her in person, and a grateful Remembrance of her and your kindness will ever be retained in our minds.

My feelings it is true have been wounded at some part of your letter which I conceive to be unnecessarily harsh, but Still I am desirous as you say to wind up this business amicably, and I hope it will be so terminated as that we shall remain good Friends.

I am Sir Yours &c.

RM

To Alexander Hamilton, 31 May 1796

Philada May 31. 1796

Dear Sir

I am sorry that the Omission & inaccuracy of description in the Mortgage Deed as expressed in your letter of the 26 Inst. should have occasioned you any farther Trouble in Mr Churchs Business. The Omission of the name was owing to that Tract not having been conveyed to the parties for whom it was intended by Colo Ogden, who made an Agreement short of my terms the Object being to discharge thereby Colo Smiths Mortgage but as Colo Walker will not discharge the Mortgage I will not agree to the Bargain of Mr. Ogden as it was not consanant to my Orders either as to price or terms of Payment. I have therefore conveyed the Tract to Mr Garrett Cottringer whose name is now inserted in the new Mortgage executed by me, and as I want no other depositary than yourself I will send both Mortgages by the Young Gentn. you have sent hither. It may be well however to have a line from you declaratory that the two are for the same purpose & that the Payment of the Bond will discharge both. Accept my thanks for the friendly terms of your last letter and be assured of my constant regard.

Yrs. RM

P.S. Suppose you were to make up a Company to purchase the 50,000 acres conveyed to Mr Cottringer, give me two Dollars ℔ acre, discharge Colo Smith's mortgage which is for 50,000 Dolls Six ℔ Cent stock and pay me the bal.? You will get four Dolls an acre in about 12 Mos. and Colo Walker will give longer credit than that I suppose, or I will sell at 2 Dolls ℔ acre as much as will discharge that Mortgage altho my Son Tom writes that Lands are risen so much that he advises me not to sell.

To Alexander Hamilton, 17 June 1796

Phila June 17 1796

Dear Sir

I was disappointed in not seeing you as expected before your departure. In reply to your favor of the 9th. I must first tell you, that if certain Negotiations which I am working at succeed I will pay you sooner than you expect, but if they fall through as many others have done I will at all Events take up my Note by paying Principal and Interest within nine months from this date & as much sooner as I can, besides if at any particular time before the Period abovementioned you need a part, let me know it, and I will Struggle hard (if needful) to get it.

I am Dr Sir Yrs

RM

To Alexander Hamilton, 27[–30] June 1796

Phila. June 27 [–30] 1796

dear Sir

Your favor of the 20th I have received & will most chearfully comply with your requisition by remitting $1500 which if I can shall go in this letter and if in the Course of my negotiations I can meet with notes or drafts upon New York suitable for the remaining Payment they shall be sent you, but if I do not obtain Such you may rely that I will fulfill my Promise in regard to that Payment or it shall be as you propose half in six & half in 12 mos.

Yrs.
RM

June 30   I could not bear to send this without the $1500. You will find herein a draft of Joseph Higbee upon at 30 days for that sum you can get it discounted & charge me with the Cost letting me know the amount. You will see by this that I did not neglect you altho' you did not receive it immediately.

RM

To George Washington, 25 August 1796

Philada August 25th 1796

Sir.

In the year 1791—I purchased of the State of Massachusetts a Tract of Country lying within the boundaries of the State of Newyork which had been Ceded by the latter to the former State under the Sanction & with the Concurrence of the Congress of the United States, This Tract of Land is bounded to the East by the Genesee River, to the North by Lake Ontario, to the West partly by Lake Erie & partly by the Boundary Line of the Pensylvania Triangle & to the South by the North Boundary Line of the State of Pensylvania, A Printed Brief of my Title I take the liberty to transmit Herewith, To perfect this Title it is necessary to purchase of the Seneca Nation of Indians their Native right, which I should have done soon after the purchase was made of the State of Massachusetts, but that I felt myself restrained, from doing so by Motives of Public consideration. The War between the Western Indian Nations & the United States did not extend to the Six Nations of which the Seneca's Nation is one, and as I apprehended that if this Nation should sell its right during the existance of that War, they might the more readily be induced to join the Enemies of my Country I determ(ined) not to make the purchase whilst that War lasted. When peace was made with the Indian Nations I turned my thoughts towards the purchase which is to me an object very interesting, but upon its being represented that a little longer patience untill the Western Posts should be delivered up by the British Government might still be of public utility I concluded to wait for that event also which is now happily accomplished, and there seems no obstacle remaining to restrain me from making the purchase, especially as I have reason to believe the Indians are desirous to make the Sale[.] the delays which have already taken place & which arose solely from the considerations above mentioned have been *extremely detrimental to my private affairs,* but still being desirous to comply with Formalities prescribed by Certain Laws of the United States, altho' those Laws probably do not reach my Case, I now make application to the President of the United States and request that He will Nominate and appoint a Commissioner to be present and Preside at a Treaty which He will be pleased to Authorize to be held with the Seneca Nation for the purpose of enabling me to make a purchase in Conformity with the Formalities required by sd Laws of the Tract of Country for which I have already paid a very large Sum of Money. My right to the preemption is unequivocal, and the Land is become so necessary to the growing Population and surrounding Settlements that it is with difficulty that the white People can be restrained from Squatting or setting down upon these Lands, which if they should do, it may probably bring on Contentions with the Six Nations. This will be prevented by a timely fair & honorable purchase[.] This proposed Treaty ought to be held immediately before the Hunting Season, or another year will be lost, as the Indians Cannot be Collected during that Season, The loss of another year under the payments I have made for these Lands, would be ruinous to my affairs, and as I have paid so great deferrence to Public considerations whilst they did exist, I expect & hope that my request will be readily granted now when there can be no cause for delay, especially If the Indians are willing to sell, which will be tested by the offer to buy. With the most perfect Esteem & respect I am Sir Your most Obedt & most hble Servt

R.M.

To George Washington, 23 December 1796

Philada [c.23 Dec. 1796]

Sir

On the 25th of August last I had the honor to state in my letter of that date what had been the tenor of my Conduct in regard to the pre-emption right which I had acquired by purchase of the State of Massachusets to a Tract of Country within the State of New York and to request of the President of the United States that He would "Nominate and appoint a Commissioner to be present and preside at a Treaty which he would be pleased to Authorize to be held with the Seneca Nation of Indians for the purpose of enabling me to purchase the Native right to the said Tract of Country &c.["]

On the 27th of August I received a Note from the Secretary of State enclosing an Opinion of the Attorney General by which it would appear that The President had not Authority to appoint Such Commissioner without the advice & Consent of the Senate, Upon the receipt of this opinion I forbore to pursue my object untill the Senate Should be in Session & now that they are so & when There cannot exist any reason for further delay, I beg leave to refer to my said Letter that of the Secy of State with the oppinion of the Atty General and to renew the request that a Commissioner may be Nominated for the approbation of the Senate in order that a Treaty may be held with the Seneca Nation of Indians at such Time & place as may hereafter be fixed for the purpose.

R.M.

To Alexander Hamilton, 31 December 1796

Philada. Decr. 31st. 1796

Dear Sir

You will find annexed hereto the Copy of a letter just received from Charles Bridgen Esqr. and enclosed my Answer, which after reading You will be kind enough to send to him. I suppose myself to be founded in saying that the suit contemplated, cannot be brought against me, otherwise no Man whose Name is on another Mans paper, can be safe, At any rate I request your Aid as a professional Man and will Chearfully pay such Compensation as you shall say is right for the Service you render me or the trouble this Application may Occasion you. I have no property in the State of New York that Mr Bridgen can come at even if his Suit could be Maintained, therefore He had better seek for payment in the regular Course against the drawer of the Bill.

I am Dr Sir Your Obedt Servant

Robt. Morris

To Alexander Hamilton, 7 January 1797

Philada. Jany. 7th. 1797

Dear Sir

I have arranged with Capt Chas Williamson for the debt Contracted with Colo Wm S. Smith in August 1791 of which fifty Thousand Dollars. in Six ℔ Ct Stock remains to be transferred and delivered & for the performance thereof I have given to Capt. Williamson Assignee of Colo Smith a satisfactory Security, in Consequence Whereof that Tract of Land in the Genesee Country for which I gave Colo Smith a Deed of Conveyance is to be reconveyed to me, and a Suit which was instituted by Colo Walker in the Court of Chancerry is to be withdrawn & rendered Null & Void, for a more full & perfect information of these matters I refer you to the enclosed Copies of the Articles of Agreement between Colo Smith and me, and of the Defeazant executed by him. The Original of the latter is with me, the Original of the former and the Deed of Conveyance were left with Colo Smith and I suppose are now in the hands of Colo. Walker who Acted as Atty to Capt Williamson, the latter will do every thing to be done for restoring to me my Title to the Tract of Land West of the Genesee River free of all incumbrance either by means of my Deed to Colo Smith or of the suit in Chancerry, but I must request your immediate care and attention as a professional Man to see this done in all due Form & without loss of time for which I will chearfully pay the Compansation you will say is right.

I am Dr Sir Your Obed Servt

Robt Morris.

To Alexander Hamilton, 23 January 1797

Philada Jany. 23d. 1797

Dr Sir

Your letter of the 21st inst. is just received none of a previous date in reply to mine of 31st Ulto ever reached me, nor have I received from you any acknowledgement of the receipt of my letter to you of 7th Inst. which was sent by Captn Williamson in order to have the mortgage to Colo Smith removed & the suit in Chancery brought by Colo Walker discharged. This latter is a very important business as you know and I am anxious to know the needfull therein has been done agreably to the promise of Captn Williamson. With respect to the suit meditated by Mr Bridgen I wish measures to be stopped untill Mr Nicholson the drawer of the bill (who is soon expected) shall return from the City of Washington where he now is when I will consult him and make in consequence such propositions as may be acceptable to the parties unless in the meantime the affair should be adjusted with Ralph Mather the last endorser who I suspect to be the real owner of the bill as I have heard of his endeavoring to make a negotiation on the first bill of the suit whilst Mr Bridgen threatens a suit on the second. I will address you again on this business soon as Mr Nicholson arrives & in the mean time I rely on your taking care of Dr Sir

Yr Obedt Servt

RM

P S I am not sure that Mr Mather offered the same bill for negotiation but I suppose it to be so.

To Alexander Hamilton, 27 February 1797

Philada. Feby 27th. 1797

Dear Sir

Mr Tilghman authorizes me to tell you that our Law respecting endorsements is exactly the same as the Law of England & that 20 ℔ Ct is the Amot of Damages on protested Bills drawn here upon Europe.

Mr. Nicholson is returned to this City & I think the holders of his bill should Apply to him for payment. I think he would make some arrangement with them so as to secure the payment and allow compensation for time. I wish you would mention this to them; I will aid the Negotiation if they will open one.

I am very anxious to have the affair of the Genesee Tract settled as proposed in my last, that is, to have the Chancery Suit withdrawn or dismissed and the Deed or Mortgage assigned to Mr. Cottringer, or done away so that the property Revest in me, one or the other I pray to have done immediately & give preferrance to that which you may think best for me. But I pray that no longer delay may be offered as my intended operations require it & are essential. Let me hear from you & be assured of the Esteem & regard of Dr Sir

Your Obed Servt.

Robt Morris

To Alexander Hamilton, 3 March 1797

Philada March 3d 1797

Dear sir

On the day I wrote you last, Mr Westerloe left at my House Yours of the 23d. I expect the pleasure of his company soon. I hope Mr Bridgon's Clients will as was proposed in my last letter to you come or send to Mr Nicholson who is disposed to put their demand upon the most satisfactory footing in his power, & I expect the business may be so settled as that the Money will be forth coming sooner than by Legal process it can be obtained, for as I am not properly the payer, altho' responsible, I shall resist as long as I can if they pursue me instead of seeking paymt from the real debtor or principal who is willing to arrange the matter to their Content. I want sadly to have the affair of the Genesee Land finished by Colo Walker it is become indispensible to have it done in one or other of the modes mentioned in my last letter if the Assignment of Colo Smiths Deeds or Mortgage is made to Mr Cottringer he can release such parts as I convey. And the remainder will not be subject to Attachment. The President has nominated a Commr to preside at the Treaty which I intend to hold with the Indians, and I expect the senate will this day give their assent so that I hope it may not be long before I make a purchase but my wish is to have this as little known as possible. I mention it to you that you may advise Mr Church to give Mr Marshall two Dollars an Acre for the 10,000 Acres mortgaged to him I could now sell it for 2/ N York currency on a credit shorter than the time I am to pay Mr Church and I am confident that it will be worth four, to six or eight dolls pr Acre by that time. My wants cause me to desire a Sale and if I must sell had not Mr Church better to take the benefit than let others do it. The moment the Indian title is obtained there will be a rush of People into that Country that will raise the price of land beyond that or any other part of America, & the settlements will be made by Men of property, & respectable character who are now laying by Money, and preparing themselves for the purpose. Nothing is more certain than these things & Mr Church has the opportunity of doubling trebling or Quadrupling his money, tell him therefore to embrace it.

I am Dr Sir Yours &c.

RM

To Alexander Hamilton, 27 March 1797

Philada. March 27th. 1797

Dear Sir

I wrote a few lines from Mr Nicholsons house on Saturday whilst waiting to see Mr Mather; he did not come there untill I was obliged to come away, but Mr Nicholson informs me he came afterwards and that they are likely to effect an Arrangement for the Bill of Exchange and that Mr Mather has written to stay any proceedings in New York untill they hear again from him. This being a debt of Mr Nicholsons I am desirous that he should settle it, but should he fail I must ultimately do it, and if in the end it falls to my lot, I now request that you will use your discretion, and make the best Arrangement you can for me. I pledge my honor that there is no other encumbrance on the 100000 Acres of Genesee land Mortgaged to Mr Church than that Mortgage and I am extreemly averse to suffering any other to go on it. I want Mr Church to buy it. He may do that now, so as to double his Money on me, respecting this I wrote you some time ago to which you did not reply.

I am Dr Sir Yours &c.

RM

To George Washington, 10 April 1797

Philad[elphi]a April 10th 1797

Dear Sir

I forwarded by Post the letter mentiond in the annexed from Mr Parish, under a Blank Cover to your address (being then hurried). You will judge wether the Contents of the annexed will be any gratification to Mr La Fayette to whom I pray my Compts. Mrs Morris & Maria desire their best & affectionate regards to Mrs Washington & Miss Custis. We were happy in the Company of Master Custis yesterday He is astonishingly improved and is a manly fine Fellow. I pray to be also presented to Mrs Washington & Miss Custis and that you will ever consider me as most sincerely attached to you & yours

Robt Morris

To Alexander Hamilton, 20 May 1797

Philada. May 20th. 1797

Dear Sir

I cannot account for the little notice that has been taken of some of my latest letters to you, but I hope the present will obtain your favourable attention. When Capt. Williamson agreed to give up the Lien which my Deed gave to Colo Smith, it was expressly mention'd by me & agreed by him that the Suit which had been Commenced in the Court of Chancerry by Colo Walker should be withdrawn & the injunction that had been issued & served on me was to be removed, otherwise I could not make use of the remaining property. Mr Sterett to whom I have Conveyed 175 M Acres in searching the Public Offices & obtaining Certificates got out of the Chancerry Court those which you will find inclosed herein, which as they now stand would be an effectual Bar to any thing been done with the Lands. I pray therefore that you will obtain a discharge of the injunction & let a proper Certificate thereof be added to these & then the whole be returned to me & let this be done with all possible expedition as these Papers are to be sent immediately to Europe. I wro⟨te⟩ also to Colo Walker for the Deed I gave to Colo Smith. He did not think it worth while to Answer my letter. I have known the time when he would have thought differently & perhaps I may notwithstanding present appearances, See that time again. I ought to have had that Deed with the others & this Chancerry business should have been finished. As I cannot think that you mean to Neglect me, I shall be thankfull if you will have these things done for Dr Sir

Your faithfull Friend & Servant

Robt Morris

PS Mr Sterett told me that you had an Idea that the Land Conveyed to him was the same that is mortgaged to you. I do not know but their may be ⟨some⟩ interference in a part & ⟨there⟩fore a Conditional ⟨ad⟩dition was made to the Deed.

RM

To Alexander Hamilton, 23 May 1797

Philada. May 23d. 1797

Dear Sir

Your letter of yesterday is arrived and the Contents are very Acceptable, I hope the business in the Chancerry Court will soon be dismissed and the Certificate returned to me with that addition.

Accept my Congratulations on the arrival of Mr Church & his Family and I will thank you to present Mrs Morris's & mine to Mr

& Mrs. Church with the Assurance of the pleasure it will give us to See them here. I find by a letter from Mr Marshall that Mr Church would not Treat with him for the purchase of the 100,000 Acres of Genesee Lands Mortgaged to you, but he has found another Person that will and therefore He desires me to forward a Copy of the Mortgage I gave to you, with a declaration that there are no other Incumbrances & that you will assign or release the Mortgage upon receiving the principal & interest of the debt for which it was given. Thus you see my Dear Sir I am obliged to give you trouble, altho I wish to spare it & in order to take it off of you personally I should be glad that you would get an Authenticated Copy from the Office where it is recorded with a Certificate that there are no other incumbrances upon record, and have a declaration drawn & endorsed on the said Copy to be signed by you purporting that you promise & bind yourself to assign or release the Original Mortgage upon receipt of the principal Sum & interest for which it was given, all this except the signing your Name may be done by a person employed for the purpose & I will chearfully pay the Cost. Expedition is necessary as I have an opportunity of sending the Papers by a Gentln whom I wish to be the bearer and he will soon depart. I must also request that you will examine to see that the Certificates & declaration are such as will be likely to give satisfaction to an European purchasor. I am not in a situation to answer offhand as was formerly the case, every claim on my justice, I ought most certainly to pay that which you call for and I will immediately cast about to see how it can be accomplished; respecting which you shall Soon hear again from Dr Sir

Your Obedt & faithfull Friend & Servant

Robt Morris

To Alexander Hamilton, 2 June 1797

Philada. June 2d. 1797

Dear Sir

Your letter of yesterday is this moment recd and I take my pen upon the first impulse to tell you not to be uneasy, I will pay you every farthing principal & interest, have patience for my measures to operate & rely yourself with Confidence. The Nature of your debt ties me at all events & it shall be paid. As to Mr Church's Security how can it be doubted. I told you before that Mr Marshall is in treaty for the Land at Two Dollrs ℔ Acre & writes for the Papers I wrote to you for. I beg you to send them as Speedily as possible. I think they will enab(le) me to pay him off long before the time stipulated.

I am to be sure disagreeably situated, but my affairs are retrievable if I could get the Common aid of Common times and I will struggle hard. Keep All this to Yourself. I will address you again by & by. But send me the Papers written for.

Yours Sincerely

Robt Morris

To Alexander Hamilton, 9 September 1797

Hills near Philada. Septr. 9th. 1797

Dear Sir

I have received your favour of the 29th. with the Papers enclosed therewith and should have acknowledged the receipt of them immediately but that I observed you had inserted a larger Sum as the bala. of my Note than I thought could be due thereon & lest you may not have kept a regular acct of the payments I have made

401

on that account I wrote Mr Cottringer to make an extract from My Books & you will find it herein. I wish I could remit you the balance, but that is not yet in my power, I hope it may [be] soon.

I was much disappointed at not seeing you when in Philada. I went thither on purpose one Sunday Morning & sent my Son Charles to every place I could think of to bring you to dine with us, but he was unsuccessful and I regretted it much & more so afterwards when I found you had departed without giving me a call at this place.

I am most truly your obedt. Servant

Robt Morris

To Alexander Hamilton, 2 October 1797

Hills near Philada. Octr. 2d. 1797

Dear Sir

I cannot help feeling some chagrin when I find you constantly treating the debt I owe you as if you were in danger of loosing it, because I wish to stand higher in your confidence than it seems is the case. I have assured you that you should not loose and I am happy to see my way clear to effect the payment pretty soon, perhaps some influen⟨ce o⟩n your part over those who are to pay may ⟨b⟩e necessary, and as soon as I receive a Copy of the Treaty made with the Indians I will write again and explain myself on this point in the mean while I am as ever Dr Sir

Your Obedt hble servt.

Robt Morris

To Alexander Hamilton, 27 October 1797

Hills [near Philadelphia] October 27th 1797

Dear Sir

In my last letter to you I said I saw the means of discharging my debt to you in consequence of the purchase made of the Indians and that your influence might be usefull in the recovery of the money, it is thus; Doctor Craigie in Co with Watson & Greenleaf purchased of Mr Saml. Ogden with my consent 100000 acres of Genesee land for which they paid, except $12500 Watson and Greenleaf were half and Doctr Craigie half, unfortunately at the solicitation of Greenleaf when he was settling accounts with Mr Watson I released the latter of his responsibility and took Greenleaf's Bond for their half. Doctor Craigie is to pay me the other half in specie or in certain Bonds which he then held of mine those Bonds I have satisfied by a sale of lands to him since; therefore he is to pay me $6250 in specie in 60 days after the Indian title is acquired to the 100000 Acres of land, that title was acquired on the 15th day of September last being the date of the Indian Deed of conveyance for the whole Country of which that 100000 Acres is a part and none of the Indian reservations are near it. I wrote to Mr Craigie last Week and enclosed a Copy of the instructions I gave for the survey and sent that letter open under cover to his relation and Agent Mr Seth Johnston of New York but have not heard from either of them. I do not Know of or suspect any demur to this payment unless they or either of them should have possessed themselves of some of the notes in circulation on which unfortunately my Name is. I think you have influence with both these Gentln and in your last letter dated the 5th inst. you promise the exertion of it. I request that you will apply to them upon this subject as if the debt was assigned to you and prevail on them to pay without any attempt at defalcation. If they agree I will send you an order or assignment as you may think best, you had best in your first application only to mention that you are to receive this Money & hear what they have to say, if they agree to pay all is well, if they make any objections I will send you the papers on which the debt rests. There are two orders in the hands of Mr Hazlehurst amount to about £500 to £600 which I am to get up or they will stop the Amot. these I expect to obtain in time. I shall await your Answer and remain   Dr Sir yrs

RM

To Alexander Hamilton, 1 November 1797

Hills [near Philadelphia] Novr. 1st. 1797

Dear Sir

I wrote to you some days ago, but have not yet heard in reply. I take the liberty to enclose herein a letter for Mr. Church and to ask your interference. If it is only his Money that he is Seeking I will get it for him, and I would fain hope that he does not wish to take advantage of my Necessities and obtain my property at less than its worth.

I am willing to Sell it at a fair price to him if he chooses, but if he really does not wish to have the Land, procure for me a little time and I will do him ample justice.

If he were pressed by Necessity I could not think hard of his pressure, but as that is not the case and I am willing to pay for indulgence I hope he will grant it, and you will oblige me by letting Mr Rd. Harison and myself know what to expect. I hope I am not imposing a disagreable task on you, but that you will do the needfull for a real Friend.

Your hble servt.

Robt Morris

To John B. Church, 1 November 1797

Hills near Philada Novr 1st 1797

Sir

I informed you some time since that I was in Treaty for money to pay the interest due to you, it so happened that I could not bring the agreement to a close before the Citizens of Philadelphia began to disperse on account of the Yellow fever, and since they did so, it has been next to impossible to get any business done. They are now returning to their homes and I shall renew my negotiations and doubt not but in a short time I shall be able to secure the money to pay the interest due as well as that which is coming due. Under this expectation I request your patience for a little longer time and you shall hear from me again I hope with the remittance. I shall not object to pay interest for the delay of the payment which ought to have been made on the 1st Jany last.

Yrs.
RM

To George Washington, 6 November 1797

Hills near Philad[elphi]a Novr 6th 1797

Dear Sir

As I make a point to trouble you with as few introductions as possible, I will make no other appology for the present one. This letter will be delivered by Mr Danl Lister an English young Gentn r⟨ecommende⟩d to me by Mr Richd Penn, Mr James Marshall & others as worthy of Attention & Civilities. He is going to the Southward after having travelled through the Eastern & Middle States and has asked me for this introduction, saying that he could not return contentedly without seeing the Saviour of this

Country. Thus you see that your well earned Fame subjects your time & attention to be taxed by Strangers. I pray that my respects may be presented to Mrs Washington & Miss Custis and that you will ever believe me to be with sincere attachment Dr Sir Your most Obedt Servt

Robt Morris

To Alexander Hamilton, 23 November 1797

Hills [near Philadelphia] Novr. 23d. 1797

Dear Sir

I have this minute received your favour of the 20th inst. and sit down immediately to acknowledge my fear that the mistake respecting Doctr Cragies Bond is with me, I am seperated from the Bulk of my Papers and when I wrote you respecting it I had only his letter agreeing for the purchase of the Land and terms of payment, not hearing from you I sent to Town a few days ago for the Bond intending to Send it to you, but it could not be found amongst my Papers and then it occurred for the first time, that Colo. Ogden must have it, as he made the Sale of that Land to Greenleaf Watson & Cragie, and I have Greenleafs Bond for their half, which I have just put in Suit against him, for I had at his request in the days of my Confidence in him released Mr Watson and taken him alone of which I now repent as I do of every transaction between him & me. I beg your pardon for having given you this trouble, and I will immediately turn my attention to another source of reimbursement for you. My promise to you on this point is sacred and shall be fullfilled, you will speedily hear again from me in regard to it. I hope Mr Church has too much Spirit and too high a Sense of honor to entertain a desire of possessing himself of my property at less than its Value, and at its

Value I am willing to Sell it to him. I trust to your assurance of serving me in this business and remain as ever Dr Sir

Your Sincere Friend & Servant

Robt Morris

To Alexander Hamilton, 7 February 1798

Hills [near Philadelphia]
Feby 7th 1798

Dear Sir

You will find annexed the exact statement of your Acct with me for the ten thousand dollars which you lent me with the Interest computed to the 27th Novr last Balance in your favour on that day being $6002.25. This Balance my Son Tom is to assume with interest from that date accordingly I have closed the Acct in my Books by charging you and crediting him for the same which I hope will meet with your & his approbation. I shall ever be gratefull for your Kindness in this transaction and lament that it should have been attended with inconvenience as to loss it was ever my determination to secure you against, Mr Rees is still here settling his own affair, he has the Deed the execution of which he will prove (being one of the Witnesses) before a Master in Chancery or Judge of your State so as to entitle it to be recorded.

Yrs
RM

To Thomas Jefferson, 2 March 1801

Philada. March 2d. 1801

Dear Sir

I was this day honoured with the receipt of your letter of the 26th. ulto. and immediately sent in quest of James Tate the person of whose Character You enquire, he came, and I communicated to him your intentions, he told me that he is now employed in the Custom House & that he thought it a duty he owed to the Collector Mr Latimer to consult him previous to any determination on his own part, altho his inclination would lead him to engage in your service because he conceived himself to be capable of performing the duties of the Station, I then gave him your letter to shew to Mr Latimer, and he has just returned with a line from that Gentleman to me which for your satisfaction is enclosed herein. James Tate served me in the Capacity of Steward or upper Servant for three or four years; I always considered him as Capable faithfull, attentive, sober & honest; my misfortunes dismissed him from my service, there was no other cause that I know of, It is however proper to observe that he is a man of *Temper* this to me was no inconvenience but on the contrary as I put up with some things, his Spirit saved me the trouble with subordinate Servants in many instances and in a smaller degree required the interference of *The Master*, (Mrs Morris who returns her esteem for you) desires me to tell you, as a thing she deems highly important, that he is very cleanly, which I mention perhaps with more pleasure from a selfish motive as I expect (notwithstanding my present situation and age) some day or other to partake of your hospitality. I think it proper however to tell you that in my days of affluence I was generally well Served by my domesticks, and that I attributed to Mrs. Morris the merit of an attentive superintendance which caused the performance of domestick duty. The Eye of a Master or Mistress is ever usefull in this respect. We had here a plentifull

Market Tate knew the people that brought good things he knew how to buy & how they ought to be cooked & Served. I reposed in him a confidence of which he was proud & for which I thought him gratefull it is some years since we parted, he has since kept a Tavern & I cannot answer for the habits or manners he may since that time have acquired but Mr. Latimer's letter is much in his favour He has a Wife & three Children, his Wife is as he tells me very capable of taking the charge of the linen &c of any family and if he engages with you one at least of his children will remain behind with its Grandmother. He will attend you immediately if your answer to this letter requires it, and I have told him that if his Conduct in your service meets & Merits your approbation that your liberality will induce you to place him at parting in some situation that will enable him to provide for a growing family. permit me to assure you that my esteem & Respect for your personal Character has never abated from party considerations as many of your friends & foes well know, for I have invariably averred that your administration if you came into the chief Magistracy, would be governed by good sense and strict integrity, pardon me if you think I should have been silent on this head & believe that I am very truly dear Sir

Your most obedt Servt

Robt Morris

To Thomas Jefferson, 6 May 1801

Philada. May 6th. 1801

Dear Sir,

As I know that you take pleasure in patronizing ingenious men of merit, I expect you will not think this an improper intrusion. The bearer of this letter is Mr Henry Foxall who has for a considerable time past been employed in Casting Cannon for the use of the United States, He is well skilled in the Iron business in all its branches & has performed his engagements with the Secy at War, Secy of the Navy &c I believe to their perfect satisfaction and certainly has made the best cannon they have received, He was in my Service for a time & has since been concerned with My Son and we have every reason to consider him as an honest, faithfull, industrious Man perfectly master of his business, and as he is usefully engaged for public Service I beg to recommend him to your notice & protection if found deserving

With perfect respect I am Dr Sir, Your obt hble servt

Robt. Morris

To Thomas Jefferson, [on or before 29 January 1802]

[on or before 29 Jan. 1802]

Dear Sir

When I had the honor of seeing you, it escaped my recollection to mention the subject contemplated in the enclosed note; mr Fitzsimons told me the blank therein was occasioned by his having forgot at the time of writing it wether he had ten or twelve chairs. This furniture is elegant and well suited for your appartments, perhaps better than any other in America, and it may be had for less than its real value by an appraismt of any Gentn. you may think proper to name for the purpose, excuse this intrusion on behalf of my friend and accept the assurance of the respectfull attachment of Dr Sir

Your obedt & hble servt

Robt Morris

Letter List

The following letters in this book are available on the
National Archives Founders Online

1776 (page 9)

To John Jay, 23 September 1776

To George Washington, 21 December 1776

To George Washington, 23–24 December 1776

To George Washington, 26 December 1776

To George Washington, 30 December 1776

1777 (page 17)

To George Washington, 1 January 1777

To John Jay, 12 January 1777

To John Jay, 4 February 1777

To George Washington, 12 February 1777

To the American Commissioners, 18 February 1777

To George Washington, 27 February 1777

To George Washington, 6–15 March 1777

To the American Commissioners, 7 March 1777

To the American Commissioners, 28 March 1777

To John Jay, 1 April 1777

To George Washington, 10 May 1777

To George Washington, 21 June 1781

To Benjamin Franklin, 22 June 1781

To John Jay, 29 June 1781

To George Washington, 2 July 1781

To John Jay, 4 July 1781

To George Washington, 5 July 1781

To John Jay, 7 July 1781

To John Jay, 9 July 1781

To Benjamin Franklin, 13 July 1781

To John Jay, 13 July 1781

To Benjamin Franklin, 14 July 1781

To Benjamin Franklin, 19 July 1781

To Benjamin Franklin, 21 July 1781

To George Washington, 23 July 1781

To John Jay, 15 August 1781

To George Washington, 22 August 1781

To The States, 22 August 1781

To Benjamin Franklin, August 28[–September 7] 1781

To George Washington, 28 August 1781

To George Washington, 6 September 1781

To George Washington, 6 September 1781

To George Washington, 6 September 1781

To George Washington, 20 March 1782

To Benjamin Franklin, 22 March 1782

To Benjamin Franklin, 23 March 1782

To George Washington, 3 April 1782

To Benjamin Franklin, 8 April 1782

To Alexander Hamilton, 15 April 1782

To George Washington, 15 April 1782

To Benjamin Franklin, 17 April 1782

To George Washington, 22 April 1782

To Alexander Hamilton, 2 May 1782

To Benjamin Franklin, 17 May 1782

To Benjamin Franklin (Two Letters), 18 May 1782

To Alexander Hamilton, 20 May 1782

To Benjamin Franklin, 29 May 1782

To Alexander Hamilton, 4 June 1782

To George Washington, 4 June 1782

To George Washington, 4 June 1782

To Benjamin Franklin, 10 June 1782

To George Washington, 12 June 1782

To Office of Finance 12th-13 June 1782

To George Washington, 21 June 1782

To Benjamin Franklin, 26 June 1782

To George Washington, 29 June 1782

To Benjamin Franklin, 1 July 1782

To Alexander Hamilton, 2 July 1782

To Benjamin Franklin, 5 July 1782

To George Washington, 9 July 1782

To Alexander Hamilton, 12 July 1782

To Alexander Hamilton, 19 July 1782

To Alexander Hamilton, 22 July 1782

To George Washington, 5 August 1782

To George Washington, 8 August 1782

To George Washington, 9 August 1782

To George Washington, 13 August 1782

To George Washington, 17 August 1782

To George Washington, 20 August 1782

To George Washington, 22 August 1782

To Alexander Hamilton, 28 August 1782

To Alexander Hamilton, 29 August 1782

To George Washington, 29 August 1782

To George Washington, 30 August 1782

To Alexander Hamilton, 6 September 1782

To George Washington, 9 September 1782

To Alexander Hamilton, 12 September 1782

To George Washington, 12 September 1782

To Alexander Hamilton, 17 September 1782

To George Washington, 19 September 1782

To George Washington, 19 September 1782

To John Adams, 25 September 1782

To John Adams, 25 September 1782

To Benjamin Franklin (Two Letters), 25 September 1782

To George Washington, 25 September 1782

To John Adams, 27 September 1782

To Benjamin Franklin (Two Letters), 27 September 1782

To Benjamin Franklin, 28 September 1782

To Benjamin Franklin, 30 September 1782

To Benjamin Franklin, 1 October 1782

To Alexander Hamilton, 5 October 1782

To Alexander Hamilton, 5 October 1782

To Alexander Hamilton, 5 October 1782

To Benjamin Franklin, 5 October 1782

To Alexander Hamilton, 5 October 1782

To Benjamin Franklin, 5 October 1782

To George Washington, 5 October 1782

To Benjamin Franklin (Three Letters), 7 October 1782

To Alexander Hamilton, 15 October 1782

To George Washington, 15 October 1782

To Alexander Hamilton, 16 October 1782

To George Washington, 16 October 1782

To Alexander Hamilton, 23 October 1782

To Benjamin Franklin, 27 October 1782

To Alexander Hamilton, 28 October 1782

To George Washington, 30 November 1782

To George Washington, 3 December 1782

To George Washington, 17 December 1782

To George Washington, 19 December 1782

To George Washington, 26 December 1782

To George Washington, 27 December 1782

To George Washington, 31 December 1782

1783 (page 263)

To Benjamin Franklin, 2 January 1783

To Benjamin Franklin, 3 January 1783

To Benjamin Franklin, 11 January 1783

To Benjamin Franklin, 13 January 1783

To John Adams, 19 January 1783

To Benjamin Franklin, 19 January 1783

To George Washington, 20 January 1783

To George Washington, 21 January 1783

To George Washington, 20 January 1783

To George Washington, 21 January 1783

To George Washington, 5 February 1783

To George Washington, 17 February 1783

To George Washington, 27 February 1783

To George Washington, 3 March 1783

To George Washington, 25 March 1783

To Alexander Hamilton, Theodorick Bland, Thomas FitzSimons, Samuel Osgood, and Richard Peters, 14 April 1783

To Alexander Hamilton, 16 April 1783

To Benjamin Franklin, 29 April 1783

To John Adams, 12 May 1783

To Benjamin Franklin, 12 May 1783

To Alexander Hamilton, Richard Peters, and Nathaniel Gorham, 15 May 1783

To Benjamin Franklin (Two Letters), 26 May 1783

To Benjamin Franklin from, 27 May 1783

To George Washington, 29 May 1783

To Benjamin Franklin, 30 May 1783

To John Jay, 31 May 1783

To George Washington, 5 June 1783

To John Jay, 26 July 1783

To George Washington, 12 August 1783

To George Washington, 20 August 1783

To George Washington, 2 September 1783

To George Washington, 5 September 1783

To George Washington, 10 September 1783

To Benjamin Franklin, 17 September 1783

To John Adams, 20 September 1783

To Benjamin Franklin, 30 September 1783

To Benjamin Franklin, 2 October 1783

To George Washington, 10 October 1783

To George Washington, 15 October 1783

To John Adams, 23 October 1783

To Benjamin Franklin, 4 November 1783

To John Adams, 5 November 1783

To George Washington, 26 November 1783

To John Jay, 27 November 1783

1784 (page 319)

To Benjamin Franklin, 17 January 1784

To Benjamin Franklin, 12 February 1784

To Benjamin Franklin, 13 February 1784

To George Washington, 14 February 1784

To Thomas Jefferson, 25 February 1784

To Thomas Jefferson, 8 April 1784

Robert Morris' contribution to the foundation of the United States of America is often overlooked but not forgotten. Here he is forever depicted in this scene from *The Apotheosis of Washington* painted by Constantino Brumidi in 1865. The painting shows Robert Morris receiving a bag of gold from Mercury, commemorating his financial services during the Revolutionary War.

Bibliography

Print

Oberholtzer, Ellis Paxson. *Robert Morris, Patriot And Financier.* Wentworth Press, 2019.

Rappleye, Charles. *Robert Morris: Financier of the American Revolution.* Simon & Schuster, 2011.

Smith, Ryan K. *Robert Morris's Folly: The Architectural and Financial Failures of an American Founder (The Lewis Walpole Series in Eighteenth-Century Culture and History).* Yale University Press, 2014.

Sumner, William Graham. *Robert Morris (1892). By: William Graham Sumner: Robert Morris, Jr. (January 20, 1734 – May 8, 1806), a Founding Father of the United States.* CreateSpace Independent Publishing Platform, 2017.

Unger, Harlow Giles. *Robert Morris: Washington's 'Magick Money Man'.* Independently published, 2023.

Online

Descendents of the Signers of the Declaration of Independence (https://www.dsdi1776.com/signer/robert-morris/)

Founder of the Day (https://www.founderoftheday.com/founder-of-the-day/robert-morris)

History.com (https://www.history.com/articles/robert-morris-financier-revolutionary-war)

National Archives: Founders Online (https://founders.archives.gov/)

Also by Michael Aubrecht and Heritage Books Inc.

The Long Roll: Wartime Experiences of the Civil War Drummer Boy

The Long Roll

Wartime Experiences of the
Civil War Drummer Boy

By Michael Aubrecht
Foreword by Daniel Glass

"The Long Roll" called troops to arrange themselves in line prior to attack and it was the responsibility of the drummer boys to command the men to muster. The army relied on the services of these boys as musicians and as communicators. Just like their counterparts, these boys were regulars who suffered the same hardships and risks as the men. When they were not acting in the role of musicians, they served as stretcher bearers, witnessing firsthand the horrors of war and the carnage it inflicted upon those who fell. Whether drumming on the march or bearing the wounded, these courageous boys quickly grew up in a man's war.

About the Author

Michael Aubrecht is an experienced author, historian and producer with a genuine passion for preserving and presenting the past through film and the written word. He lives in historic Fredericksburg, Virginia surrounded by 18th and 19th century historical sites. Michael has written multiple books to include *Historic Churches of Fredericksburg, The Civil War in Spotsylvania County, The Long Roll* and *Thomas Jefferson and the Virginia Statute for Religious Freedom.* He has published many articles for print and online magazines to include *Patriots of the American Revolution* and *Emerging Civil War.* Michael co-wrote and produced the documentary "The Angel of Marye's Heights," hosts the YouTube series "The Naked Historian" and manages the Facebook page entitled Today's History Lesson. Michael has lectured at many venues, including the Manassas Museum and the University of Mary Washington. Michael's books have been Amazon Best-Sellers in their category and he was a finalist in the International Book Awards.

Visit Michael online at: https://michaelaubrecht.wordpress.com/

www.ingramcontent.com/pod-product-compliance
Lightning Source LLC
Chambersburg PA
CBHW060129280326
41932CB00012B/1465